BIOINFORMATICS COMPUTING

Bryan Bergeron

PRENTICE HALL
PROFESSIONAL TECHNICAL REFERENCE
UPPER SADDLE RIVER, NJ 07458
WWW.PHPTR.COM

ISBN 0-13-100825-0

9 790131 008259

93999

Library of Congress Cataloging-in-Publication Data

Bergeron, Bryan P.
  Bioinformatics computing / Bryan Bergeron.
    p. cm.
  Includes bibliographical references.
  ISBN 0-13-100825-0
  1. Molecular biology--Data processing. 2. Bioinformatics. I. Title.

QH506 .B47 2002
572.8--dc21

2002038177

Editorial/production supervision: *Vanessa Moore*
Full-service production manager: *Anne R. Garcia*
Cover design director: *Jerry Votta*
Cover design: *Talar Agasyan-Boorujy*
Manufacturing buyer: *Alexis Heydt-Long*
Executive editor: *Paul Petralia*
Technical editor: *Ronald E. Reid, Ph.D., Professor and Chair, University of British Columbia*
Editorial assistant: *Richard Winkler*
Marketing manager: *Debby vanDijk*

© 2003 Pearson Education, Inc.
Publishing as Prentice Hall Professional Technical Reference
Upper Saddle River, New Jersey 07458

PRENTICE
HALL
PTR

Prentice Hall books are widely used by corporations and government agencies
for training, marketing, and resale.

For information regarding corporate and government
bulk discounts, please contact:
Corporate and Government Sales
Phone: 800-382-3419; E-mail: corpsales@pearsontechgroup.com

Printed in the United States of America
10   9   8

ISBN 0-13-100825-0

Pearson Education LTD.
Pearson Education Australia PTY, Limited
Pearson Education Singapore, Pte. Ltd.
Pearson Education North Asia Ltd.
Pearson Education Canada, Ltd.
Pearson Educación de Mexico, S.A. de C.V.
Pearson Education—Japan
Pearson Education Malaysia, Pte. Ltd.

About Prentice Hall Professional Technical Reference

With origins reaching back to the industry's first computer science publishing program in the 1960s, Prentice Hall Professional Technical Reference (PH PTR) has developed into the leading provider of technical books in the world today. Formally launched as its own imprint in 1986, our editors now publish over 200 books annually, authored by leaders in the fields of computing, engineering, and business.

Our roots are firmly planted in the soil that gave rise to the technological revolution. Our bookshelf contains many of the industry's computing and engineering classics: Kernighan and Ritchie's *C Programming Language*, Nemeth's *UNIX System Administration Handbook*, Horstmann's *Core Java*, and Johnson's *High-Speed Digital Design*.

PH PTR acknowledges its auspicious beginnings while it looks to the future for inspiration. We continue to evolve and break new ground in publishing by providing today's professionals with tomorrow's solutions.

CONTENTS

Chapter 2 • DATABASES 42

Chapter 3 • NETWORKS 104

Chapter 7 • DATA MINING   260

Chapter 8 • PATTERN MATCHING   302

Chapter 9 • MODELING AND SIMULATION   342

PREFACE

Bioinformatics Computing is a practical guide to computing in the burgeoning field of bioinformatics—the study of how information is represented and transmitted in biological systems, starting at the molecular level. This book, which is intended for molecular biologists at all levels of training and practice, assumes the reader is computer literate with modest computer skills, but has little or no formal computer science training. For example, the reader may be familiar with downloading bioinformatics data from the Web, using spreadsheets and other popular office automation tools, and/or working with commercial database and statistical analysis programs. It is helpful, but not necessary, for the reader to have some programming experience in BASIC, HTML, or C++.

In bioinformatics, as in many new fields, researchers and entrepreneurs at the fringes—where technologies from different fields interact—are making the greatest strides. For example, techniques developed by computer scientists enabled researchers at Celera Genomics, the Human Genome Project consortium, and other laboratories around the world to sequence the nearly 3 billion base pairs of the roughly 40,000 genes of the human genome. This feat would have been virtually impossible without computational methods.

No book on biotechnology would be complete without acknowledging the vast potential of the field to change life as we know it. Looking beyond the computational hurdles addressed by this text, there are broader issues and implications of biotechnology related to ethics, morality, religion, privacy, and economics. The high-stakes economic game of biotechnology pits proponents of custom medicines, genetically modified foods, cross-species cloning for species conservation, and creating organs for transplant against those who question the bioethics of stem cell research, the wisdom of creating frankenfoods that could somehow upset the ecology of the planet, and the morality of creating clones of farm animals or pets, such as Dolly and CC, respectively.

Even the major advocates of biotechnology are caught up in bitter patent wars, with the realization that whoever has control of the key patents in the field will enjoy a stream of revenues that will likely dwarf those of software giants such as Microsoft. Rights to genetic codes have the potential to impede R&D at one extreme, and reduce commercial funding for research at the other. The resolution of these and related issues will result in public policies and international laws that will either limit or protect the rights of researchers to work in the field.

Proponents of biotechnology contend that we are on the verge of controlling the coding of living things, and concomitant breakthroughs in biomedical engineering, therapeutics, and drug development. This view is more credible especially when combined with parallel advances in nanoscience, nanoengineering, and computing. Researchers take the view that in the near future, cloning will be necessary for sustaining crops, livestock, and animal research. As the earth's population continues to explode, genetically modified fruits will offer extended shelf life, tolerate herbicides, grow faster and in harsher climates, and provide significant sources of vitamins, protein, and other nutrients. Fruits and vegetables will be engineered to create drugs to control human disease, just as bacteria have been harnessed to mass-produce insulin for diabetics. In addition, chemical and drug testing simulations will streamline pharmaceutical development and predict subpopulation response to designer drugs, dramatically changing the practice of medicine.

Few would argue that the biotechnology area presents not only scientific, but cultural and economic challenges as well. The first wave of biotechnology, which focused on medicine, was relatively well received by the public—perhaps because of the obvious benefits of the technology, as well as the lack of general knowledge of government-sponsored research in biological weapons. Instead, media stressed the benefits of genetic engineering, reporting that millions of patients with diabetes have ready access to affordable insulin.

The second wave of biotech, which focused on crops, had a much more difficult time gaining acceptance, in part because some consumers feared that engineered organisms have the potential to disrupt the ecosystem. As a result, the first genetically engineered whole food ever brought to market, the short-lived Flavr Savr™ Tomato, was an economic failure when it was introduced in the spring of 1994—only four years after the first federally approved gene therapy on a patient. However, Calgene's entry into the market paved the way for a new industry that today holds nearly 2,000 patents on engineered foods, from virus-resistant papayas and bug-free corn, to caffeine-free coffee beans.

Today, nearly a century after the first gene map of an organism was published, we're in the third wave of biotechnology. The focus this time is on manufacturing military armaments made of transgenic spider webs, plastics from corn, and stain-removing bacilli. Because biotechnology manufacturing is still in its infancy and holds promise to avoid the pollution caused by traditional smokestack factories, it remains relatively unnoticed by opponents of genetic engineering.

The biotechnology arena is characterized by complexity, uncertainty, and unprecedented scale. As a result, researchers in the field have developed innovative computational solutions heretofore unknown or unappreciated by the general computer science community. However, in many areas of molecular biology R&D, investigators have reinvented techniques and rediscovered principles long known to scientists in computer science, medical informatics, physics, and other disciplines.

What's more, although many of the computational techniques developed by researchers in bioinformatics have been beneficial to scientists and entrepreneurs in other fields, most of these redundant discoveries represent a detour from addressing the main molecular biology challenges. For example, advances in machine-learning techniques have been redundantly developed by the microarray community, mostly independent of the traditional machine-learning research community. Valuable time has been wasted in the duplication of effort in both disciplines. The goal of this text is to provide readers with a roadmap to the diverse field of bioinformatics computing while offering enough in-depth information to serve as a valuable reference for readers already active in the bioinformatics field. The aim is to identify and describe specific information technologies in enough detail to allow readers to reason from first principles when they critically evaluate a glossy print advertisement, banner ad, or publication describing an innovative application of computer technology to molecular biology.

To appreciate the advantage of a molecular biologist studying computational methods at more than a superficial level, consider the many parallels faced by students of molecular biology and students of computer science. Most students of molecular biology are introduced to the concept of genetics through Mendel's work manipulating the seven traits of pea plants. There they learn Mendel's laws of inheritance. For example, the Law of Segregation of

Alleles states that the alleles in the parents separate and recombine in the off-spring. The Law of Independent Assortment states that the alleles of different characteristics pass to the offspring independently.

Students who delve into genetics learn the limitations of Mendel's methods and assumptions—for example, that the Law of Independent Assortment applies only to pairs of alleles found on different chromosomes. More advanced students also learn that Mendel was lucky enough to pick a plant with a relatively simple genetic structure. When he extended his research to mice and other plants, his methods failed. These students also learn that Mendel's results are probably too perfect, suggesting that either his record-keeping practices were flawed or that he blinked at data that didn't fit his theories.

Just as students of genetics learn that Mendel's experiment with peas isn't adequate to fully describe the genetic structures of more complex organisms, students of computer science learn the exceptions and limitations of the strategies and tactics at their disposal. For example, computer science students are often introduced to algorithms by considering such basic operations as sorting lists of data.

To computer users who are unfamiliar with underlying computer science, sorting is simply the process of rearranging an unordered sequence of records into either ascending or descending order according to one or more keys—such as the name of a protein. However, computer scientists and others have developed dozens of searching algorithms, each with countless variations to suit specific needs. Because sorting is a fundamental operation used in everything from searching the Web to analyzing and matching patterns of base pairs, it warrants more than a superficial understanding for a biotechnology researcher engaged in operations that involve sorting.

Consider that two of the most popular sorting algorithms used in computer science, quicksort and bubblesort, can be characterized by a variety of factors, from stability and running time to memory requirements, and how performance is influenced by the way in which memory is accessed by the host computer's central processing unit. That is, just as Mendel's experiments and laws have exceptions and operating assumptions, a sorting algorithm can't simply be taken at face value.

For example, the running time of quicksort on large data sets is superior to that of many other stable sorting algorithms, such as bubblesort. Sorting long lists of a half-million elements or more with a program that implements the bubblesort algorithm might take an hour or more, compared to a half-second for a program that follows the quicksort algorithm. Although the performance of quicksort is nearly identical to that of bubblesort on a few hundred or thousand data elements, the performance of bubblesort degrades rapidly with increasing data size. When the size of the data approaches the number of base pairs in the human genome, a sort that takes 5 or 10 seconds using quicksort might require half a day or more on a typical desktop PC.

Even with its superb performance, quicksort has many limitations that may favor bubblesort or another sorting algorithm, depending on the nature of the data, the limitations of the hardware, and the expertise of the programmer. For example, one virtue of the bubblesort algorithm is simplicity. It can usually be implemented by a programmer in any number of programming languages, even one who is a relative novice. In operation, successive sweeps are made through the records to be sorted and the largest record is moved closer to the top, rising like a bubble.

In contrast, the relatively complex quicksort algorithm divides records into two partitions around a pivot record, and all records that are less than the pivot go into one partition and all records that are greater go into the other. The process continues recursively in each of the two partitions until the entire list of records is sorted. While quicksort performs much better than bubblesort on long lists of data, it generally requires significantly more memory space than the bubblesort. With very large files, the space requirements may exceed the amount of free RAM available on the researcher's PC. The bubblesort versus quicksort dilemma exemplifies the common tradeoff in computer science of space for speed.

Although the reader may never write a sorting program, knowing when to apply one algorithm over another is useful in deciding which shareware or commercial software package to use or in directing a programmer to develop a custom system. A parallel in molecular biology would be to know when to describe an organism using classical Mendelian genetics, and when other mechanisms apply.

Given the multidisciplinary characteristic of bioinformatics, there is a need in the molecular biology community for reference texts that illustrate the computer science advances that have been made in the past several decades. The most relevant areas—the ones that have direct bearing on their research—are in computer visualization, very large database designs, machine learning and other forms of advanced pattern-matching, statistical methods, and distributed-computing techniques. This book, which is intended to bring molecular biologists up to speed in computational techniques that apply directly to their work, is a direct response to this need.

ORGANIZATION OF THIS BOOK

This book is organized into modular, stand-alone topics related to bioinformatics computing according to the following chapters:

- *Chapter 1: THE CENTRAL DOGMA*
  This chapter provides an overview of bioinformatics, using the Central Dogma as the organizing theme. It explores the relationship of molecular biology and bioinformatics to computer science, and how the purview of computational bioinformatics necessarily extends from the molecular to the clinical medicine level.

- *Chapter 2: DATABASES*
  Bioinformatics is characterized by an abundance of data stored in very large databases. The practical computer technologies related to very large databases are discussed, with an emphasis on object-oriented database methods, given that traditional relational database technology may be ill-suited for some bioinformatics needs. Data warehousing, data dictionaries, database design, and knowledge management techniques related to bioinformatics are also discussed in detail.

- *Chapter 3: NETWORKS*
  This chapter explores the information technology infrastructure of bioinformatics, including the Internet, World Wide Web, intranets, wireless systems, and other network technologies that apply directly to sharing, manipulating, and archiving sequence data and other bioinformatics information. This chapter reviews Web-based resources for researchers, such as GenBank and other systems maintained by NCBI, NIH, and other government agencies. The Great Global Grid and its potential for transforming the field of bioinformatics is also discussed.

- *Chapter 4: SEARCH ENGINES*
  The exponentially increasing amounts of data accessible in digital form over the Internet, from gene sequences to published references to the experimental methods used to determine specific sequences, is only accessible through advanced search engine technologies. This chapter details search engine operations related to the major online bioinformatics resources.

- *Chapter 5: DATA VISUALIZATION*
  Exploring the possible configurations of folded proteins has proven to be virtually impossible by simply studying linear sequences of bases. However, sophisticated 3D visualization

techniques allow researchers to use their visual and spatial reasoning abilities to understand the probable workings of proteins and other structures. This chapter explores data visualization techniques that apply to bioinformatics, from methods of generating 2D and 3D renderings of protein structures to graphing the results of the statistical analysis of protein structures.

- *Chapter 6: STATISTICS*

The randomness inherent in any sampling process—such as measuring the mRNA levels of thousands of genes simultaneously with microarray techniques, or assessing the similarity between protein sequences—necessarily involves probability and statistical methods. This chapter provides an in-depth discussion of the statistical techniques applicable to molecular biology, addressing topics such as statistical analysis of structural features, gene prediction, how to extract maximal value from small sample sets, and quantifying uncertainty in sequencing results.

- *Chapter 7: DATA MINING*

Given an ever-increasing store of sequence and protein data from several ongoing genome projects, data mining the sequences has become a field of research in its own right. Many bioinformatics scientists conduct important research from their PCs, without ever entering a wet lab or seeing a sequencing machine. The aim of this chapter is to explore data-mining techniques, using technologies, such as the Perl language, that are uniquely suited to searching through data strings. Other issues covered include taxonomies, profiling sequences, and the variety of tools available to researchers involved in mining the data in GenBank and other very large bioinformatics databases.

- *Chapter 8: PATTERN MATCHING*

Expert systems and classical pattern matching or AI techniques—from reasoning under uncertainty and machine learning to image and pattern recognition—have direct, practical applicability to molecular biology research. This chapter covers a variety of pattern-matching approaches, using molecular biology as a working context. For example, microarray research lends itself to machine learning, in that it is humanly impossible to follow thousands of parallel reactions unaided, and several gene-prediction applications are based on neural network pattern-matching engines. The strengths and weakness of various pattern-matching approaches in bioinformatics are discussed.

- *Chapter 9: MODELING AND SIMULATION*
  This chapter covers a variety of simulation techniques, in the context of computer modeling events from drug-protein interactions and probable protein folding configurations to the analysis of potential biological pathways. The application of event-driven, time-driven, and hybrid simulation techniques are discussed, as well as linking computer simulations with visualization techniques.

- *Chapter 10: COLLABORATION*
  Bioinformatics is characterized by a high degree of cooperation among the researchers who contribute their part to the whole knowledge base of genomics and proteomics. As such, this chapter explores the details of collaboration with enabling technologies that facilitate multimedia communications, real-time videoconferencing, and Web-based application sharing of molecular biology information and knowledge.

HOW TO USE THIS BOOK

For readers new to bioinformatics, the best way to tackle the subject is to simply read each chapter in order; however, because each chapter is written as a stand-alone module, readers interested in, for example, data-mining techniques, can go directly to Chapter 7, "Data Mining." Where appropriate, "On the Horizon" sidebars provide glimpses of techniques and technologies that hold promise but have either not been fully developed or have yet to be embraced by the bioinformatics community. In addition, readers who want to delve deeper into bioinformatics are encouraged to refer to the list of publications and Web sites listed in the Bibliography.

THE LARGER CONTEXT

Bioinformatics may not be able solve the numerous social, ethical, and legal issues in the field of biotechnology, but it can address many of the scientific and economic issues. For example, there are technical hurdles to be overcome before advances such as custom pharmaceuticals and cures for genetic diseases can be affordable and commonplace. Many of these advances will require new technologies in molecular biology, and virtually all of these advances will be enabled by computational methods. For example, most molecular biologists concede that sequencing the human genome was a relatively trivial task compared to the challenges of understanding the human proteome. The typical cell produces hundreds of thousands of proteins, many of which are unknown and of unknown function. What's more, these proteins fold into shapes that are a function of the linear sequence of amino acids they contain, the temperature, as well as the presence of fats, sugars, and water in the microenvironment.

As the history of the PC and the Internet has demonstrated, the rate of change in technological innovation is accelerating, and the practical applications of computing to unravel the proteome and other bioinformatics challenges are growing exponentially. In this regard, bioinformatics should be considered an empowering technology with which researchers in biotechnology can take a proactive role in defining and shaping the future of their field—and the world.

ACKNOWLEDGMENTS

Thanks to Jeffrey Blander of Harvard Medical School and Ardais Corporation; David Burkholder, Ph.D., of Medical Learning Company; and the bioinformatics faculty at Stanford University, including Christina Teo, Meredith Ngo, Vishwanath Anantraman, Russ Altman, M.D., Ph.D., Douglas Brutlag, Ph.D., Serafim Batzoglou, Ph.D., and Betty Cheng, Ph.D., for their insight and constructive criticism.

Special thanks to Ronald Reid, Ph.D., for reviewing the material from the perspective of an expert molecular biologist; Miriam Goodman, for her unparalleled skill as a wordsmith; my managing editor at Prentice Hall, Paul Petralia, for his encouragement, vision, and support; and Prentice Hall production editor, Vanessa Moore, and copy editor, Ralph Moore.

Bryan Bergeron
October 2002

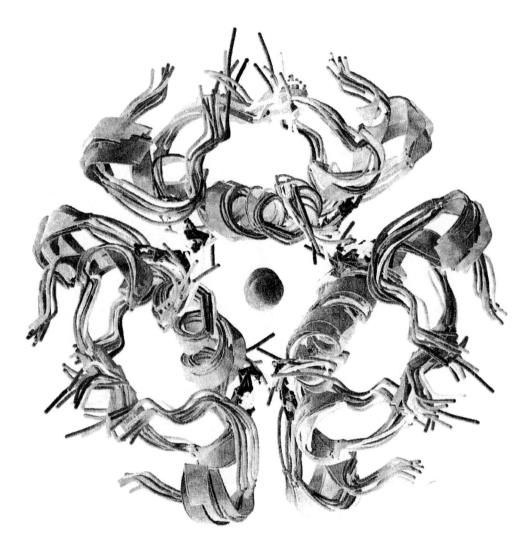

➤ Human Insulin, PDB entry 1AIO. Image produced with PDB Structure Explorer, which is based on MolScript and Raster3D.

CHAPTER

The Central Dogma

If I have seen further it is by standing on the shoulders of Giants.
— Isaac Newton

To many pre-genomic biologists, computational bioinformatics seems like an oxymoron. After all, consider that the traditional biology curriculum of only a few years ago was heavily weighted toward the qualitative humanities, while advanced numerical methods, programming, and computerized visualization techniques were the purview of engineers and physicists. In a strict sense, bioinformatics—the study of how information is represented and transmitted in biological systems, starting at the molecular level—is a discipline that does not need a computer. An ink pen and a supply of traditional laboratory notebooks could be used to record results of experiments. However, to do so would be like foregoing the use of a computer and word-processing program in favor of pen and paper to write a novel.

From a practical sense, bioinformatics is a science that involves collecting, manipulating, analyzing, and transmitting huge quantities of data, and uses computers whenever appropriate. As such, this book will use the term "bioinformatics" to refer to computational bioinformatics.

Clearly, times have changed in the years since the human genome was identified. Post-genomic biology—whether focused on protein structures or public health—is a multidisciplinary, multimedia endeavor. Clinicians have to be as fluent at reading a Nuclear Magnetic Resonance (NMR) image of a patient's chest cavity as molecular biologists are at reading X-ray crystallography and NMR spectroscopy of proteins, nucleic acids, and carbohydrates. As such, computational methods and the advanced mathematical operations they support are rapidly becoming part of the basic literacy of every life scientist, whether he works in academia or in the research laboratory of a biotechnology firm.

The purpose of this chapter is to provide an overview of bioinformatics, using the Central Dogma as the organizing theme. It explores the relationship of molecular biology and bioinformatics to computer science, and how informatics relates to other sciences. In particular, it illustrates the scope of bioinformatics' applications from the consideration of nucleotide sequences to the clinical presentation and, ultimately, the treatment of disease. This chapter also explores the challenges faced by researchers and how they can be addressed by computer-based numerical methods that encompass the full range of computer science endeavors, from archiving and communications to pattern matching and simulation, to visualization methods and statistical tools. Specifically, the section called "The Killer Application" examines at least one of the biotechnology industy's (biotech's) holy grails, that of using bioinformatics techniques to create designer drugs. "Parallel Universes" provides a historical view of how the initially independent fields of communications, computing, and molecular biology eventually converged into an interdependent relationship under the umbrella of biotechnology. "Watson's Definition" explores the Central Dogma, as defined by James Watson, and "Top-Down Versus Bottom-Up" explores the divergent views created by scientists who are working from first principles and those working from heuristics. The "Information Flow" section examines the parallels of information transfer in communications systems and in molecular biology. Finally, the convergence of computing, communications, and molecular biology is highlighted in "Convergence of Science and Technology."

THE KILLER APPLICATION

In the biotechnology industry, every researcher and entrepreneur hopes to develop or discover the next "killer app"—the one application that will bring the world to his or her door and provide funding for R&D, marketing, and production. For example, in general computing, the electronic spreadsheet and the desktop laser printer have been the notable killer apps. The spreadsheet not only transformed the work of accountants, research scientists, and statisticians, but the underlying tools formed the basis for visualization and mathematical modeling. The affordable desktop laser printer created an industry and elevated the standards of scientific communications, replacing rough graphs created on dot-matrix printers with high-resolution images.

As in other industries, it's reasonable to expect that using computational methods to leverage the techniques of molecular biology is a viable approach to increasing the rate of innovation and discovery. However, readers looking for a rationale for learning the computational techniques as they apply to the bioinformatics that are described here and in the following chapters can ask "What might be the computer-enabled 'killer app' in bioinformatics?" That is, what is the irresistible driving force that differentiates bioinformatics from a purely academic endeavor? Although there are numerous military and agricultural opportunities, one of the most commonly cited examples of the killer app is in personalized medicine, as illustrated in Figure 1-1.

Instead of taking a generic or over-the-counter drug for a particular condition, a patient would submit a tissue sample, such as a mouth scraping, and submit it for analysis. A microarray would then be used to analyze the patient's genome and the appropriate compounds would be prescribed. The drug could be a cocktail of existing compounds, much like the drug cocktails used to treat cancer patients today.

Alternatively, the drug could be synthesized for the patient's specific genetic markers—as in tumor-specific chemotherapy, for example. This synthesized drug might take a day or two to develop, unlike the virtually instantaneous drug

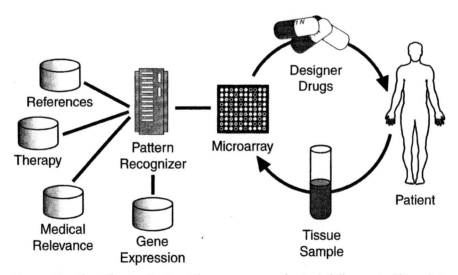

Figure 1-1 The Killer Application. The most commonly cited "killer app" of biotech is personalized medicine—the custom, just-in-time delivery of medications (popularly called "designer drugs") tailored to the patient's condition.

cocktail, which could be formulated by the corner pharmacist. The tradeoff is that the drug would be tailored to the patient's genetic profile and condition, resulting in maximum response to the drug, with few or no side effects.

How will this or any other killer app be realized? The answer lies in addressing the molecular biology, computational, and practical business aspects of proposed developments such as custom medications. For example, because of the relatively high cost of a designer drug, the effort will initially be limited to drugs for conditions in which traditional medicines are prohibitively expensive. Consider the technical challenges that need to be successfully overcome to develop a just-in-time designer drug system. A practical system would include:

- **High throughput screening**—The use of affordable, computer-enabled microarray technology to determine the patient's genetic profile. The issue here is affordability, in that microarrays costs tens of thousands of dollars.
- **Medically relevant information gathering**—Databases on gene expression, medical relevance of signs and symptoms, optimum therapy for given diseases, and references for the patient and clinician must be readily available. The goal is to be able to quickly and automatically match a patient's genetic profile, predisposition for specific diseases, and current condition with the efficacy and potential side effects of specific drug-therapy options.
- **Custom drug synthesis**—The just-in-time synthesis of patient-specific drugs, based on the patient's medical condition and genetic profile, presents major technical as well as political, social, and legal hurdles. For example, for just-in-time synthesis to be accepted by the FDA, the pharmaceutical industry must demonstrate that custom drugs can skip the clinical-trials gauntlet before approval.

Achieving this killer app in biotech is highly dependent on computer technology, especially in the use of computers to speed the process testing-analysis-drug synthesis cycle, where time really is money. For example, consider that for every 5,000 compounds evaluated annually by the U.S. pharmaceutical R&D laboratories, 5 make it to human testing, and only 1 of the compounds makes it to market. In addition, the average time to market for a drug is over 12 years, including several years of pre-clinical trials followed by a 4-phase clinical trial. These clinical trials progress from safety and dosage studies in Phase I, to effectiveness and side effects in Phase II, to long-term surveillance in Phase IV, with each phase typically lasting several years.

What's more, because pharmaceutical companies are granted a limited period of exclusivity by the patent process, there is enormous pressure to get drugs to market as soon as a patent is granted. The industry figure for lost revenue on a drug because of extended clinical trials is over $500,000 per day. In addition, the pharmaco-economic reality is that fewer drugs are in the pipeline, despite escalating R&D costs, which topped $30 billion in 2001.

Most pharmaceutical companies view computerization as the solution to creating smaller runs of drugs focused on custom production. Obvious computing applications range from predicting efficacy and side effects of drugs based on genome analysis, to visualizing protein structures to better understand and predict the efficacy of specific drugs, to illustrating the relative efficacy of competing drugs in terms of quality of life and cost, based on the Markov simulation of likely outcomes during Phase IV clinical trials.

Despite these obvious uses for computer methods in enabling the drug discovery and synthesis process, the current state of the art in these areas is limited by the underlying information technology infrastructure. For example, even though there are dozens of national and private genome databases, most aren't integrated with each other. Drug discovery methods are currently limited to animal and cell models. One goal of computerizing the overall drug discovery process is to create a drug discovery model through sequencing or microarray technology. The computer model would allow researchers to determine if a drug will work before it's tried on patients, potentially bypassing the years and tens of millions of dollars typically invested in Phases I and II of clinical trials.

In addition to purely technological challenges, there are issues in the basic approach and scientific methods available that must be addressed before bioinformatics can become a self-supporting endeavor. For example, working with tissue samples from a single patient means that the sample size is very low, which may adversely affect the correlation of genomic data with clinical findings. There are also issues of a lack of a standardized vocabulary to describe nucleotide structures and sequences, and no universally accepted data model. There is also the need for clinical data to create clinical profiles that can be compared with genomic findings.

For example, in searching through a medical database for clinical findings associated with a particular disease, a standard vocabulary must be available for encoding the clinical information for later retrieval from a database. The consistency and specificity in a controlled vocabulary is what makes it effective as a database search tool, and a domain-specific vehicle of communication. As an illustration of the specificity of controlled vocabularies, consider that in the domain of clinical medicine, there are several popular controlled vocabularies in use: There is the Medical Subject Heading (MeSH), Unified Medical Language System (UMLS), the Read Classification System (RCS), Systemized Nomenclature of Human and Veterinary Medicine (SNOMED), International Classification of Diseases (ICD-10), Current Procedural Terminology (CPT), and the Diagnostic and Statistical Manual of Mental Disorders (DSM-IV).

Each vocabulary system has its strengths and weaknesses. For example, SNOMED is optimized for accessing and indexing information in medical databases, whereas the DSM is optimized for description and classification of all known mental illnesses. In use, a researcher attempting to document the correlation of a gene sequence with a definition of schizophrenia in the DSM may have difficulty finding gene sequences in the database that correlate with schizophrenia if the naming convention and definition used to search on are based on MeSH nomenclature.

A related issue is the challenge of data mining and pattern matching, especially as they relate to searching clinical reports and online resources such as PubMed for signs, symptoms, and diagnoses. A specific gene expression may be associated with "M.I." or "myocardial infarction" in one resource and "coronary artery disease" in another, depending on the vocabulary used and the criteria for diagnosis.

Among the hurdles associated with achieving success in biotech are politics and the disparate points of view in any company or research institution, in that decision makers in marketing and sales, R&D, and programming are likely to have markedly different perspectives on how to achieve corporate and research goals. As such, bioinformatics is necessarily grounded in molecular biology, clinical medicine, a solid information technology infrastructure, and business. The noble challenge of linking gene expression with human disease in order to provide personal medicine can be overshadowed by the local issues involved in mapping clinical information from one hospital or healthcare institution with another. The discussion that follows illustrates the distance between where science and society are today, where they need to be in the near future, and how computational bioinformatics has the potential to bridge the gap.

PARALLEL UNIVERSES

One of the major challenges faced by bioinformatacists is keeping up with the latest techniques and discoveries in both molecular biology and computing. Discoveries and developments are growing exponentially in both fields, as shown in the timeline in Figure 1-2, with most of the significant work occurring within the past century. Initially, developments were independent and, for the most part, unrelated. However, with time, the two became inseparably intertwined and interdependent.

Consider, for example, that at the dawn of the 20th Century, Walter Sutton was advancing the chromosome theory just as transatlantic wireless communications was being demonstrated with a spark-gap transmitter using Morse code. The state of the art in computing at the time was a wearable analog time

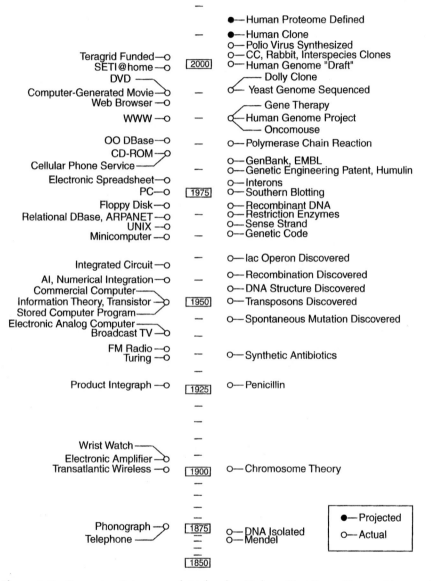

Figure 1-2 Computer Science and Molecular Biology Timelines. The rapid rate of change in the 20th Century is significant for both computing and biology, as seen from this timeline of discoveries and inventions for both areas.

computer—the newly invented wristwatch. The remarkable fact about the status of computing, communications, and biology at the dawn of the 20th Century is that all three were nascent curiosities of a few visionaries. It's equally remarkable that the three technologies are so pervasive today that they are largely taken for granted.

Two key events in the late 1920s were Alexander Fleming's discovery of penicillin and Vannevar Bush's Product Integraph, a mechanical analog computer that could solve simple equations. In the 1930s, Alan Turing, the British mathematician, devised his Turing model, upon which all modern discrete computing is based. The Turing model defines the fundamental properties of a computing system: a finite program, a large database, and a deterministic, step-by-step mode of computation. What's more, the architecture of his hypothetical Turing Machine—which has a finite number of discrete states, uses a finite alphabet, and is fed by an infinitely long tape (see Figure 1-3)—is strikingly similar to that of the translation of RNA to proteins. Turing theorized that his machine could execute any mathematically defined algorithm, and later proved his hypothesis by creating one of the first digital electronic computers.

By the early 1940s, synthetic antibiotics, FM radio, broadcast TV, and the electronic analog computer were in use. The state of the art in computing, the electronic Differential Analyzer occupied several rooms and required several workers to watch over the 2,000 vacuum tubes, thousands of relays, and other components of the system. Not surprisingly, for several years, computers

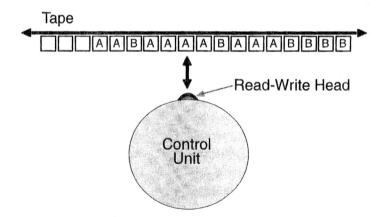

Figure 1-3 The Turing Machine. The Turing Machine, which can simulate any computing system, consists of three basic elements: a control unit, a tape, and a read-write head. The read-write head moves along the tape and transmits information to and from the control unit.

remained commercial curiosities, with most of the R&D activity occurring in academia and most practical applications limited to classified military work. For example, the first documented use of an electronic analog computer was as an antiaircraft-gun director built by Western Electric Company. Similarly, the first general-purpose electronic analog computer was built with funds from the National Defense Research Committee. This trend of government and military funding of leading-edge computer and communications technologies continues to this day.

With the declassification of information about the analog computer after World War II, several commercial ventures to develop computers were launched. Around the same time, Claude Shannon published his seminal paper on communications theory, "A Mathematical Theory of Communication." In it, he presented his initial concept for a unifying theory of transmitting and processing information. Shannon's work forms the basis for our understanding of modern communications networks, and provides one model for communications in biological systems.

As illustrated in Figure 1-4, Shannon's model of Information Theory describes a communication system with five major parts: the information source, the transmitter, the medium, the receiver, and the destination. In this model, the information source, which can be a CD-ROM containing the sequence information of the entire human genome or a human chromosome, contains the message that is transmitted as a signal of some type through a medium. The signal can be a nucleotide sequence in a DNA molecule or the dark and light patches on a metal film sandwiched between the two clear plastic plates of a CD-ROM. The medium can be the intracellular matrix where DNA is concerned, or the clear plastic and air that the laser must pass through in order to read a CD-ROM. Regardless of the medium, in the propagation of

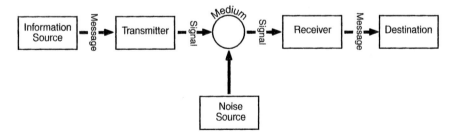

Figure 1-4 Information Theory. Shannon's model of a communications system includes five components: an information source, a transmitter, the medium, a receiver, and a destination. The amount of information that can be transferred from information source to destination is a function of the strength of the signal relative to that of the noise generated by the noise source.

the desired signal through the medium, it is affected to some degree by noise. In a cell, this noise can be due to heat, light, ionizing radiation, or a sudden change in the chemistry of the intracellular environment causing thermal agitation at the molecular or nucleotide level. In the case of a CD-ROM, the noise can be from scratches on the surface of the disc, dirt on the receiver lens, or vibration from the user or the environment.

When the signal is intercepted, the receiver extracts the message or information from the signal, which is delivered to the destination. In Shannon's model, information is separate from the signal. For example, the reflected laser light shining on a CD-ROM is the signal, which has to be processed to glean the underlying message—whether it's the description of a nucleotide sequence or a track of classical music. Similarly, a strand of RNA near the endoplasmic reticulum is the signal that is carried from the nucleus to the cytoplasm, but the message is the specific instruction for protein synthesis.

Information theory specifies the amount of information that can be transferred from the transmitter to the receiver as a function of the noise level and other characteristics of the medium. The greater the strength of the desired signal compared to that of the noise—that is, the higher the signal-to-noise ratio—the greater the amount of information that can be propagated from the information source through the medium to the destination. Shannon's model also provides the theoretical basis for data compression, which is a way to squeeze more information into a message by eliminating redundancy. Shannon's model is especially relevant for developing gene sequencing devices and evaluation techniques.

Returning to the timeline of innovation and discovery in the converging fields of molecular biology and computer science, Watson and Crick's elucidation of the structure of DNA in the early 1950s was paralleled by the development of the transistor, the commercial computer, and the first stored computer program. Around the same time, the computer science community switched, en masse, from analog to digital computers for simulating missile trajectories, fuel consumption, and a variety of other real-world analog situations. This virtually overnight shift from analog to digital computing is attributed to the development of applied numerical integration, a basic simulation method used to evaluate the time response of differential equations. Prior to the development of numerical integration, simulating analog phenomena on digital computers was impractical.

The 1950s were also the time of the first breakthrough in the computer science field of artificial intelligence (AI), as marked by the development of the General Problem Solver (GPS) program. GPS was unique in that, unlike previous programs, its responses mimicked human behavior. Parallel developments in molecular biology include the discovery of the process of spontaneous mutation and the existence of transposons—the small, mobile DNA sequences that can replicate and insert copies at random sites within chromosomes.

The early 1970s saw the development of the relational database, object-oriented programming, and logic programming, which led in turn to the development of deductive databases in the late 1970s and of object-oriented databases in the mid-1980s. These developments were timely for molecular biology in that by the late 1970s, it became apparent that there would soon be unmanageable quantities of DNA sequence data. The potential flood of data, together with rapidly evolving database technologies entering the market, empowered researchers in the U.S. and Europe to establish international DNA data banks in the early 1980s. GenBank, developed at the Los Alamos National Laboratory, and the EMBL database, developed at the European Molecular Biology Laboratory, were both started in 1982. The third member of the International Nucleotide Sequence Database Collaboration, the DNA Data Bank of Japan (or DDBJ), joined the group in 1982.

Continuing with the comparison of parallel development in computer science and molecular biology, consider that shortly after the electronic spreadsheet (VisiCalc) was introduced into the general computing market in the late 1970s, the U.S. Patent and Trademark Office issued a patent on a genetically engineered form of bacteria designed to decompose oil from accidental spills. These two events are significant milestones for computing and molecular biology in that they legitimized both fields from the perspective of providing economically viable products that had demonstrable value to the public.

The electronic spreadsheet is important in computing because it transformed the personal computer from a toy for hobbyists and computer game enthusiasts to a serious business tool for anyone in business. Not only could an accountant keep track of the business books with automatic tabulation and error checking performed by electronic spreadsheet, but the electronic spreadsheet transformed the personal computer into a research tool statisticians could use for modeling everything from neural networks and other machinelearning techniques, to performing what-if analyses on population dynamics in the social sciences. Similarly, the first patent for a genetically engineered life form, issued in 1980, served to legitimize genetic engineering as an activity that could be protected as intellectual property. While detractors complained that turning over control of the genome and molecular biology methods to companies and academic institutions provided them with too much control over what amounts to everyone's genetic heritage, the patent opened the door to private investments and other sources of support for R&D.

Other developments in the 1980s included significant advances in the languishing field of AI, thanks to massive investment from the U.S. Government in an attempt to decode Russian text in real time. In addition, by 1985, the Polymerase Chain Reaction (PCR) method of amplifying DNA sequences—a cornerstone for molecular biology research—was in use.

The next major event in computing, the introduction of the World Wide Web in 1990, roughly coincided with the kickoff of the Human Genome

Project. These two events are significant in that they represent the convergence of computing, communications, and molecular biology. The Web continues to serve as the communications vehicle for researchers in working with genomic data, allowing research scientists to submit their findings to online databases and share in the findings of others. The Web also provides access to a variety of tools that allow searching and manipulation of the continually expanding genomic databases as well. Without the Web, the value of the Human Genome Project would have been significantly diminished.

By 1994, the Web was expanding exponentially because of increased public interest around the time the first genetically modified (GM) food, Calgene's Flavr Savr™ Tomato was on the market. Cloning of farm animals followed two years later with the birth of Dolly the sheep—around the time the DVD was introduced to the consumer market.

At the cusp of the 21st Century, the pace of progress in both computer science and molecular biology accelerated. Work on the Great Global Grid (GGG) and similar distributed computing systems that provide computational capabilities to dwarf the largest conventional supercomputers was redoubled. By 1999, distributed computing systems such as SETI@home (Search for Extraterrestrial Intelligence) were online. SETI@home is a network of 3.4 million desktop PCs devoted to analyzing radio telescope data searching for signals of extraterrestrial origin. A similar distributed computing project, Folding@home, came online in 2001. It performed molecular dynamics simulations of how proteins fold. The project was started by the chemistry department at Stanford University. It made a virtual supercomputer of a network of over 20,000 standard computers.

Like most distributed computing projects, SETI@home and folding@home rely primarily on the donation of PC processing power from individuals connected to the Internet at home (hence the @home designation). However, there are federally directed projects underway as well. For example, the federally funded academic research grid project, the Teragrid, was started in 2001—around the time Noah, the first interspecies clone and an endangered humpbacked wild ox native to Southeast Asia, was born to a milk cow in Iowa. This virtual supercomputer project, funded by the National Science Foundation, spans 4 research institutions, providing 600 trillion bytes of storage and is capable of processing 13 trillion operations per second over a 40-gigabit-per-second optical fiber backbone. The Teragrid and similar programs promise to provide molecular biologists with affordable tools for visualizing and modeling complex interactions of protein molecules—tasks that would be impractical without access to supercomputer power.

On the heels of the race to sequence the majority of coding segments of the human genome—won by Craig Venter's Celera Genomics with the publication of the "rough draft" in February of 2000—IBM and Compaq began their race to build the fastest bio-supercomputer to support proteomic research. IBM's

Blue Gene is designed to perform 1,000 trillion calculations per second, or about 25 times faster than the fastest supercomputer, Japan's Earth Simulator, which is capable of over 35 trillion operations per second. Blue Gene's architecture is specifically tuned to support the modeling, manipulation, and visualization of protein molecules. Compaq's Red Storm, in contrast, is a more general-purpose supercomputer, designed to provide 100 trillion calculations per second. As a result, in addition to supporting work in molecular biology, Red Storm's design is compatible with work traditionally performed by supercomputers—nuclear weapons research. Interestingly, IBM and Compaq are expected to invest as much time and money developing Red Storm and Blue Gene as Celera Genomics invested in decoding the human genome.

As demonstrated by the timelines in biology, communications, and computer science, the fields started out on disparate paths, only to converge in the early 1980s. Today, bioinformatics, like many sciences, deals with the storage, transport, and analysis of information. What distinguishes bioinformatics from other scientific endeavors is that it focuses on the information encoded in the genes and how this information affects the universe of biological processes. With this in mind, consider how bioinformatics is reflected in the Central Dogma of molecular biology.

WATSON'S DEFINITION

The Central Dogma of Molecular Biology, as originally defined by James Watson, is deceptively simple: DNA defines the synthesis of protein by way of an RNA intermediary. Documenting, controlling, and modifying this process, which is illustrated from a high-level structural perspective in Figure 1-5, is the focus of bioinformatics. It's also the basis for genetic engineering, mapping the human genome, and the diagnosis and treatment of genetic diseases. For example, genetic engineering involves modifying the process so that new proteins are synthesized; these new proteins in turn form the basis of everything from new drugs to new types of plants and animals.

The simplified version of the Central Dogma, shown in Figure 1-5, in which DNA is duplicated through replication, transcribed to RNA, which is in turn translated to protein, only hints at the complexity of the information transfer process that is the driving force for bioinformatics. Consider that the archive of an individual's genetic information or genome is encoded in DNA as a sequence of four different nitrogenous bases on a sugar-phosphate backbone. This deoxyribonucleic acid can adopt a variety of conformations, including the infamous right-handed double helix first described by Watson and Crick in 1953. The sequence of four nitrogenous bases—some combination of Adenine (A), Thymine (T), Cytosine (C), and Guanine (G)—in each strand of the

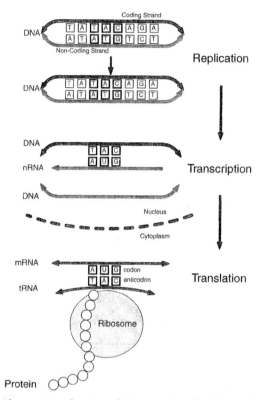

Figure 1-5 The Central Dogma of Molecular Biology. DNA is transcribed to messenger RNA in the cell nucleus, which is in turn translated to protein in the cytoplasm. The Central Dogma, shown here from a structural perspective, can also be depicted from an information flow perspective (see Figure 1-9).

double helix mirror each other in a predefined manner; Adenine on one strand always binds with Thymine on the other, and Cytosine always binds with Guanine.

In human cells, DNA is organized and compressed into 23 pairs of chromosomes, with one member of each pair inherited from each parent. Most of this DNA—on the order of 98.5 percent—is considered "junk," in that its function is unknown. The remainder of the DNA is in the genes—the stretches of DNA involved in the transcription process.

Not only are there duplications in the remaining DNA, but there are additional non-coding nucleotide sequences. Interrupting the sequences of base pairs that will be expressed (the exons), there are interruptions in the sequence by segments that aren't expressed (the introns). Like the much larger expanses of "junk DNA" in the chromosome, these smaller interruptions in the DNA have unknown functions. Whether some of the non-coding DNA are remnants of provirus infections during hominoid evolution or somehow involved in compacting the DNA is open to conjecture.

In the process of RNA synthesis within the cell nucleus, DNA is transcribed to single-stranded nuclear RNA (nRNA), which is then processed to form mature messenger RNA (mRNA), as illustrated in Figure 1-6. Small nuclear RNA (snRNA) is involved in this maturation process, which includes excising the introns from the mRNA strands and concatenating the remaining exons according to their original order in the mRNA. As an information transport medium, RNA differs from DNA in that it's single-stranded, much shorter, and the nitrogenous base Uracil (U) is substituted for Thymine.

Mature mRNA is transported through the nuclear membrane to the cytoplasm where the translation of mRNA to protein occurs with the aid of ribosomes. These ribosomes contain a variety of different proteins and an

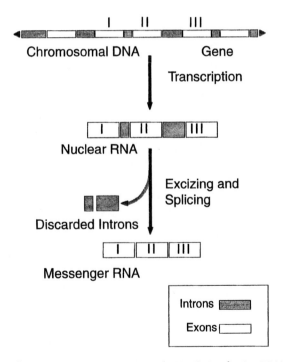

Figure 1-6 Messenger RNA (mRNA) Synthesis. DNA is transcribed to nuclear RNA (nRNA) this is in turn processed to mature mRNA in the nucleus. Maturation involves discarding the junk nucleotide sequences (introns) that interrupt the sequences that will eventually be involved in translation (exons).

assortment of RNA molecules, collectively known as ribosomal RNA (rRNA). These short-lived but abundant rRNAs are involved in the binding of mRNA to the ribosome during the translation process.

The translation of mRNA to protein is facilitated by transfer RNA (tRNA), which associates with the 20 common amino acids (there are 22 genetically encoded amino acids) and controls the sequential binding of the amino acids according to the 3-letter base sequences (codons) on the mRNA. In this way, the tRNA is responsible for positioning the correct amino acid residue at the ribosome, as dictated by the base pair sequence in the mRNA.

Information is transmitted in transcription and translation processes through three-letter words and an alphabet of four letters. Because there are 3 base sequences, there are 4^3 or 64 possible codons (see Figure 1-7), 3 of which are used as stop codons, and 1 for the start codon, to mark the end and start of translation, respectively. The remaining codons are used as redundant

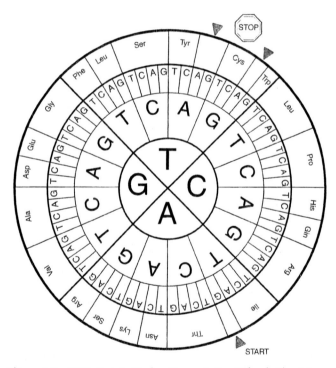

Figure 1-7 RNA-Protein Codon Transcription Wheel. The 64 possible codons represent the 20 common amino acids, as well as one start (ATG) and three stop (TAG, TAA and TGA) markers. Redundancies normally occur in the last nucleotide of the three-letter alphabet.

representations of the amino acids. In most cases, the first two bases are fixed, and the redundancy occurs in the last base. For example, the codons CCC, CCT, CCA, and CCG all code for the amino acid Proline.

During translation, amino acids are added to the growing protein sequence one at a time as the ribosome moves from codon to codon along the mRNA. The starting point for translation is marked by a start codon. At the end of the coding sequence, marked by a stop codon, the translation ends and the protein is released by the ribosome. Before the protein is transported outside of the cell to perform or promote a variety of tasks, it is usually modified by adding a sugar, for example, and it takes on a characteristic folded three-dimensional form—the focus of proteomics research.

TOP-DOWN VERSUS BOTTOM-UP

Although times were simpler when Mendel was tending his garden of *Pisum sativum* in the 1860s, the scientific method used by the father of genetics is virtually identical to that used by a contemporary molecular biologist. There is the formation of a hypothesis followed by observation and controlled, documented experiments that produce results. These data are in turn interpreted to determine whether they support or refute the hypothesis. Regardless of whether the experiments focus on the color of pea plant petals in a monastery garden or on the results of a microarray assay performed on a murder suspect's DNA, data are generated, and they must be accurately recorded for interpretation and future reference.

Mendel recorded experimental findings with paper and pen, and he shared his hypothesis and experimental methods and results with the scientists of the time through traditional journal publishing mechanisms. His opus, "Experiments in Plant Hybridization," appeared in the obscure *Transactions of the Brunn Natural History Society*, where it was promptly ignored by scientists in the hundred or so organizations that subscribed to the journal.

In part because his journal article describing his experiment with peas was very limited in distribution, and in part because the relevance of his work was at best unclear, Mendel failed to stir the imaginations of the thinkers of the time. After all, many of his observations were practiced by the horticulturists of the day; quantifying the breeding practice wasn't viewed as a contribution to science. As a result, he lost interest in genetics and turned to administration. When he died in obscurity in 1884, Mendel was an unknown in the world of science.

Mendel's work illustrates the tension between the top-down and bottom-up approaches to experimental and applied biology. For example, consider how a clinician's top-down view of the human condition contrasts with that of molecular biologist regarding what contributes to health. As shown in Figure 1-8, heredity, as defined by an individual's genetic structure, is only one of many variables that a clinician evaluates in assessing overall health. Environmental factors, including radiation and a variety of chemical and biological agents can modify an individual's genetic structure, resulting in cancer or genetic changes that may be passed on to offspring. In addition, clinicians focus on the normal aging process, trauma from accidents, parasitic infestation, and infection by bacteria and viruses. Lifestyle factors, including smoking, drug use, diet, exercise, and factors that contribute to stress are also considered.

In contrast, molecular biologists typically take a bottom-up approach to evaluating the human condition, working from first principles. Nucleotide sequences and genetic mutations that predispose the individual or the popula-

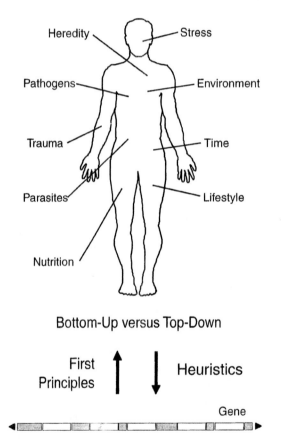

Figure 1-8 Observations and Heuristics. Top-down approaches are often based on heuristics and observations, whereas bottom-up approaches are usually based on first principles.

tion to diseases are the primary focus. Neither approach is correct nor incorrect. The simultaneous top-down and bottom-up approaches to evaluating the human condition are common research methods of virtually every field. A bottom-up approach starts at the most detailed level, and seeks the big picture from the details. For instance, the examination of DNA sequences to study the human organism is analogous to studying alphabets to research written language. Eventually, the interrelated works converge on some greater understanding of the underlying culture (the human organism)—the point of expressing thought and feelings through language.

The dual top-down and bottom-up views of the human condition illustrate the interrelatedness of high-level observations and nucleotide sequences as well as the practical significance of perspective. For example, many animals, plants, and insects directly affect human health in ways that may not be obvious from first principles derived from human nucleotide sequences. Many plants produce beneficial compounds, while animals and insects are common vectors for parasites and pathogens. An individual's genetic constitution may provide information on what is best for his or her survival, but it may not indicate what is best for the population as a whole. For example, there are times when individuals must suffer so that the general population can survive and thrive.

Consider the interrelatedness of public health and molecular biology. Public health officials rely on population statistics, education levels, vaccination compliance, and other predictors of disease prevention. For example, thanks to efforts orchestrated in part by the World Health Organization, smallpox was eradicated from the general population in the last century through vaccination. For the sake of protecting the entire population, the health of a subset of the population was jeopardized. Many children were subject to side effects of the smallpox vaccine, which ranged from fever to death.

From a slightly different perspective, consider that while smoking is considered detrimental to the health of the population as a whole, there are exceptions. For individuals at risk for developing Parkinson's Disease, smoking can reduce the risk of developing this neurologic disorder. This protective effect of smoking is only present with patients with a genetic profile that makes them susceptible to developing Parkinson's. Individuals without genetic susceptibility can increase their chances of contracting Parkinson's if they smoke. Given the relatively low incidence of Parkinson's Disease (less than 1 person per 1,000, predominantly in their 50s), prescribing smoking for the general population would have a negative effect on public health overall.

Another example of the need for simultaneous top-down and bottom-up approach to studying the human organism is the interrelatedness of personal and public health. A significant issue worldwide is the interrelatedness of sickle-cell anemia and the *Plasmodium falciparum* parasite responsible for malaria. Sickle-cell anemia is caused by a change in the chemical composition of the hemoglobin protein that carries the oxygen inside of the red blood cells. These chemical changes in hemoglobin cause the molecule to elongate, distorting the shape of the whole red blood cell. These sickle-shaped red blood cells can damage the capillaries around them and the tissues that depend on the vessels for oxygen and nourishment, resulting in clotting, and, in some cases, death of surrounding tissues.

The homozygous form of sickle-cell disease that is associated with an anemia is universally fatal; few individuals suffering from sickle-cell disease live beyond 20. What's more, in a population free of Anopheline mosquitoes carrying the *Plasmodium falciparum* parasite, individuals with the sickle-cell trait (heterozygotes) are also at a distinct disadvantage to those without the trait. However, in malaria-infested areas of the world, the sickle-cell trait has a protective effect against the malaria parasite. Women with the trait have more offspring, compared to women without the trait, and more of their offspring reach maturity because they are relatively unaffected by malaria.

Although malaria can be cured by drug therapy, treatment is extensive and usually associated with numerous side effects. However, because the DNA of the *Plasmodium falciparum* parasite was sequenced in 2002, there is increased likelihood of an engineered drug that will free those infected from extensive medical regimens.

The pharmaceutical industry provides additional examples of the tension between bottom-up and top-down approaches to evaluating the human condition. Consider that when the antibiotic penicillin was discovered by Alexander Fleming, he observed, by chance, that bacterial growth on a piece of bread was inhibited by a contaminating mold. When it was first used as an antibiotic, penicillin was effective against the majority of bacterial infections. To a practicing clinician, there was no need to understand penicillin's mechanism of action. All that mattered was whether the antibiotic was effective in inhibiting or eradicating a particular pathogen, and the potential side effects, such as allergic reactions.

As soon as penicillin was introduced into the general patient population, bacteria developed a resistance through mutation and the natural selection process. As a result, many patients were unable to benefit from penicillin as an antibiotic, and the market for synthetic pharmaceuticals was born. Since the 1950s, many synthetic derivatives of penicillin have been widely used for a variety of diseases. For example, ampicillin is one of the most useful of these derivatives and serves as a highly effective agent against bacterial infections. As with penicillin, the side effects are normally relatively minor, and usually limited to minor allergic reactions.

Because bacteria can mutate faster than pharmaceutical firms can create engineered antibiotics, newly introduced antibiotics have shorter useful lifetimes than their predecessors. Clinicians attempt to minimize the growing of resistant strains of bacteria by using analogs of penicillin and other first-generation antibiotics whenever possible. However, because antibiotic-resistant bacteria are increasing in relative numbers, more powerful drugs have to be introduced to the market frequently. For example, the cephalosporin class of synthetic antibiotics has a much wider spectrum of activity against pathogens than penicillin and its derivatives.

Synthetic, engineered antibiotics such as the cephalosporins are resistant to the penicillinases produced by penicillin-resistant bacteria and are therefore useful in treating bacterial infections that don't respond to penicillin derivatives. However, bacteria are also developing resistance to the cephalosporins. In addition, these later-generation antibiotics also tend to have more significant side effects than penicillin-based drugs. For example, common side effects of cephalosporins range from stomach cramps, nausea, and vomiting, to headache, fainting, and difficulty breathing.

Molecular biologists are in a constant time-limited battle with mutating bacteria. One of the latest trends in the pharmaceutical industry is the synthesis of drugs that interfere with the bacteria at multiple sites. As a result, for a pathogen to survive, it must develop multiple mutations in one generation—an unlikely event. A dual-site antibiotic interferes with two or more processes that not only function independently within the bacteria but aren't linked in any way. However, developing these next-generation antibiotics requires the use of new visualization techniques, simulations, and other computationally intensive processes—as well as the data on a pathogen's nucleotide sequence. The relevance and relatedness of the pharmaceutical industry's rush to bring product to market to address bacterial resistance and other issues can be appreciated from an information flow perspective.

INFORMATION FLOW

Shannon's information theory applies equally to the flow of information during replication as it does to translation, as depicted in Figure 1-9. For example, in the replication of DNA during mitosis, the information source is the original DNA, and the message is represented by the nucleotide sequence of some combination of Adenosine, Tyrosine, Guanine, and Cytosine. This message is transmitted and reconstituted as a second DNA molecule.

During the replication process, there is a possibility that the noise in the system will upset this ideal information transfer process. For example, a random mutation may occur during the replication process because of, for example, ionizing radiation. Similarly, viruses and other sources of noise may interfere with the replication process, resulting in an imperfect copy of the original DNA molecule.

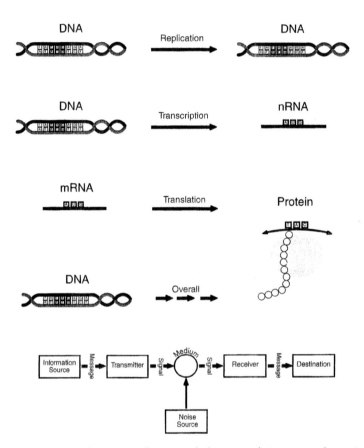

Figure 1-9 Information Theory and the Central Dogma. Information theory applies equally to the replication, transcription, translation, and the overall process of converting nucleotide sequences in DNA to protein.

Viewing the Central Dogma from the perspective of Information Theory enables researchers to apply computer-based numerical techniques to models and evaluate the underlying processes. Evaluating the Central Dogma in terms of information flow also brings metrics into play—such as the effectiveness of the underlying data archiving capacity, the effectiveness of the information flow process, error rate, the degree of data compression, and the degree of uncertainty in the data translation process.

Each of these concepts is related to computer science information theory technologies and approaches. For example, DNA functions as a data archive and, as such, can be evaluated as any other information archive. There are issues of information capacity, how data are represented within the DNA molecule, whether there is provision for automatic error correction, the longevity of the information, the various sources of error at different points in the system, and how the information embedded in DNA is shared with other systems.

Even though there are apparently only about 40,000 coding genes in the human genome, a typical human DNA strand would extend several feet if uncoiled. The physical compression of the nucleotide sequences into tightly coiled chromosomes has parallels in the digital processing world where there is a constant tradeoff between storage capacity and access speed.

As a final example, consider that there is a degree of uncertainty inherent in the communication of information from DNA to protein. For example, the process of information flow can be analyzed to model the sources and types of errors (such as mutations) in the flow of information from nucleotide sequences in DNA to protein in the cytoplasm. In addition to modeling and simulation, resolving or at least quantifying this uncertainty entails the use of data mining, pattern matching, and various other forms of statistical analysis.

From Data to Knowledge

In viewing the Central Dogma as an information flow process, it's useful to distinguish between data, knowledge, and metadata. For our purposes, the following definitions and concepts apply:

- *Data* are numbers or other identifiers derived from observation, experiment, or calculation.
- *Information* is data in context—a collection of data and associated explanations, interpretations, and other material concerning a particular object, event, or process.
- *Metadata* is data about the context in which information is used, such as descriptive summaries and high-level categorization of data and information.

In addition to data, information, and metadata, the concepts of knowledge and understanding are worth noting because these terms often surface in the computer science literature. There's a trend, for example, to re-label databases as knowledgebases—a term borrowed from the AI research community. *Knowledge* is a combination of metadata and an awareness of the context in which the metadata can be successfully applied. In the same context, *understanding* is the personal, human capacity to render experience intelligible by relating specific knowledge to broad concepts.

Both knowledge and understanding are normally considered uniquely human. For example, a so-called knowledgebase of protein folding rules may contain contextual information of folding as a function of the extracellular environment, but the program using the knowledgebase doesn't have an awareness of when this context applies. Furthermore, one of the major failings of expert systems—pattern matching programs that use heuristics or IF-THEN rules stored in a database in order to make decisions—is the inability to fail gracefully when they are used outside of the narrow domain for which they are designed.

Similarly, although understanding is often touted as the inevitable holy grail of AI research, even with the current rate of innovation in computer science, it will be well into the middle of the 21st Century before machines demonstrate understanding. To illustrate how the concepts of data, information, and metadata compare with those of the Central Dogma in evaluating the human condition, consider that to a practicing clinician, a reasonable perspective on a disease such as hereditary disease like neurofibromatosis would be:

- *Data* (from direct observation)
  Patient Age: 5. Physical Exam Findings: Freckling in the armpits and masses on and just below the surface of the skin.
- *Information* (from a molecular disease database)
  Neurofibromatosis is a genetic disorder causing tumors to form on nerve tissue anywhere in the body. The pattern of inheritance is autosomal dominant.
- *Metadata* (from an online publications database)
  The incidence of neurofibromatosis is about one out of every 2,500 people worldwide. It is associated with difficulty seeing, hearing, and in some cases (NF2), with paralysis and early death. In contrast, type 1 (NF1) is more of a cosmetic disorder.

For the clinician, the importance of the databases—whether they contain data, information, or metadata—is to aid in correctly diagnosing the patient and to correctly counsel the parents about the possibility of the disease occurring in children born later. Because neurofibromatosis is an autosomal dominant disease, the clinician would expect each additional offspring to have a 50-50 chance of having the abnormality and could counsel the parents accordingly. This example illustrates how, in general, progressing from data to metadata involves moving from more to less granularity, from direct to indirect observation, and from the verifiable to the theoretical.

For a geneticist studying neurofibromatosis, the relevant data, information, and metadata would likely include:

- *Data* (from NCBI's Map View)
  Position of NF2 gene on chromosome 22, in area 22q12 (see Figure 1-10).

- *Information* (from an online molecular disease database)
  The NF2 gene has been mapped to chromosome 22 and is thought to be a so-called "tumor-suppressor gene."
- *Metadata* (from an online publication database)
  The pattern of inheritance is autosomal dominant, caused by a spontaneous mutation in the egg or sperm before fertilization.

To the typical practicing clinician, the position of the gene on chromosome 22 and even the fact that it's a tumor suppressor gene is of no practical interest. In treating the patient and, more importantly, offering genetic counseling to the parents, the inheritance pattern and how the mutation occurs are much more relevant than whether the responsible gene is on chromosome 2 or 22. However, for the researcher, the position on the gene and proximity to other genes is of paramount importance in the core data to be gleaned from online databases. How the condition appears on the patient—brown spots on the skin, for example—is of peripheral interest at best.

Gene Locus
Neurofibromatosis (NF2)

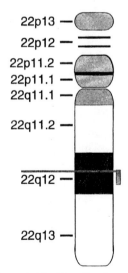

Figure 1-10 Visualization of NF2 Gene on Chromosome 22. As it would appear through National Center for Biological Information's Web-based Map View program, the NF2 gene appears at position 22q12 on chromosome 22.

This difference in perspective affects what constitutes data, information, and metadata, and illustrates the multiple uses of the genomic databases and the difficulty the database designers have in assuming typical users. From the molecular biologist's perspective, the hierarchy of data, information, and metadata is based on first principles. These differences are relative and a matter of degree, in that what is considered data by one researcher might be considered information or metadata by another. For example, to typical clinical researchers, molecular disease databases may represent the finest-grained level of data in which they have an interest. In this case, even the details of protein structure are too far removed from their research interests to constitute relevant data. The typical molecular biologist dealing with DNA sequences regards protein structure as information that provides context to the data—nucleotide sequences.

CONVERGENCE

From the previous discussions, it should be no surprise that the co-evolution of computer science and molecular biology has led to the current state where bioinformatics and computer science are inextricably linked. In this regard, the primary roles of computers in bioinformatics are to serve as controllers, information archives, asynchronous communications devices, and numerical processors. To highlight the part technology plays in molecular biology research—these roles—consider the prototypical DNA sequencing process, depicted in Figure 1-11.

In automated gene sequencing, purified genomic or complementary DNA is first fragmented by restriction enzymes, and these fragments are separated by size on a gel. This is followed by isolating single fragments and using the Sanger chain-termination method to sequence each fragment individually with chain-terminating ddNTS (dideoxy nucleoside triphosphates) labeled with fluorochromes according to the base present. For example, a green fluorochome is typically used for Adenine (A), red for Tyrosine (T), blue for Cytosine (C), and yellow for Guanine (G).

The fragments arising from the Sanger method are then separated by size through polyacrylamide gel electrophoresis. A scanning argon laser is used to excite the fluorochromes attached to the ddNTP, terminating the different fragments and thus identifying a sequence for the fragment. The sequence data are then stored in a database for later analysis.

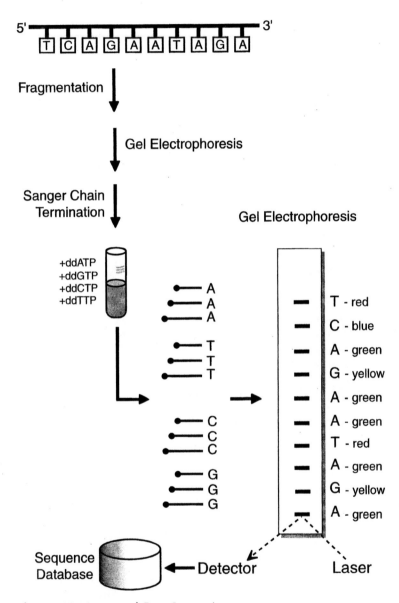

Figure 1-11 Automated Gene Sequencing.

Before examining the gene sequencing process in terms of computer-mediated and enabled control, information archiving, asynchronous communications, and numerical processing, consider that the data can be characterized as:

- **Valuable**—Because the sequencing data are valuable, they are worth archiving for future use and for sharing with others, whether internal to the R&D laboratory or through worldwide publication. In this example, the equipment for sequencing is typically in the $300K range, with additional funds required for trained personnel and supplies. As such, the replacement cost for data inadvertently lost can be significant.
- **Plentiful**—A single gene sequencing run can produce thousands of data points, and sequencing a gene can result in millions of data points.
- **Incomplete**—Even though data are plentiful, they are often considered incomplete because even though the nucleotide sequence of a genome may be nearly complete, there are typically major gaps in data on the proteins that code from the DNA or RNA sequences.
- **Of questionable quality**—Even though the sequencing process may be under computer control, there are limits of data accuracy, repeatability, precision, and reliability. There is a variety of potential error sources that can affect the quality of data, from failure of the detector to register florescent dyes correctly to inconsistencies in pattern matching.

Now, consider the four basic application areas of computers in bioinformatics, summarized in Table 1-1 and described in more detail there.

Control

As noted in Table 1-1, control encompasses technologies including equipment control, robotics, and automatic data collection. For example, the typical gene sequencing machine, like most automated laboratory equipment, is under the control of an embedded computer. Everything from timing the overall process to recording the fluorescing colors as the dyes on the DNA fragments are excited by the laser is controlled by a computer that is an integral part of the underlying electronics. Not only would it be practically impossible to manually track the tens of thousands of base sequences as they are read by the optical scanner, but the computer-enabled pattern-matching function makes the system tenable. Although a desktop computer can be used in control applications, most often computer controllers are integrated or embedded into the device, and support a standard interface for communications with an external PC.

Table 1-1 Application Areas of Computers in Bioinformatics. There is considerable overlap in the technologies associated with each application area.

Application Area	Associated Technologies
Process Control	Equipment control Robotics Automatic data collection
Archiving	Databases IT infrastructure Vocabulary
Numerical Processing	Pattern matching Simulation Data mining Search engines Statistical analysis Visualization
Communications	Desktop publishing Web publishing Internet

Control is unique in the computer science arena in that it involves directly interfacing the physical world with the digital one through stepper motors (electric motors that rotate a fixed number of degrees in fixed steps), robotic arm assemblies, event counters, and other input and output devices other than the traditional keyboard, mouse, and monitor. However, except for this feature, the underlying computing issues, from complexity and logic to language, are relevant to computing and numerical processing, archiving, and communications. These computing concepts are introduced here.

For example, in addition to the Turing model, digital computing is inexorably tied to Boolean logic, advanced in the 1840s by the self-taught professor of mathematics, George Boole. That is, in addition to the arithmetic operations such as addition, subtraction, and multiplication, the digital computers deal with operations such as AND and OR, illustrated by the truth tables in Figure 1-12. As shown in the truth table for the AND operator, the output is high (1) only when both inputs (A AND B) are high. Conversely, as shown on the truth table for the OR operator, the output is high when either inputs (A OR B) are high.

Although digital computers have evolved considerably since Turing's day, the basic elements are the same. Memory, in the form of RAM, ROM, or

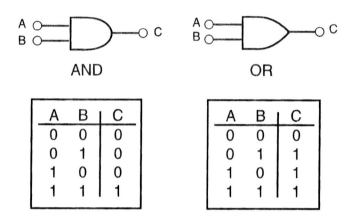

Figure 1-12 Boolean Operators. The AND and OR logic operators form the basis of digital computer operations. Compare the truth tables for each operator with the translation wheel in Figure 1-7.

hard-disk storage, together with the digital microprocessor, forms the basic building blocks for a digital computer, as illustrated in Figure 1-13. As the brains of a microcomputer, the microprocessor directs the flow of data within the computer and performs mathematical operations on the data. Within the microprocessor, the Arithmetic Logic Unit (ALU) performs mathematics and Boolean logic operations according to the truth tables in Figure 1-12. Registers provide temporary storage, a clock provides for the timing of events, and a common bus supports communications among the components. The most important component, from a process control perspective, is the input/output unit that communicates data to and from external devices, such as the instructions to the stepper motors that control the positioning of samples in a gene sequencing machine and accept the output of optical scanners.

One of the distinguishing characteristics of the digital computer is the development of several layers of abstraction above the hardware through the use of a software program referred to as the operating system. The significance of the operating system for end users of computer systems is a relatively recent phenomenon. Prior to the introduction of the PC, programmers and users never interacted with the operating system. It was the computer operator's job to work with the utilities that read data from punched cards, tape, and large disk packs. For everyone else, the user interface consisted of a key-punch machine that could create a single line of code or data. Rearranging lines of code consisted of rearranging stacks of punched cards. Still, users could write in FORTRAN or other high-level languages, without having to worry about the individual registers in the microprocessor.

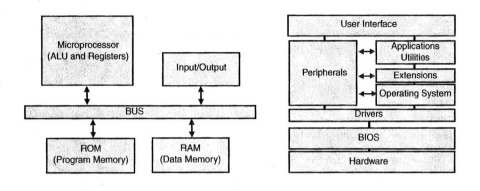

Physical Architecture   Abstraction

Figure 1-13 Digital Computer Physical Architecture (left) versus Abstraction (right). Process control applications emphasize input/output hardware (left), which corresponds to the peripherals abstraction (right).

Operating systems allow users to upgrade their underlying hardware, often without having to learn new applications. They allow users with different hardware—even with different underlying operating systems—to share data. The transition hasn't been smooth, however, and there are still incompatibility issues because of the constant evolution of Macintosh, Windows, UNIX, Linux, and other operating systems. The operating system has undergone tremendous market and technologic evolution since its introduction, with thousands of operating system–specific applications and utilities forced into evolutionary dead ends in the process. Today, UNIX, Microsoft Windows, and Linux rule the desktop PCs, and even these systems are in flux as the developers jostle for market share.

Although process control programmers may have to deal with the base hardware and basic input/output system (BIOS), written in Assembly language, most programmers use a higher-level language. In this way, programmers don't have to concern themselves with the intricacies of the underlying microprocessor or other hardware, but work at a level of abstraction with a "virtual machine," as shown in Figure 1-13.

Although a process control program can be written in Assembly language, abstraction allows the programmer to focus on the real-world problems, such as controlling the progression of a laser beam across a sample of dyed base sequences. The level of abstraction is often a function of the language used to communicate to the hardware. There are dozens of computer languages, many developed for niches in the digital computer world. For example, LISP (LISt Processing) and Perl have been used extensively in pattern-matching research, and SIMULA is popular in the simulation and modeling world. BASIC, PASCAL, and Smalltalk have enjoyed popularity in academic settings, because they are easy to use or demonstrate important programming concepts. MUMPS continues to be used for medical databases, and PHP, XML, Python, and JAVA are increasingly popular for Web development. FORTH, one of the first process control languages, developed initially to control observatory telescopes, continues to be used in equipment controllers. Outside of relatively small niche areas, many of these languages turned out to be evolutionary dead ends, in favor of industry standard BASIC and C++.

As the number of transistors in a microcomputer and the number of lines of code in operating systems climb into the millions, there is the challenge of dealing with increasing complexity. Complexity theory explains how extremely small errors in initial conditions within complex systems—a single mistake in a million-line piece of code, for example—can grow to influence behavior on a much larger scale. It's no surprise that PCs occasionally fail or crash because of "memory leaks" and other non-specific reflections of a system characterized by complexity. Sometimes, the results are more insidious, such as the math errors caused by a defect in Intel's original Pentium chip.

Fortunately, technologies have been developed in an attempt to resolve potential problems before they surface. For example, decision tables—matrices of possible input and output states—can help identify combinations of input conditions that should be tried when testing a microprocessor. When the number of possible input conditions rises to the hundreds, decision tables and other state-validation tools make an otherwise impossible task doable.

Archiving

As illustrated by the gene sequencing machine, the end result of processing the DNA fragments is volumes of data that must be stored for a variety of uses. For example, the sequence data can be compared with other investigators' data to look for inconsistencies or validation. The data can be processed locally in order to visualize the most likely protein structures that would result from translation of the nucleotide sequences. In addition, the data can be submitted to one of the national databases to support the work of other microbiologists or to give the researcher academic credit for the electronic publication. As such, a reason for creating biological databases is to support the analysis and communication of data, information, and metadata relevant to molecular biologists. In many respects, the functions of archiving, processing, and communications overlap significantly.

Just as the transfer of data from DNA to RNA to protein relies on an information infrastructure, data archives rely on an information technology (IT) infrastructure. This IT infrastructure includes network and database technologies as well as standard vocabularies to store and access information. Even though sequencing and other molecular biology data is vast and growing daily, there are huge gaps in our understanding of the relationships of databases to each other and with higher-level disease databases. One of the motivations for constructing archives and linking them together is so that this gap can be closed as quickly as possible.

For the molecular biologist involved in developing or using databases, it's important to consider the processes involved in managing data before focusing on the technology. That is, the process of data collection, use, and dissemination should drive technology. After all, Mendel's notebooks didn't dictate his experiments with garden-variety peas, but they empowered him by leveraging his capacity to recall previous experiments, to plan for future experiments, and publish his findings.

Numerical Processing

Computers are recognized foremost for their computational or numerical-processing capabilities. In bioinformatics, applications for numerical-processing techniques range from sequence analysis, microarray data analysis, and site prediction to gene finding, protein structure prediction, and phylogenetic analysis. These applications in turn rely on methods ranging from pattern matching, simulation, and data mining to machine learning, statistics, cluster analysis, and decision trees. For example, consider the pattern-matching challenge associated with multiple string alignment—aligning multiple polypeptide sequences—as a means of discovering potential homologous relationships between proteins. Because millions of calculations may be involved in examining three or four relatively short sequences, the much more formidable task of matching multiple sequences of several hundred polypeptides in length is usually computationally prohibitive on even the fastest desktop hardware.

In numerical-processing applications such as pattern matching, speed of computation is valued over all else. As every computer hardware manufacturer knows, speed sells. A PC or workstation that was leading-edge two years ago now seems slow, given that the next processor will provide leaps in processing power according to the prediction of Intel Computer's CEO, Gordon Moore. Moore's Law, which states that microprocessor capacity doubles every 18 months, has held up thus far, and will likely do so for the next decade. Processing speed is critical for analysis of biological data, especially when there are vast amounts of processing-associated visualization, sequence alignment, and sequence prediction. For example, Craig Venter of Celera Genomics backed up his statement of "Speed matters, discovery can't wait" with an $80 million supercomputer. Similarly, for the researcher using Web-based tools to search for sequences, the processing time required for each search effectively limits the number of searches that can be performed in a working day.

In addition to string matching and manipulation operations using string-manipulation capabilities inherent in languages such as Perl, JAVA, or PHP, the most significant pattern-matching tools are rules-based expert systems, artificial neural networks, and genetic algorithms. Rules-based systems, all of which have been developed on the digital computer, rely on IF-THEN clauses. For example:

```
IF First Codon = "T" AND Second Codon = "A"
   AND (Third Codon = "A" OR Third Codon ="G")
THEN Codon = "Stop"
```

Rules-based systems are often developed in a language such as LISP and then recoded in JAVA, C++, XML, or another efficient language.

Another class of pattern-matching programs is machine learning, typified by the artificial neural network (or neural net). Unlike expert systems, neural nets don't rely on conventional algorithmic programming techniques, but work by altering the strength of connections between input and output nodes. The advantage of artificial neural networks over conventional, algorithm-based systems is that they can learn from examples, and generalize this learning to new situations. For example, the input nodes can be associated with amino acid sequences and the output nodes can be associated with specific protein folding patterns. When a novel amino acid sequence is presented to the neural net, it can make a guess as to the folding pattern of the protein. A rule-based system, like a conventional algorithm-based system, would simply fail with a novel sequence. In addition to protein structure prediction, neural networks are used as "gene finders," typified by the applications GRAIL, GeneParser, and Genie.

Artificial neural networks are commonly created in layers, with one or more hidden layers sandwiched between the input and output layers. It is the hidden layer that does most of the work involved in classifying or recognizing the pattern presented to the input layer. Learning is represented by the relative strengths of the connections between the individual nodes, which are defined during training of the network. That is, the internal simulation is inherently analog in nature, even though the input and output states are mapped to binary values. During training, important pathways are strengthened, and unimportant ones diminish with experience (repeated training).

In the elementary artificial neural network schematic shown in Figure 1-14, the network consists of three input and two output nodes, with each input node connected to both output nodes. The possible truth table shown in the figure is the result of the specific training of the network. Other truth tables would result from other training.

Amino Acid Sequence

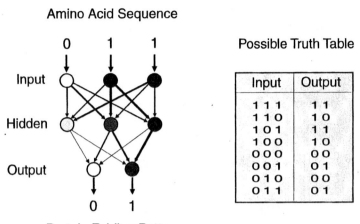

Protein Folding Pattern

Figure 1-14 Artificial Neural Network. This machine-learning technology relies on tightly interconnected input, hidden, and output layers to map input patterns to output patterns. One of many possible truth tables (right) illustrates the mapping of input to output patterns. Learning is signified by the thickness of lines joining nodes, and node values are indicated by color (white = 0 and black = 1). Hidden nodes can take on values between 0 and 1.

Artificial neural networks and other forms of machine learning are only one form of pattern matching that have application in bioinformatics. Other approaches to pattern matching include techniques such as genetic algorithms, which work by identifying the best fit for a function that is used to select future generations. Hybrid systems of artificial neural networks supplemented by genetic algorithms rule-based expert systems, and conventional, algorithmic programming hold particular promise in bioinformatics.

In addition to simulating neural networks, the numerical processing capabilities of a computer are commonly used to simulate the interactions of various proteins and drugs at their active sites. Data-mining applications include searching patterns of known gene structures for newly discovered patterns. Search engines are similarly instrumental to uncovering patterns or key works in local or online databases. Pairwise sequence comparison, based on either BLAST or Smith-Waterman dynamic programming techniques, form the basis for most sequence alignment operations. Using online tools based on BLAST, it's possible for anyone with a connection to the Internet to evaluate all possible ways of aligning one sequence against another in a reasonable time, even though the number of such possible alignments grows exponentially with the length of the two sequences.

Statistical analysis is an important component of searching and pattern matching, especially in dealing with uncertainty. For example, in the multiple sequence alignment problem in Figure 1-15, statistical methods can be used to determine the best alignment of the four polypeptide strings consistent with an alignment score that rewards perfect matches, and penalizes for imperfect matches and the number and length of the gaps introduced in the final sequence. Non-statistical methods of multiple sequence alignment can be used as well.

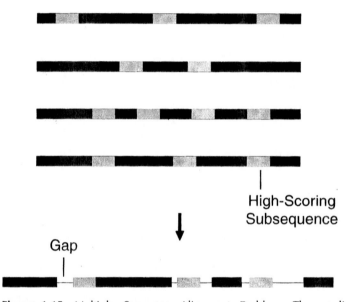

Figure 1-15 Multiple Sequence Alignment Problem. The unaligned polypeptide sequences are shown at the top of the figure, and the resultant sequence with gaps is shown at the bottom. Statistical and non-statistical methods can be used to identify the optimum position of gaps and the relative location of the high-scoring polypeptide sequences, as a starting point for evolutionary modeling, for example.

The most numerically intensive application of computers to bioinformatics is in predicting protein structure, especially when the modeling process begins with first principles—so-called *ab initio* modeling. Once a protein has been modeled, any number of online or desktop applications can be used to visualize the structures in three dimensions. Although affordable workstations can handle most visualization needs, modeling protein structure and interactions often requires distributed computer systems or supercomputers.

It's important to note that many of the numerical techniques used in bioinformatics provide *an* answer, but not necessarily *the* answer to data analysis, classification, and prediction problems. For example, a neural network can be trained to predict the location of exons on a segment of DNA, but the answer is never a certainty until it is verified experimentally. Similarly, numerical methods can be used to predict the structure of proteins, but the accuracy of the prediction varies significantly, depending on the methods used and the problem set. The challenge is identifying the methodology that provides adequate results with the time and computer resources available.

Communications

As a communications system, the computer is like an asynchronous communications medium, typified by server-based e-mail. Data are deposited in the system and retrieved later. As in an e-mail system, the information can be retrieved by the person who originally created it, or more often by another party. Similarly, biological database systems can be private or public, where the former is intended to provide asynchronous communications to the same user, and the latter approximates sending mail to others.

From a data-management perspective, computers are increasingly used as *asynchronous* communications devices. That is, unlike a telephone or other synchronous communications device, communications through computer networks don't necessarily occur in real-time and are independent of any clock. Instead, communications are event driven. For example, in the normal operation of a database server, data are sent to a computer where they may be stored for a few microseconds or for a decade before they are output to a printer or monitor. When computers are configured as a communication device, the users who generate the data tend to be different from the users who receive the results, and the response time may be hours or days.

The difference between e-mail and a typical biological database is that contribution to biological databases such as GenBank are meant for others, but the identity of the recipients is unknown and largely unknowable by the sender. Unlike an e-mail that is automatically deleted by the server after the e-mail is read, the data in a biological database is considered permanent or at least not altered by the process of accessing the data.

The communications of sequencing and protein structure information is hindered because of the lack of a standard format for creating and storing gene data, even within companies. Several contenders for the standard include Gene Expression Markup Language (GEML), based on the eXtensible Markup Language (XML), and Microarray Markup Language (MAML). The latter is based on collaboration between the National Center for Biotechnology Information, Stanford University, and the European Bioinformatics Institute.

ENDNOTE

The history of innovation and development in computing and molecular biology is much more complicated than that suggested by the timeline in Figure 1-2 or by the Central Dogma. The flow of information through replication, transcription, and translation is more involved than described here, and there are unknowns and exceptions to most of the theories put forth by investigators. For example, the Central Dogma is only partially correct, in that the flow of information isn't unidirectional as Watson initially proposed. In contrast to the Central Dogma, information can flow from external sources into the genome. For example, retroviruses or RNA-based viruses such as HIV copy their genetic information into the host cell's DNA, where the cell's machinery obediently duplicates the retrovirus.

In addition, there are many more unknowns than the role of introns and other apparently non-coding DNA in the chromosomes. Many of the proteins in the human proteome haven't been cataloged, and the roles of those that have been cataloged are poorly understood. Similarly, the processes of replication, transcription, and translation are exceedingly complex, involving hundreds of thousands of operations mediated by hundreds of factors, only a few of which are understood. Furthermore, the information-transfer process described by the Central Dogma differs somewhat from that used by mitochondria and some microorganisms.

What's more, it's possible that the source of much of the work in bioinformatics—the human genome—is inherently biased. Because much of the sequence data is derive from analysis of Craig Venter's DNA, with minimal contributions from five other donors, the data necessarily reflect Venter's genotype. Although it was recognized early on that his DNA carries a variant gene associated with abnormal fat metabolism and Alzheimer's disease, other variants carried by Venter that have not yet been studied may be considered normal for the human genome until more research is performed. Undoubtedly, over the next decade, when scientists finally finish and verify the genome sequence, other discoveries will be made as well. For example, it's unclear what the sequences in the centromeres will reveal, especially because the sequences in those regions of each chromosome have been resistant to sequencing techniques used on the other parts of the chromosomes.

Similarly, developments in computer science have not been as straightforward as suggested by the timeline. For example, the promise of AI, the darling of the computer science community throughout the 1980s, never materialized. After the massive military funding for language translation evaporated, the few companies that attempted to survive in the commercial world folded. Even the notable academic systems, such as MYCIN—the first rule-based expert system in medicine—were never put to practical use. What survives today are the various pattern-recognition methods and object-oriented programming techniques that are invaluable in genome and proteome research.

The timeline offered here also glosses over much of the human struggle involved in the discoveries and triumphs in both molecular biology and computing. For example, James Watson was initially in charge of the Human Genome Project, but resigned after only a few years because of a feud with the director of the National Institutes of Health over gene patenting. His successor, Francis Collins was then embroiled in competition with Craig Venter's private research institute over methodology. Although Venter prevailed and won the race to decode the majority of what is currently understood to be the human genome, the commercial viability of his company is less certain. Similarly, there is turmoil—and millions of dollars at stake—over determining who should be credited with the basic sequencing technique.

Just as the hype of what AI was supposed to deliver served to kill the industry for many years, many of the favored genomics research firms have performed less profitably than expected on Wall Street. Some genetically engineered drugs have not taken off as expected, and companies such as Genetech have been forced to turn to modifications of conventional pharmaceuticals to stay in business.

When exploring the computational methods described in this book, the reader is encouraged to apply basic business metrics to the information. For example, what is the added value of each step in the computerization process? How can the computing method described save time, provide a more accurate result, or save valuable resources? In the end, computers and computational methods are simply tools. Like a sculptor, chipping away at the rock covering a statue, it's up to the readers to select the tools that can best help create their vision.

➤ Prefoldin Chaperone, PDB entry 1FXK. Image produced with PDB Structure Explorer, which is based on MolScript and Raster3D.

CHAPTER 

Databases

What a piece of work is man! How noble in reason!
How infinite in faculty! In form, and moving, how express
and admirable! In action how like an angel! In apprehension
how like a god! The beauty of the world! The paragon of
animals! And yet, to me, what is this quintessence of dust?
— William Shakespeare, Hamlet

omputers serve four interdependent functions in bioinformatics: commu-nications, computation, control, and storage. Embedded computer con-trollers in sequencing machines, fermentation tanks, and bioreactors direct the programmable robotic arms that automate intricate processes and mark-edly decrease the need for human operators. When time is of the essence, computer-controlled devices are superior to manual operations, in part because they can operate virtually unattended around the clock. Venter's company, Celera Genomics—followed by government-funded sequencing lab-oratories—was able to make unprecedented gains in sequencing throughput primarily through computer-directed robots that automated the tedious sequencing process.

As a communications device, not only has the computer helped researchers craft more journal articles in less time than at any other point in history, but an increasingly large proportion of academic research information appears online. Up until the mid-1990s, newly discovered nucleotide sequences from human and other species of DNA were published in printed journals, requiring that researchers interested in using computer techniques to explore the sequence either key in the sequences by hand or use optical character recognition (OCR) systems to automatically capture the printed sequences and translate them into in machine-readable form. Today, no researcher would think of consulting a printed journal for a nucleotide sequence, but would immediately turn to either one of the numerous public databases on the Web or one of the value-added commercial databases. Furthermore, if a printed journal article isn't referenced by one of the electronic databases, such as PubMed, then the chances of the article ever being read in any form are low.

As computational devices in bioinformatics, computers are used for tasks that range from searching for nucleotide sequences and visualizing protein folding patterns to simulating complex 3D protein-protein interactions, for applications ranging from drug discovery to biomaterials research and development. As an example of computer processing power focused on numeric computation in bioinformatics, consider that Celera Genomics' network of 800 Compaq AlphaServers has the capacity to compare up to 250 billion genomic sequences per hour generated by its hundreds of robotic gene sequencing machines. Even lesser-endowed companies and academic centers are creating high-performance Beowulf clusters for bioinformatics work. These massively parallel systems that are constructed from dedicated PC hardware are generally affordable and available to anyone.

Researchers at another pharmacological powerhouse, GlaxoSmithKline (GSK), are studying how individual variations in the genetic code cause adverse drug reactions in some patients. To pursue this research, GSK partners with biotech research firms who store clinical data from drug trials and correlate it with the patient's genetic information to create a genetic profile of patients at risk. Similarly, clinicians with the Mayo Clinic in Minnesota are working with researchers to identify gene markers that indicate which patients should respond to specific anticancer therapy. Elsewhere, pharmaceutical research firms are using genetic traits to predict whether a patient will respond to therapy as well as the likelihood of serious side effects. Several biotech startups are developing panels of DNA tests that will allow clinicians to quickly determine how patients metabolize drugs so that dosage regimens can be tailored to their individual metabolism.

All of these activities revolve around database technology. For example, both communications and computation operations in bioinformatics depend on data that have to be maintained. Electronic databases maintain data in a persistent, non-volatile form that allows operations to be repeated and compared with other operations, with the results communicated to other researchers and developers. The electronic database—a file composed of records, each containing fields together with a set of operations for searching, sorting, recombining, and other functions—is the silicon, plastic, and iron-oxide equivalent of the experimenter's private notebook, and the basis for electronic publishing to the scientific community.

As an illustration of how central databases are to the molecular biology research and development, consider a sampling of the public bioinformatics databases listed in Table 2-1. Perhaps the best-known of the hundreds of DNA sequence databases accessible through the Internet are the international nucleotide sequence database collaborators GENBANK, supported by the National Center for Biological Information (NCBI), the DNA DataBank of Japan (DDBJ), and the European Molecular Biology Laboratory (EMBL). Another major database, PubMed, which is maintained by the U.S. National Library of Medicine, is a key resource for biomedical literature.

Table 2-1   Public Bioinformatics Databases Accessible via the Internet.

Database Type	Example	Note
Nucleotide Sequence	GenBank	One of the largest public sequence databases
	DDBJ	DNA DataBank of Japan
	EMBL	European Molecular Biology Laboratory
	MGDB	Mouse Genome Database
	GSX	Mouse Gene Expression Database
	NDB	Nucleic Acid Database
Protein Sequence	SWISS-PROT	Swiss Institute for Bioinformatics and European Bioinformatics Institute
	TrEMBL	Annotated supplement to SWISS-PROT
	TrEMBLnew	Weekly, pre-processed update to TrEMBL
	PIR	Protein Information Resource
3D Structures	PDB	Protein DataBank
	MMDB	Molecular Modeling Database
	Cambridge Structural Database	For small molecules
Enzymes and Compounds	LIGAND	Chemical compounds and reactions

Table 2-1 Public Bioinformatics Databases Accessible via the Internet. *(continued)*

Database Type	Example	Note
Sequence Motifs (Alignment)	PROSITE	Sequence motifs
	BLOCKS	Derived from PROSITE
	PRINTS	A superset of BLOCKS
	Pfam	Protein families database of alignments and hidden Markov models
	ProDOM	Protein Domains
Pathways and Complexes	Pathway	Metabolic and regulatory pathway maps
Molecular Disease	OMIM	Online Mendelian Inheritance in Man
Biomedical Literature	PubMed	Contains Medline
	Medline	Medical Literature
Vectors	UniVec	Used to identify vector contamination
Protein Mutations	PMD	Protein Mutant Database
Gene Expressions	GEO	Gene Expression Omnibus
Amino Acid Indices	Aaindex	Amino Acid Index Database
Protein/Peptide Literature	LITDB	Literature database for proteins and peptides
Gene Catalog	GENES	KEGG Genes Database

The nucleotide sequence databases and PubMed represent the extremes of the spectrum from sequences of base pairs to their relevance in disease and the practice of medicine. Other online databases, such as the protein sequence database SWISS-PROT, and the Online Mendelian Inheritance in Man (OMIM) database—a molecular disease database that links human genes and genetic disease—provide data that is somewhere between the two ends of the spectrum. For example, SWISS-PROT contains sequence motifs (where a motif is a small structural element that is recognizable in several proteins, such as the alpha helix) that are often associated with particular functions, linking structure and function. Popular representatives of so-called alignment databases are PROSITE and BLOCKS, for sequence motif and motif alignment data, respectively.

Public structural databases are represented by the Cambridge Structural Database for small molecules and the Protein Data Bank (PDB) for macromolecules. The PDB, which is maintained by the Research Collaboratory for Structural Bioinformatics (RCSB), includes publicly available 3D structures of proteins, nucleic acids, and carbohydrates, as determined by X-ray crystallography and NMR spectroscopy. The PDB serves as the source data for other databases, such as the Molecular Modeling Database (MMDB), which is used to construct 3D images of the molecules involved.

In addition to the public databases, there are a rapidly increasing number of private databases created and maintained by for-profit companies and laboratories associated with academic institutions. For example, the LifeSeq database from Incyte Genomics, Inc. contains gene sequences from humans, rats, and mice. Regardless of whether databases are public or private, most have particular functions and uses in bioinformatics, and entire books could easily be devoted to their construction, maintenance, and use. However, because of volatility in the commercial database space and evolving associations among academic laboratories, the specifics of particular databases will change markedly over time. As such, it's more important for the reader to understand the general concepts and issues that apply to all biological databases, whether they're custom, in-house systems or public databases administered by the federal government.

For example, one characteristic of biological databases that is virtually universal is the enormity of their contents. To the delight of the sagging post-eCommerce information technology industry, the data-handling requirements associated with even modest biological databases often necessitate considerable investment in hardware, software, and personnel. Consider that as of mid-2002, GenBank, the repository of nucleotide sequences for a variety of species that forms the basis for much bioinformatics research, contained data on over 17 billion base pairs stored in over 15 million sequence records. Similarly, Incyte Genomics' LifeSeq commercial database contained over a terabyte (1,000 gigabytes) of data, with a system capacity of 70 terabytes. Many companies in the bioinformatics space have database system capacities in excess of 200 terabytes (200,000 gigabytes, equivalent to about 310,000 CD-ROMs), in the form of multiple, refrigerator-sized racks of hard drives. Creating archives is an inherent challenge in any database system. So is integrating information in different formats from multiple databases. The difficulty of these tasks is accentuated by the sheer enormity of the volume of data involved.

Given the central role databases and database technology plays in bioinformatics, at a minimum, researchers, managers, and scientists in the field should not only become fluent in the language of database technology, but should also understand how biomedical databases form the basis of all bioinformatics research and development efforts. In addition, readers should appreciate that database technology is most valuable in the biotech industry when it enables the integration of research, development, clinical activity, manufacturing, and selling and marketing. Data take on added value when they leave the confines of a workstation and become incorporated into shared public and private databases, applications, and products.

To this end, this chapter gives an overview of database technology and its uses in bioinformatics, with a focus on shared or multi-user database systems. Topics range from the database management process, database models, interfacing databases to the Internet for collaboration, archiving, to the practical challenges associated with establishing a local database. The likely future of bioinformatics database technology is also discussed. The first section, "Definitions," provides a review of key definitions that readers should be familiar with to understand the following discussions. The "Data Management" section provides a functional overview of the typical data-management challenges faced by researchers in the biotechnology field. These researchers typically work with locally generated data, the public genomic databases, and data from collaborators in associated areas, such as clinical medicine. The "Data Life Cycle" section continues the functional overview by exploring the normal life cycle of data, from creation to disposal, and how this cycle can be managed. "Database Technology" reviews the more technical issues associated with biomedical databases, from the architecture of databases and database management systems to database models and data capture. The "Implementation" section illustrates how an understanding of these technical issues translates to practical database installations. Finally, "Endnote" looks to the near horizon and suggests impending developments in biomedical databases and the challenges of moving forward to a fully integrated biomedical database system.

DEFINITIONS

Databases, which provide the long-term memory of computer operations, take on a variety of names, depending on their structure, contents, use, and amount of data they contain. Two technologies often confused with databases are disk servers and file servers. A disk server is a node in a local area network that acts as a remote disk drive. A disk server can be divided into multiple volumes, some of which are shared by all users on the server, and others of which can be accessed only by a specific user, as defined by username and password login. At the next level in sophistication is the file server, which can be thought of as a disk server with intelligence. A file server not only stores files, but manages the network requests for them and maintains order as users request and modify files.

The file server, like the disk server, supports movement and cataloging of files, but, unlike a true database, the contents of a file server are unavailable without the use of some other application. With both disk servers and file servers, separate applications must be used to open documents for reviewing and editing. In this regard, most disk and file servers work like extensions to the computer operating system. Files can be identified, copied, deleted, and otherwise managed at a very high level. For our purposes, file servers and disk servers can be considered as extensions to the internal workstation hard drive that may be configured as a shared volume so that collaborators on the same network can share data stored on the server.

At the simplest level of a true database is the data repository, a database used as an information storage facility, with minimal analysis or querying functionality. A data repository is a structured, systematically collected storehouse of data distilled or mirrored from a single application, such as a sequencing machine, microarray analyzer, or clinical system (see Figure 2-1).

One advantage of using a data repository instead of the original database in the host application or device is that longitudinal studies are possible because all data in the host application are mirrored and stored in the repository. For example, because of storage limitations, or because the local database is always in use, it may be virtually impossible for a researcher to compare data from multiple runs of a sequencing machine. Another advantage of using a data repository instead of the original database is that it offloads the query functions that are available through native applications to the database management system that enables efficient control and management of the data repository.

Next up the hierarchy of complexity and capability is the data mart, a searchable database system, organized according to the user's likely needs. Like a data repository, a data mart has a narrow focus on data that is specific to a particular research project or task. That is, a data mart contains a subset of the data contained in other databases as opposed to an indiscriminate mass copying of all the data from another database. The major difference between a data mart and a data repository is that a data mart contains data extracted or mirrored—copied in real time—from multiple application databases.

One step up from the data mart is the data warehouse, a central database, frequently very large, that can provide authenticated researchers with access to all of an institution's information. That is, a data warehouse is usually populated with data from a variety of non-compatible sources, such as sequencing machines, clinical systems, or national genomic databases. Because a data warehouse combines data from a variety of application-oriented databases into a single system, data from disparate sources must be cleaned, encoded, and translated so that a standard set of analytical tools can be used with the data. Furthermore, the data in a data warehouse are nonvolatile in that new data are appended to the database and never replace existing data. In addition, the data warehouse is considered time-variant in that the data are time-stamped.

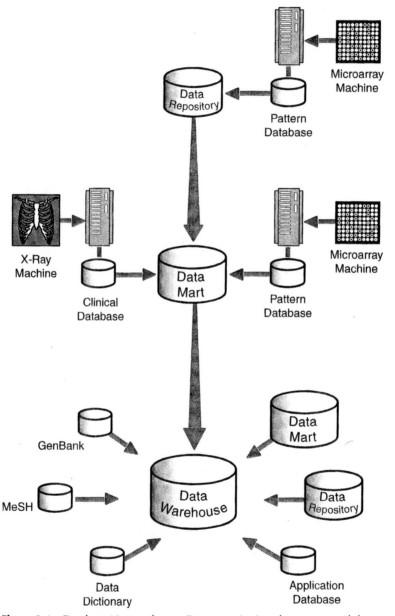

Figure 2-1 Database Nomenclature. Data repositories, data marts, and data warehouses differ primarily in the diversity of data sources that contribute to their contents.

The data warehouse is also distinguished from application-specific databases in the way the data destined for incorporation in a data warehouse are selected, prepared, and loaded, and how the underlying database is optimized for use. Once data to be included in a data warehouse have been identified, the data are cleaned, merged, and the original database structures are manipulated to mirror those of the data warehouse. For example, data redundancy may be intentionally built-in to the data warehouse architecture, thereby minimizing the processing required for a typical query, which in turn maximizes the efficiency of the underlying database engine.

It's important to note that when the specialized vocabulary is peeled away, data repositories, data marts, and data warehouses are simply databases. The three architectures share the usual issues of database design, provision for maintenance, security, and periodic modification. Similarly, data repositories, data marts, and data warehouses are built with some form of a database management system, a program that allows researchers to store, process, and manage data in a systematic way.

One of the uses of a fully functional data warehouse or data mart is that it supports data mining—the process of extracting meaningful relationships from usually very large quantities of seemingly unrelated data. Specialized data-mining tools allow researchers to perform complex analyses and predictions on data. A prerequisite to data mining and the archiving process in general is the availability of a controlled vocabulary that provides a single term for a given concept. This controlled vocabulary is most often implemented as part of a data dictionary—a program that maps or translates identical concepts that are expressed in different words, phrases, or units into a single vocabulary. A popular controlled vocabulary is the Medical Subject Heading (MeSH), maintained by the U.S. National Library of Medicine, and used with the government-sponsored PubMed biomedical literature database.

Related to the concept of databases is the data archive—a non-volatile holder for data that are infrequently accessed—that is optimized for data recovery and data longevity. Strictly speaking, an archive needn't be a database. Archives are commonly made on multi-gigabyte tape cartridges that are stored offsite in environmentally controlled conditions to minimize the chances of data loss.

Armed with these core definitions, the reader can proceed with this chapter, which considers databases from a functional, data-management perspective before exploring the core technologies.

DATA MANAGEMENT

A central tenet in applied information technology is that process should drive technology. If there is an obvious need that is only partially or inefficiently addressed, it's much easier to introduce a technology to address the need than it is to eradicate the need through technology alone. There are exceptions, of course, in that some individuals will adopt a new technology simply because it's new. Marketing professionals refer to these prospects as innovators and early adopters—technophiles who take joy in owning the first model of a new technology before it's available to the public or their peers. However, for most of the population—the early and late majority—technology is a means to an end.

For most researchers in bioinformatics, database technology is the means to handling the enormity of data and information that is created, manipulated, and communicated every day. Consider the various components in the biological data-management scenario in the pharmacogenomic laboratory depicted in Figure 2-2.

This data-management scenario is similar to that followed by several commercial biotech ventures, such as deCODE Genetics, the commercial venture in Iceland that is headed by a former Harvard Medical School professor who recognized the advantage of having access to a genetically homogeneous population for pharmacogenomic R&D. Because the majority of Iceland's population dates back only to the time of the original Viking settlers around 800 AD, and there are meticulous records of family history, every native's genetic heritage is available online through a government-run database. In addition, the researchers at deCODE, through a hotly debated arrangement with the Icelandic government, purchased the exclusive rights to access every citizen's medical records, most of which are in electronic form.

Because of the similarity of the genetic code in the closed population, DNA samples from families that suffer from particular diseases can be compared to those of closely related families who are disease-free. Through data mining, researchers at deCODE hope to identify the genes responsible for a variety of diseases, such as osteoarthritis. The competitive advantage of the company isn't the latest sequencing or microarray machines; it's their ability to integrate data from Iceland's family tree and medical record databases with deCODE's own patient DNA database and to manage that data in a way that supports the company's research objectives.

In this scenario, patient medical records are combined with genomic data in order to associate genes with particular diseases. Researchers in the laboratory also have access to the public and private online databases, such as those from the National Center for Biological Information and Celera Genomics, respectively. In addition to numerous application-specific databases in the clinical departments and local databases associated with the sequencing machines, researchers query local data repositories of aggregated data, data marts, and a data warehouse. Some of the information technology components in this scenario, such as the data sources, are obvious, whereas others, such as standards for data formats, would only be apparent to the researchers who work in the environment on a daily basis.

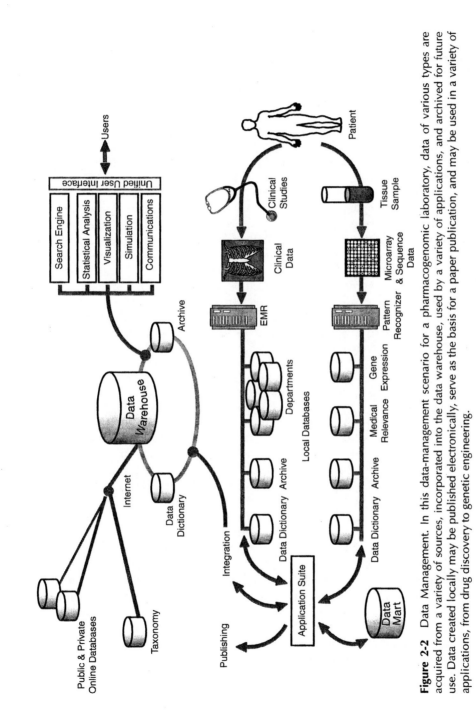

Figure 2-2 Data Management. In this data-management scenario for a pharmacogenomic laboratory, data of various types are acquired from a variety of sources, incorporated into the data warehouse, used by a variety of applications, and archived for future use. Data created locally may be published electronically, serve as the basis for a paper publication, and may be used in a variety of applications, from drug discovery to genetic engineering.

Pharmacogenomics and Aggression

To illustrate the data-management issues associated with a biotech research effort that depends on multiple, disparate systems and accompanying databases, assume that the laboratory depicted in Figure 2-2 focuses on understanding the genetic basis for aggression, with a goal of creating new, more effective medications to control the behavior. The challenge is formidable on a number of fronts. For example, there is no universally accepted definition for aggression. The standard source for the definitions of human behavior for clinicians and third-party payers in the U.S., the Diagnostic and Statistical Manual of Mental Disorders, Fourth Edition-Text Revision (DSM-IV-TR), doesn't contain a definition of aggression or violence. Furthermore, some clinicians use the terms "agitation" and "aggression" interchangeably. However, the DSM-IV-TR describes agitation as excessive, nonproductive, and repetitious motor activity—such as pacing, fidgeting, and an inability to sit still—secondary to feelings of inner tension. Other clinicians view agitation and aggression as representing the spectrum of behaviors from simple anxiety to overt physical aggression against others.

Despite the lack of a clear definition, a commonly used method of classifying the behavior of individuals thought to be aggressive is to use a questionnaire and then evaluate the results according to rating scales designed to systematically evaluate the signs of aggression. For example, the Overt Aggression Scale (OAS), quantifies verbal aggression (from making loud noises to threatening violence), physical aggression against self (from pulling hair to deep cuts), physical aggression against objects (from slamming doors to breaking windows), and physical aggression against other people (from threatening gestures to breaking bones). However, even this widely recognized scale isn't all-inclusive. For example, it doesn't distinguish between acute and chronic aggression. Although there is no universally accepted boundary between acute and chronic aggression, a one-month timeframe is often used as the breakpoint. The distinction between acute and chronic aggression has practical significance because patients diagnosed with chronic aggression are eligible for insurance coverage for behavioral modification and pharmacological treatment, including the use of antipsychotic drugs, while drugs for patients diagnosed with acute aggression are not covered by insurance.

Researchers in the lab might use an online literature reference database, such as PubMed, to identify prior research in academia and perhaps published reports from other companies working on the genetic basis of aggression. A reasonable place to start in the search for prior research would be the National Library of Medicine's online MeSH browser, shown in Figure 2-3. The browser offers a definition for the term "aggression," and provides two MeSH trees to indicate there are two applicable contexts—behavioral symptoms and social behavior.

MeSH Heading	Aggression
Tree Number	F01.145.126.125
Tree Number	F01.145.813.045
Annotation	human & animal; "aggression" in French is translated "stress" & indexed under a STRESS heading; "agressologie" = STRESS
Scope Note	A form of behavior which leads to self-assertion; it may arise from innate drives and/or a response to frustration; may be manifested by destructive and attacking behavior, by covert attitudes of hostility and obstructionism, or by healthy self-expressive drive to mastery. (Dorland 27th ed)
Allowable Qualifiers	CL DE PH PX RE
Unique ID	D000374

Behavior and Behavior Mechanisms [F01]

Behavior [F01.145]

Behavioral Symptoms [F01.145.126]

Affective Symptoms [F01.145.126.100]

➤ Aggression [F01.145.126.125]

Agonistic Behavior [F01.145.126.125.100]

Catatonia [F01.145.126.156]

Child Reactive Disorders [F01.145.126.159]

Coprophagia [F01.145.126.175]

Delusions [F01.145.126.200]

Depersonalization [F01.145.126.300]

Depression [F01.145.126.350]

Encopresis [F01.145.126.837]

Enuresis [F01.145.126.856]

Hearing Loss, Functional [F01.145.126.875]

Malingering [F01.145.126.925]

Mental Fatigue [F01.145.126.937]

Obsessive Behavior [F01.145.126.950]

Paranoid Behavior [F01.145.126.962]

Schizophrenic Language [F01.145.126.975]

Self-Injurious Behavior [F01.145.126.980]

Stress, Psychological [F01.145.126.990]

Figure 2-3 National Library of Medicine Medical Subject Heading Descriptor Data and Tree Structure for "Aggression." The tree structure puts the term in the context of a behavioral symptom. A second tree that defines a social behavior context for the term is not shown here.

In addition, the browser lists the Allowable Qualifiers for aggression that can be used to restrict or limit search results. As defined on the MeSH site (*www.nlm.nih.gov/mesh/MBrowser.html*), these qualifiers are:

- **CL (classification)**—Used for taxonomic or other systematic or hierarchical classification systems.
- **DE (drug effects)**—Used with organs, regions, tissues, or organisms and physiological and psychological processes for the effects of drugs and chemicals.
- **PH (physiology)**—Used with organs, tissues, and cells of uni- and multi-cellular organisms for normal function. It is used also with biochemical substances, endogenously produced, for their physiologic role.
- **PX (psychology)**—Used with non-psychiatric diseases, techniques, and named groups for psychologic, psychiatric, psychosomatic, psychosocial, behavioral, and emotional aspects, and with psychiatric disease for psychologic aspects; used also with animal terms for animal behavior and psychology.
- **RE (radiation effects)**—Used for effects of ionizing and non-ionizing radiation upon living organisms, organs and tissues, and their constituents, and upon physiologic processes. It includes the effect of irradiation on drugs and chemicals.

The most relevant of these qualifiers for the researcher's work is probably drug effects (DE), to identify articles that deal with the physical and psychological aspects of drugs and chemicals dealing with aggression. In addition, articles dealing with radiation effects (RE) may also be relevant, especially if the articles describe radiation-induced genetic mutations associated with aggression in rats or primates.

With the relevant MeSH search terms and contexts defined, the next step would be to conduct an online search of the biomedical literature dealing with aggression using the online bibliographic database PubMed. The search on PubMed would likely return citations such as Antonio Moniz's surgical removal of the frontal lobes of the brain to control aggressive behavior—a procedure for which he won the Nobel prize in medicine in the late 1940s. The search would also reveal work on twin studies in Denmark in the late 1980s that suggests aggressiveness is a personality trait with a genetic component because twins raised apart have similar aggressiveness scores.

The PubMed search would also reveal work on attempting to identify the genetic basis for aggression in other animals, including lobsters, rats, and fruit flies. For example, researchers at Harvard and the University of Basel in Switzerland experimented with fruit flies to quantify aggressive behavior as a function of genetic makeup. Pairs of fruit flies were allowed to fight over females and the genetic profiles of the winners were studied for systematic differences among those of more submissive losers. One difference noted in the study is that there are significant variations in levels of certain neurotransmitters, including serotonin and dopamine, in the brains of the more aggressive combatants. However, these studies leave many questions unanswered, such as the contribution of physical strength or experience to winning a bout. As in human conflicts, the better fighter, not necessarily the more aggressive fighter, may be victorious.

Armed with information on aggression from the medical literature, the researchers might hypothesize that a new drug that moderates the production of serotonin in the brain may be useful in controlling aggressive behavior. They establish a study using volunteers who have been screened according to the Overt Aggression Scale and they use a battery of clinical studies to rule out non-genetic causes for aggressive behavior. The clinical examination includes a general history and physical, with a neurological examination, medication history, and mental status examination, as well as Chest X-ray, EEG, MRI, and lumbar puncture. The objective of this testing is to identify patients in which abnormal behavior might be due to causes such as head trauma, infection, or brain tumors. For example, meningitis, an infection of the spinal fluid, can result in behavior consistent with aggression and apprehension. Volunteers for the study would also be subject to standard laboratory tests, including urine drug screening, blood-alcohol concentration, serum drug concentrations, and a thyroid profile to screen for patients who are taking illicit drugs or who have metabolic diseases that could contribute to abnormal behavior. These and similar clinical data are stored in an electronic medical record (EMR) in the format described in Table 2-2.

Table 2-2 Typical Electronic Medical Record (EMR) Contents. The EMR contains both objective signs, such as physical examination findings, as well as subjective patient symptoms, including chief complaint and review of systems.

Data Category	Description
Chief Complaint	Patient's primary reason for the medical visit
History of Present Illness	History of onset of clinical signs and symptoms
Medications	Current list of medications the patient is using
Past Medical History	Relevant past medical history, including hospital admissions, surgeries, and diagnoses
Family History	History of family diseases, such as diabetes, cancer, heart disease, and mental illness

Table 2-2 Typical Electronic Medical Record (EMR) Contents. The EMR contains both objective signs, such as physical examination findings, as well as subjective patient symptoms, including chief complaint and review of systems. *(continued)*

Data Category	Description
Social History	Use of drugs, smoking, job stability, housing, living conditions, incarceration
Review of Systems	Patient's recollection of symptoms and current medical problems, such as trouble sleeping at night or panic episodes, and results of tests
Physical Examination	The clinician's hands-on examination of the patient, including head, eyes, ears, nose, throat, chest, and extremities
Labs	Includes blood glucose, cholesterol, and drug levels
Studies	X-ray, MRI, CT, and EKG
Progress notes	Record of temporal progression of signs and symptoms, labs, and studies for the length of the study or admission

The components of the EMR report rarely exist in a single, unified database, but reside in the separate, domain-specific databases that may exist within a single hospital or clinic or be dispersed geographically across a region or country. Regardless of their relative proximity to each other, laboratory, radiology, cardiology, hematology, internal medicine, and other clinical departments typically maintain their own medical-record systems. What's more, each application may be supported by a different operating system, use a different underlying database—some of which may be outdated—and execute on a completely different hardware platform. For example, the pharmacy system might run under UNIX on a Sun Server using a Sybase database, whereas the clinical radiology system might run under VMS on a VAX server with an Oracle database. Within each department or clinic, these differences are usually irrelevant unless data have to be shared with other departments. The traditional method of creating a composite view of a patient's clinical status is to generate custom reports, which is time-consuming and expensive. The modern approach to the EMR is to create one or more central databases derived from, and yet completely independent of, each of the application databases, and to optimize these databases for research and analysis.

In order to create a comprehensive record that can be queried, the data from the various clinical systems have to be integrated, usually with the assistance of a data dictionary that translates various clinical databases to common formats so that the data can be more easily combined. The data dictionary is, in simplest terms, a collection of information about naming, classification, structure, usage, and administration of data that originates from a variety of sources. The data dictionary is perhaps most useful in addressing the problem of data element ambiguity. For example, within a biotech enterprise composed of variety of commercial and in-house applications, a given data element may be defined differently within different applications.

Patient age might be defined in months within a clinical pathology system, whereas patient age within the microarray database and the data dictionary might be represented in years. The data dictionary can be used to reconcile the two systems, providing an appropriate data transform between the two representations. For example, the appropriate transforms to move between the representations used by the pathology and microarray systems for patient age might be:

PatientAge (Data Dictionary) = PatientAge (Microarray) = PatientAge (Pathology)/12

The data dictionary can also impose a standard vocabulary on the system so that clinical findings can be identified unambiguously. For example, one clinical system might refer to heart attack as "M.I.," another as "Myocardial Infarction," and yet another as "Heart Attack." By imposing a standard vocabulary, the data dictionary allows data from the various systems to be combined into a unified view of the patient that can be more easily mined for patterns. This view is typically maintained in a data mart, as illustrated in Figure 2-4. The data mart contains a subset of the data that resides in the individual databases combined with contents from these databases translated into a standard format that can be efficiently mined for data.

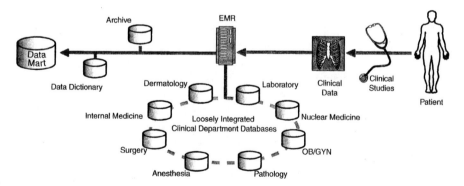

Figure 2-4   Integration of Clinical Data. To create an EMR capable of supporting efficient data mining, a data dictionary is used to impose a standard format and vocabulary on data stored in the clinical data mart.

A parallel situation exists in the bioinformatics component of the patient data management. As depicted in Figure 2-5, patients provide DNA source material for analysis in the form of tissue samples, which are processed for microarray analysis, generating thousands of data points. These data are then processed by a pattern-recognizer program to identify significant patterns. Researchers rely on local databases of gene expression, medical relevance, and a data dictionary to provide a common language and format for the data. Links to the large public genomic databases provide additional reference material. As with the clinical data, the composite genomic data are stored in a data mart for efficient manipulation and analysis through a suite of applications. Ideally, relevant data from clinical applications are combined in the data mart as well.

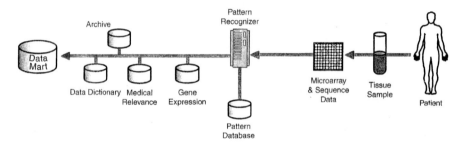

Figure 2-5   Integration of Bioinformatics Data. Like clinical data, bioinformatics data from a variety of sources and in numerous formats are combined in a data mart to enhance data management.

One advantage of building and maintaining a data mart that combines data from genomic and clinical sources is that data can be manipulated and visualized by applications that offer a single, combined view of the data that may provide a unique insight into their correlation and relevance. As shown in Figure 2-6, when clinical laboratory (Serotonin), psychological (Overt Aggression Scale or OAS), and genetic (Gene) data are readily available in a common format, they can be combined to provide a quick qualitative and quantitative view of how behavior, gross biology, and genomic information relate to each other and how they correlate with aggressive behavior.

In addition to locally generated clinical and genetic data, the typical pharmacogenomic laboratory has access to data in private and public online databases. Ideally, subsets of often-used data are integrated with local data in the laboratory's data warehouse, making the data readily available for searching, statistical analysis, visualization, simulation, and communications. In addition

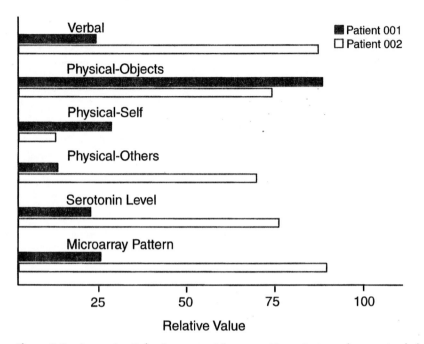

Figure 2-6 Aggressive Behavior versus Microarray Data. A view of aggressive behavior in two closely related patients as a function of clinical laboratory (Serotonin), psychological (Overt Aggression Scale or OAS), and genetic (Gene) data. Compared to Patient 002, Patient 001 has a relatively high score on the physical aggressiveness against the objects component of the OAS, and low scores on serum serotonin and microarray patterns.

to homogenizing and standardizing data representations through a data dictionary, the data warehouse serves as the central repository for the laboratory's intellectual property that can be easily archived. Although separate archives are typically maintained for genomic and clinical systems, an additional archive of the central data warehouse provides assurance that the data that have been cleaned, reformatted, indexed, and otherwise enhanced in value aren't lost to human error or natural disaster.

As illustrated in Table 2-3, the applications typically used to manipulate and analyze genomic data range from sequence searching to visualization. For example, researchers can upload new sequence data to the major databases through applications such as AceDB, Audit, BankIt, Sakura, Sequin, or WebIN. Most laboratories have access to these and similar applications through the Internet, as well as a suite of internally developed and commercial applications.

Table 2-3 Genomic Applications. A variety of public and private applications are available for analysis of genomic data, many of which are designed to work on the large public databases. Listed here are publicly funded applications.

Application	Examples
Sequence Search	BLAST, BLASTN, CLUSTALW, FASTA, MOTIF, PBLAST, TBLASTIN
Submission	AceDB, Audit, BankIt, Sakura, Sequin, WebIN
Information Retrieval	Entrez, DBGET, IDEAS
Linkage	LocusLink
Portal	KEGG
Structure Match	CD, DALI, SCOP, Searchlite, Structure Explorer, VAST
Visualization	CAD, Cn3D, Mage, RasMol/WebMol, SWISS-PDBViewer, VRML, WebMol
Protein-Protein Interactions	BRITE
Microarray Gene Expression Profiles	Expression
Open-Reading Frame Locator	ORF Finder

Continuing with the example of research on aggression, the data warehouse might contain a compilation of data on the fruit fly's genome, with a particular focus on the sequence that relates to genes responsible for serotonin production. Researchers might want to compare sequences in the fruit fly's genome with those in the human genome suspected of contributing to serotonin neurotransmitter control, using an application such as the BLAST sequence alignment tool. One consideration in using one of the online applications is data format.

The most popular data formats in bioinformatics include FASTA, PHYLIP, MAML (Microarray Markup Language), NEXUS, PAUP, FASTA+GAP, and MmCIF. Some formats are specific to particular data types and applications. For example, MmCIF is used to describe 3D structures, whereas FASTA is used to describe sequence data. As shown in Figure 2-7, the FASTA format begins with a single-line description, followed by lines of sequence data. The description line is distinguished from the sequence data by a greater-than (>) symbol in the first column. Sequences, which should be shorter than 80 characters in length, are represented in the standard International Union of Biochemistry-International Union of Pure and Applied Chemistry (IUB/IUPAC) amino acid and nucleic acid codes. Exceptions are that lower-case letters are accepted and are mapped into upper-case; a single hyphen or dash can be used to represent a gap of indeterminate length; and in amino acid sequences, U and * are acceptable letters.

FASTA FORMAT

A sequence in FASTA format begins with a single-line description, followed by lines of sequence data. The description line is distinguished from the sequence data by a greater-than (">") symbol in the first column. An example sequence in FASTA format is:

```
>gi|532319|pir|TVFV2E|TVFV2E envelope protein
ELRLRYCAPAGFALLKCNDADYDGFKTNCSNVSVVHCTNLMNTTVTTGLLLNGSYSENRT
QIWQKHRTSNDSALILLNKHYNLTVTCKRPGNKTVLPVTIMAGLVFHSQKYNLRLRQAWC
HFPSNWKGAWKEVKEEIVNLPKERYRGTNDPKRIFFQRQWGDPETANLWFNCHGEFFYCK
MDWFLNYLNNLTVDADHNECKNTSGTKSGNKRAPGPCVQRTYVACHIRSVIIWLETISKK
TYAPPREGHLECTSTVTGMTVELNYIPKNRTNVTLSPQIESIWAAELDRYKLVEITPIGF
APTEVRRYTGGHERQKRVPFVXXXXXXXXXXXXXXXXXXXXXXXXVQSQHLLAGILQQQKNL
LAAVEAQQQMLKLTIWGVK
```

Sequences, which should be shorter than 80 characters in length, are expected to be represented in the standard International Union of Biochemistry-International Union of Pure and Applied Chemistry (IUB/IUPAC) amino acid and nucleic acid codes, with these exceptions: lower-case letters are accepted and are mapped into upper-case; a single hyphen or dash can be used to represent a gap of indeterminate length; and in amino acid sequences, U and * are acceptable letters. Before submitting a request, any numerical digits in the query sequence should either be removed or replaced by appropriate letter codes (e.g., N for unknown nucleic acid residue or X for unknown amino acid residue). The nucleic acid codes supported are:

```
A --> adenosine            M --> A C (amino)
C --> cytidine             S --> G C (strong)
G --> guanine              W --> A T (weak)
T --> thymidine            B --> G T C
U --> uridine              D --> G A T
R --> G A (purine)         H --> A C T
Y --> T C (pyrimidine)     V --> G C A
K --> G T (keto)           N --> A G C T (any)
                           -   gap of indeterminate length
```

For programs that use amino acid query sequences, such as BLASTP and TBLASTN, the accepted amino acid codes are:

```
A  alanine                 P  proline
B  aspartate or asparagine Q  glutamine
C  cystine                 R  arginine
D  aspartate               S  serine
E  glutamate               T  threonine
F  phenylalanine           U  selenocysteine
G  glycine                 V  valine
H  histidine               W  tryptophan
I  isoleucine              Y  tyrosine
K  lysine                  Z  glutamate or glutamine
L  leucine                 X  any
M  methionine              *  translation stop
N  asparagine              -  gap of indeterminate length
```

Figure 2-7 The FASTA Format. This is a standard data format for use with online sequencing databases.

Complexity

The pharmacogenomic laboratory exploring the genetic basis for aggression illustrates several key characteristics of data management in the biotech industry. Foremost is the complexity of data management, as summarized in Table 2-4. There are numerous data sources, including the volunteer patients, clinical studies, genomic studies, and public and private online databases. Similarly, there are a variety of applications that can be brought to bear on genomic and clinical data and the biomedical literature, including search engines, statistical analysis applications, visualization tools, simulations, communication applications, database management systems, electronic medical record (EMR) systems, and genomic analysis recognition and manipulation, including sequence recognition.

Table 2-4 Complexity and Data Management. The typical R&D environment in a biotech firm encompasses an array of data sources, applications, formats, interfaces, and integration tools.

Data Category	Examples
Data Sources	Patient, Clinical Studies, Genomic Studies, Public Databases, Private Databases
Applications	Search Engines, Statistical Analysis, Visualization, Simulation, Communications, Database Management System, Electronic Medical Record, Genomic
Databases	Public, Private, Taxonomy, Clinical, Genetic, Local, External, Archives
Data Formats	FASTA, PHYLIP, MAML, NEXUS, PAUP, FASTA+GAP, and MmCIF, Proprietary Clinical Formats, Local Application Formats
Interfaces	Local Databases, Online Databases, Data Warehouse, Application
Integration Tools	Data Dictionary, Network, Standards

Furthermore, many of the dozens of databases involved in pharmacogenomic research and development use proprietary formats. This is especially true of clinical systems, many of which are specialty-specific. For example, standard image formats for radiology databases include Digital Imaging and Communications in Medicine (DICOM) and the American College of Radiology/National Electrical Manufacturers Association (ACR/NEMA) standards.

These standards were developed primarily to facilitate multi-vendor connectivity to promote the development of Picture Archiving and Communications Systems (PACS), but they have no provision for linking images with genomic systems, such as gene expression databases.

The typical research laboratory must develop and maintain numerous interfaces between applications and databases to provide the logical connectivity for data communications through the network infrastructure. The simple network illustrated in Figure 2-2 glosses over the inner complexity of the dozens of standards used through a typical information system, a problem at least partially addressed by data dictionaries and conversion utilities. For example, few laboratories or medical facilities provide the degree of connectivity suggested by this discussion. The vast majority of hospitals in the U.S. use paper charts to record patient history and physical findings, for example.

Perhaps 5 percent of hospitals have a functional EMR, and most of these are partial implementations that provide only summary information. Furthermore, these systems typically require researchers and clinicians to learn several arcane languages and procedures to access all data that may be relevant to a given patient. For example, clinicians may have to log in to a pathology system to check urinalysis results, a radiology system to read the report on a patient's latest image studies, and an admission, discharge, transfer (ADT) system to verify the patient's insurance provider. Similarly, although many clinical studies are multimedia-rich, most radiology and pathology images, EKG tracings, pulmonary function test curves, and other graphical materials are maintained in separate databases that aren't connected to the main hospital or clinic network.

One approach to minimizing or hiding the complexity of the data-management process is to create a single, integrated user interface. Just as the Windows or Macintosh operating systems hide the complexity of computer operations from users, a unified user interface to a network of disparate applications can hide the complexity of the data sources and various applications used to manipulate the data. This unified user interface may take the form of a Web portal or the workstation's operating system. For example, the flavors of UNIX for the PC, Macintosh, and dedicated UNIX workstations each provide various views of local and networked applications. The challenge with hiding complexity this way is that the constant changes in how data are actually managed in the background requires parallel updating of the user interface that provides a front end to the system.

The data-management process is much more involved than simply sending data to a database and retrieving it later. As discussed in the following sections, the databases used in bioinformatics research presents a variety of challenges, many of which pertain to all phases of the data life cycle, issues such as security, standards, interoperability, longevity of data, access and version control, the use of encryption, and minimizing access time. The data life cycle and the relevant issues that arise at each stage in the life of data are discussed in the rest of this chapter. Finally, issues that pertain to data repositories are discussed: database technology, database architecture, and data base management systems.

DATA LIFE CYCLE

In the data-management process, data are authored by clinicians and researchers and generated directly by research and test equipment, used by a variety of applications, repurposed or modified for other uses, and archived for future study. Eventually, the data are disposed of, freeing the data warehouses and other hardware from the overhead of maintaining low-value data. The overall process, from data creation to disposal, is normally referred to as the data life cycle, as depicted in Figure 2-8. The highlights of each stage are described there.

Data Creation and Acquisition

The process of data creation and acquisition is a function of the source and type of data. For example, in the scenario depicted in Figure 2-8, data are generated by sequencing machines and microarrays in the molecular biology laboratory, and by clinicians and clinical studies in the clinic or hospital. Depending on the difficulty in creating the data and the intended use, the creation process may be trivial and inexpensive or extremely complicated and costly. For example, recruiting test subjects to donate tissue biopsies is generally more expensive and difficult than identifying patients who are willing to provide less-invasive (and painful) tissue samples.

In addition to cost, the major issues in the data-creation phase of the data life cycle include tool selection, data format, standards, version control, error rate, precision, and accuracy. These metrics apply equally to clinical and genomic studies. In particular, metrics such as error rate, precision, and accuracy are more easily ascribed to machine-generated data, whether from clinical laboratory studies or microarray analysis. For example, optical character recognition (OCR), which was once used extensively as a means of acquiring sequence information from print publications, has an error rate of about two characters per hundred, which is generally unacceptable.

Subjective information created by hands-on clinical analysis and entered into the computer system through the use of manual transcription, voice recognition data-input systems, or desktop or handheld computers, is much more difficult to validate. What's more, there is significant variation in subjective interpretation of clinical studies. For example, five seasoned radiologists will

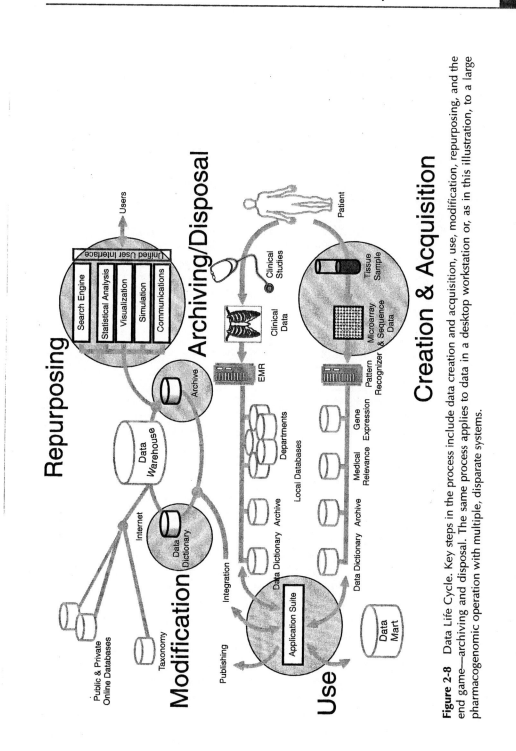

Figure 2-8   Data Life Cycle. Key steps in the process include data creation and acquisition, use, modification, repurposing, and the end game—archiving and disposal. The same process applies to data in a desktop workstation or, as in this illustration, to a large pharmacogenomic operation with multiple, disparate systems.

typically provide five different interpretations of the same chest film or other radiographic study. In addition to the quality of the initial clinical observation, there are errors introduced by the hardware, software, and processes involved in capturing data, from keyboard and mouse to optical character recognition, and voice recognition.

The creation and acquisition of patient data raises several ownership and privacy concerns. One of the greatest challenges regarding acquisition of clinical data is the Health Insurance Portability and Accountability Act (HIPAA), which mandates security and privacy of patient data. The act requires all health plans, clearinghouses, and providers of healthcare services to adopt national standards for electronic transactions and information security by mid-2004. Technologies that support user authentication, from password-protection schemes to biometric security technologies and data encryption are key to ensuring compliance with the act. Although there is not yet a parallel guideline for genomic data, it is likely that legislation in this area will materialize as soon as public awareness of the privacy issues becomes widely apparent.

Use

Once clinical and genomic data are captured, they can be put to a variety of immediate uses, from simulation, statistical analysis, and visualization to communications. Issues at this stage of the data life cycle include intellectual property rights, privacy, and distribution. For example, unless patients have expressly given permission to have their names used, microarray data should be identified by ID number through a system that maintains the anonymity of the donor.

Data Modification

Data are rarely used in their raw form, without some amount of formatting or editing. In addition, data are seldom used only for their originally intended purpose, in part because future uses are difficult to predict. For example, microarray data may not be captured expressly for comparison with clinical pathology data, but it may serve that purpose well. The data dictionary is one means of modifying data in a controlled way that ensures standards are followed. A data dictionary can be used to tag all microarray data with time and date information in a standard format so that they can be automatically correlated with clinical findings (see Figure 2-9).

Data that are modified or transformed by the data dictionary are normally stored in a data mart or data warehouse so that the transformed data are readily available for subsequent analysis without investing time and diverting computational resources by repeatedly reformatting the data. In the example in Figure 2-9, the relationship between microarray data and clinical data, such as activity at a particular gene locus and overt aggression score, can be more easily computed because the data can be sorted and compared by date of birth. That is, the more likely transformed data will be used in analysis in the future, the more valuable the data warehouse and the data dictionary.

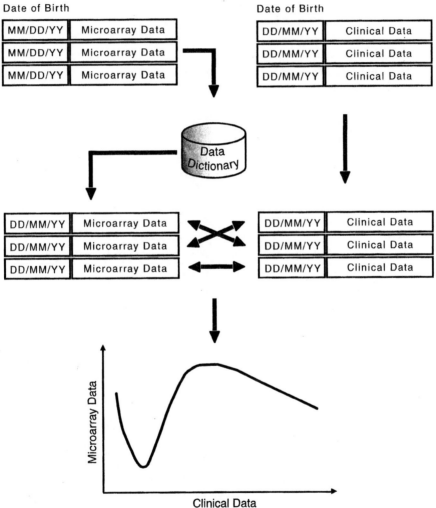

Figure 2-9 Data Dictionary-Directed Data Modification. The time and date header for microarray data can be automatically modified so that it can be easily correlated with clinical findings.

Archiving

Archiving, the central focus of the data life cycle, is concerned with making data available for future use. Unlike a data repository, data mart, or data warehouse, which hold data that are frequently accessed, an archive is a container for data that is infrequently accessed, with the focus more on longevity than on access speed. In the archiving process—which can range from making a backup of a local database on a CD-ROM or Zip® disk to creating a backup of an entire EMR system in a large hospital—data are named, indexed, and filed in a way that facilitates identification later. While university or government personnel archive the large online public databases, the archiving of locally generated data is a personal or corporate responsibility. Regardless of who takes responsibility for the process, the issues associated with archiving are numerous, as suggested by Table 2-5.

Table 2-5 Archiving Issues. Key issues in bioinformatics in the archival process range from the scalability of the initial solution to how to best provide for security.

Issue	Description
Indexing	Vocabulary, metadata, language, completeness, efficiency
Space Requirements	Index space versus data space
Hardware Requirements	Hard drives, network
Scalability	Ability to expand functionality without investing in new hardware and software
Database Design	Data model
Archival Process	Responsibilities for overseeing the process
Space Requirements	Current and projected archival capacity
Completeness	Relative quantity of total data that are archived
Media Selection	Compatibility, speed, capacity, data density, cost, volatility, durability, and stability
Location	Local, server-based, or network
Infrastructure Requirements	Network and computer hardware

Table 2-5 Archiving Issues. Key issues in bioinformatics in the archival process range from the scalability of the initial solution to how to best provide for security. *(continued)*

Issue	Description
Relative Value	Value of data vs. archival overhead
Hardware Configuration	RAID and other configurations
Longevity	Technical obsolescence of media and MTBF rating of related equipment
Security	Limited access to data

The archiving stage of the data life cycle usually involves making decisions about the most appropriate software, hardware, storage medium and archiving process to use. There are the obvious issues of media cost and longevity, security standards, the type of hardware to use to store the data, and the software that will facilitate storage and later retrieval. For example, selecting the optimal storage medium for the archiving process is a function of the frequency with which archived data are accessed, the budget, and the volume of data involved.

The hardware involved in the archiving process may include a PC-based CD-ROM burner, a large database server that's networked to a number of workstations and routinely backed up onto magnetic tape, or a network-based storage that may be located offsite. As discussed later in this chapter, each option has security, cost, and performance issues. The software tools selected for archiving data also define the usability and performance of the data archive, especially regarding data indexing and retrieval functions.

After data have been created and, if necessary, modified for use, and before it can be archived, it's typically named, indexed, and filed to facilitate locating it in the future. As such, the filing system, naming conventions, and accuracy and specificity of indexing limit the efficiency with which the data can be located later. For example, each document can be assigned one or more keywords, but if the keywords aren't appropriate, the keyword vocabulary is undefined or not enforced, or too few keywords are used, then a document may be effectively lost in the system. Not only the choice and number of keywords, but the indexing hierarchy can make data hard to find.

The process of data archiving is far more important than the associated technology, in that the best software and hardware are useless if they aren't used. Of the technical issues involved in archiving gene sequences, microarray analysis, and other bioinformatics data, scalability is typically the most important. Even relatively small laboratories generate megabytes of data every week, which is fueling demand for very-large-capacity archival storage devices.

One of the primary determinants of archive capacity is the storage media—the physical material used to form a tape, disk, or cartridge. In addition to capacity, media can be characterized in terms of compatibility, speed, data density, cost, volatility, durability, and stability. Compatibility is the ability of media to function within a particular software and hardware environment. Speed is a multi-faceted performance characteristic that encompasses both the time to locate data (seek time) and the time to write it to or download it from the media (data transfer rate), all of which are functions of the construction of the supporting hardware and electronics. Seek time may be several hundred milliseconds for a CD-ROM, a few milliseconds for a hard drive, and a few microseconds for a flash memory card. Capacity—the maximum amount of data the media can store—is a function of the media construction, the tolerance of the casing or cartridge for tape- and disk-based media, and the technology used to read and write the data. Capacity is also a function of data density, which is in turn a function of the media, the drive mechanism, and the error coding and compression technologies. Error-control and compression schemes in hard drives and other media allow higher data densities than the raw media would support otherwise.

Cost is a function of the raw materials involved in the creation of media, but has more to do with what the market will bear and what the competition has to offer. Volatility, a characteristic normally ascribed to solid-state memory, refers to the status of the data when external power is removed. Flash memory, like magnetic disk or tape, is considered relatively non-volatile, and can hold data for years without loss.

Durability refers to the physical properties of the media that contribute to the longevity of the surface, mechanisms, and housing, if any, during normal use. For example, the bearings and other components in the rotational system of a hard drive undergo wear and tear over time. Stability reflects the physical properties of the media in a given environment that contribute to the longevity of the media and therefore the data, in a dormant state. For example, the bearings, metal, and plastic parts are subject to the same problems that beset every complex electro-mechanical device. Lubrication dries out, leaving bearings dry and without protection, rubber becomes brittle, plastic parts deform, and dust and lint accumulate in the cooling system. Furthermore, the magnetic patterns induced in the iron-oxide coating on the disk platters fade over the years, especially in the heat. Similarly, the plastic-based optical media of a CD-ROM is susceptible to damage from high humidity, rapid and extreme temperature fluctuations, and contamination from airborne pollution. Over time, oil from our fingers can also damage the plastic surface of a CD-ROM. Fluctuations in temperature and humidity can also cause shrinking and expansion of magnetic tape, distorting the position of data tracks, resulting in data loss.

The longevity or life expectancy of the devices in an archive system is usually expressed in the Mean Time Between Failure (MTBF) rating. The MTBF, an estimate of the failure rate of a device during its expected lifetime, is one metric that can be used to estimate the life span of an archive. Typical MTBF ratings for tape drives and commercial-grade hard drives are over 20 years. However, this figure assumes ideal conditions of constant low temperature and humidity, freedom from biological agents, static-electricity discharges, and mechanical abuse. Another consideration is that even if a tape survives a decade or more in fireproof safe, it's likely that the data it contains will be inaccessible because of changes in tape-drive standards. Most of the disk packs, tapes, and magnetic cartridges that were standard archival media a decade ago are incompatible with current computer hardware.

Archives vary considerably in configuration and in proximity to the source data. For example, servers typically employ several independent hard drives configured as a Redundant Array of Independent Disks (RAID system) that function in part as an integrated archival system. The idea behind a RAID system is to provide real-time backup of data by increasing the odds that data written to a server will survive the crash of any given hard drive in the array. RAID was originally introduced in the late 1980s as a means of turning relatively slow and inexpensive hard disks into fast, large-capacity, more reliable storage systems.

RAID systems derive their speed from reading and writing to multiple disks in parallel. The increased reliability is achieved through mirroring or replicating data across the array and by using error-detection and correction schemes. Although there are seven levels of RAID, level 3 is most applicable to bioinformatics computing. In RAID-3, a disk is dedicated to storing a parity bit—an extra bit used to determine the accuracy of data transfer—for error detection and correction. If analysis of the parity bit indicates an error, the faulty disk can be identified and replaced. The data can be reconstructed by using the remaining disks and the parity disk.

For example, in Figure 2-10, disks A–D are dedicated to data and disk P is used to store the parity bit. In this case, an odd number of "1" bits corresponds to a high ("1") parity bit. When data are written in parallel to the data disks, the corresponding parity bit is stored on the parity disk. Immediately after the data are written to the data disks, the data are read and the parity bits are compared. The discrepancy noted in Figure 2-10 is typical of a case when there is an error on one disk. The error on disk "C" can be repaired, or if groups of errors are suddenly becoming apparent indicating imminent disk failure, then the entire disk can be replaced.

Another approach is to create archives on separate media on a regular basis and transport the media offsite to a safe location that would survive natural or man-made disaster at the main computing facility. A related tactic is to use network-based storage from a third-party vendor and export data to the offsite storage electronically. However, third-party archives have greater security risks than archives that can be controlled and maintained locally.

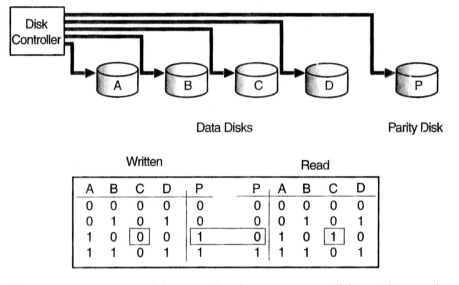

Figure 2-10   RAID-3. Data disks are read and written to in parallel, providing speed, while a dedicated parity disk provides increased reliability through error detection and correction. In this example, an error in disk C is detected by a different parity bit (P), indicating that the data read from disks A–D don't agree with what was written to the disks. Although the parity bit is usually based on a comparison of bytes on the data disks, bits (0 or 1) are used here for clarity.

Repurposing

One of the major benefits of having data readily available in an archive is the ability to repurpose it for a variety of uses. For example, linear sequence data originally captured to discover new genes are commonly repurposed to support the 3D visualization of protein structures.

One of the major issues in repurposing data is the ability to efficiently locate data in archives. The difficulty in locating data once it's been incorporated into a storage system depends on the volume of data involved. Efficient retrieval is a function of the hardware and database management software, the effectiveness of the user interface, and the granularity of the index. For example, nucleotide sequence data indexed by chromosome number would be virtually impossible to locate if the database contains thousands of sequences indexed to each chromosome.

Issues in the repurposing phase of the data life cycle include the sensitivity, specificity, false positives, and false negatives associated with searches. The usability of the user interface is also a factor, whether free-text natural language, search by example, or simple keyword searching is supported. In addition, the provisions for security can affect the ease with which data can be located and repurposed. An overly complex security procedure that requires revalidation of user identity every five minutes could deter even the most well-intentioned researcher.

Disposal

The duration of the data life cycle is a function of the perceived value of the data, the effectiveness of the underlying process, and the limitations imposed by the hardware, software, and environmental infrastructure. Eventually, all data die, either because they are intentionally disposed of when their value has decreased to the point that it is less than the cost of maintaining it, or because of accidental loss. Often, data have to be archived because of legal reasons, even though the data is of no intrinsic value to the institution or researcher. For example, most official hospital or clinic patient records must be maintained for the life of the patient. As such, earmarking data for disposal is normally based on the quality and relevance of the data, as opposed to the age of the data. Researchers in a laboratory working with sequence data might be investigating single genes in turn, moving from one gene to the next. When sequence data from one gene is no longer necessary, it can be discarded from the local data warehouse leaving room for the next gene's sequence data—whether the data are stored on an internal disk in a Linux workstation or a central data warehouse.

Managing the Life Cycle

Managing the data life cycle is an engineering exercise that's a compromise between speed, completeness, longevity, cost, usability, and security. For example, the media selected for archiving will not only affect the cost, but the speed of storage and longevity of the data. Similarly, using an in-house tape backup facility may be more costly than outsourcing the task to networked vendor, but the in-house approach is likely to be more secure. These tradeoffs are reflected in the implementation of the overall data-management process.

DATABASE TECHNOLOGY

The purpose of a database is to facilitate the management of data, a process that depends on people, processes, and as described here, the enabling technology. Consider that the thousands of base pairs discovered every minute by the sequencing machines in public and private laboratories would be practically impossible to record, archive, and either publish or sell to other researchers without computer databases. At the current stage of database technology evolution, bioinformatics databases are housed on large hard drives in locker- or refrigerator-sized local servers and online sequence databases such as GenBank. Thanks to modern computer technology, a modern bioinformatics researcher can compare and contrast the genomes of a dozen species while sitting on the beach with a laptop computer connected through a wireless modem to the Internet. While this image makes for good advertising copy, in practice, most researchers are tied to wet laboratories that generate, manipulate, and store vast quantities of experiment-specific data. In this context, the database technology empowers researchers to store their data in a way that it can be quickly and easily accessed, manipulated, compared to other data, and shared with other researchers.

The concept of a database is necessarily colored by the current state of the technology. Just as a state-of-the-art bioinformatics workstation, operating at Gigahertz clock speeds with a gigabyte or more of RAM and banks of hundred-gigabyte hard drives, would easily outperform one of the early supercomputers, database technology is constantly evolving. Within our lifetimes, the contents of GenBank will easily fit into the working memory of a handheld computer, and our concept of what constitutes a "large" database will have to be adjusted accordingly. Even so, there is more to the concept of a database—whether it's referred to as a repository, data warehouse, data mart, or local database—than raw capacity.

The volatility of the data, the concept of working memory, and the interrelatedness of data, regardless of the volume of data involved, are distinguishing features of the various forms of memory systems or databases. For example, from the perspective of working memory, the function of a data warehouse is to move data from a variety of sources and prepare the data for incorporation into working memory. Similarly, a data warehouse or other database is distinguished from an archive in that the data in an archive are much further removed from working memory. An archive might be stored on optical platters, magnetic tapes, or other media that is held in an offsite fireproof safe or underground building. Furthermore, the archive is typically engineered for longevity and the ability to be reconstituted, and not for speed of access. A database, in contrast, is a live, working system that forms the centerpiece for biotech R&D activities.

Functionally, the relationship between various database technologies can be compared to the information stored in the body, as depicted in Figure 2-11. Just as it's inefficient to have papers strewn about an office, out of order, difficult to identify, and distracting the user's attention from the documents that should be addressed, our genetic information is stored in the genome, tightly packed, out of harm's way, and yet accessible. The data are there, as in an archive, but not immediately available. Focusing on the individual chromosomes, data are more readily available, but still packed away so that they don't interfere with cellular processes. As subsets of data are moved out of the chromosome to the work environment, through the process of transcription, data are more readily available for use. Finally, at the translation stage, the data serve as the basis for the current work (as data do for computer applications), whether creating proteins according to the Central Dogma, or attempting to locate a matching gene in a pattern-matching application.

The analogy depicted in Figure 2-11 highlights the concept of working memory. Data are pulled from archives, whether they reside in the double helix of a chromosome or on a tape cartridge, and are put in position where they can either be acted upon or direct other activities. In the cell, the activity is protein synthesis. In the workstation, this activity can be identifying a nucleotide sequence, predicting the 3D structure of a protein, or modeling how multiple proteins interact at the molecular level.

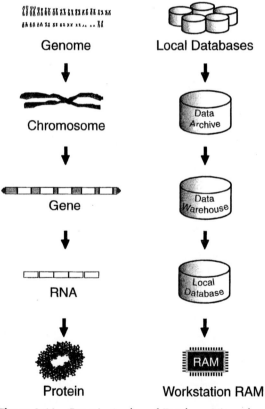

Figure 2-11 Organic Analog of Database Hierarchy. The database hierarchy has many parallels to the hierarchy in the human genome. Data stored in chromosomes, like a data archive, must be unpacked and transferred to a more immediately useful form before the data can be put to use.

For example, as illustrated in Figure 2-12, a pattern-matching program that is searching for a match in a long nucleotide sequence works on the sequence in local, high-speed, active (and volatile) memory—the computer's RAM. As soon as the length of nucleotide sequence that can fit in RAM is searched, it is discarded and replaced by a new sequence that is copied (akin to transcription) from the hard disk, flash memory, or other non-volatile storage media. Just as RNA is discarded after it has been involved in the translation process to make room for the next set of instructions from the DNA, the data in RAM are constantly refreshed and updated under the direction of the computer's CPU.

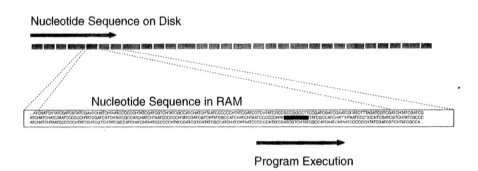

Figure 2-12   Working Memory. Limited working memory in volatile RAM is used for program execution, whereas an expansive disk or other non-volatile memory serves as a container for data that can't fit in working memory.

Volatility, working memory, and the volume of data that can be handled are key variables in memory systems such as databases. In addition, there is the quality of interrelatedness; just as the genes in the chromosomes are associated with each other by virtue of their physical proximity, the data in a database are interrelated in a way that facilitates use for specific applications. For example, nucleotide sequences that will be used in pattern-matching operations in the online sequence databases will be formatted according to the same standard—such as the FASTA standard.

As reflected in the data life-cycle model discussed earlier, the data-archiving process involves indexing, selecting the appropriate software to manage the archive, and type of media as a function of frequency of use and expected useful life span of the data. From an implementation perspective, the key issues in selecting one particular archiving technology over another depends on the size of the archive, the types of data and data sources to be archived, the intended use, and any existing or legacy archiving systems involved. For example, the size of the archive is measured in terms of the number of items and the space requirements per item. Text-only archives of nucleotide or amino acid sequences generally require less space per item than archives of 3D images of protein molecules and other multimedia. Not only are space requirements generally much greater for multimedia data than they are for text, but images usually require additional keywords and text associated with them so that they can be readily located in an archive.

Similarly, a single source of data is generally much easier to work with than data from multiple, disparate sources in different and often non-compatible formats. In addition, hardware and software used in the archiving process should reflect the intended use of the data. For example, seldom-used data can be archived using a much less powerful system, compared to data that must be accessed frequently. Finally, it's rare to have the opportunity to initiate a digital archiving program from scratch. Normally, there is some form of existing (legacy) system in place whose data has to be converted to be suitable for archiving.

The simplest approach to managing bioinformatics data in a small laboratory is to establish a file server that is regularly backed up to a secure archive. To use the hardware most effectively, everyone connected to the server copies their files from their local hard drive to specific areas on the server's hard drive on a daily basis. The data on the server are in turn archived to magnetic tape or other high-capacity media by someone assigned to the task. In this way, researchers can copy the file from the server to their local hard drive as needed. Similarly, if the server hardware fails for some reason, then the archive can be used to reconstitute the data on a second server.

As noted earlier, from a database perspective, file servers used as archives have several limitations. For example, because the data may be created using different applications, perhaps using different formats and operating systems, searching through the data may be difficult, especially from a single interface other than with the search function that is part of the computer's operating system. Even then, there is no way of knowing what particular files hold. For example, the files in a library of 3D protein-folding images created in a graphics modeling package may be labeled according to one researcher's experiment and not for general use. That is, there is typically no automated way of instituting a controlled vocabulary for all users to abide by.

There are other practical limitations as well. For example, in a small workgroup of perhaps a dozen researchers, it's tempting to make an open file-sharing system without security procedures. However, this practice can result in accidental loss of information through inadvertent deletion or modification of files. In addition, without a database, it's difficult to control for versions or updated copies of particular files, other than with file-naming conventions. Furthermore, combining data from different applications in a meaningful way to assist in analysis may be arduous and time-consuming without a database system in place.

The need for greater control over the intellectual capital of a biotech R&D laboratory usually necessitates the understanding and use of database technology. Just as particular wet-lab equipment provides a mix of features that supports some experiments and yet hinders others, databases are available in a wide spectrum of designs that are optimized for specific types of operations at the expense of others. The overall architecture, the underlying models supporting the database, and the database management system that supports the model provided by one database system may be ideal for managing nucleotide sequence data, but unwieldy for managing 3D protein structures, for example. Furthermore, a homegrown database that is developed without knowledge of outside standards may be unusable or inefficient when used with public-domain software, such as the locally executable BLAST application.

Database Architecture

One of the greatest challenges in bioinformatics is the complete, seamless integration of databases from a variety of sources. This is not the case now, primarily because when databases such as GenBank and SWISS-PROT were designed, their architectures were designed primarily to support their particular function. Working with other systems was a secondary concern. However, with the proliferation of data and the standardization on the Web as the main means of access to these data, integration has become a major concern. Without some form of database integration, the researcher who seeks to correlate a symptom such as aggression with a genetic abnormalities must query several databases to compare clinical behavior with genetic abnormalities. Furthermore, because the amount of data in many of the molecular biology databases is growing at an exponential rate, there usually aren't sufficient resources to modify the basic architecture of these databases.

There are exceptions, such as PubMed Central, where data from disparate databases, each with their own data formats and underlying architectures, have been combined into one common structure. However, because of the time and cost involved in converting database architectures, a better approach, when the option is available, is to use an architecture that not only supports immediate needs, but that also makes provision for future integration with other database systems. For this reason, knowledge of database architecture is key to anyone practicing bioinformatics. In addition, an understanding of database architectures can facilitate working with existing or legacy systems.

From a structural or architectural perspective, database technology can be considered either centralized or distributed. In the centralized approach, typified by the data warehouse, data are processed in order to fit into a central database. In a distributed architecture, data are dispersed geographically, even though they may appear to be in one location because of the database management system software. In each case, the goal is the same—providing researchers with some means of rapidly accessing and keeping track of data in a way that supports reuse. This is especially critical in large biotech laboratories, where large, comprehensive patient and genomic databases support data mining and other methods that extract meaningful patterns from potentially millions of records.

A centralized architecture, such as that illustrated in Figure 2-13, concentrates all organizational activity in one location. This can be a formidable task, as it requires cleaning, encoding, and translation of data before they can be included in the central database. For example, once data to be included in a data warehouse have been identified, the data from each application are cleaned (typos and other errors are identified and removed or corrected) and merged with data from other applications. In addition, there are the usual issues of database design, provision for maintenance, security, and periodic modification.

A data warehouse isn't simply a large hard disk, but a database system implemented on a tiered storage system that reflects access time, cost, and data longevity constraints. For example, some data may reside on fast magnetic media, such as hard disks, and other data may reside on slower optical media. The goal is to keep the right information flowing to the right people in the most intelligent form as quickly and efficiently as possible, which includes making provision for the storage of both frequently and seldom-accessed data.

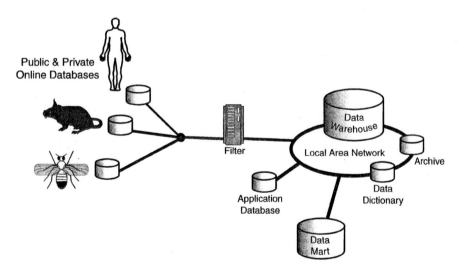

Figure 2-13   Centralized Database Architecture. A centralized database, such as a data warehouse, combines data from a variety of databases in one physical location.

In contrast to a centralized architecture, distributed database architecture is characterized by physically disparate storage media. One advantage of using a distributed architecture is that it supports the ability to use a variety of hardware and software in a laboratory, allowing a group to use the software that makes their lives easiest, while still allowing a subset of data in each application to be shared throughout the organization. Separate applications, often running on separate machines and using proprietary data formats and storage facilities, share a subset of information with other applications. A limitation of this common interface approach, compared to a central database, is that the amount of data that can be shared among applications is typically limited. In addition, there is the computational overhead of communicating data between applications.

A challenge of using an integrated approach is developing the interfaces between the databases associated with each application. When there are only a few different applications and operating systems to contend with, developing custom interfaces between different databases may be tenable. However, with multiple applications and their associated databases, the number of custom interfaces that must be developed to allow sharing of data becomes prohibitive. For example, with 5 different databases, 9 different custom interfaces would have to be developed. For 6 different databases, 11 interfaces would be needed. Because of the work involved, a typical scenario is incomplete integration, as shown in Figure 2-14.

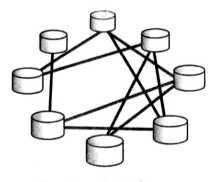

Custom Interfaces   Common Interface

Figure 2-14 Distributed Database Integration. Distributed databases can be configured to share data through dedicated, one-to-one custom interfaces (left) or by writing to a common interface standard (right). Custom interfaces incur a work penalty on the order of two times the number of databases that are integrated.

A better solution to integrating incompatible databases is to write interfaces to a common standard. For example, in clinical medicine, most application vendors are compatible with the Health Level 7 (HL7) interface protocol, which allows Radiology, Laboratory, and Pathology systems to exchange a subset of their data, such as patient demographics, diagnosis, drug allergies, and current medications.

Full database integration is much more than simply moving data to a single hard disk. A file server can store data from dozens of various applications and yet have no integration between applications. Similarly, just as a single hard disk can be formatted so that it appears as several logical volumes or drives, a distributed physical architecture can function like a logical centralized database. Taking this analogy one step further, there are hybrid database architectures that combine aspects of centralized and distributed architectures to provide enhanced functionality or reduced cost. For example, the Storage Area Network (SAN) architecture is based on a separate, dedicated, high-speed network that provides storage under one interface (see Figure 2-15). With the appropriate software, a SAN can be configured to provide the functionality of a central data warehouse, including provision for making available an unlimited subset of the data from each application database.

In addition to SANs, there is a variety of other network-dependent database architectures. For example, Network Attached Storage (NAS) is one method of adding storage to a networked system of workstations. To users on the network, the NAS acts like a second hard drive on their workstations. However, a NAS device, like a file server, must be managed and archived separately. A similar approach is to use a Storage Service Provider (SSP), which functions as an Application Service Provider (ASP) with a database as the application.

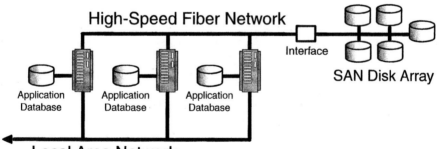

Figure 2-15 Storage Area Network Architecture. A SAN is a dedicated network that connects servers and SAN-compatible storage devices. SAN devices can be added as needed, within the bandwidth limitations of the high-speed fiber network.

With the increased reliance on the Internet, outsourcing storage through Internet-based SANs and SSPs is often used instead of purchasing huge servers in-house. The advantage of technologies such as SANs and SSPs is that they can provide virtually unlimited storage as part of huge server farms that may be located in geographically disparate areas. The downside is loss of control over the data and archiving process, as well as the risk that company providing the service may fail, resulting in the loss of valuable research and production data. In addition, like NAS, SANs and SSPs only address additional storage space, not integration.

Database Management Systems

The database management system (DBMS) is the set of software tools that works with a given architecture to create a practical database application. The DBMS is the interface between the low-level hardware commands and the user, allowing the user to think of data management in abstract, high-level terms using a variety of data models, instead of the bits and bytes on magnetic media. The DBMS also provides views or high-level abstract models of portions of the conceptual database that are optimized for particular users. In this way, the DBMS, like the user interface of a typical application, shields the user from the details of the underlying algorithms and data representation schemes.

In addition to providing a degree of abstraction, the DBMS facilitates use by maximizing the efficiency of managing data with techniques such as dynamically configuring operations to make use of a given hardware platform. For example, a DBMS should recognize a server with large amounts of free RAM and make use of that RAM to speed serving the data. A DBMS also ensures data integrity by imposing data consistency constraints, such as requiring numeric data in certain fields, free text in others, and image data elsewhere. A researcher isn't allowed to insert a numerical sequence in the space assigned for a nucleotide sequence, for example.

The DBMS also guards against data loss. For example, a DBMS should support quick recovery from hardware or software failures. A DBMS can guard against data corruption that might result from two simultaneous operations on a given data item. The most common example is prohibiting two users from simultaneously manipulating the same data. In addition, a DBMS adds security to a database, in that a properly constructed DBMS allows only users with permission to have access to specific data, normally down to the level of individual files. Multi-level user password-protection schemes can be used to allow only graphic designers to view intermediate graphic data, and those in marketing to view only final versions. Using intranets that limit data communications within a predefined group of workstations can add greatly to the security of a database.

A key issue in working with a DBMS is the use of metadata, or information about data contained in the database. Views are one application of metadata—a collection of information about naming, classification, structure, and use of data that reduces inconsistency and ambiguity. For example, as shown in Figure 2-16, one way to think about the application of metadata is to consider the high-level biomedical literature a means of simplifying and synthesizing the underlying complexity of molecular disease, protein structure, protein alignment, and protein and DNA sequence data. From this perspective, data are base pair identifiers derived from observation, experiment, or calculation, information is data in context, such as the relationship of DNA sequences to protein structure, and metadata is a descriptive summary of disease presentations that provides additional context to the underlying information. The use

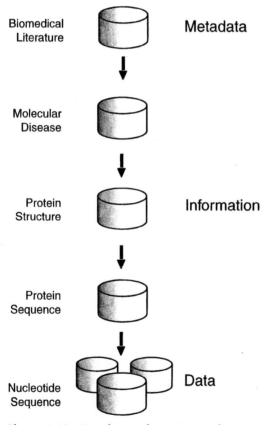

Figure 2-16 Metadata, Information, and Data in Bioinformatics. Metadata labels, simplifies, and provides context for underlying information and data.

of metadata as an organizational theme makes the centralized data-management approach easier to maintain and control. For example, a simple file-server system typically lacks the contextual framework and interrelatedness of information and data provided by a database management system. As a result, there is no automated way to manage the contents of individual files and folders that may be included on the file server.

Commonly used commercial DBMS packages in bioinformatics include products from Microsoft, Oracle, Sybase, IBM, MySQL AB, and InterSystems. In addition, there are dozens of proprietary and academic systems developed for particular niche applications that many bioinformatics researchers employ as well. Regardless of whether the technology is rooted in academia or business, virtually every DBMS can be described using three levels of abstraction: the physical database, the conceptual database, and the views. The point of using these abstractions is that they allow researchers to manipulate huge amounts of data that may be associated in very complex ways by shielding database designers and users from the underlying complexity of computer hardware. The physical database is the low-level data and framework that is defined in terms of media, bits, and bytes. This low-level abstraction is most useful for anyone who has to deal directly with data and files.

The conceptual database, at a somewhat higher level of abstraction than the physical database, is concerned with the most appropriate way to represent the data. This level of abstraction more closely approximates the needs of database designers who deal with DBMS data representation and efficiency issues such as the data-dictionary design. The conceptual database is defined in terms of data structures (an organizational scheme, such as a record) and the properties of the data to be stored and manipulated. The most common methods of representing the conceptual database are the entity-relationship model and the data model.

The entity-relationship model focuses on entities and their interrelationships in a way that parallels how we categorize the world. For example, common database entities in bioinformatics are the human being, protein sequences, nucleotide sequences, and disease processes about which data are recorded. Similarly, every entity has some basic attribute, such as name, size, weight (a particular protein may have a known weight), or charge. Relationships within the model are classified according to how data are associated with each other, such as one-to-one, one-to-many, or many-to-many. For example, a length of DNA may be translated to one mRNA sequence (a one-to-one relationship) and a gene may give rise to several proteins (a one-to-many relationship). These and other relationships can be used to maintain the integrity of data. For example, a gene (one entity) may generate more than one protein, but the gene, having a one-to-one relationship with a nucleotide sequence, shouldn't be associated with more than one nucleotide sequence. The data model can enforce this one-to-one relationship.

The conceptual database can also be represented as a data model. Like entity-relationship models, data models provide a means of representing and manipulating large amounts of data. A data model consists of two components—a mathematical notation for expressing data and relationships, and operations on the data that serve to express manipulations of the data. Like entity-relationship models, data models may also contain a collection of integrity rules that define valid data relationships. These various components work together to provide a formal means of representing and manipulating data.

The most common data models supported by DBMS products are flat, network, hierarchical, relational, object-oriented, and deductive data models, as illustrated graphically in Figure 2-17. Even though long strings of sequencing data lend themselves to a flat file representation, the relational database model is by far the most popular in the commercial database industry and is found in virtually every biotech R&D laboratory. However, virtually every data model illustrated in Figure 2-17 has applications in bioinformatics, from flat to semi-structured.

The flat data model is simply a table without any embedded structure information to govern the relationships between records. As a result, a flat file database can only work with one table or file at a time. Strictly speaking, a flat file

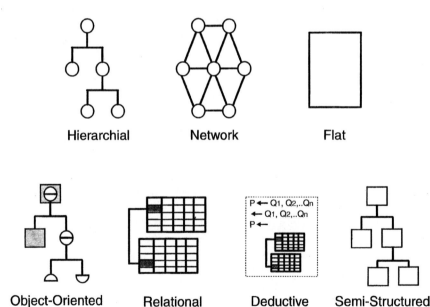

Figure 2-17 Data Models. The most common data models in bioinformatics are relational, flat, and object-oriented.

doesn't really fit the criteria for a data model because it lacks an embedded structure. However, the lack of an embedded structure is one reason for the popularity of the flat file database in bioinformatics, especially in capturing sequence data. A sequence of a few dozen characters may be followed by a sequence of thousands of characters, with no known relationship between the sequences, other than perhaps the tissue sample or sequence run. As such, a separate flat file can be used to efficiently store the sequence data from each sample or run. In order to make the management of large amounts of sequence or other data more tenable, a model with an embedded structure is required.

The relational model, developed in the early 1970s, is based on the concept of a data table in which every row is unique. The records or rows in the table are called tuples; the fields or columns are variably referred to attributes, predicates, or classes. Database queries are performed with the select operation, which asks for all tuples in a certain relation that meet a certain criterion—for example, a query such as "Which authors write about neurofibromatosis?" To connect the data of two or more relations, an operation called a join is performed. A record is retrieved from the database by means of a key, or label, that may consist of a field, part of a field, or a combination of several fields. Supporting this data model so that it's easy for someone to direct a search for the record that contains the particular value of the key is the purpose of a relational DBMS. Consider querying a bibliographic database with an "author_subject_table," using the Structured Query Language (SQL) statement:

```
SELECT *.* FROM author_subject_table
   WHERE subject = "Neurofibromatosis"
```

A useful feature of the relational model is that records or rows from different files can be combined as long as the different files have one field in common. Theoretically, records with a common field can be combined or joined with an unlimited number of files. The price paid for this flexibility is extended access time. That is, in a database design that doesn't take likely use patterns into account, performance suffers. A large amount of processor time will be spent extracting information from the system as the database program performs joins and other operations. This performance penalty is a reason for not simply polling application databases for data. It's far better, from a performance perspective, to move the data into a separate data repository, a second database that is optimized for the desired searching and analysis.

The attraction of the ubiquitous relational model is that it is mature, stable, reliable, well understood, and well suited for a number of different applications in bioinformatics. The basic concepts involved with the relational model are easily grasped; data are populated into rows and columns in a table, and tables are associated with one another by joining fields that match in the two tables. However, the relational model has several limitations. Because the relational model is based on rows and columns, it's most efficient working with scalar data such as names, addresses, and laboratory values. That is, all relationships between objects must be based on data values as opposed to a location or place-holder in the database. This limitation often requires the database designer to create additional relations to describe logical associations between data elements. For example, in a relational database containing both nucleotide and amino acid sequences, the researcher can't relate the two without the aid of tables that relate nucleotide sequences to proteins and protein sequences to specific amino acids.

An even greater limitation of the relational model from a bioinformatics perspective is that the metaphor of rows and columns often isn't a natural fit for sequence or protein shape data. Recall that one reason for using a DBMS is to allow users to think of data management in abstract, high-level terms, instead of the underlying algorithms and data representation schemes. Although tables of rows and columns can be considered a simplification over hard disk platters, they can seem obtuse to a researcher working with thousands of sequences, genes, and other data that don't fit neatly into a tabular metaphor. That is, the relational model often doesn't hide the complexity of genomic data. As a result, various other data models are used by professionals in the biotech industry.

One alternative to the relational model is the hierarchical model, which predates the relational model by a decade. Unlike the flexible relational model, permanent hierarchical connections are defined when the database is created. Within the hierarchical database model, the smallest data entity is the record. That is, unlike records in a relational model, records within a hierarchical database are not necessarily broken up into fields. In addition, connections within the hierarchical model don't depend on the data. The hierarchical links, sometimes called the structure of the data, can best be thought of as forming an inverted tree, with the parent file at the top and children files below. The relationship between parent and children is a one-to-many connection, in that one parent may produce multiple children.

The basic operation on the hierarchical database is the tree walk, proceeding from parent to child. Data can be retrieved only by traversing the levels of the hierarchy according to the path defined by the succession of parent fields. This unidirectional convention causes certain relationships to be difficult to extract from the database, even though they may be explicit in the data. For example, one characteristic of the hierarchical model is that information must often be repeated. Returning to the author-subject database example, under the topic of neurofibromatosis, if an author wrote more than one paper on the subject, the author's name and contact information would be repeated throughout the database.

The hierarchical model was once very popular in medicine, in the form of the Massachusetts General Hospital Utility Multi-Programming System (MUMPS) database language, which was used to develop one of the first electronic medical record (EMR) systems. A reason for the initial popularity of MUMPS in the early 1960s was that the data model is a good fit for clinical data, which tends to follow a standard topic outline, which is hierarchical. For example, patients at the top of the hierarchy have child nodes containing the elements of the EMR, including chief complaint, diagnosis, and laboratory results, as defined in Table 2-2. The limitation, noted earlier, is that for every patient admission, certain data must repeated, such as the patient's address, billing information, and other demographic information.

The hierarchical model remains significant in bioinformatics if only because a library of clinical information resides in databases following this model. For example, a descendent of MUMPS called simply M is the standard for EMRs in the Veterans Administration hospitals throughout the U.S.

Because of the storage inefficiency of the hierarchical model for some types of data, the network model was developed in the late 1960s. For example, the network model is more flexible than the hierarchical one because multiple connections can be established between files. These multiple connections enable the user to gain access to a particular file more effectively, without traversing the entire hierarchy above that file. Unlike the one-to-many relationship supported by the hierarchical model, the network model is based on a many-to-one relationship. The network model is significant in bioinformatics in that it may play a significant role in the architecture of the Great Global Grid and other Web-based computing initiatives.

One of the most significant alternatives to the relational database model is the object-oriented model in which complex data structures are represented by composite objects, which are objects that contain other objects. These objects may contain other objects in turn, allowing structures to be nested to any degree. This metaphor is especially appealing to those who work with bioinformatics data because this nesting of complexity complements the natural structure of genomic data (see Figure 2-18).

The object-oriented model combines the natural structure of the hierarchical model with the flexibility of the relational model. As such, the major advantage of the object-oriented model is that it can be used to represent complex genomic information, including non-record-oriented data, such as textual sequence data and images, in a way that doesn't compromise flexibility. Furthermore, with an object-oriented DBMS, it's possible to use arbitrary data types, and complex relationships can be queried without having to create resource-intensive joins between tables. The object-oriented model is considered optimum for handling genomic data, because it allows combinations of data to be treated as single entities. Instead of thinking about a gene with exons, introns, mRNA, nucleotide sequences, associated proteins, and their

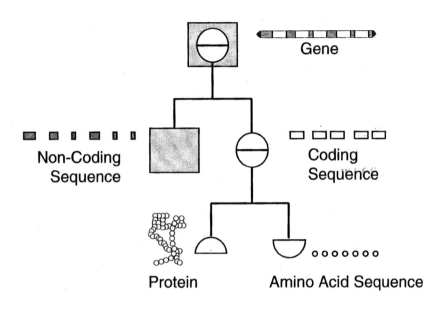

Figure 2-18 Object-Oriented Data Representation. The object-oriented data model is natural for hiding the complexity of genomic data.

3D shapes as a separate sound file, a separate video file, and a separate text document, researchers can simply work with the gene object.

Although the object-oriented approach holds great promise in bioinformatics, it still lags far behind relational technology in the global database market. In addition, because of the flexibility and power of the relational design, many of the object-oriented DBMS products on the market are based on extensions of commercial relational database packages. Because of the added overhead, the performance of these hybrid object-oriented systems is necessarily less than that of either a pure relational or an object-oriented system.

In addition to object-oriented models built on relational model technology, a variety of other models that are optimum for bioinformatics work can be constructed from relational technology. For example, the deductive model is an extension of the relational database with a logic programming interface based on the principles of logic programming. The logic programming interface is composed of rules, facts, and queries, using the relational database infrastructure to contain the facts.

The database is termed deductive because from the set of rules and the facts it is possible to derive new facts not contained in the original set of facts. Unlike logic programming languages such as PROLOG, which search for a single answer to a query using a top-down search, deductive databases search from bottom-up, starting from the facts to find *all* answers to a query.

For example, using the format "patient (Patient ID, Sex, Mother Carrier, Father Trait)," data in the deductive database describing a sex-linked recessive gene such as red-green color blindness could be represented in a relational table as in Table 2-6.

Table 2-6   Data for a Deductive Database. Columns, from left to right, represent Patient ID, Sex, Mother Carrier, and Father Trait.

Patient ID	Sex	Mother Carrier	Father Trait
001	Male	Yes	Yes
002	Female	Yes	No
003	Male	No	Yes
004	Female	No	Yes
005	Male	Yes	No
006	Male	No	No
007	Female	Yes	Yes

A relevant rule in a deductive database would be:

Potential Carrier ← (Sex = Female) AND (Mother Carrier = Yes)

That is, the patient is a potential carrier if the sex of the patient is female and the patient's mother is a known carrier. Males with the gene exhibit the disease, or red-green color blindness. However, because the gene involved in color blindness is maternal, then the state of the father's color acuity is irrelevant.

The query:

← Patient ID (X, potential carrier)

Would return the list of patients that should be tested for the genetic anomaly, in this case Patient 002 and Patient 007 from Table 2-6. Despite the obvious uses of deductive databases in bioinformatics, most deductive databases are either academic projects or internally developed and have yet to enter the ranks of commercial relational database products.

One more model worth mentioning is loosely defined as the semi-structured model. This model is a hybrid between a flat file and a hierarchical model, typically written as a text document in eXtensible Markup Language

(XML). The major advantage of the semi-structured model (which, like a flat file, isn't really a model per se) includes the ability to revise the structure to match new requirements on-the-fly. Like the hybrid model, however, there is a likely repetition of data.

Regardless of the model, at the highest level of abstraction of the DBMS is the view. That is, views are abstract models of portions of the conceptual database. Each view describes some of the database entities, attributes, and relationships between entities in a format convenient for a specific class of user or application. For example, researchers in a pharmacogenomic firm working with an application to report sequencing results do not need to know about patient findings. Similarly, clinicians in the pharmacology department may not need access to sequence results, but may require access to patient files. Thus, there may be one view of the database for the sequencing department and one for the proteomics department. As described in the following section, the view abstraction has application in user interface design.

INTERFACES

Databases don't stand alone, but communicate with devices and users through external and user interfaces, respectively. Getting data into a database can come about programmatically as in the creation of a data warehouse or data mart through processing an existing database. More often, the data are derived from external sources, such as user input through keyboard activity, or devices connected to a computer or network.

Common sources of input data include mouse and keyboard activity, voice recognition, bar-code readers, wireless devices, and RF-ID tags. Electronic data recorders, sequencing machines, and a variety of test equipment can also provide data for inclusion in the database, according to device communications standards. A variety of standards, such as the IEEE 1073 Point of Care Medical Device Communications standard, define the format, speed, and protocol of communications between workstations and external devices (see Figure 2-19).

Getting data into a database is of little value unless the data can also be retrieved. As illustrated in Figure 2-19, the most common methods for extracting data from a database are based on the Internet or an intranet and languages such as the Common Gateway Interface (CGI), the PHP: Hypertext Processor (PHP), and Java. In each case, the user issues a command from the workstation that is interpreted in the server. Results of the database query are then processed by language system and HTML is sent to the user's browser. In this scenario, the computational overhead is borne by the server.

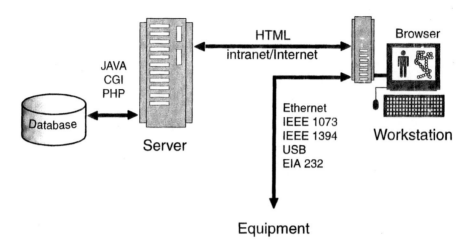

Figure 2-19   External Interfaces. Databases communicate with equipment and users through a variety of external interfaces.

Each system handles high-level database queries differently. For example, to perform a query using CGI, the user submits a query through a Web browser and the server executes a program, a CGI script, and the user's query is passed to the database via CGI. The program then returns information to the server via CGI, and this information is formatted into an HTML Web page that is displayed through the user's browser.

Similarly, the PHP interface offloads database query functions to the server, which handles the query, formats results, and conveys these to the user via standard HTML. Although PHP, which was originally referred to as Personal Home Page/Forms Interpreter (PHP/FI), is less established than CGI, it is considerably more powerful as a database interface. For example, unlike other scripting languages for Web page development, PHP offers excellent connectivity to most of the common databases, including Oracle, Sybase, MySQL, ODBC and many others. Java is also a server-side language that shares many of the database interface features of CGI and PHP. In addition, like PHP, Java uses a language that loosely resembles C.

CGI, PHP, and Java are all dependent on the server hardware for performance, and don't make additional demands for space or execution time on the workstations that are accessing data. This is in contrast with JavaScript, which has little to do with Java. JavaScript runs on the client side of the interface and, as such, can be malicious because of JavaScript viruses. JavaScript, while providing interactivity to Web pages, is much less useful as a database query tool compared to CGI, PHP, or Java.

Regardless of the language used to extract data from a database, the data have to be displayed on the user's monitor in an appropriate, understandable, and attractive way. This component of the user interface is most easily handled with a separate style sheet that defines the characteristics for the display device. In this paradigm, data to be displayed are first extracted from the database and coded in XML, a markup language for the Web that classifies content, but doesn't define how it should be displayed. A separate style sheet, in the form of an Extensible Stylesheet Language (XSL) document, specifies how the data are to be displayed in the user's browser.

Using the XML/XSL approach, modifying the manner in which data are displayed can be done without changing the XML Document, and involves simply modifying the relevant style sheet. Similarly, if the data change, only the XML document need be changed, not the style sheet. For example, consider the differences in how wireless content appears in HTML, XML, and XSL for the following database report.

Genetic History: The patient's *mother* is *carrier* for *BCG1*.

In standard HTML, which combines data and formatting instructions, the source code could appear as:

```
<HTML>
<BOLD> Genetic History: </BOLD>
The patient's
<I> mother </I>
 is a
<I> carrier </I>
for
<I> BCG1 </I>.
</HTML>
```

Notice that <BOLD> and </BOLD> are the HTML instructions to display in boldface type whatever comes between these two tags. Similarly <I> and </I> are the instructions to italicize the type between these two commands. By decoupling content from format instructions, changes in content can be made without the need to modify the formatting instructions given in the style sheets. Here's an example (formatted for clarity), using XML to categorize the data and XSL source code to describe formatting:

```
<PHRASE>
<GENETIC_CATEGORY> Genetic History: </ GENETIC_CATEGORY >
The
<SUBJECT> patient's </SUBJECT>
<PARENT> mother </PARENT>
```

```
is
<GENOTYPE> recessive </GENOTYPE>
for
<GENE> BCG1 </GENE>
.

   </PHRASE>
```

Assuming that the data are destined to be displayed on a wireless PDA with a monochrome display, one that supports bold and italic text formatting, the associated XSL source code could take the form:

```
FORMAT "GENETIC_CATEGORY" = BOLD
FORMAT "PARENT" = ITALICS
FORMAT "GENOTYPE" = ITALICS
FORMAT "GENE" = ITALICS
```

Furthermore, because the data in XML is decoupled from the display information in XSL, the symptom can be displayed in italics on the PDA and, for example, in red bold text on a laptop with a color display.

IMPLEMENTATION

Even with all of the public-domain databases accessible through the Internet, there will be research tasks that necessitate using a local database. The reasons vary from a need to collect, analyze, and publish sequence information inside a small laboratory to establishing a massive data warehouse as part of a pharmacogenomic R&D effort. In either case, the general issues and challenges are the same, albeit in different degrees of severity. As shown in Table 2-7, the major database implementation issues range from the storage capacity requirements and cost to scalability and security.

Table 2-7   Bioinformatics Database Implementation Issues.

Issue	Description
Accessibility	Ease of use, support for multiple mental models and database abstractions
Archiving	Support for the archival process, including software and hardware, and offsite storage facilities
Capacity	Local and remote data storage capacity, including space for expansion of the database

Table 2-7 Bioinformatics Database Implementation Issues. *(continued)*

Issue	Description
Connectivity	Connectivity through local and wide area networks, intranets, and the Internet
Control	Internal vs. third-party control of data, which may be an issue with storage service providers and other Internet-based commercial storage options
Cost	Initial, operating, and indirect (need to upgrade current network hardware and software, purchase additional peripherals) costs
Data Dictionary	Design, implementation, and maintenance of the data dictionary
Data Formats	Data formats supported by the database
Data Input	Hardware, software, and processes involved in feeding data into the database, from keyboard and voice recognition to direct instrument feed and the Internet
Data Model	Flat files, relational, hierarchical, network, object-oriented, or semi-structured
DBMS Software	Robustness, scalability, performance, cost, vendor reputation (if commercial), support available (if open source)
Dependencies	Dependence on primary databases for populating the database, especially regarding update frequency provision for validating data to minimize propagation of errors
Disaster Recovery	Procedural, hardware, and software provisions for disaster recovery, including error recovery mechanisms
Export/Import Capabilities	Provisions for importing and exporting data to and from different file formats
Hardware Requirements	Hard disks, controllers, backup hardware, production and staging servers for large database projects
Indexing	Indexing methodology, including selection and use of the most appropriate controlled vocabulary
Integration	Integration with other databases

Table 2-7   Bioinformatics Database Implementation Issues. *(continued)*

Issue	Description
Intellectual Property	Ownership of sequence data, images, and other data stored in and communicated through the database
Interfaces	Connectivity with other databases and applications
Legacy Systems	How to deal with legacy data and databases
Licensing	For vendor-supplied database systems, the most appropriate licensing arrangement
Life Span	The MTBF for the hardware as well as the likely useful life of the data
Load Testing	The maximum number of simultaneous users that can be supported by the DBMS
Maintenance	Cost and resource requirements
Media	The most appropriate disk, tape cartridges, and CD-ROM media
Normalization	Avoiding errors by representing data one way, one time, and in one place
Operating Environment	Ensuring proper power and operating temperature and humidity
Operating System	UNIX, Linux, Windows, MacOS, or mini/mainframe OS
Output	Format of database output
Performance	Access time and data throughput
Privacy	Provision for preserving confidentiality of data
Query Language	Proprietary or standard query language
Redundancy	Hot backups, shadowing, and RAID systems
Resource Requirements	Hardware, software, and operating and development personnel

Table 2-7   Bioinformatics Database Implementation Issues. *(continued)*

Issue	Description
Scalability	Ability to handle greater data volume with added hardware and/or software upgrades
Security	Limits on user access, from username-password combinations to biometrics, as well as encryption of sessions
Stand-Alone vs. Network	And multi- vs. single user
Standards	From media format to operating system, query language, and data models
Utilities	Availability of software tools for data recovery
Vendor Viability	Commercial viability of the hardware and software vendors supplying database tools and platform

For example, a milestone in designing and implementing a database is defining the type of data to be stored. This decision will then imply the most appropriate data model and type of DBMS to employ. If the data are nucleotide sequences, then a reasonable choice would be a semi-structured database based on XML-tagged text files. However, if the data are images of 3D protein structures and keywords, then either an object-oriented or a relational database would likely be more appropriate. Even though the representation of rows and columns may not be optimum for mapping protein structures onto a database, factors such as support from a commercial relational database vendor and support might dictate use of a relational product.

Consider the process involved in creating a central data warehouse of a scale appropriate for the pharmacogenomic laboratory discussed at the beginning of this chapter. The six-stage process usually involves these phases: planning; data consolidation; data transformation; selective archiving; data distribution; and ongoing maintenance.

In the planning stage, arguably the most important phase of data warehouse development, representatives from administration, R&D, and information technology departments decide exactly what to include in the data warehouse. Ideally, the data warehouse content should reflect the questions likely to be asked. For example, researchers might want to correlate microarray values with specific clinical diagnoses, and administrators might want to compile summaries of average sequence run costs. Because of practical cost, resource, and performance limitations, it's normally impossible to store every data element from every application in a data warehouse. The planning phase directly impacts the eventual cost and functionality of the data warehouse.

In the consolidation phase, the selected data from each application database are restructured. This typically involves adding fields and relations to reflect how the data will be used in the data warehouse. The goal in the consolidation phase is to provide an efficient framework that supports queries likely to be asked, as determined in the planning stage.

The data transformation stage of data warehouse development involves transforming the consolidated data into a more useful form through summarization and packaging. In summarization, the data are selected, aggregated, and grouped into views more convenient and useful to users. Packaging involves using the summarized data as the basis of graphical presentations, animations, and charts.

Selective archiving involves moving older or infrequently accessed data to tape, optical, or other long-term storage media. Archiving saves money by sparing expensive magnetic, high-speed storage, and minimizes the performance hit imposed by locally storing data that is no longer necessary for outcomes analysis.

The distribution phase makes data contained in the data warehouse available to users. Providing for distribution encompasses front-end development so that users can easily and intuitively request and receive data, whether in real-time or in the form of routine reports. Push technologies, including e-mail alerts, can be used to distribute data to specific users. The Web is also a major portal for accessing the data.

Maintenance is the final, ongoing stage of data warehouse development. However, creating a data warehouse involves much more than simply designing and implementing a database. Even if there is a process in place for extracting, cleaning, transporting, and loading data from sequence machines, bibliographic reference databases, and other molecular biology applications, and distribution tools are both powerful and intuitive, the data warehouse may not be sustainable in the long-term. For example, the process of extracting, cleaning, and reloading data can be prohibitively expensive and time-consuming. A sustainable data warehouse provides a real benefit to users to the degree that not only is the return worth the original development, but that it is valuable enough to warrant continual redesigning and evaluation to meet changing demands.

Infrastructure

From a hardware perspective, implementing a database requires more than servers, large hard drives, perhaps a network and the associated cables and electronics. Power conditioners and uninterruptible power supplies are needed to protect sensitive equipment and the data they contain from power surges and sudden, unplanned power outages. Providing a secure environment for data includes the usual use of username and passwords to protect accounts. However, for higher levels of assurance against data theft or manipulation, secure ID cards, dongles, and biometrics (such as voice, fingerprint, and retinal recognition) may be appropriate.

Secure ID cards are credit card–sized pseudorandom number generators that are synchronized with a similar generator on the server. Users enter the 16-digit number displayed on the secure ID card for their password to gain access to the system. Biometric security systems use personal biological characteristics, such as a fingerprint, voice, or the pattern of capillaries on the retinae to verify the identity of a user. Dongles are hardware keys that applications look for on either the serial or USB port of a workstation before users can access their data and applications. Dongles can be considered as a form of hardware-based encryption. Dedicated, high-speed hardware capable of high-speed encryption and decryption are available options as well.

Encryption is the use of a key or code to scramble a message so that it can only be deciphered by someone with knowledge of the key and the algorithm used to encrypt the original message. From a practical perspective, encryption is the processing of data so that it's at least challenging for casual eavesdroppers to read, even if the data are intercepted.

For Web-based databases, Secure Socket Layer (SSL) is the dominant security protocol. Information transmitted over the Web using SSL is automatically encrypted, and only when the user's Web browser and the computer serving content have the same key can they communicate. Both Netscape and Internet Explorer support the optional use of SSL.

One of the limitations of SSL is that it's wedded to the client/server architecture, where a secure session is established, through which any amount of data may be securely transmitted for the duration of the session. A complementary communications protocol that makes use of encryption is Secure Hypertext Transfer Protocol (S-HTTP), a protocol that is designed to transmit individual messages securely over the Web. That is, SSL provides a secure communications channel for the length of the connection between the client and the server, regardless of whether or not data is flowing from one to the other. In contrast, S-HTTP is more appropriate for short communications that only uses the channel when data are moving from sender to receiver.

Regardless of whether SSL or S-HTTP is used, at the core of communications over the Internet is an encryption technology called Public Key Encryption (PKE), which is based on a pair of keys or data strings. One key is public, known or at least knowable to everyone, and one key is private, known only to the sender. The private key, which is not shared with anyone, is used to decrypt information that's been encrypted by someone using the public key. In other words, encoding uses a generally available public key and decoding is performed using a private key available only to the intended recipient. PKE is like a physical padlock, where one key is used to lock a padlock and another key to open it.

ENDNOTE

Looking to the immediate future, the database technologies that will most likely have a significant impact on bioinformatics are the ones that deal with systems integration, the process in which disparate computer applications and systems can share data. Because the applications in a typical biotech laboratory are often cobbled together from different vendors and custom, in-house development, and may be running on multiple generations of hardware, system integration is still a custom-programming task. As a result, integrating every database in an organization can take months of effort, considerable expense, and have only mixed results. Part of the challenge is that, due to the relative youth of the bioinformatics arena, the market has yet to respond to the need for commercial integration tools that address the specific needs of the community. Two areas in which rapid innovation is required for database integration and overall improved interoperability of bioinformatics tools are vocabulary standards and DBMSs.

Although organizations such as NCBI and the National Library of Medicine are actively involved in developing tools for the molecular biologist working in the field of bioinformatics, a vocabulary of bioinformatics has yet to be defined. As a result, most data warehouses and data dictionaries are based on ad-hoc compilations of existing vocabularies with additions made on an as-needed basis. Part of the challenge of creating a standard bioinformatics vocabulary is determining the appropriate level of granularity needed to adequately describe everything from nucleotide sequences and protein structure to species data. This challenge is intensified as the focus of bioinformatics research shifts from nucleotide sequencing to proteomics, which necessarily includes phenotypic expression data stored in clinical systems. As a result, an all-encompassing vocabulary must increasingly incorporate data in the medical record and public health as well.

In the area of DBMSs, although the relational model currently dominates the market, the complexity of clinical and laboratory data is driving many researchers to seriously consider other DBMS technologies, such as object-oriented DBMSs. While there is a great deal of interest in object-oriented approaches to supporting bioinformatics computing, the information technology community is still expressing caution toward the technology. This is partly because many object-oriented database systems are incomplete, in that they lack backup and recovery functions. In addition, data models often conflict, the languages supported by vendors are proprietary, scalability is unproven, and the systems require huge amounts of memory and computational resources. In the recent past, vendors have partially addressed these and other limitations of ODBMs, but performance and scalability concerns remain.

Several vendors are building what they consider the next generation of bioinformatics database systems, but it's uncertain which of these systems will establish a standard. As such, the most promising technologies in the systems integration arena are aimed at the general computing market, such as Web Services, Storage Area Networks, Storage Service Providers, or Application Service Providers. Time will tell which of these models, if any, can be shown to be economically—as opposed to simply technologically—viable. In most cases, this translates to technologies that are transparent to the research workflow, thereby augmenting current processes and contributing to effectiveness of R&D.

By far the most significant challenges surrounding the effective use of database technology in bioinformatics relate to issues of security, privacy, and bioethics, and how these issues will eventually affect legislation that will either support or hamper advances in the field. Consider the privacy and security issues associated with having an individual's medical records and DNA analysis available online and instantly available to teachers, employers, the courts, police, the FBI, and, inevitably, hackers. For now, the challenge is achieving the level of database integration that would make these issues a reality. At best, integration is limited to what Internet and intranet technology can support, through both fixed or hard-wired links and, more commonly, through dynamic links provided by online search engines. As described in Chapter 4, "Search Engines," significant progress in molecular biology database integration is being made in this arena.

➤ Ebola Virus structure, superimposed over its PDB summary information. Image produced with PDB Structure Explorer, which is based on MolScript and Raster3D.

CHAPTER

Networks

People seldom improve when they have
no other model but themselves to copy after.
— Oliver Goldsmith

Comparing a data network to a living organism, the hardware provides the skeleton or basic infrastructure upon which the nervous system is built. Similarly, a few hundred meters of cable running through the walls of a laboratory is necessary but insufficient to constitute a network. Rather, the data pulsing through cables or other media in a coordinated fashion define a network. This coordination is provided by electronics that connect workstations and shared computer peripherals with the networks that amplify, route, filter, block, and translate data. Every competent bioinformatics researcher should have a basic understanding of the limits, capabilities, and benefits of specific network hardware, if only to be able to converse intelligently with hardware vendors or to direct the management of an information services provider.

According to Chaos Theory, the ability to adapt and the capacity for spontaneous self-organization are the two main characteristics of complex systems—systems that have many independent variables interacting with each other in many ways and that have the ability to balance order and chaos. In this regard, computer networks qualify as complex systems, always at the edge of failure, but still working. In some sense, it's difficult to define success and failure for these systems, in part because of the so-called law of unintended consequences that stipulates these systems can provide results so beneficial, so out of proportion to the intended "success" that they overshadow the significance of the intended goal. Consider that gunpowder was intended as an elixir to prolong life, or that the adhesive on 3M Post-It Notes® was intended to be a superglue, Edison's phonograph was intended to be a telephone message recorder, and Jacquard's punch card was intended to automate the loom, not to give the computer its instructions or determine presidential elections. Such is the case with the Internet, one of the greatest enabling technologies in bioinformatics, allowing researchers in laboratories anywhere on the globe to access data maintained by the National Center for Biological Information (NCBI), the National Institutes of Health (NIH), and other government agencies.

The Internet was never intended to serve as the portal to the code of life, but was a natural successor to the cold war projects in the 1950s and early 1960s. During this time, the military establishment enjoyed the nearly unanimous respect and support of politicians and the public. Universities with the top science and engineering faculties received nearly unlimited funding, and the labors of the nation's top scientists filtered directly into industry. Military demand and government grants funded the development of huge projects that helped establish the U.S. as a Mecca for technological developments in computing and communications networks.

The modern Internet was the unintended outcome of two early complex systems: the ARPANET (Advanced Research Project Agency Network) and the SAGE system (semiautomatic ground environment), developed for the military in the early 1950s and 1960s, respectively. SAGE was the national air defense system comprised of an elaborate, ad hoc network of incompatible command and control computers, early warning radar systems, weather centers, air traffic control centers, ships, planes, and weapons systems. The communications network component of the SAGE system was comprehensive and extended beyond the border of the U.S. and included ships and aircraft. It was primarily a military system, with a civil defense link as its only tie with civilian communications system.

Government-sponsored R&D increasingly required reliable communications between industry, academia, and the military. Out of this need, and spurred by the fear of disruption of the civilian communications grid through eventual nuclear attack, a group of scientists designed a highly redundant communications system, starting with a single node at UCLA in September of 1969. By 1977, the ARPANET stretched across the U.S. and extended from Hawaii to Europe. The ARPANET quickly grew and became more complex, with an increasing number of nodes and redundant cross-links that provided alternate communications paths in the event that any particular node or link failed.

Although the ARPANET's infrastructure was an interdependent network of nodes and interconnections, the data available from the network was indistinguishable from data available from any standalone computer. The infrastructure of the system provided redundant data communications, but no quick and intuitive way for content authors to cross-link data throughout the network for later access—the mechanism that allows today's Internet users to search for information. In 1990, ARPANET was replaced by the National Science Foundation Network (NSFNET) to connect its supercomputers to regional networks. Today, NSFNET operates as the high-speed backbone of the Internet.

Fortunately, and apparently coincidentally, during the period of military expansion in the 1950s and 1960s, federally funded researchers at academic institutions explored ways to manage the growing store of digital data amid the increasingly complex network of computers and networks. One development was hypertext, a cross-referencing scheme, where a word in one document is linked to a word in the same or a different document.

Around the time the ARPANET was born, a number of academic researchers began experimenting with computer-based systems that used hypertext. For example, in the early 1970s, a team at Carnegie-Mellon University developed ZOG, a hypertext-based system that was eventually installed on a U.S. aircraft carrier. ZOG was a reference application that provided the crew with online documentation that was richly cross-linked to improve speed and efficiency of locating data relevant to operating shipboard equipment.

In addition to applications for the military, a variety of commercial, hypertext-based document management systems were spun out of academia and commercial laboratories, such as the Owl Guide hypertext program from the University of Kent, England, and the Notecards system from Xerox PARC in California. Both of these systems were essentially stand-alone equivalents of a modern Web browser, but based on proprietary document formats with content limited to what could be stored on a hard drive or local area network (LAN). The potential market for these products was limited because of specialized hardware requirements. For example, the initial version of Owl Guide, which predated Apple's HyperCard hypertext program, was only available for the Apple Macintosh. Similarly, Notecards required a Xerox workstation running under a LISP-based operating system. These and other document management systems allowed researchers to create limited Web-like environments, but without the advantage of the current Web of millions of documents authored by others.

In this circuitous way, out of the quest for national security through an indestructible communications network, the modern Internet was born. Today, the Internet connects bioinformatics researchers in China, Japan, Europe, and worldwide, regardless of political or national affiliation. It not only provides communications, including e-mail, videoconferencing, and remote information access. Together with other networks, the Internet provides for resource sharing and alternate, reliable sources of bioinformatics data.

As an example of how important networks are in bioinformatics R&D, consider that the typical microarray laboratory involved in creating genetic profiles for custom drug development and other purposes generates huge amounts of data. Not only does an individual microarray experiment generate thousands of data points, usually in the form of 16-bit tiff (tagged image file format) files, but the experimental design leading up to the experiments, including gene data analysis, involves access to volumes of timely data as well. Furthermore, analysis and visualization of the experimental data requires that they be seamlessly and immediately available to other researchers.

The scientific method involves not only formulating a hypothesis and then generating creative and logical alternative solutions for methods of supporting or refuting it, but also a hypothesis that will withstand the scrutiny of others. Results must be verifiable and reproducible under similar conditions in different laboratories. One of the challenges of working with microarrays is that there is still considerable art involved in creating meaningful results. Results are often difficult to reproduce, even within the same laboratory. Fortunately, computational methods, including statistical methods, can help identify and control for some sources of error.

As shown in Figure 3-1, computers dedicated to experimental design, scanning and image analysis, expression analysis, and gene data manipulation support the typical microarray laboratory. The microarray device is only one small component of the overall research and design process. For example, once the experiment is designed using gene data gleaned from an online database, the microarray containing the clones of interest has to be designed and manufactured. After hybridization with cDNA or RNA from tissue samples, the chips are optically scanned and the relative intensity of fluorescent markers on the images are analyzed and stored. The data are subsequently subject to further image processing and gene expression analysis.

In this example, the server provides a gateway or access point to the Internet to access the national databases for gene data analysis. Individual computers, running different operating systems, share access to data generated by the microarray image scanner as soon as it's generated. For example, even though a workstation may be running MacOS, UNIX, Linux, or some version of the Windows operating system, and the microarray image scanner controller operates under a proprietary operating system, the network provides a common communications channel for sharing and capturing data from the experiment as well as making sense of it through computer-based analysis. The network also supports the sharing of resources, such as printers, modems, plotters, and other networked peripherals. In addition, a wireless extension of the network allows the researchers to share the wireless laptop for manipulating the data,

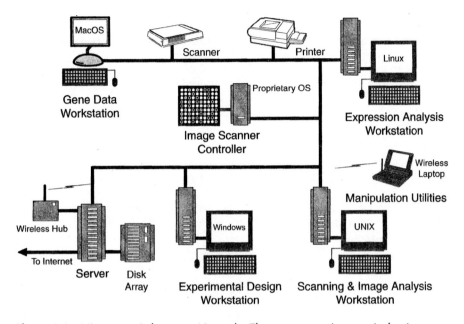

Figure 3-1 Microarray Laboratory Network. The computers in a typical microarray laboratory present a mixture of data formats, operating systems, and processing capabilities. The network in this example, a wired and wireless local area network (LAN), supports the microarray laboratory processes, from experimental design and array fabrication to expression analysis and publishing of results.

such as by transforming spot data from the image analysis workstation to array data that can be manipulated by a variety of complex data-manipulation utilities. In this context, the purpose of the LAN is to provide instantaneous connectivity between the various devices in the laboratory, thereby facilitating the management, storage, and use of the data.

Consider the process without the network depicted in Figure 3-1. The gene analysis workstation would have to be connected directly to the Internet—a potentially dangerous proposition without a software or hardware firewall or safety barrier to guard against potential hackers. Similarly, the results of any analysis would have to be separately archived to a floppy, Zip® disk, or CD-ROM. In addition, sharing experimental data would require burning a CD-ROM or using other media compatible with the other workstations in the laboratory. Simply attaching a data file to an e-mail message or storing it in a shared or open folder on the server would be out of the question. Data could also be shared through printouts, but because the computers aren't part of a network, each workstation requires its own printer, plotter, modem, flatbed scanner, or other peripherals. For example, unless the expression analysis workstation has its own connection to the Internet, results of the experiment can't be easily communicated to collaborating laboratories or even the department in an adjoining building. Furthermore, even though many of the public online bioinformatics databases accept submissions on floppy or other media, the practice is usually frowned upon in favor of electronic submission.

Without the wireless component of the LAN, researchers in the lab would not be able to instantly explore the data generated by the scanning and analysis workstation, but would have to wait until the other researchers operating a workstation have time to write the data to a disk or other media. More importantly, every workstation operator would be responsible for backing up and archiving their own data—a time-consuming, high-risk proposition. It's far more likely, for example, that a researcher in the laboratory will fail to manually archive local data on a regular basis than it is for a central, automated backup system to fail.

This brief tour of this prototypical microarray laboratory highlights several applications of networks in bioinformatics. The underlying advantage of the network is the ability to move data from one computer to another as quickly, transparently, and securely as possible. This entails accessing online databases, publishing findings, communicating via e-mail, working with other researchers through integrated networked applications known as groupware, and downloading applications and large data sets from online sources via file transfer protocol (FTP) and other methods.

Although many of these features can be had by simply plugging in a few network cards and following a handful of instruction manuals, chances are that several key functions won't be available without considerably more knowledge of network technology. For example, selecting and configuring a network requires that someone make educated decisions regarding bandwidth, reliability, security, and cost. Furthermore, mixed operating system environments typical of bioinformatics laboratories, which tend to have at least one workstation running Linux or UNIX, presents challenges not found in generic office networks.

What's more, it may not be obvious from the simple network depicted in Figure 3-1 that bioinformatics networks present unique networking challenges that typically can't be addressed by generic network installations. The first is that there is a huge amount of data involved. The network isn't handling short e-mail messages typical of the corporate environment, but massive sequence strings, images, and other data. In addition, unlike networks that support traditional business transaction processing, data are continually flowing from disk arrays, servers, and other sources to computers for processing because the data can't fit into computer RAM. As a result, the network and external data sources are in effect extensions of the computer bus, and the performance of the network limits the overall performance of the system. It doesn't matter whether the computer processor is capable of processing several hundred million operations per second if the network feeding data from the disks to the computer has a throughput of only 4–5 Mbps.

This chapter continues the exploration of the Internet, intranets, wireless systems, and other network technologies that apply directly to sharing, manipulating, and archiving sequence data and other bioinformatics information. The following sections explore network architecture—how a network is designed, how the components on the system are connected to the network, and how the components interact with each other. As illustrated in Figure 3-2, this includes examining networks from the perspective of:

- Geographical scope
- Underlying model or models used to implement the network
- Signal transmission technology
- Bandwidth or speed
- Physical layout or topology
- Protocol or standards used to define how signals are handled by the network
- Ownership or funding source involved in network development
- Hardware, including cables, wires, and other media used to provide the information conduit from one device to the next
- Content carried by the network

This chapter also explores the practical network implementation issues, especially network security, and considers the future of network technology.

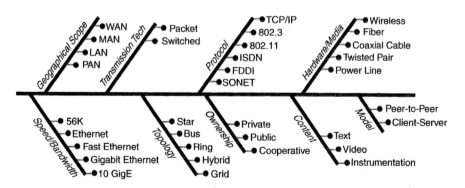

Figure 3-2 Network Taxonomy. Networks can be characterized along a variety of parameters, from size or geographical scope to the contents carried by the network.

GEOGRAPHICAL SCOPE

The geographical extent of a network is significant because it affects bandwidth, security, response time, and the type of computing possible. For example, it is only because of the high-speed Internet backbone that real-time teleconferencing and model sharing are possible on a worldwide basis.

Although the geographical boundaries are somewhat arbitrary the networks are commonly referred to as personal area networks (PANs), LANs, metropolitan area networks (MANs), or wide area networks (WANs), as depicted in Figure 3-3. Although many networks are interconnected, they can also function alone.

PANs, which are limited to the immediate proximity of the user, or about a 10-meter radius, are typically constructed using wireless technology. LANs extend to about 100-meters from a central server, or a single floor in a typical research building. MANs take over where LANs leave off, covering entire buildings and extending tens of kilometers. MANs are typically implemented with digital subscriber line (DSL), cable modem, and fixed wireless technologies.

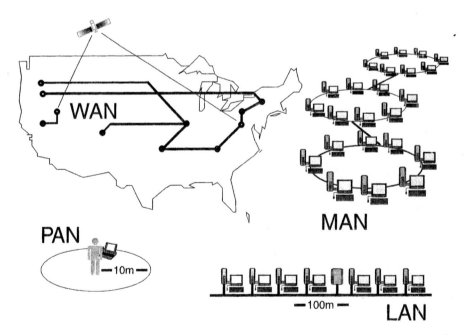

Figure 3-3 Network Geographical Scope. Bioinformatics R&D incorporates network resources on worldwide (WAN), institution-wide (MAN), and laboratory-wide (LAN and PAN) levels.

WANs extend across the continent and around the globe, and are typically composed of a combination of terrestrial fixed satellite systems, coaxial cable, and fiber optical cable. The public switched telephone network and the Internet are examples of WANs.

Grid computing, in which multiple PCs are interconnected to form a distributed supercomputer, can take advantage of LAN, MAN, and WAN technology, as a function of computer processing speed, network connection bandwidth, and the effectiveness of the software that coordinates activities among computers on the grid. For example, relatively slow-speed DSL and cable modem connections are used by many of the experimental grid systems, such as the Folding@home project at Stanford University. The system uses standard DSL and cable modem networks, which provide between 125 Kbps and 1 Mbps throughput, to connect over 20,000 PCs to form a grid computer. The higher-speed grid systems are necessarily limited to MAN distances using conventional Internet connections or WAN distances with much higher-speed network connections. For example, the Department of Energy's Science Grid project is based on a 622 Mbps fiber network running a suite of software that includes Globus grid software.

COMMUNICATIONS MODELS

In the traditional client-server model, a server provides data to one or more clients. In contrast, in a peer-to-peer network, every computer acts as a server and client to other computers on the network. As such, a particular computer might function as a server one moment and as a client the next (see Figure 3-4).

The simplest type of computer network to construct in a small workgroup is a peer-to-peer network. In this model, every workstation acts as both a server and a client for every other workstation (see Figure 3-4). The disadvantage of the peer-to-peer model is uneven use of resources, in that the workstations with the most relevant content are accessed more often than workstations with less-frequently accessed content. The result is decreased performance for computational tasks of the frequently accessed workstations. Another limitation of this design is that data management is more challenging. Everyone in the workgroup must perform tasks such as archiving and updating antiviral utilities, for example.

In contrast, a client-server model employs a central server to provide programs and data files that can be accessed by client workstations on the network. An advantage of this model is that the network operating system running on the server provides for security, tiered access privileges, and no degradation of individual workstation performance because files are accessed from the server. In addition, the data and programs on the central server can be more easily and consistently archived, backed up, accessed, and shared.

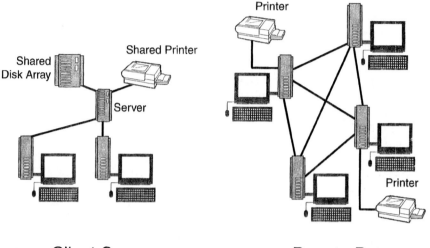

Figure 3-4   Communications Models.

TRANSMISSIONS TECHNOLOGY

One of the major technological innovations initiated by pioneers of the Internet was the development of alternatives to the traditional switched network model first used by telephone switchboard operators at the turn of the 19th century. Even though some communications networks, including many of the cell phone networks, still follow the switched model, computer networks such as the Internet are based on a more complex but bandwidth-sparing packet model. The major disadvantage of the much simpler switching model is that it can't provide more communications channels than there are switches.

As shown in Figure 3-5, in a switched communications network, once a connection is established, it monopolizes the circuit until the switch is released, even though the data has been transferred from source to destination and the connection may remain idle. As such, the switching circuit in the figure is capable of supporting only six simultaneous bi-directional communications channels. That is, the communications path through the network is identical, regardless of which party originates the message.

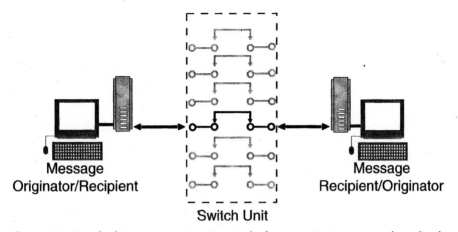

Figure 3-5 Switched Communications. In switched communications networks, a fixed, continuous bi-directional connection is established between the message source and recipient.

Packet communications makes use of the pauses and breaks in typical communications allowing a single physical communications circuit to establish multiple, virtual channels. In the packet paradigm, messages are parsed into small segments and packaged into labeled packets by the message disassembler and packet generator (see Figure 3-6). These packets travel via various routes through the network to the destination, as determined by the traffic density at nodes along the way. Because packets are dynamically routed to different nodes as a function of the momentary demand for virtual communications channels, some packets may arrive ahead of others, out of the original sequence.

At the destination, the data packets are captured by the packet organizer and re-assembled in their original order by the message assembler. Even though the recipient is capable of receiving information at any time, the communications channel is capable of carrying packets to and from other subscribers. That is, the recipient can receive messages at any time without blocking the use of the communications channel for other communications. This is in contrast with switched communications, which holds the channel captive until the subscriber releases it, even if no data are being transferred. Even though packet communications uses separate channels for two-way communications, it is nonetheless several orders of magnitude more bandwidth-efficient than switched communications. This is especially true with intermittent communications with relatively long periods of idle time, such as sending and receiving e-mail or reading content on the Web.

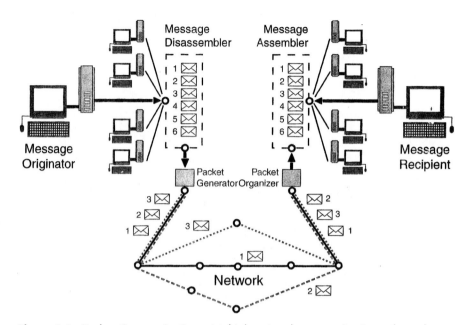

Figure 3-6 Packet Communications. Multiple, virtual communications channels are established by breaking up messages into small packets and reassembling them at the destination.

PROTOCOLS

Bioinformatics R&D involves the generation, capture, management, and repurposing of vast amounts of data. Furthermore, robotic sequencers, nucleotide pattern matchers, and other sources of data can communicate with workstations and other devices on the network only to the extent that the network supports the appropriate protocols or sets of standards that enable unencumbered communications. One of the primary benefits of a computer network is interoperability—the ability of different computers running different operating systems to share data and resources over a network. Furthermore, the more devices that can communicate with each other over a network, the more valuable the network becomes. This interoperability can occur by accident, by a single powerful vendor defining standards, or, more commonly, by a proposal put forth by a recognized standards organization.

The key standards organizations that define or suggest network protocols include the Open Systems Interconnection (OSI) group, the Institute of Electrical and Electronics Engineers (IEEE), the Consultative Committee on International Telegraphy and Telephony/International Telecommunications

Union-Telecommunications Sector (CCITT/ITU-T), the American National Standards Institute (ANSI), and the Exchange Carriers Standards Association (ECSA), also known as the Alliance for Telecommunications Industry Solutions (ATIS).

These organizations define protocols by consensus. Unlike laws enacted by the Federal Communications Commission (FCC) or other government agencies, there is no legal penalty for ignoring a standard—other than potential economic peril. As such, most companies abide by these and other protocols.

OSI, begun by the International Organization for Standardization in the late 1970s, defines high-level communications architectures, including the OSI Reference Model (see Table 3-1). The model, which defines everything from the physical medium to the semantics of the messages on the network, corresponds to the original ARPANET model. TCP/IP, the model upon which the current Internet is based, omits layers 5 and 6, the session and presentation levels. As such, TCP/IP illustrates the status of standards in the bioinformatics industry. Because the field is expanding so rapidly, there are multiple "standards," each of which solves a particular problem.

Table 3-1 The OSI Reference Model. OSI defines the communications process into seven different categories that deal with communications and network access.

Layer	Name	Focus
7	Application	Semantics
6	Presentation	Syntax
5	Session	Dialog coordination
4	Transport	Reliable data transfer
3	Network	Routing and relaying
2	Data Link	Technology-specific transfer
1	Physical	Physical connections

The IEEE develops standards for the entire computing industry, including wired and wireless networks. Unlike the OSI protocols, these standards define specific low-level functionality, such as operating frequency, bandwidth, message format, signal voltage, and connector style for computer networks. For example, the IEEE-802.3 10BaseT standard defines Ethernet over ordinary twisted pair cable. The standard defines the cable, the connector type, pin connections, voltage levels, and noise immunity requirements. The most important IEEE standards in bioinformatics are listed in Table 3-2.

Table 3-2   Key Network Protocols.

Standard	Description
IEEE 488	Computer to electronic instrument communications; also known as GPIB and HPIB
IEEE-802	LAN and MAN standards
IEEE-802.3	Ethernet; the most common LAN specification
IEEE-802.3 10Base-T	Ethernet over twisted pair cable
IEEE-802.11	Wireless LANs
IEEE-802.11a	5 GHz, 54 Mbps wireless LAN; shorter range than 2.4 GHz systems, higher bandwidth, and more channels than WiFi
IEEE-802.11b	2.4 GHz, 11 Mbps wireless LAN; the most common, most mature; limited channels, also known as WiFi
IEEE-802.11e	2.4 GHz, 11 Mbps wireless LAN; enhanced quality of service
IEEE-802.11g	2.4 GHz, 22 Mbps wireless LAN; higher-bandwidth version of 802.11b, limited channels
IEEE-802.11i	2.4 GHz, 11 Mbps wireless LAN; enhanced security
CCITT/ITU-T ISDN	Digital communications over standard phone lines
CCITT/ITU-T X.25	Switched packet communications
ANSI FDDI	High-speed (200 Mbps) fiber backbone LAN
ECSA SONET	Very high-speed (10 Gbps) optical network standard
DARPA TCP/IP	The protocol of the Internet

The relatively short list of standards in Table 3-2 may give the false impression that there are only a few basic standards that network manufacturers abide by. In reality, there are dozens of extensions to these and other protocols. For example, the extensions shown for IEEE 802.11 illustrate how the standard for wireless LANs has several extensions, each of which provides for significant differences in the frequency, bandwidth, and feature of the communications. The relative contribution of each factor to the overall bioinformatics project depends on the nature of the project. For example, when working with 3D images, bandwidth becomes an issue.

The CCITT/ITU-T develops international network standards that generally involve the telephone network. For example, a prominent standard developed by CCITT/ITU-T is Integrated Services Digital Network (ISDN). The ISDN standard defines digital communications at a rate of up to 128 Kbps over ordinary twisted pair cable. The X.25 protocol, also known as packet switched network, forms the basis for packet communications that is similar to that used by the Internet. ANSI is a U.S. equivalent of the CCITT/ITU-T, in that it publishes voluntary protocols for use by the U.S. computer industry. The most significant ANSI standard that applies to computer networks is the Fiber Distributed Data Interface (FDDI). This networking standard defines a fiber-optic network that operates between 100 and 200 Mbps. A FDDI LAN is often called a Backbone LAN because it's used to join LANs together. The ECSA, a relatively new domestic standards organization, is involved in defining network interconnection standards. An example of a significant ECSA protocol is the Synchronous Optical Network (SONET) a very high-speed (in excess of 10 Gbps) optical communications network.

The most significant protocol used on the Internet is TCP/IP, developed by the Defense Advanced Research Project Agency (DARPA). The Transmission Control Protocol (TCP) component of the standard defines rules for exchanging information with other Internet points at the packet level. In addition, the Internet Protocol (IP) standard defines exchange of information at the Internet address level. TCP/IP, the protocol that defines communications on the Internet, is a packet system. It is the TCP component of the standard that defines how a message is broken down into packets, sized appropriately, and then transmitted over the Internet.

BANDWIDTH

Given the amount of data generated by a typical bioinformatics laboratory, adequate network bandwidth—commonly expressed as speed or throughput in thousands or millions of bits per second (bps)—is essential to efficient computation and communications. As shown in Figure 3-7, the applications operating on data retrieved from a storage area network disk array are typically supported by a tiered network system comprising a Gigabit Ethernet. This protocol provides 1 Gbps communications throughput between the storage area network disk array and the servers. A Fast Ethernet protocol provides 100 Mbps interprocess communications between the server-based applications. Finally, a standard Ethernet provides 10 Mbps throughput between workstations, which make relatively light throughput demands.

Although it's tempting to simply put every device on Gigabit Ethernet, there is a cost and maintenance issue with a Gigabit or other high-speed network

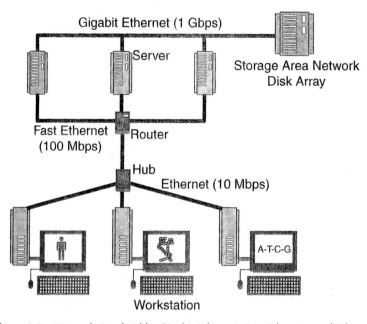

Figure 3-7 Network Bandwidth. Gigabit Ethernet, Fast Ethernet, and Ethernet provide a tiered network system that provides a compromise between system data throughput, cost, and maintenance.

compared to Fast or regular Ethernet. For example, Gigabit Ethernet has a limited range compared to regular Ethernet. In addition, whereas standard Ethernet works well over twisted pair and coaxial cable, most Gigabit Ethernet installations are based on fiber cable and expensive fiber-based electronics.

What constitutes "standard" and "high-speed" is a moving target, in that applications in the general networking industry are pushing standard and Fast Ethernet toward retirement. For example, Fast Ethernet isn't especially fast compared to the latest Gigabit Ethernet standard, 10 GigE, which provides a throughput of about 10 Gbps. As network electronics compatible with 10 GigE proliferate and Gigabit Ethernet electronics for workstations become more affordable, the throughput on virtually every scientific network, like the minimum workstation clock speed, will be in the giga-range.

TOPOLOGY

The physical layout of a network, referred to as its topology, is a function of the practical constraints imposed by the environment, the protocols that must be supported, and the cost of installation. The most common protocols used with LANs, Ethernet and token ring, assume a bus and ring topology, respectively. The star topology is often used as a hub to connect several networks and in wireless networks, where multiple devices connect via radio frequency, it links to a central wireless access point or wireless hub.

The three pure topologies—ring, bus, and star—illustrated in Figure 3-8, rarely exist alone. More likely, they are part of a hybrid network such as a small workgroup connected by bus to a star network in another workgroup, perhaps supporting computers running under a different operating system as well.

The practical implications of network topologies are material and labor costs associated with running cable and purchasing and installing the new network electronics. For example, in establishing a laboratory with a new network, running cables from one workstation position to the next to support a bus topology is usually cheaper and less labor-intensive than running cables from each workstation and device position to a central closet to support a star topology. However, although wiring a laboratory to support a star topology is much more expensive in terms of cable required and the labor involved in pulling all cables to a central closet, the cables pulled for a star topology can be easily reconfigured in a bus to support Ethernet or token ring protocols.

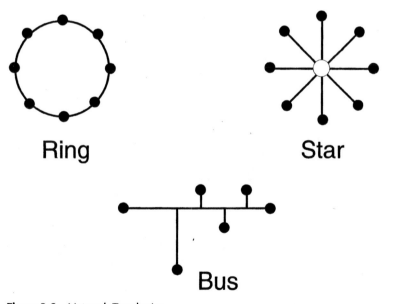

Figure 3-8   Network Topologies.

Similarly, a network wired in a ring topology can easily be converted to support an Ethernet bus by breaking the ring and installing the appropriate electronics. These modifications are illustrated in Figure 3-9. This conversion of topologies is most difficult going from ring or bus topology to a star topology, because the electronics in the hub or center of the star typically controls each spoke of the hub individually, normally requiring a separate cable from the hub to each device.

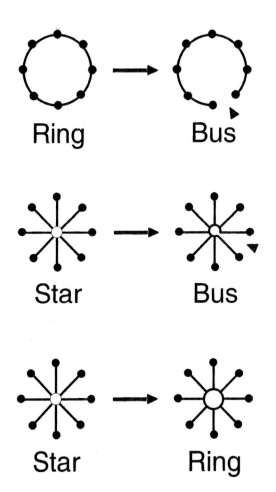

Figure 3-9   Network Topology Conversion. Network topologies initially configured to support one protocol can be modified to support others. For example, a star topology can be converted to a bus or ring topology, and a ring can be converted to a bus topology.

HARDWARE

The major network hardware components are the media and network electronics, as described here.

Media

At the lowest level of the hardware infrastructure is the media used to connect the workstations, sequencing machines, and microarray readers in a network. The most common media are coaxial cable, twisted pair wiring, fiber optics, and, for wireless networks, the ether (see Figure 3-10).

Coaxial Cable. Coaxial cable is popular as a medium for LANs because it's inexpensive and provides the greatest flexibility in installation; it can be folded and kinked with minimal signal loss. The coaxial design, where the center conductor is shielded by a copper or aluminum mesh or foil, provides

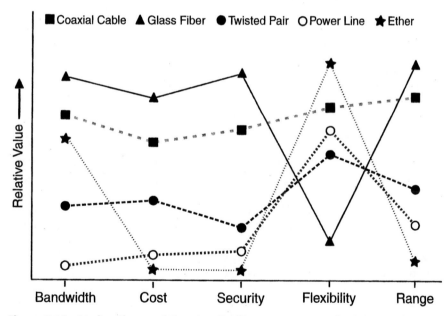

Figure 3-10 Media Characteristics. Bandwidth, cost, security, flexibility, and range reflect the innate physical characteristics of the media as well as the current state of the art in the associated electronics. In this example, ether refers to wireless LAN signals; satellite and point-to-point microwave communications links provide the bandwidth comparable to that of fiber and coaxial cable.

a relatively secure connection and a high bandwidth. However, from a security perspective, it's virtually impossible to determine if an eavesdropper has tapped a run of coaxial cable. In addition, unlike fiber, it's possible for someone with a sensitive receiver and antenna to remotely pick up signals traveling through coaxial cable, amplify them, and decode the digital stream. This is especially true in coaxial cable designs in which the outer shield is formed by a copper or aluminum wire mesh, which provides incomplete shielding of the inner wire compared to cable made with a solid foil outer shield.

Fiber. As summarized in Figure 3-10, of the most popular media used in networks, glass fiber provides the greatest bandwidth, highest level of security, greatest range, and resistance to electrical noise. Although fiber provides a working range of up to several kilometers with standard electronics, it's less flexible to install compared to copper cable. For example, unlike twisted pair or coaxial cable, fiber can't be snaked through very tight turns because the glass fiber is more fragile than the copper or aluminum wire used in the coaxial cable, twisted pair, or power line cable.

From a security perspective, fiber is the superior medium because, unlike the other copper cables or wireless, there is no radio frequency signal that can be intercepted by a nearby receiver. A wire run in parallel with a twisted pair or coaxial cable acts as an antenna to pick up the signals traversing through the cable that can be amplified and interpreted. In contrast, the light in a fiber cable is confined to the optical fiber, which is additionally shielded by a tough sheath. Furthermore, whereas coaxial cable or twisted pair can be tapped without detection, tapping into a fiber strand results in a marked, detectable drop in signal level because of the loss associated with a physical tap.

Twisted Pair. Twisted pair cable, the wiring used in virtually every office and residence for telephone communications, is a comprise between cost, bandwidth, security, and availability. It's more affordable than coaxial cable or fiber, but the bandwidth isn't as great, and security is a much greater concern. When used with radio frequency network signals, twisted pair cables don't perfectly cancel out the signals traversing the two wires, but act as antennas. As a result, not only are signals in the cable more readily intercepted, but the twisted pair cable is more susceptible to electrical noise in the environment. For this reason, twisted pair may not be able to be used in laboratory settings in which electronic equipment may interfere with the network signals, or in which the radiated network signals may interfere with sensitive laboratory equipment. One option is to use shielded twisted pair cable, but this usually involves running the special cable in walls because standard telephone twisted pair cable is unshielded.

Power Line Cable. Power line cable is a low-cost, low-bandwidth solution to networking. Although it may be suitable for exchanging text-only e-mails and other small files, the limitations of the medium prevent it from being a serious network medium for bioinformatics applications. It may be a viable as part of a redundant backup network system, however.

Ether. As a conduit for light or radio frequency signals, the ether provides the greatest flexibility of the options listed here, but also presents the greatest security risk. Typical internal installations for wireless LANs are limited to the same floor in a building. However, within that space, users may have complete mobility with laptops or desktop workstations that are frequently moved. Optical LANs, based on infrared (IR) links are line-of-sight only, and are limited to a single work area.

Radio frequency communications are also commonly used between buildings, in the form of microwave links. These links tend to be line-of-sight and limited to perhaps 30 miles, depending on terrain and buildings that may interfere with line-of-sight communications. Unlike the radio frequency technology used with LANs, the bandwidth of these links is on the same order as coaxial cable. Similarly, radio frequency satellite links that extend thousands of miles support high-bandwidth transmission rates comparable to that provided by coaxial cable and fiber media.

Note that the media characteristics summarized in Figure 3-10 reflect the physical properties of the media as well as the current state of the art in network electronics. For example, although wireless LANs are limited to a range of about 200 meters because of legal restrictions on the power of the electronics, the ether is capable of supporting communications across virtually infinite distances, and satellite-based wireless Internet connectivity is a viable alternative to wire, fiber, and cable in remote areas. Similarly, although glass fiber is less expensive than coaxial cable, the associated electronics and connectors are more expensive and more difficult to use.

The type of media used for Internet access depends primarily on the types of service available, and secondarily on the bandwidth, security, and cost constraints. For example, the TV cable companies that offer Internet service use coaxial cable to feed cable modems. Conversely, DSL companies provide access to the Internet through the same type of twisted pair used by the telephone companies. Because of the losses associated with ordinary twisted pair cable, DSL service is limited by the distance from a telephone switching station, and the maximum bandwidth diminishes with distance from the station. Many academic institutions and some well-funded biotech firms have access to the Internet through high-bandwidth, secure fiber.

In contrast to the media used for Internet access, the choice of media that can be used to support an internal LAN is more a function of cost, bandwidth requirements, security, ease of installation, and type of existing wiring, if any. For example, many older buildings have spare twisted pair cables running throughout their structure from the telephone service. In some of these buildings, running cables through asbestos or concrete structures many be prohibitively expensive or time-consuming, making wireless the only viable media. Another option is to use the power wiring as a data network medium. However, because the wire isn't twisted but is run parallel, it's more susceptible to noise than the other common types of media, resulting in a significantly lower maximum bandwidth.

Network Electronics

The media running from office to office and across the country become a useful communications channel with the addition of electronics capable of sending and receiving signals through the media. These electronics serve a variety of functions, including:

- Generating signals destined for a recipient somewhere in the network
- Coordinating signals through media in order to minimize interference
- Amplifying and conditioning signals so that they can continue error-free to their destination
- Blocking signals from certain paths to minimize interference in those paths
- Routing signals down the quickest or least-expensive route from source to destination
- Translating signals originally designed to work with one protocol so that they are compatible with networks designed to support other protocols
- Connecting different networks
- Monitoring the status of the network, including the functioning of network electronics and the amount of data on segments of the network

Although there are hundreds of devices on the market that transmit, receive, manage, convert, block, redirect, and monitor signals on the network, most fit into the categories listed in Table 3-3.

Several of the network devices listed in Table 3-3 are illustrated in context in Figure 3-11 on page 130. However, it's important to note that the physical layout of the network depicted in this figure may have little relation to the logical

Table 3-3 Network Electronics. In addition to these major classifications, many devices combine features common to multiple categories.

Device	Application
Bridge	Connects multiple network segments and forwards data between them
Content Filter	Prevents access of restricted external Web content
Firewall	Prevents unauthorized users from accessing the network
Gateway	Links two networks that use different protocols
Hub	Provides a central connection point for a network configured in a star topology
Modem	Connects a workstation or LAN to an outside workstation or network, such as the Internet
Monitor	Monitors activity on the network by node and by network segment
Router	Sends data transmissions only to the portion of a network meant to receive them
Satellite	Transmits signals from a server in orbit
Server	Supplies files and applications to clients
Switch	Selects network paths at high speeds
UPS	Provides uninterruptible power for network electronics, especially servers
Wireless Hub	Provides mobile, cable-free access to servers, shared resources, and the Internet from anywhere within range of the hub
Wireless Modem	Allows workstations and laptops to communicate with a wireless hub (access point)

functioning of the network electronics. For example, even though the workstations or clients are connected directly to the printer, all printing requests or jobs may be directed to the print server, which manages the printing queue and buffers printing requests, freeing the processors in the workstation clients to handle other computations instead of devoting machine cycles to managing individual print jobs.

Servers

The centerpiece of most bioinformatics networks is a server (or more than one) that supplies files and applications to workstations, printers, and other clients. Servers are typically high-speed dedicated computers with several GB of RAM, multi-GB fast hard drives, and over-engineered power supplies that can withstand power surges and other challenges. Servers vary in size and shape, degree of redundancy, performance, expansion options, amount of noise generated in normal operation, the type of operating system supported, management software, security features, power supply design, amount of cache memory, and price.

Servers are no longer relegated to footlocker-sized cases, but are available in units as small as a pizza box that can be easily stacked in racks to provide high server densities. Related to form factor is the operating environment, in that the compact size often necessitates the use of high-volume fans that not only move large quantities of air over the densely populated motherboards, but that generate considerable noise as well. As such, servers may need to be mounted in a separate room or closet, away from researchers whose work the noise may disrupt. Also related to form factor is the provision for redundancy in the two most common server failure points—the mechanical disks and the power supplies. Many server designs provide internal redundant disks and power supplies that take over as soon as the main units fail.

The typical server used in a bioinformatics laboratory has between 1 and 8 GB of RAM, several hundred GB of disk storage distributed between 2 and 8 drives, 2 power supplies, BIOS password protection, and virus protection. Performance, as measured by throughput in Mbps average response time in milliseconds, and thousands of requests handled per second, is a function of the processor, operating system, amount of RAM available, cache memory, and overall design.

The most common server operating systems are Microsoft Windows 2000, Linux, Solaris, UNIX, and Microsoft .NET. Windows 2000 commands about a third of the server market, in part because of the familiar graphical user interface (GUI) and compatibility with relatively inexpensive server hardware. The relatively new Microsoft .NET Server is Windows 2000–based with added Web development tools. Linux, an increasingly popular operating system for servers and bioinformatics workstations, accounts for only about 5 percent of the overall server operating system market. An advantage of using Linux as a server operating system is cost savings and an abundance of license-free (albeit Spartan) utilities. Linux is considered more stable and reliable than Windows 2000, but more difficult to use. In comparison, Solaris commands a little over 15 percent of the server market, followed by IBM AIX and HP's UX. These various flavors of UNIX account for over a third of the server market, especially in high-end applications, such as massive sequence databases.

In addition to generic servers that serve content to clients on the network, there are specialized server designs, such as cache, file, print, mail, proxy, and terminal servers. A cache server dynamically pulls frequently accessed content from the main servers and maintains the content in cache for later use. The purpose of a cache server is to speed content to clients and to reduce network traffic at the server site. One of the challenges with cache servers is ensuring that the cached files are current and synchronized with the files on the source server. Cache servers usually double as proxy servers, which are designed to intercept and manage client requests in a way that provides increased security by matching incoming messages with outgoing requests. A proxy server acts as a filter that passes valid requests on to a file or Web server or, if it's configured as a cache server, serves the content from its cache. Because the functionality of proxy, firewall, and caching servers is so tightly integrated, they are commonly combined in a single device.

A file server is a server configured to allow workstation clients on the network to use the disk storage on the server for collaborative work, to facilitate archiving, and to provide additional disk storage. File servers typically contain large, high-speed hard drives and comprehensive data management software. Print servers provide buffering and queuing for networked printers.

Web servers provide HTML pages or files to a Web client. A mail server hosts the e-mail system for users on the network, providing processing and storage for e-mail messages. Terminal servers connect several terminals, including dial-up modems, to a single LAN connection. A terminal server has a single network interface and several ports for terminal connections, allowing several terminals to be connected to the network by a single LAN cable.

Remote access servers, also known as communications servers, provide access to users seeking to use a network remotely, especially while traveling away from the main office. A remote access server is typically configured with a firewall and a router to provide security and to limit the remote access to a specific subset of the network. For example, a remote access server may allow access to e-mail and non-confidential files. In this way, if a hacker manages to somehow gain access to the network through the remote access server, he won't be able to destroy or steal confidential data. A remote access server is typically configured with one or more telephone modems so that remote users can call in to the network and read their e-mail and access files from any location with telephone access.

Bridges

A bridge connects two or more network segments and forwards packets between them, amplifying the signal to compensate for the loss associated with splitting a signal across multiple segments. So-called dumb bridges are protocol-specific and are designed to connect networks running the same

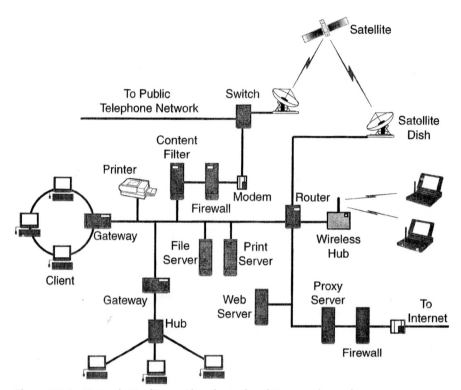

Figure 3-11   Network Hardware. The physical architecture shown here may support a markedly different logical architecture.

protocol. These devices simply accept data packets from one segment of a network and forward them on to the other segments. They have no built-in intelligence.

In addition to these bridges, several varieties of bridge design provide processing, enabling data sharing between otherwise incompatible networks. For example, encapsulating bridges encapsulate network data with header information so they are compatible with devices in the destination network. A translating bridge goes one step further and actually translates the data from the source network so that the protocol is compatible with that of the destination network. A filtering bridge, also called a multi-port bridge, directs data from the source network to a specific segment of the destination network, thereby reducing unnecessary traffic on some segments of the network. In addition, there are numerous bridge designs that combine filtering, routing, and security functions.

Routers

A router directs data to the portion of a network meant to receive it rather than broadcasting data to every node of a network. Instead of merely passing information like a dumb bridge, routers monitor network activity and change traffic patterns if necessary to maintain efficiency or throughput. Intelligent routers dynamically reconfigure the communications path to improve availability and reliability.

Routers are rarely used alone but are combined with other devices. For example, routers are located at every gateway and are often included as part of a network switch. Routers are also commonly combined with a network bridge in the form of a brouter. In contrast to switches, routers are typically used at the edges of a network, where intelligence is needed to determine the best path for data.

Switches

A switch is a device that selects a circuit for sending data through a network. A switch, which tends to be simpler, faster, and less expensive than a router, lacks information about the network that a router may use in determining the best circuit or path to use to move data from one part of a network to another. Switches, which lack the intelligence of a router, are normally used in the network backbone and at gateways, where speed is of the essence. Also called LAN switches, data switches, and packet switches, they typically contain buffer memory to hold packets briefly until network resources become available.

Gateways

A gateway links two networks running different protocols by functioning as a router and providing translation and amplification of network signals. Because gateways can connect networks using different protocols, they are slower than simple routers.

Hubs

A standard wired hub is the center of a network physically connected in a star configuration. These hubs generally have little intelligence and serve primarily as a common connection point. However, hubs can also be complex devices that provide bridging and routing between multiple LAN architectures.

Wireless hubs, also known as access points, function like wired hubs but use different protocols that provide for different levels of interoperability. With a wireless hub, a wireless LAN can be established quickly with only a server and wireless modem cards (or PCMCIA cards for laptops). Except for the wired connection to the Internet, there is no need to drill holes in walls and pull cables to individual workstations.

Content Filters

A content filter is a device that prevents workstations from accessing specific types of external Web content, such as high-bandwidth streaming video entertainment. Content filters, which can also be implemented in software, maximize available network bandwidth for work-related content.

Firewalls

A firewall is a dedicated device or suite of programs running on a server that protects a network from unauthorized external access. Firewalls are especially relevant in establishing collaborative intranets that allow, for example, researchers in China to work with information in a U.S. laboratory's intranet around the clock. A flexible firewall is one component in a system that allows external collaborators to freely access the laboratory's internal intranet. Firewalls are typically used in conjunction with routers, gateways, and proxy servers to limit access to internal network resources.

Modems

Modems (short for modulator/demodulator) provide connectivity between a workstation or network with a remote network such as the Internet. Telephone modems translate digital data into analog signals for transmission over a twisted pair telephone line and convert incoming analog data into digital form. Telephone modems have a maximum bandwidth of about 56 Kbps. Cable modems provide the same digital-to-analog and analog-to digital conversion as telephone modems, but they connect to a cable TV circuit and provide a bandwidth of about 1.5 Mbps.

A wireless modem, the equivalent of a telephone modem or NIC, allows a computer to access a wireless hub or access point through radio frequency (RF), or, less frequently, IR light. Wireless modems are protocol-specific, in that they only work with access points following the same communications standard.

Satellites

Orbiting satellites are special cases of servers connected to workstation clients through long-distance radio frequency links. The major complicating factor is, the need for local uplink and downlink hardware, including a satellite dish, on the client side. The capabilities of communications satellites are defined by their orbit—GEO (geostationary earth orbit), MEO (medium earth orbit), or LEO (low earth orbit)—as well as their operating frequency and bandwidth. The orbit affects the availability and reliability of communications, the terrestrial antenna requirements, and the latency or lag time associated with transmit and receive operations.

For example, a GEO satellite provides continental coverage and can be used with a fixed terrestrial antenna, but has a significant latency because the satellite is orbiting at 36,000 kilometers. In contrast, a LEO satellite provides only a few Km ground coverage but latency is low because of the 500 to 2000 km orbit. Latency is an issue when data need to be frequently retransmitted because of errors, which is often the case when the receiver is operating at the fringe of the satellite coverage area. As a result, a LEO satellite can provide greater throughput than a GEO satellite, all else being equal.

Network Interface Cards

A Network Interface Card (NIC) is a card or, more often, the part of the workstation motherboard that provides the client-side connectivity to the network. The NIC is connected to the network through a variety of media, including coaxial cable, twisted pair, and fiber.

Network Monitors

A network monitor is a specialized device that can monitor or sniff packets and determine throughput of hardware, as well as detect sources of error, such as a defective network interface card. A network monitor can also be implemented in the form of a software utility running on a workstation attached to the network.

Uninterruptible Power Supplies

An Uninterruptible Power Supply (UPS) is a battery and power-filtering device that can provide emergency power for up to several hours, allowing the hardware to be automatically shut down without data loss. UPSs, especially those with built-in power conditioners, protect sensitive equipment and the data they contain from power surges and sudden, unplanned power outages.

CONTENTS

Networks are sometimes defined by the nature of the content they carry. For example, some networks capable of sustained high-bandwidth connections are dedicated to video and other multimedia, whereas others are limited to text. Networks may also be relegated to database or equipment communications. The former is especially prominent in bioinformatics, in the form of storage area networks. These networks, typically based on fiber optics, are maintained for high-speed communications between disk arrays and computers involved in sequencing and other applications that require almost constant access to data stored on high-speed hard drives.

SECURITY

Network security is an increasingly important factor in bioinformatics because of the central role that online databases, applications, and groupware such as e-mail play in the day-to-day operation of a bioinformatics facility. Opening an intranet to the outside world through username and password-protected restricted access may be the basis for collaboration as well as a weak point in the security of the organization. In addition, because many biometric laboratories are involved, even if indirectly, with applied genomics, there is a group of politically active opponents to this research. The computer-savvy members of these activist groups represent a potential threat to network security.

Every network presents a variety of security holes through which potential hackers and disgruntled or simply curious employees can implement random threats, such as viruses. Many of these threats are network- and operating system–specific. For example, Microsoft typically announces a service pack within a few weeks after the introduction of a server-based operating system to patch security holes discovered by users.

The most secure method—physical isolation from outside networks—isn't usually a viable option. Even a closed network without dial-in or any other wired access to other networks can be breached by someone with enough motivation and time. For example, wireless networks are notorious for their potential to disseminate data to nearby listeners. A hacker with a high-gain antenna, receiver, and laptop computer can monitor wireless network activity from a mile or more away. A similar setup, configured to a slightly different frequency, can be used to reconstruct whatever data is displayed on a video screen, including username and password information. Every cable, peripheral, and display device emits a radio frequency signal that can be captured, amplified, and read. For this reason, computer facilities used by military contractors are frequently located in shielded, windowless rooms that minimize the chances of the radiation emitted from a computer reaching someone who is monitoring the building.

Although it may be practically impossible to maintain security from professional industrial spies, a variety of steps can be taken to minimize the threat posed by modestly computer-savvy activists and the most common non-directed security threats. These steps include using antiviral utilities, controlling access through the use of advanced user-authentication technologies, firewalls, and, most importantly, low-level encryption technologies.

Antiviral Utilities

In addition to threats from hackers, there is a constant threat of catastrophic loss of data from viruses attached to documents from outside sources, even those from trusted collaborators. The risk of virus infection can be minimized by installing virus-scanning software on servers and locally on workstations. The downside to this often-unavoidable precaution is decreased performance of the computers running antiviral programs, as well as the maintenance of the virus-detection software to insure that the latest virus definitions are installed.

Authentication

The most often used method of securing access to a network is to verify that users are who they say they are. However, simple username and password protection at the firewall and server levels can be defeated by someone who either can guess or otherwise has access to the username and password information. A more secure option is to use a synchronized, pseudorandom number generator for passwords. In this scheme, two identical pseudorandom number generators, one running on a credit card–sized computer and one running on a secure server, generate identical number sequences that appear to be random to an observer.

The user carries a credit-card sized secure ID card that displays the sequence on an LCD screen. When a user logs in to the computer network, she uses the displayed number sequence for her password, which is compared to the current number generated by a program running the server. If the sequences match, she is allowed access to the server. Otherwise, she is locked out of the network. Because the number displayed on the ID card—and in the server—changes every 30 seconds, the current password doesn't provide a potential intruder with a way in to the system. The major security hole is that a secure ID card can be stolen, which will provide the thief with the password, but not the username.

More sophisticated methods of user authentication involve biometrics, the automated recognition of fingerprint, voice, retina, or facial features. Authentication systems based on these methods aren't completely accurate, however, and there are often false positives (imposters passing as someone else) and false negatives (an authentic user is incorrectly rejected by the system) involved in the process. In addition to errors in recognition, there are often ways of defeating biometrical devices by bypassing the image-processing components of the systems. For example, fingerprints are converted into a number and letter sequence that serves as the key to gaining access to network assets; anyone who can intercept that sequence and enter it directly into the system can gain access to the network.

A researcher employed by a biotech firm to analyze nucleotide sequences probably has no need to examine the files in a 3D protein visualization system in the laboratory a few doors down from his office. Similarly, payroll, human resources, and other administrative data may be of concern to the CFO, but not to the manager of the microarray laboratory. Authentication provides the information necessary to provide tiered access to networked resources. This access can be controlled at the workstation, the server, and firewall levels to limit access to specific databases, applications, or network databases.

Firewalls

As introduced in the discussion of network hardware, firewalls are stand-alone devices or programs running on a server that block unauthorized access to a network. Dedicated hardware firewalls are more secure than a software-only solution, but are also considerably more expensive.

Firewalls are commonly used in conjunction with proxy servers to mirror servers inside a firewall, thereby intercepting requests and data originally intended for an internal server. In this way, outside users can access copies of some subset of the data on the system without ever having direct access to the data. This practice provides an additional layer of security against hackers.

Encryption

Encryption, the process of making a message unintelligible to all but the intended recipient, is one of the primary means of ensuring the security of messages sent through the Internet and even in the same building. It's also one of the greatest concerns—and limitations—of network professionals. Many information services professionals are reluctant to install wireless networks because of security concerns, for example.

Although cryptography—the study of encryption and decryption—predates computers by several millennia, no one has yet devised a system that can't be defeated, given enough time and resources. Every form of encryption has tradeoffs of security versus processing and management overhead, and different forms of encryption are used in different applications (see Table 3-4).

Of the encryption standards developed for the Internet, most are based on public key encryption (PKE) technology. One reason that PKE is so prominent is because it's supported by the Microsoft Internet Explorer and Netscape Navigator browsers. PKE is a form of asymmetric encryption, in that the keys used for encryption and decryption are different. Aside from the added complexity added by the use of different keys on the sending and receiving ends, the two forms of encryption and decryption are virtually identical. As such, the illustration of PKE in Figure 3-12 assumes symmetric encryption for the purpose of clarity.

PKE allows two sequencing laboratories—in Figure 3-12, one in a biotech firm in San Francisco (left) and one in a research facility in Cambridge (right)— to securely exchange data. Assuming a researcher in San Francisco wants to

Table 3-4 Encryption Standards. PGP (Pretty Good Privacy) is one of the more popular encryption standards used on the Internet. Most of these standards are based on PKE technology.

Standard	Description
AES	Advanced Encryption Standard—Eventual replacement for DES, based on 128-bit encryption.
DES	Data Encryption Standard—Used by the government, based on 64-bit encryption.
IDEA	International Data Encryption Algorithm—Used by the banking industry, developed by the Swiss Federal Institute of Technology, 128-bit encryption.
PGP	Pretty Good Privacy—Popular on the Internet, effective, free, simple to use.
RSA	Rivest-Shamir-Adelman System—Popular in business and government.
S-HTTP	Secure Hypertext Transfer Protocol—For transmitting individual messages over the Internet.
SSL	Secure Sockets Layer—Developed by Netscape Communications Corp. for the Internet.

send a message to the lab in Cambridge, he first acquires the public key (26) of the facility in Cambridge and, using his private key, generates a session key (2). That is, the private key for the lab in San Francisco is 8, the lab's public key is 16, and the key for this particular session with the lab in Cambridge is 2. A subsequent communication with the lab in Cambridge might use a session key of 4, 7, or some other random number. Similarly, the private key for the lab in Cambridge is 6 and the public key is 26. The session key is 2, identical to the session key used by the lab in San Francisco.

To decrypt a message from the lab in San Francisco, the lab in Cambridge uses its private key (6) and the public key (16) from the lab in San Francisco to generate a session key (2) that is identical to the key used by lab in San Francisco to encrypt the message. Note that only their respective owners know the value of the private keys and that the public keys are generally available. The session key is a function of the other lab's public key. For clarity, not shown is the public key infrastructure, which provides authentication of the public and private keys.

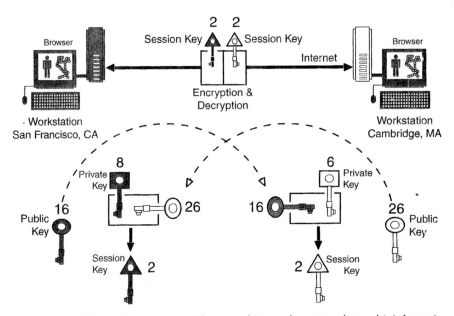

Figure 3-12   PKE. Workstations in California and Massachusetts exchange bioinformatics data by first exchanging public keys. These public keys are then used with private keys to generate a session key, which defines encryption and decryption. Although true PKE is asymmetric, the session keys illustrated here are identical (symmetrical) for clarity.

A more secure symmetrical encryption approach, and one used by most governments and corporations to send secure communications over networks, is to use a multi-digit key. The greater the key length, the more difficult and time-consuming it is to crack. The goal is to create a key that is long enough to either deter someone from attempting to hack the code, or one that requires so much computer time to decrypt that the encrypted message is of no value by that time.

Process

More important than the specific encryption algorithm or user-authentication technology used is the process of implementing a security strategy. For example, the best firewall, proxy server, and user-authentication system is valueless if a researcher has a habit of losing his secure ID card. Similarly, a wireless hub capable of supporting the latest security standards is vulnerable to attack if the person who configures the hub doesn't take the time to enable the security features. Similarly, a researcher who leaves her username and passwords on a Post-It Note stuck to her monitor provides a security hole for everyone from the janitorial staff to a visitor who happens to walk past her office.

OWNERSHIP

Networks are often characterized by the way they are funded. Private networks are owned and managed by private corporations. For example, many of the major pharmaceutical corporations have internal bioinformatics R&D groups that manage workflow and data with the help of privately owned and highly secure networks. These private networks may be completely isolated, connect to the Internet through a secure firewall, or communicate with academic and commercial collaborators through dedicated, secure lines. Private networks may also be open to researchers and other companies—for a fee.

In contrast, public networks such as the Internet and the public telephone network are at least partially funded by public coffers. They are also freely open to anyone who is capable of paying for their services. Cooperative networks are supported and managed by their users. One of the best-known cooperative networks was BITNET (Because It's Time Network), started by universities in the early 1980s. Before it was replaced by NSFNET (National Science Foundation Network) in the early 1990s, it connected about 3,000 mainframe computers at universities in the U.S., Canada, South America, Europe, Asia, and Australia.

IMPLEMENTATION

The National Science Foundation (NSF), Department of Energy, and other government agencies, often in collaboration with industry and academia, have virtually unlimited resources available for developing and maintaining networks that have bioinformatics applications. However, for small- to medium-sized biotech firms and bioinformatics departments within pharmaceutical companies, implementing in-house databases presents a formidable challenge. Part of this challenge is that the traditional information services department is ill-equipped to deal with the throughput issues that typically must be addressed by a bioinformatics-compatible network. The typical corporate CIO needs background education on how to implement gigabit fiber networks dedicated to data storage as well as high-speed routers and associated network electronics.

Despite the differences between bioinformatics computing and traditional institutional computing, the process for implementing a high-speed bioinformatics network is identical to that of implementing any other major network. The major steps in the implementation process are the same, regardless of whether they are performed by staff in the bioinformatics laboratory or corporate information services staff. These steps include:

1. **Create a Requirements Specification.** This document includes a high-level description of the tasks to be supported by the network, such as routing sequencing data from sequencing machines to analysis workstations and data warehouses, as well as the desired response times and storage capacities. For example, the requirements specification document may stipulate the need to support 35 workstations, provide access to storage in excess of 1 terabyte with an access time of less than 50 milliseconds, with tiered password protection, and secure, high-speed access to the Internet.

2. **Create a Functional Specifications Document.** The functional specifications document defines, in detail, how the high-level needs outlined in the requirements specification will be met. This document quantifies many of the qualitative terms in the requirements specification to the degree that anyone competent in information sciences can determine exactly what equipment, personnel, and costs will be associated with the project. Once the functional specifications document has been finalized, the remaining steps are largely straightforward.

3. **Select Hardware.** Assuming the functional specifications document is complete, the next step is selecting network and workstation electronics and media. Often the functional specifications document is authored with particular hardware and software in mind, which further simplifies the selection process.

4. **Select Software.** Again, following the functional specifications document, this step of the implementation process involves selecting the network operating system, as well as database publishing software and tools such as PHP, XML, CGI, Java, or JavaScript editors and runtime systems.

5. **Select Utility.** Software and hardware utilities, such as network monitors and antiviral utilities, should be defined during the design process, not as an afterthought.

6. **Select Internet Access Service.** Most larger institutions have high-speed Internet access available throughout their offices. However, bandwidth requirements may necessitate alternate Internet services, such as supplementing a corporate-wide cable modem service with a high-speed dedicated line, satellite link, or high-speed microwave link.

Each of the steps in the implementation process requires different levels of expertise with the bioinformatics requirements, the information technology capabilities, and the likely return on investment of each approach. As a result, network implementation is necessarily a collaborative process involving programmers, hardware technicians, vendors, management, and perhaps the assistance of a consultant.

MANAGEMENT

After a network is established, it must be managed to realize its full potential. Network management issues include making provision for disaster recovery, load balancing, bandwidth management, and maintaining network security. For example, disaster recovery plans and support for inevitable network electronics and media failure should consider fire, electrical disturbances, power outages, or intentional destruction. Part of disaster recovery planning includes securing redundant systems, such as running extra cables when installing a wired network, and installing a bank of 56K dial-up modems available for Internet access in the event that the high-speed Internet connection fails.

Load balancing, in the context of network management, refers to a method of distributing data volume among multiple paths so that the throughput of the overall system is maximized. For example, if there are two equivalent network paths, one carrying 10 percent of the network traffic and the other 90 percent, then the first path is underutilized, and the second path is likely degraded because the routers and other electronics are saturated with traffic. Load balancing involves configuring routers and other network electronics so that the network traffic is spread as evenly as possible among the various network segments and devices to maximize throughput of the network.

Bandwidth management involves load balancing as well as upgrading equipment when necessary in order to support the increasing computational needs of bioinformatics R&D. Bandwidth management is in part dependent on the cost and availability of higher-bandwidth electronics and the work involved in laying new cable.

Perhaps the greatest management challenge is maintaining adequate security. This task entails monitoring the Internet on a daily basis to check for word of new viruses or security holes in the operating system, and installing the appropriate software patches and utilities to address the new threats.

ON THE HORIZON

The most significant changes on the horizon for networking include a higher degree of interconnectivity, greater bandwidth, and increased access to supercomputer-level computational resources. Much of the research in this area is federally funded, while some is being undertaken by deep-pocketed corporations such as IBM. The most notable federally funded initiatives include the Very High-Bandwidth Network Service (vBNS) initiative by the NSF that provides connectivity between about 45 and 155 Mbps. In addition, the Next-Generation Internet (NGI) initiative is aimed at supporting the NSF and other agencies in developing advanced networks, such as Grid computing.

The goal for most of this advanced network research is aptly referred to as ubiquitous computing—the anywhere, anytime access to computing power and data. For example, the Grid, when and if it is established, will put affordable supercomputer power in the hands of researchers who would otherwise be limited to workstation power. Virtual reality, simulation, data mining, and other bioinformatics endeavors that demand high-bandwidth computational support are expected to be commonplace as the focus of bioinformatics research extends from sequence analysis to gene expression and proteomics.

Many challenges remain before ubiquitous computing is an everyday reality. For example, the primary impediment to distributing information to a grid of computers that cover a large geographic area is security because each node in the grid represents a potential security risk. Similarly, the extension of the wireless Web is limited as much by the need for a high-bandwidth network infrastructure as it is by security concerns. After all, consider that genomic data that might indicate a subject's predisposition for, as an example, Alzheimer's disease or schizophrenia, are data that could indelibly ruin that person's prospect for employment and lower his social standing in his community.

ENDNOTE

Bioinformatics is populated by a disparate group of specialists—mathematicians, statisticians, biologists, fellows, pharmaceutical scientists, marketers, programmers, clinicians, forensic scientists, and public health officials—each of whom has different needs, work styles, vocabularies, and focus. For example, clinicians may be primarily interested in visualization tools, whereas statisticians may be focused on statistical analysis tools and large samples of data.

As many biotech firms have discovered, it's virtually impossible for one application to fulfill every need to everyone's satisfaction. However, networks provide the glue and, with the Web and other interfaces, veneers that can be used to make a suite of tools appear and work as one. With the appropriate network technology, professionals of all disciplines can work on data and share their findings in a way that matches their mental model of the workspace and promotes efficient use of R&D resources.

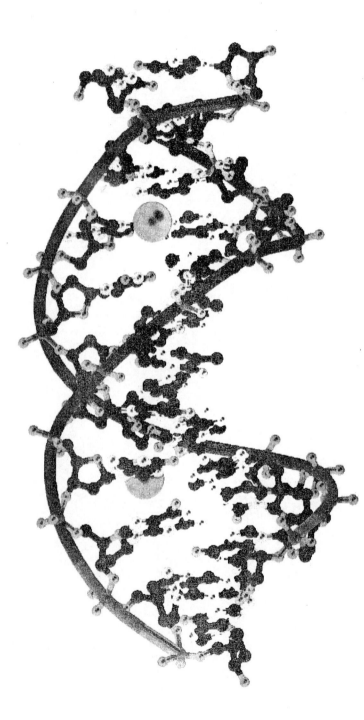

➤ Crystal structure of a DNA duplex containing 8-hydroxydeoxyguanine-adenine base pairs. PDB entry 178D. Image produced with PDB Structure Explorer.

CHAPTER

Search Engines

A little knowledge that acts is worth more
than much knowledge that is idle.
— Kahil Gibran, the prophet

I n the year 2020, a visit with your dentist will likely consist of a teleconference with an intelligent software robot (or "bot") that guides you through a self-administered test for acid-producing bacilli on and around your teeth. Based on the test results, which will be communicated wirelessly through the communications grid, the bot will prescribe a mouthwash to displace your native bacilli with a genetically engineered version that is specific to your genetic profile. The mouthwash, a custom prophylaxis designed to protect you from caries and heart disease, arrives the next day by Priority Mail, direct from the factory.

Making this scenario a practical reality requires someone or some intelligent agent to establish or discover the links between the bacteria in your oral cavity and tooth decay, your predisposition for heart disease, your work environment, personal habits, and a multitude of internal and external factors. These factors include your genetic profile, the relationship between your proteome, bacteria in your oral cavity, your history of encounters with pathogens, prior diseases, as well as your likelihood of developing caries, heart disease, and other diseases, based on factors such as your genetic profile, family history of disease, diet and exercise habits, and work-related stress level.

Figure 4-1 illustrates a partial view of this mesh of interrelationships, in which everything is related to everything else to some degree. The linking isn't limited to relationships between major categories such as demographics and medical history, but links exist within each sub-mesh as well. For example, within the genomic profile, there are links to nucleotide sequences, protein sequences, enzyme profiles, and disease predisposition. At issue is the fact that these links may not be explicit, or even known. In this regard, linking or associating facts from disparate fields is a metaphor for knowledge. The dynamic links or associations that are defined by a human- or computer-directed search represent knowledge discovery when the user becomes aware of the links and the contexts in which they can be successfully applied.

Today, most of the potential links between data in digital form aren't readily available because the relevant data, when they exist, are in disparate databases. In addition, each database is typically based on different and incompatible database technologies and uses different languages and vocabularies to

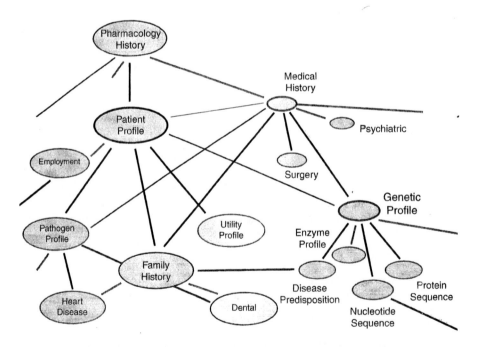

Figure 4-1 Relationship Mesh. Dynamic links created by searching medical, genomic, and other databases can make use of this multi-dimensional mesh of relationships.

access data. These incompatibilities are especially significant when non-textual data, such as 3D images of protein structures, accessed by author-specified keywords, need to be linked with nucleotide sequences in other databases. Because each database is typically created as a stand-alone application to support one function, linking between databases is most often an afterthought. Although static links between databases can be established programmatically, a more common approach is to create links dynamically by using search engines. In addition, even when static links are established between databases, extracting meaningful content from these linked databases invariably involves using a search engine of some sort.

As anyone who has surfed the Internet has discovered, a search isn't necessarily successful, and may turn up nothing or thousands of irrelevant links. Thus, the relevance of the dynamic database links created by interacting with a typical Web-accessed search engine is primarily a function of the search engine's selectivity and sensitivity, the ingenuity and knowledge of the search engine user, and the availability of relevant content. In addition, the amount of irrelevant content and its similarity with the desired content, together with the peculiarities of database design, limit the ease of finding the sought-after data.

The exponentially increasing amounts of data accessible over the Internet, from gene sequences and clinical disease findings to related issues in other fields, is primarily accessible through search engine technologies. As such, this chapter explores the status of search engine technology, focusing on bioinformatics resources, within the context of the overall knowledge management of online data.

"The Search Process" section of this chapter introduces many of the challenges and concepts involved in a typical search of molecular biology databases accessible through the Internet, based on the Entrez integrated searching environment. "Search Engine Technology" explores the various technologies that researchers can use to differentiate required data from the noise, from portals and intelligent agents, to natural-language processing (NLP) and other user interface tools. In particular, this section explores dynamic, search-based linking as a form of database integration. The "Searching and Information Theory" section explores the basic Information Theory model as it relates to online searching, and defines the concepts of the sensitivity and specificity of a search, and the issues of false positives and negatives in search results.

"Computational Methods" explores several exact and approximate search algorithms, and provides an overview of methods applicable to searching for text as well as sequence data. The "Searching, Dynamic Linking, and Knowledge Management" section explores searching and the underlying process of dynamic linking from the perspective of knowledge management. The "On the Horizon" section examines the likely future of search engine technologies designed to access online resources, especially those related to the prospect of ubiquitous computing. Finally, "Endnote" explores the technical challenge of not only providing a unified image of scientific knowledge in the hard and biological sciences, but of the societal implications of achieving this capability.

THE SEARCH PROCESS

Pursuing a solution to a molecular biology problem with bioinformatics methods invariably involves significant backtracking, stepping, and jumping around from one database to the next. In support of this typical work process, integrated information-retrieval systems have been created to provide a mesh of "hard" or pre-computed links between the key online molecular biology databases. By far, the most popular of these integrated systems is the National Center for Biotechnology Information's Entrez, which includes many of the key molecular biology databases listed in Table 4-1.

Table 4-1 Databases Included in the Entrez System.

Database	Description
PubMed	Biomedical literature.
Protein	Protein sequences from the Protein Information Resource (PIR), SWISS-PROT, Protein Research Foundation (PRF), and Protein Data Bank (PDB), and from the translated coding regions from DNA sequences in GenBank, the European Molecular Biology Laboratory (EMBL) and the DNA Database of Japan (DDBJ).
Nucleotide	Nucleotide sequence data from GenBank, EMBL, and DDBJ, the Genome Sequence Data Base (GSDB), and patent sequences from U.S. Patent and Trademark Office (USPTO) and other international patent offices.
Structure	Experimental data from crystallographic and NMR structure determinations obtained from the Protein Data Bank (PDB).
Genome	Views of genomes, chromosomes, contiged sequence maps, and integrated genetic and physical maps.
PopSet	Aligned nucleotide and protein sequence data submitted as a set resulting from a population, a phylogenetic, or mutation study.
OMIM	Human genes and genetic disorders.

Table 4-1   Databases Included in the Entrez System. *(continued)*

Database	Description
Taxonomy	Names of all organisms represented NCBI's genetic database.
Books	A collection of biomedical books.
ProbeSet	The Gene Expression Omnibus (GEO) gene expression and hybridization array.
3D Domains	Protein domains from NCBI's Conserved Domain Database.

The Entrez system supports both inter- and intra-database linking. For example, not only are there links between PubMed and the Nucleotide database and between proteins and the nucleotide sequences from which the proteins were generated (see Figure 4-2), but there are BLAST-computed links between all similar sequences within the Nucleotide database.

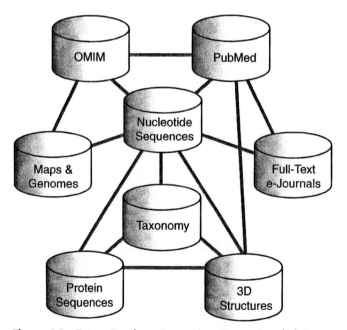

Figure 4-2   Entrez Database Integration. Entrez is a link-integrated search system for accessing a growing number of linked molecular biology databases. In addition to the major databases shown here, Entrez includes PopSet, ProbeSet, and 3D Domains.

There are two versions of the Entrez system—one that uses an application that runs locally on the user's workstation, called Networked Entrez, and one that is accessible through a Web browser (see Figure 4-3). Networked Entrez communicates directly to the NCBI's dispatcher through a client-server connection. Each version provides the same core functionality—that of providing a single interface through which all databases in the Entrez suite of databases can be accessed. However, because the Networked Entrez can make use of local computing power, it can execute much faster than the browser-based version. In addition, it provides a more flexible user interface with multiple windows and graphical viewers for genome sequences and 3D protein structures.

The major downside of Networked Entrez is that data outside of the Entrez system aren't available by simply clicking on hypertext links, as they are in the Web version of Entrez. A minor limitation of the local version is that it must be updated periodically in order to have the latest version. The most obvious benefit of a Web-delivered system that runs under a browser is that updates to the interface and the underlying search engine are transparent and instantaneous. The burden of application maintenance is fully on the shoulders of the NCBI staff and their affiliates, freeing users from having to manually update local copies of a search engine or user interface.

Trading a more flexible user interface and faster execution for lack of instant connectivity to other online resources and the need to periodically update the local application is more of a personal decision that doesn't affect the quality of data available through the Entrez system. Both versions of Entrez provide a common user interface, specifying subjects, ranges, Boolean operators, and other search criteria. Search results may be reviewed in a variety of formats, saved to disk or to the clipboard, or printed. In addition, the results can be incrementally refined if the user continually narrows the search criteria, working from the results of previous searches that are temporarily maintained in the system's memory. The discussion that follows assumes that the more popular Web browser version of Entrez is used.

The major search features of the Entrez system include a variety of tools to define and refine a database search (see Figure 4-4). These tools support selecting a database, linking, imposing limits on searches, using indexes and the search history in searches, and saving results to a clipboard. In addition, the tools support searching by a variety of topics, searching within a specified range, truncating searches, using Boolean operators to narrow searches, and advanced search authoring capabilities to supplement menu-driven search commands.

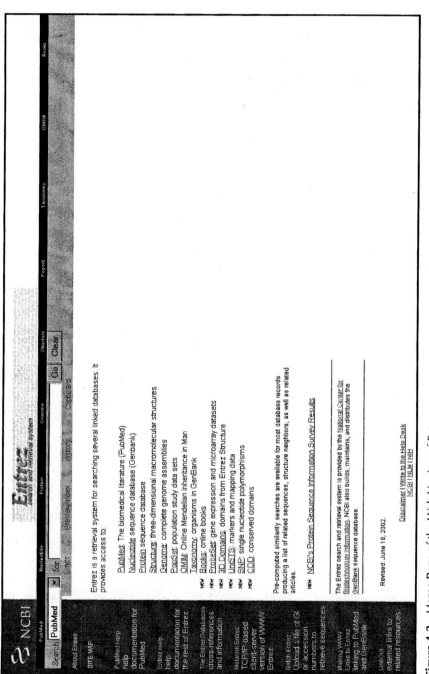

Figure 4-3   Home Page of the Web Version of Entrez.

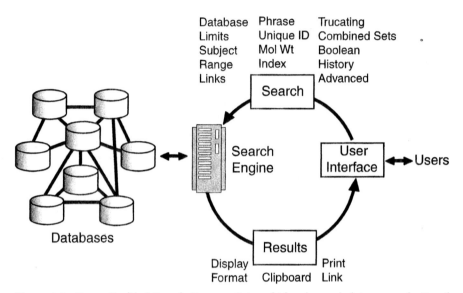

Database Phrase   Trucating
Limits   Unique ID Combined Sets
Subject   Mol Wt   Boolean
Range   Index   History
Links   Advanced

Figure 4-4 Entrez-Enabled Search Process. Entrez hides the underlying complexity of online molecular biology databases, facilitating the iterative process of submitting search criteria, viewing results, and refining or narrowing the search until the desired results are achieved.

The Search

The first step in the process of initiating a search in the Entrez system is to define, through the use of a pull-down menu system, which database to search. Once a database is selected, the next step is to specify a search topic. Entrez supports searching by subject, subject phrase, author, unique identifier, and, where applicable, molecular weight. Search topics are defined by keying terms into a free-text query box. As in the most popular general-purpose search engines on the Web, such as Google and Yahoo!, the words in a phrase are automatically treated as a Boolean AND unless they are included in double quotes. That is, the sequence of words in a non-quoted phrase is ignored. Conversely, a quoted phrase results in a much narrower search, because word order and position are additional search criteria.

A search can also be specified by a unique identifier, which can be an accession number for the complete sequence record in a database or a sequence number assigned by NCBI. The format for the accession number depends on the database. For example, the format of an accession number in GenBank is one letter followed by five digits, compared to a series of six or seven digits followed by a letter for the PRF database. Entrez also supports a search based on molecular weight, including a range of weights, based on calculations of protein structures. This search capability applies only to the Entrez Protein database.

Regardless of the topic, searches can be narrowed and refined by the use of Boolean operators AND, OR, and NOT, which are interpreted from left to right, except that expressions enclosed in parentheses are evaluated first. Boolean operators are especially helpful in performing advanced, manual searches that bypass menu-driven search choices. Complex, multi-parameter searches can be defined by keying a search directly in the Query field.

In addition to operations on the search topics, the results of a search can be narrowed through the use of limits. Limits can be used to restrict a search to a particular database or database field, exclude certain types of sequences, limit the search to a particular molecule type or gene location, only the master or only the parts of segmented sets of sequences, or by date. Limits, which can be used singly or in combination with other limits, are defined through standard browser pull-down menus, a free-text query box, and check boxes in the Web browser version shown in Figure 4-5.

For example, to perform a search in the Nucleotide database for mitochondria carriers that excludes working drafts of nucleotide sequences, the researcher first selects the Nucleotide database from the Search pull-down menu, then types "mitochondria carrier" in the query box, and then select Limits. From the Limits panel, the researcher puts a check next to the "exclude working drafts" check box, and then selects the "Go" button. The particular limits available are a function of the database used. For example, when the Protein database is selected, exclusion check boxes are limited to "exclude patents."

A search can be further refined through the use of indexes, which are alphabetical lists of terms from searchable database fields. The indexes available through Entrez are a function of the particular database selected. Indexes can be specified by the usual Web browser tools—by selecting terms from a pull-down menu, by typing a term into the query box, and by browsing through a scrolling list of terms.

Search histories, which are maintained by the Entrez system, can be used to review, revise, or combine results of the most recent 100 searches. Search histories, which are database-specific, are maintained as a numeric list. That is, search history sets can be combined to increase or decrease the specificity of searches within a given database. For example, the common elements of searches #45 and #56 based on the Nucleotide database can be identified by entering "#45 AND #56" in the Search field. Histories are automatically deleted by the system after one hour of inactivity.

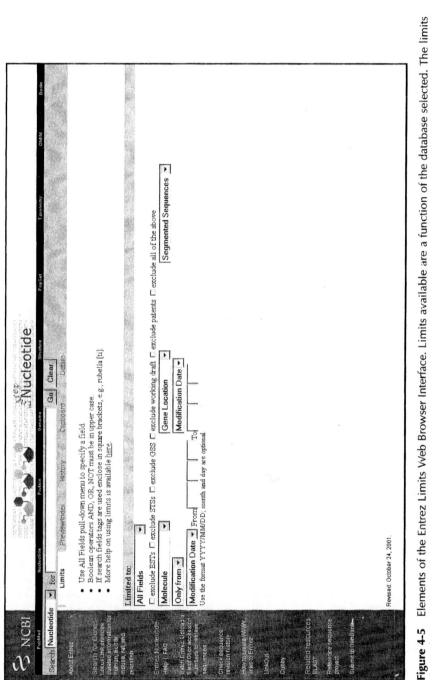

Figure 4-5 Elements of the Entrez Limits Web Browser Interface. Limits available are a function of the database selected. The limits shown here apply to the Nucleotide database.

Results

The results of an Entrez search can be displayed in a variety of formats (including FASTA), or they can be saved to a temporary clipboard area, printed directly from the browser, or saved to disk. Links to external systems, such as fee-for-use databases, are listed when available. The clipboard feature of Entrez extends the history function by providing a temporary place to save search results, in addition to the history feature that automatically saves the search criteria. Each database has its own clipboard area, which holds up to 500 items. Like the history feature, the clipboards are cleared after one hour of inactivity. However, unlike the history feature, the clipboard isn't automatic; the researcher must intentionally place results in the clipboard area for later retrieval.

SEARCH ENGINE TECHNOLOGY

Working with the Entrez system illustrates several points regarding search engine technology. The first is that the state of the art in search engine integration provides only partial, high-level integration with the growing number of rapidly expanding molecular biology databases. As a result, most intra- and inter-database links are database-specific. Furthermore, the granularity or depth of integration depends on the features that front-end or portal developers have the time and resources to implement.

Even a well-designed system such as Entrez is a compromise from the perspective of user interface. One purpose of a user interface is to hide the complexity of the underlying data structures and database systems. However, Entrez requires users to have some low-level knowledge of the databases included in the system. For example, different limits options are available as a function of the database selected, and it's up to the user to understand the lack of uniformity in options available through the user interface. That is, it's possible for a relatively naive user to try a search that will fail because he or she assumes that what works in the search of one database will also work in any other. As a result, for optimum use of Entrez or any other Internet-based, link-integrated database system, users should be familiar with the underlying databases.

The popular Entrez system also illustrates that the links available through specialized search engines, like general-purposes systems, yield results of varying quality. A researcher will quickly discard many results. Furthermore, data contained in so-called secondary databases are calculated from data contained in primary databases. Entrez supports searches on molecular weight, for example, based on molecular weights calculated from the amino acid sequence data. As a result, errors in the primary databases propagate to secondary databases in a way that may not be obvious by examining the data in the secondary database because it's internally consistent. Furthermore, errors may not be discovered until the data are validated by a wet lab experiment months or years later. The point is that data validation isn't ensured simply because databases are integrated at some level. In contrast, the process of creating a central integrated database, such as PubMed Central (PAC), necessarily involves the validation of data during the integration process. PAC provides integration of life-science journal literature in a common format and in a single repository, providing a single, unified access portal to scientific literature instead of combination of links to disparate databases, each with their own idiosyncrasies in vocabularies and infrastructures.

Working with the Entrez system demonstrates several knowledge management issues and challenges, beyond data validation. These include what to do with search results, how to update databases so that propagation of errors is controlled and traceable, how to determine who is responsible for maintenance, and how to communicate information to users on database updates and corrections. For the databases included in the Entrez system, third parties provide the maintenance. However, for private and commercial databases, these and other knowledge management activities must be assigned, monitored, and assessed.

In addition to the shortcomings of link-based database integration, Entrez also highlights the benefits of a high-level database search system. Without a system like Entrez or a related system like the NCBI Discovery Space that is designed to facilitate Single Nucleotide Polymorphism (SNP) research, users would have to alternatively login, copy, and paste or otherwise transfer results from one search to the input of another. Entrez saves users time and minimizes errors owing to mistakes made by transferring data from one database to another. Unfortunately, creating systems such as Entrez is a major endeavor. Most search engines simply create dynamic links to content that last for the duration of the session, or that at best can be saved for future reference.

Intelligent Agents

As illustrated in Table 4-2, search engine technology isn't limited to dynamically inter-linking databases, but includes a range of capabilities that apply to bioinformatics work. One particularly active area of R&D is in the area of intelligent agents—search engines with advanced pattern-matching capabilities. They automatically search multiple databases using a variety of heuristics and return results preformatted according to user preferences. Although intelligent agents vary in capabilities, in general they automatically convert simple keyword searches to advanced pattern-matching searches and, in some systems, concept searches. Instead of basing a search on a literal match for a keyword, intelligent agents increase search resolution through restriction of word proximity and exclusion of user-specified associations through Boolean operators.

Table 4-2 Search Engine Technologies. Many of the technologies applicable to general-purpose search engines can be applied to searching bioinformatics databases.

Search Engine Technology	Example
General-Purpose Intelligent Agents (Desktop)	Intelliseek, Copernic, Lexibot, WebFerret, SearchPad, WebStorm, and NetAttache
General-Purpose Intelligent Agents (Internet)	Dogpile, Ixquick, MetaCrawler, QbSearch, ProFusion, SurfWax, and Vivisimo
Internal (Intranet) Search Engines	AskMe, Cadenza
General-Purpose Search Engines	Google, Lycos, Yahoo!, Excite, AltaVista, AllTheWeb, CompletePlanet
Sequence Match (Desktop and Internet)	FASTA, BLAST and BLAST derivatives
Utilities	Connection optimizers, browser extensions, personal firewalls, file-transfer programs, download managers
Bioinformatics Portals	Entrez, SRS, BioKRIS, PubMed Central, Discovery Space
Interface Tools	Natural Language Processing (NLP), Query by example, controlled vocabulary

Intelligent agents that support concept searching perform searches based on the concept represented by the keywords entered by the user. A concept search can be as simple as executing a search on a synonym list, or as complex as inferring relationships between the keywords entered in the system. For example, an agent-mediated search on "hypertension" could perform multiple keyword searches on "hypertension" as well as "high blood pressure." A more sophisticated system could infer additional search terms, such as co-morbidities of hypertension—specific renal and retinal diseases resulting from high blood pressure, for example.

Concept-based searching is especially applicable in instances where the vocabulary may not be consistent. For example, in a patient's medical record, a clinician might record the patient's complaint of "chest pain" as "angina." A simple keyword search, whether mediated by an agent or submitted directly to a search engine, would miss the alternate phrasing.

Advanced pattern search techniques don't necessarily involve concepts or recognizable keywords. Nucleotide sequence searches use advanced techniques to identify incomplete or approximate sequence matches. At this point in the development of molecular biology databases, higher-level concept searches are still rare. However, researchers are quickly moving to provide the capability of searching a database with a term such as "obesity" and viewing not only the physiological and psychological components of obesity, but related protein structures and nucleotide sequences as well.

Portals

Entrez is an example of a portal—a pre-linked gateway to databases selected by the portal designer. Sequence Retrieval Service (SRS), and BioKRIS (as well as Entrez) are examples of portals that provide access to link-integrated databases through a variety of special support tools. For example, SRS allows users to search multiple databases simultaneously because of a powerful and unique set of link operators that dynamically link multiple databases. Portals can make better use of intelligent agents because the search engine designer can design the heuristics to fit the databases included in the portal, as opposed to working with every database on the Internet. Similarly, special operators can be defined to facilitate working with the databases encompassed by the portal.

For example, SRS uses two link operators "<" and ">" to combine two sets from different databases in the portal system, such as SWISS-PROT and PDB. The statement SWISS-PROT > PDB gives those entries in the PDB database of solved tertiary protein structures that are referenced by or linked to entries in SWISS-PROT. Conversely, the statement SWISS-PROT < PDB gives those entries in SWISS-PROT that reference or are linked to entries in PDB. As a result, the statement [swissprot-def:kinase] > PDB retrieves all kinase sequences from the SWISS-PROT protein sequence database, which are then linked to the PDB. The result is a set of all the PDB entries with atomic coordinates for all kinases for which the tertiary structure has been determined.

The SRS portal supports linking from any database to any other database in the system. If two databases are not directly connected by a link, then a series of intermediary links is created. As illustrated in Figure 4-6, SRS attempts to find the shortest possible way for linking two databases. Ideally this is the direct link as between EMBL and SWISS-PROT However, with a link request such as EMBL > PDB, when there are no nucleotide sequences in EMBL that are referenced by the PDB database of tertiary protein structures, then SRS automatically links the two databases through a SWISS-PROT intermediary, which relates both databases.

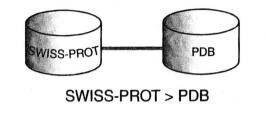

SWISS-PROT > PDB

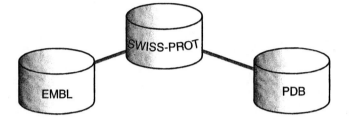

EMBL > SWISS-PROT

Figure 4-6 SRS Database Linking. When instructed to link databases without relevant references, SRS identifies the best intermediary database to support the link. In this example, a link between EMBL and PDB is automatically facilitated by SRS-directed links through the SWISS-PROT database.

User Interface Tools

Getting information out of a database is as important as putting it in. The point of human-computer communication—the user interface—is to maximize the quality and efficiency of the interchange. The better the search engine interface, the easier it is for users to interact with the data. A major function of the user interface is to decrease the cognitive load on the researcher so that the data created by the underlying application can be quickly and easily absorbed. It also provides a mechanism for the user to painlessly communicate to the application. A variety of visualization tools have been developed to aid researchers by presenting data so researchers can evaluate complex protein sequences, identify the location of genes on chromosomes, and, in general, make the otherwise unintelligible and seemingly endless strings of data intelligible. Visualization techniques are discussed in depth in Chapter 5, "Data Visualization."

From a data input perspective, the pull-down menus and check boxes supported by a standard Web browser, as demonstrated by the Web version of Entrez, represent standard user interface tools. Of the tools available to extend database search functionality within a Web browser environment, the most popular are free-text entry, query by example, and controlled vocabulary.

NLP is the technology that allows free-text searches of databases, whether in a Web browser or local application. A statement such as:

What is the molecular weight of the hemoglobin molecule?

automatically generates a different statement, for example, a SELECT statement for a SQL database of the form:

```
SELECT molecular_wt FROM protein_database
  WHERE protein = hemoglobin
```

In addition to NLP, there are a number of technologies that are useful in locating textual and graphic data in very large databases as well. One of them is image-based query by example, where the user selects from a library of images to create and then refine a search. Using this technology, the user selects an image of a protein structure and then either selects the closest fit or a representative of additional image libraries, depending on the extent of the database. The same approach is often used in commercial search engines, where the user is able to specify a search for "more like these." The system takes the exemplars and creates a search that may include terms and constraints that may not have been included in the user's initial search. The advantage of a search-by-example tool is that refining a search is relatively painless and doesn't require any particular knowledge of vocabulary, database contents, or other low-level details. However, the disadvantage of most query-by-example systems is that the search query that is actually generated is hidden from the user. As a result, an expert may not be able to manually refine the search even further. The ability to override a computer-generated search, such as the utility provided in Entrez where a user can edit the search criteria generated through the use of pull-down menus, may or may not be an issue, depending on the expertise of the user.

One of the advantages of using NLP or query by example is that it frees the user from having to learn a controlled vocabulary. An NLP engine can map concepts and use the appropriate synonyms that the underlying database management systems expect in order to provide optimum search results. However, the power of an NLP engine or an ability to manually override a search query lies in the granularity of the vocabulary used to index the data originally. For example, if all genes dealing with the heart are indexed under "cardiac," without distinguishing between normal and diseased conditions, then a researcher won't be able to narrow a search to normal heart pathology.

The optimum condition exists when the controlled vocabulary is made available to users during the search process. For example, PubMed is indexed using the Medical Subject Heading (MeSH) vocabulary, maintained by the U.S. National Library of Medicine. Knowing this, a researcher can use the online MeSH browser to identify the most appropriate search terms to use to retrieve the data of interest.

For a research group establishing an internal database, MeSH may not be the most appropriate controlled vocabulary for indexing and searching. Even within the relatively narrow domain of clinical medicine, there are several popular controlled vocabulary systems in use. In addition to MeSH, there is the Unified Medical Language System (UMLS), the Read Classification System (RCS), Systemized Nomenclature of Human and Veterinary Medicine (SNOMED), International Classification of Diseases (ICD-10), and Current Procedural Terminology (COPT). Each system has its strengths, weaknesses, and primary purpose. For example, SNOMED is optimized for accessing and indexing clinical information in human and veterinary medicine databases, whereas the COPT is optimized to identify medical procedures.

The advantage of using one of these public controlled vocabularies is that the vocabulary is immediately available. Time-consuming tasks such as removing redundancies in the vocabulary, which ultimately limits scalability, have been performed by someone else—presumably experts in the field. Another advantage is that databases indexed with a public controlled vocabulary can more readily share the database with others without having to distribute the indexing vocabulary. For example, if an academic research center wants to publish its research on SNPs and drug responses on the Internet, it can provide a simple keyword search interface to the database and simply list the appropriate search vocabulary, such as MeSH.

The major disadvantage of using a public controlled vocabulary, or its given representation, is that its granularity may not exactly fit the needs of the laboratory. Another limitation is that the public vocabulary may be updated periodically, forcing whoever manages the database to expend the resources necessary to re-index areas of the index affected by the updates. Failing to do so would likely lead to user frustration, because users may not have the latest version of the vocabulary, either because they aren't aware of the update or because they don't have access to an older version of the vocabulary for reference.

For internal databases where the user population can be informed about changes in indexing, there is much more flexibility in selecting or developing an indexing and search vocabulary. The most common approaches to developing an in-house controlled vocabulary range from a totally unconstrained ad-hoc system to creating a huge, potentially unwieldy combination of public vocabularies. The ad-hoc approach of creating a new vocabulary as data are generated is reasonable only if the vocabulary is relatively small and isn't expected to grow beyond 1,000 or 2,000 words. For larger indexing tasks requiring the breadth of a published controlled vocabulary, a reasonable approach is to modify a standard vocabulary, adding granularity in specific areas. This approach takes advantage of an extensive vocabulary that may exceed 100,000 terms, but comes at a cost of incompatibility with the published standard. The approach of combining standards is clearly the most challenging because of the inevitable redundancies and internal inconsistencies of the vocabularies used that must somehow be controlled. Whether or not the advantage of this approach—a vocabulary that exceeds several hundred-thousand terms and is likely to cover the spectrum of indexing needs—is worth the investment depends on the scope of the database project and the resources available.

Regardless of whether a controlled vocabulary is designed from scratch or is based on a published standard, the main technological issue is providing a means of using it consistently and without error. For example, without rudimentary utilities such as text auto-completion, simply misspelling a search term can render the sought-after data inaccessible.

Utilities

Many of the generic utilities originally intended to extend the functionality of browsers can be used to facilitate searching molecular biology databases. These utilities include connection optimizers, browser add-ons, personal firewalls, file-transfer programs, and download managers. Connection optimizers are designed to improve Internet connection speed and reliability. Optimizers work by allowing manual override of network communications configuration settings so that the connection throughput can be optimized for sequence data (text strings), 3D protein structures (graphics), or specific combination of data formats.

Browser extensions enhance browsers with features, such as automatic form-filling, supporting searching within a document, dictionary tools that define or complete the spelling of words on-the-fly, providing visual previews of Web pages before they are accessed, and adding buttons of frequently accessed sites to the browser. Privacy and security utilities include personal firewalls that take up where network firewalls leave off. They block advertisements, cookies, and other nuisances that can interfere with the efficient use of a browser-based search engine.

Download managers are intended to accelerate searches by opening multiple connections to one or more servers simultaneously, grabbing different parts of the file through each connection and reassembling the file on the workstation. File-transfer managers add flexibility to standard FTP clients by adding additional security through encryption, and by providing users with a graphical user interface instead of a command-line prompt. Most of these utilities are available on Windows, Linux, and UNIX environment platforms.

SEARCHING AND INFORMATION THEORY

Information Theory forms the basis for our understanding of modern communications networks, and provides a model for understanding the principles of search engines. Information Theory specifies the amount of meaningful information that can be communicated from the Web server to the browser as a function of the signal-to-noise level and the bandwidth of the medium. The greater the strength of the desired signal compared to that of the noise—that is, the higher the signal-to-noise ratio—the greater the amount of relevant data that can be propagated from the database through the Internet to the user (see Figure 4-8).

Figure 4-7 shows the application of Information Theory to search engine technology, where the molecular biology database constitutes the information source, a Web server is the transmitter, the Internet or other network serves as the medium, the search engine is the receiver, and the user's Web browser or local application is the destination. Similarly, the relevant data in the database constitutes the message to be transmitted, irrelevant data constitutes the noise source, and the message presented to the user through a Web browser consists of both relevant and irrelevant data.

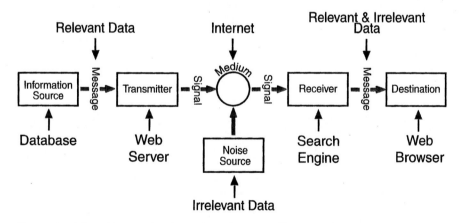

Figure 4-7 Searching and Information Theory. Following information theory, both relevant and irrelevant data reach the user through the Internet as a function of the search engine (receiver) and the relative amounts of relevant and irrelevant data in the information source.

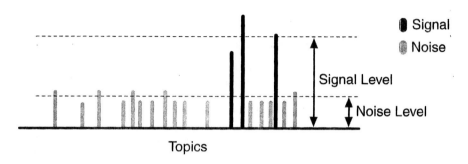

Figure 4-8 Signal-to-Noise Ratio. Line height corresponds to the amount of data available on a particular topic.

Information Theory specifies the amount of meaningful information that can be communicated from the Web server to the browser as a function of the signal-to-noise level and the bandwidth of the medium. The greater the strength of the desired signal compared to that of the noise—that is, the higher the signal-to-noise ratio—the greater the amount of relevant data that can be propagated from the database through the Internet to the user (see Figure 4-8).

Searches generally fail in one of two ways: Either they retrieve too much noise with the desired data, so that the time it takes to look through results isn't worth the trouble, or they retrieve the wrong data, because the search criteria were incorrect. The best searches are sensitive enough to return all or most of the desired data and selective enough to limit undesired data or noise to the least level possible.

One way to limit the amount of noise returned by a search is to increase the selectivity of a search by using a Boolean operator, such as AND, OR, or NOT. As illustrated in Figure 4-9, the OR operator provides the least amount of selectivity. Conversely, the AND operator provides the greatest selectivity, returning data that contains all of the keywords submitted in a query. The NOT operator generally provides an intermediate amount of selectivity. The relative selectivity of the Boolean operators assumes that there is a significant signal-to-noise ratio—that there are a significant number of Web sites or nucleotide sequences that fulfill the search requirements compared to the other results that may be returned by the search.

Regardless of the search technology used, the retrieval process is a tradeoff between sensitivity and selectivity. A non-selective search using only general terms normally returns a large amount of irrelevant data. As shown in Figure 4-10, a more selective search, while returning less noise or irrelevant data, may miss some of the desired data. Using an excessively selective search results in less noise at the expense of relevant data.

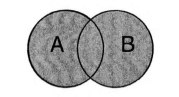

A OR B

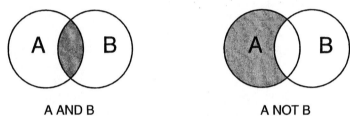

A AND B   A NOT B

Figure 4-9 Boolean Operators. Most search engines support the Boolean AND, OR, and NOT operators, illustrated graphically here. Shaded areas in each image represent the data returned by the search.

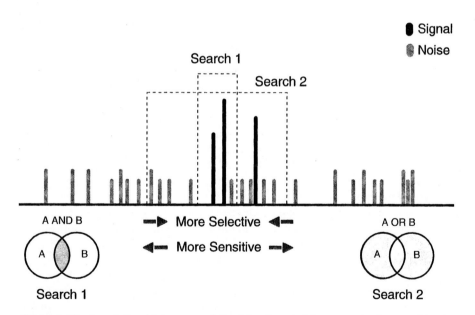

Figure 4-10 Search Sensitivity versus Selectivity. Search 1 is more selective, resulting in less noise in the search results, but also misses relevant data. Search 2 is more sensitive, including more relevant data but more noise as well.

COMPUTATIONAL METHODS

A common activity in bioinformatics work is to search through a database and locate a substring—a nucleotide sequence, for example—that matches a target string. Some computational methods provide results faster, allowing a researcher to check the results of an experiment frequently, at the expense of more false positive matches. Later, more selective, albeit slower techniques can be used to verify the results of these quick screening techniques. The performance and selectivity of a search are also a function of the search string and how the data are represented in the database to be searched.

Most programming languages provide string search capabilities, but these tend to be unacceptably inefficient when performed on large data sets typical of nucleotide sequence databases, and most don't support approximate match capabilities. Because the built-in algorithms tend to use brute-force methods that don't make use of heuristics or algorithmic tricks to increase efficiency or to accelerate the search process, special-purpose algorithms have to be used with computationally intensive tasks such as sequence searching.

Search Algorithms

Regardless of their intended purpose or design, search algorithms can be characterized by setup time, running time, and need for backtracking. The first two elements, setup time and running time, are related by the function:

$$search\ time = setup\ time + (comparisons \times characters)$$

In this relationship, *comparisons* is the number of comparisons made per character in the text body to be searched, and *characters* is the number of characters in the body of text or sequence data that is to be searched. *Setup time* is the time invested prior to the actual search, and includes programming to establish lookup tables and other data that can be used to simplify or accelerate the search once it's initiated.

A search algorithm is considered inefficient if, in the process of a search, the number of comparisons made is equal to or greater than the number of characters in the source text. For example, a search algorithm in which the number of comparisons per character is greater than one is considered inefficient. Conversely, an efficient algorithm is one that makes less than one comparison per character to complete a search. Making less than one comparison per character might seem counterintuitive at first, but this is possible through the use of heuristics that involve skipping characters and repeating characters. Heuristic techniques use previous information to identify a solution.

To illustrate the first heuristic, skipping characters, consider the search scenario in Figure 4-11 where a search for the string "RNA" progresses from left to right in the search text "The synthesis of protein is by way of an RNA intermediary". At the initial stage of this example, the search position is at the right end of the first word, as indicated by the underline "e" in "The". Now, consider the progression of the marker as the search string is compared with subsequent characters in the search text.

At each step, the number of characters in the search string—in this case, three—advances the search unless a character in the search text corresponding to the length of the search string is also in the search string. For example, in line 2 of Figure 4-11, there is no space in the search string and so the search advances three characters. However, in line 3, the "n" character in "nth" is also in the search string, but the n's don't line up. In this way, skipping continues until line 6, where the "rot" in "protein" contains the "r" character in the search string. A comparison of the first characters is made, which matches, and so the second characters are compared. This comparison fails, and the search is again advanced. In line 7, there is again a possible match, and the search string is advanced one character to verify a match, as in line 8. However, the

Search String: RNA
Search Text: The synthesis of protein is by way of an RNA intermediary

1. Th⬛ synthesis of protein is by way of an RNA intermediary
2. The s⬛nthesis of protein is by way of an RNA intermediary
3. The synt⬛esis of protein is by way of an RNA intermediary
4. The synthes⬛s of protein is by way of an RNA intermediary
5. The synthesis ⬛f protein is by way of an RNA intermediary
6. The synthesis of ⬛rotein is by way of an RNA intermediary
7. The synthesis of pro⬛ein is by way of an RNA intermediary
8. The synthesis of protei⬛ is by way of an RNA intermediary
9. The synthesis of protein⬛is by way of an RNA intermediary
10. The synthesis of protein is⬛by way of an RNA intermediary

18. The synthesis of protein is by way of an ⬛RNA⬛ intermediary

Figure 4-11 Character Skipping. The search, indicated by the marker box, progresses from left to right, skipping ahead up to three characters at a time until a character in the search string "RNA" is found in the skipped-to region of the search text.

space at the end of "protein" doesn't match the "A" in "RNA", and the search position is shifted three places to the right, as in line 10.

This process continues, stopping to check for matches whenever the next three characters contains an "r", "n", or "a". That is, if the algorithm is examining a character that doesn't occur in the search string at all, the algorithm moves ahead by the length of the entire search string. If a character does appear in the search string, the algorithm advances the search marker by the distance between that character and the right end of the string. By step 18, the search is complete, on a total of 44 characters (including spaces). The number of comparisons per character is approximately 0.4—an efficient search algorithm.

A second search heuristic makes use of repeating patterns in the search string, such as "hand to hand, door to door", and attempts to match the first repeating word, according to the algorithm described for skipping characters. When a match is made, the search string is advanced to the point that the first occurrence of the repeated word is aligned with the first occurrence of the matching term in the main text. A comparison is now made for the second occurrence of the search term in the text. Obviously, the major gain in computational efficiency and performance is obtained by the first heuristic, and the advantage of the second heuristic is dependent on the appearance of repeating words in the search pattern.

In addition to running time, another major metric for characterizing search algorithms is the need for backtracking. Some search algorithms are linear, working efficiently from the beginning of the sequence to be searched to the end, whereas others move back and forth in the text to be searched during processing. For example, the skipping search algorithm moves the index ahead by the number of characters in the search string but then backs up to compare characters if a possible match exists.

Approximate Searches

Algorithms that efficiently locate exact matches have many applications in bioinformatics, including searching for data in PubMed or some other bibliographic reference database by a specific disease or author, searching a clinical database by a specific disease or patient identification number, or searching any database where data are indexed by a known, controlled vocabulary. However, search algorithms that look for approximate matches are more useful in one of the most computationally challenging tasks in bioinformatics—that of searching sequence databases for homologies of particular sequences. Approximate match algorithms vary from the use of templates, to the use of a distance function, and the use of how words sound when spoken.

String search algorithms based on templates use metacharacters to specify the range of permissible strings that must be matched exactly. For example, the UNIX utility "grep" (general regular expression parser) uses metacharacters such as "*", "\", "$", "+", and "^" to perform a brute-force search. As such, applications such as grep don't do true approximate searches. Similarly, the Find function in the Windows operating system allows a search string such as "*research.doc" to locate Microsoft Word documents that include "MyResearch.doc", "DNAResearch.doc", and "ProteinResearch.doc". However, the search wouldn't locate documents such as "MyReserch.doc", "DNAResaerch.doc", or "ProteinRsch.doc", because of missing or transposed characters in the file names compared to the search string.

True approximate search algorithms allow approximate matches, permit the transposition of adjacent characters, substitution of characters, and assign different weights to different types of errors. An approximate match algorithm for nucleotide sequences should be able to locate nucleotide sequences despite the presence of single nucleotide polymorphism, for example. Searching with an approximate match algorithm for a nucleotide sequence that contains the string "AAGGTTAA" should be able to locate the sequence "ATGGTTAA", where the second "A" in the first string is replaced by a "T" in the second string.

Phonetic comparison algorithms, typified by Soundex and Metaphone, are examples of true approximate search algorithms that have application in bioinformatics. For example, they can be used to search bibliographic databases by author name when the exact spelling of the author's name may be unknown, or search a taxonomy database by phonetically spelling a species name. The Soundex approximate search algorithm addresses the problem of uncertain spelling by indexing and searching databases by an encoded string. These encoded strings are created by dropping vowels and silent consonants and assigning one of six values to the remaining consonants (see Table 4-3).

Table 4-3 Soundex Codes. Vowels and silent consonants are dropped from the word and the consonants are converted to a three-digit numeric codes, headed by the first character in the word. The Soundex algorithm is especially useful in performing approximate searches for names of authors, taxonomies, and other text strings that can be pronounced.

Characters	Value
AEIOUHWY	Dropped
BFPV	1
CGJKQSXZ	2
DT	3
L	4
MN	5
R	6

Soundex encoding uses the first letter of the word, followed by up to three codes, depending on the length of the word. Double consonants and repetitions of the same consonant group are dropped. For example, "protein" is converted to "P635", and "Pill", "Phil", and "Philly" are converted to "P4". Soundex errs on the side of sensitivity instead of specificity, in that it tends to pick up strings that are only vaguely similar to the search string. The major limitations of Soundex are that the first letter of a word must match exactly and that the string must be intended to be spoken. That is, Soundex isn't intended to work with a text string such as "ATTAATTGGA". Similarly, a search for a word that begins with "ph" won't find a word that actually begins with "f", even though the words may sound identical.

A major improvement on the Soundex approach of encoding search and index strings is the Metaphone algorithm. Like Soundex, Metaphone disposes of vowels—unless the word begins with a vowel. However, Metaphone encoding is based on diphthongs rather than consonants. For example, the Metaphone algorithm transforms "X" to "KS" before encoding the text string. As a result, a search using Metaphone is generally more specific than Soundex. However, the Metaphone encoding scheme doesn't overcome the limitation of being unable to encode and search for unpronounceable text strings, such as nucleotide sequence data.

When it comes to searching sequence databases for sequence homologues, the gold standard is to use a search engine based on a dynamic programming algorithm. Dynamic programming is a computationally expensive but thorough search algorithm that recursively searches through a database for a sequence that approximates the search string. Not only does a dynamic programming algorithm search a database from beginning to end, but it keeps the results of previous match attempts in memory. As a result, running a search for a sequence only a few dozen nucleotides long against a database such as the human genome database can take hours, even with a dedicated supercomputer.

Because the routine use of dynamic programming search techniques is unreasonably expensive in time and computer resources, modified versions of dynamic programming, such as the FASTA algorithm, are more practical. FASTA makes a dynamic programming approach to string search tenable by limiting the area of the sequence database that is searched. The downside to an algorithm such as FASTA is that it's possible to miss potential matches because the search isn't exhaustive.

When it comes to performing approximate searches on sequence data, by far the most popular algorithm is the Basic Local Alignment Search Tool (BLAST), which achieves computational efficiency by using heuristics that are weighted toward local sequence alignments. The BLAST heuristic assumes that sections of protein are often conserved without gaps, so that the gaps can be ignored. As such, it's able to detect relationships among sequences that share only isolated regions of similarity. BLAST is used by virtually all of the major bioinformatics centers, including NCBI. Using BLAST over the Internet, sequence searches against the full human genome can be completed in only a few seconds, even when the system is being used by multiple users.

Because of the statistical techniques used to narrow the focus of the BLAST algorithm, it can miss potential matches in a nucleotide database. To extend the capabilities of BLAST so that it finds additional matches, NCBI developed Position-Specific Iterated BLAST (PSI-BLAST) that extends the original BLAST algorithm using a position-specific scoring matrix that is capable of detecting subtle nucleotide sequence similarities. NCBI and other research centers have similarly created specialized versions of BLAST that are tuned to specific problems or areas. As described in more detail in Chapter 8, "Pattern Matching," there are versions of BLAST that are optimized for human, microbial, and malaria genomes, vector contamination, and immunoglobins.

SEARCH ENGINES AND KNOWLEDGE MANAGEMENT

The ability to search through a molecular biology database assumes that an effective knowledge management process is in place. Using the DNA sequencing process as an example, consider the steps involved in making sequence data available to a researcher through a search engine. First, there is the lengthy process of acquiring the data from a sequence machine. This involves identifying a set of clones that span a region of the genome to be sequenced, making sets of smaller clones from mapped clones, purifying DNA from the smaller clones, and finally setting up and performing the sequencing using gel electrophoresis. Then there is the verification and annotation of the sequence data. Annotation is especially critical, because it enables the sequence data to be accessed by name and linked to other databases. In this way, researchers in other labs and in other fields can access the sequence data. A newly discovered nucleotide sequence might be linked to (and linked from) a protein database, an inherited disease database, and perhaps a drug interaction database, for example. Ultimately, providing name and linking hooks to the new data facilitates discovery of associations or links between different but related fields in a way that extends our knowledge.

As involved as this initial stage of knowledge management can be, it's a waste of time and resources without a comprehensive knowledge management program. This includes a defined means of transforming data for other purposes, such as using the data in a tightly linked secondary database of clinical disease. It also includes archiving data so that they can be recovered in the event of failure in the primary database system, and providing the infrastructure capable of tracking the location of particular data elements and of controlling access to the data.

Although every component of the knowledge management process is critical, the data that are managed are of little value unless they can be easily accessed in a timely manner. From a practical perspective, knowledge management should support the retrieval of data from an online database with a search engine while making provision for security through user authentication or other methods. As such, factors that affect usability include the quality and appropriateness of the user interface, the vocabulary used to index and retrieve data, ease of use, ease of learning, and the time required for specific data to be searched for and retrieved define the value of the system.

As described earlier, using one of the integrated database systems such as Entrez, SRS, or BioKRIS can significantly reduce the time and difficulty associated with performing a successful search. Although having databases online facilitates link integration through the search process, the interface challenges begin at the time databases are first defined. The issue with creating databases of any type is that they are necessarily defined for a particular use. For example, the HomoloGene online database is optimized to manage putative homologies among the human, mouse, rat, and zebra fish genomes, whereas SWISS-PROT is optimized to locate protein sequence data. Moving outside of the molecular biology arena, the online professional databases including LexisNexis, Dialog, and Ingenta each provide comprehensive, efficient access to information in their domains. Similarly, PAC provides integration of life-science journal literature in a common format and in a single repository, providing a single, unified access portal to scientific literature instead of a combination of links to disparate databases, each with their own idiosyncrasies in vocabularies and infrastructures.

Information technology challenges aside, there is a limit to how far systems like Entrez can be further refined, because of our incomplete understanding of how a database can and should be linked. For example, molecular biology has yet to fully explain how single genes can code for multiple proteins or how all of the proteins in the human proteome interact with each other and the cellular environment under various conditions. That said, the future of bioinformatics lies clearly in the integration of disparate databases in molecular biology as well as with those in other fields to provide a unified view of life.

As an illustration of the degree of linking that will eventually be needed to even approximate this unified view, consider the experiences—which can be represented by links—typical of physician training in the United States. As listed in Table 4-4, the traditional pre-medical curriculum includes the basic sciences, including chemistry, physics, and genetics. Medical school provides exposure to pre-clinical studies such as physiology and anatomy, followed by clinical exposure to everything from nutrition and dermatology to psychology and oncology.

It's possible for someone to practice medicine without learning the interconnectedness of the underlying anatomy with the biochemical basis for disease—

Table 4-4 Typical Physician Training. The typical pre-clinical and clinical curricula, with a sampling of a possible pre-medical experience, illustrate the mesh of knowledge required for physicians to adequately understand and manage the disease process.

Pre-Medical	Pre-Clinical	Clinical
Differential Equations	Anatomy	Anesthesia
Physics	Biochemistry	Dermatology
Calculus	Microbiology	Endocrinology
Chemistry	Parasitology	Geriatrics
Genetics	Pharmacology	Hematology
Molecular Biology		Internal Medicine
Organic Chemistry		Neonatology
Strength of Materials		Nutrition
Statistics		OB/GYN
Dynamics		Oncology
Computer Science		Orthopedics
Art		Pediatrics
History		Plastic Surgery
Languages		Psychology
Sociology		Pulmonary Medicine
Psychology		Radiology
Engineering		Surgery
Management		Tropical Medicine
Biology		Urology

many advances in medicine were based on accidental discoveries, as opposed to reasoning from first principles. However, for true understanding of the disease process and how to treat it, the interconnectedness of organic chemistry, biochemistry, anatomy, and physiology generally have to be mastered. Because of human memory limitations, most clinicians specialize in relatively limited areas that they can master—that is, areas in which they can develop and maintain linkages.

An orthopedic surgeon may not need to understand the intricacies of the Central Dogma in his daily practice. Similarly, real understanding of the germ theory isn't required to perform an aseptic operation, such as a hip replacement—as long as proper procedure is followed. However, when things don't go as expected—for example, if the patient requires a new hip replacement after three years instead of the usual five—it's in the patient's best interest if the surgeon can reason from first principles, using his interlinked knowledge of skeletal and muscle anatomy, engineering, and clinical experience with hip prostheses to prevent a reoccurrence of premature failure. Often, as in the use of a search engine, the solution involves innovation—creating new links between existing knowledge.

Innovators rely on predefined links and create links on their own. For example, substituting a beneficial organism for a potentially hazardous one, as in replacement therapy, has been practiced for decades. Eating yogurt, for example, populates the stomach with benign acidophilus bacilli, displacing less beneficial bacteria. The same technique is being used with Streptococcus bacteria that have been modified by recombinant DNA techniques so as not to produce cavity-producing acids that attack the tooth's enamel. The idea is to displace the natural bacteria that cause tooth decay by using a mouthwash composed of benign bacteria that will displace the acid-producing variety.

Innovation in bioinformatics is occurring in the same way. Researchers are using the links provided by Entrez and other online services and supplementing them with their own to test new hypotheses, verify the findings or theories of others, and otherwise advance their understanding of life.

ON THE HORIZON

The current interest in bioinformatics is primarily focused on accelerating the expensive drug discovery process. Bioinformatics is currently viewed by the Pharma industry as a means of weeding out problem drugs more quickly and earlier in the R&D process. Although this view has yet to be validated by a viable product produced by bioinformatics methods alone, firms that rely heavily on bioinformatics techniques are projecting an R&D investment of 20 percent on sales. This may seem prohibitively expensive, given the industry standard of 12 percent on sales. However, the hope is that new bioinformatics methods will more accurately reject drugs that may cause serious side effects, drugs that as of now aren't discovered until millions of dollars have been invested in marketing and sales efforts.

Over the life of a drug, the initial R&D investment in bioinformatics methods could more than pay for itself if computational methods could be used to identify molecules that behave like other molecules known to cause serious side effects. Over the past 25 years, half of the dangerous side effects of drugs were recognized over 7 years after the drugs were approved. Pulling a drug from the market because of lethal side effects at this late stage is not only expensive, but these findings typically extend the FDA's approval time because of public pressure to be more vigilant.

Clearly, if bioinformatics is to solve the drug side-effect dilemma, practitioners in the field will have to work not only with gene expression and proteomic databases, but with clinical medicine databases as well. However, given the exponential growth of data in molecular biology as well as in virtually every clinical medicine domain, it's unlikely that molecular biology researchers will have sufficient knowledge or resources to manually establish and maintain links between findings in their field. Furthermore, it's even less likely that complete, up-to-date predefined links to databases in other fields can be maintained. More likely is continued work in the area of search engine technology that can create dynamic links between protein folding, DNA sequence, and inherited disease databases, as well as links between these databases and those in fields as diverse as physics, biochemistry, and the law.

ENDNOTE

One potential endpoint of creating search capabilities that dynamically and completely integrate databases in medicine, law, the genome, individual IQ and education test scores, and personal employment records is revealed in Aldus Huxley's *Brave New World*, in which everything is known about every citizen before their birth. In this novel, embryos are immunized in vitro in a central hatchery against all known infectious diseases; old age itself is a disease. Furthermore, citizens are indoctrinated at birth to the social order, based on their made-to-order genetic profile that determines whether they are leaders or obedient followers.

Another possibility is that, like other disruptive technologies—the electric light, antibiotics, the PC, and the automobile, for example—our ability to manipulate nucleotide and amino acid sequences will simply become an invisible part of the social fabric. Thanks to bioinformatics, new, more powerful drugs will be available to treat HIV and similar acquired diseases, as well as correct for genetic errors that would otherwise result in lifelong suffering for individuals and a cost burden for the healthcare system.

➤ Deoxy Human Hemoglobin. PDB entry 1A3N. Image produced with PDB Structure Explorer.

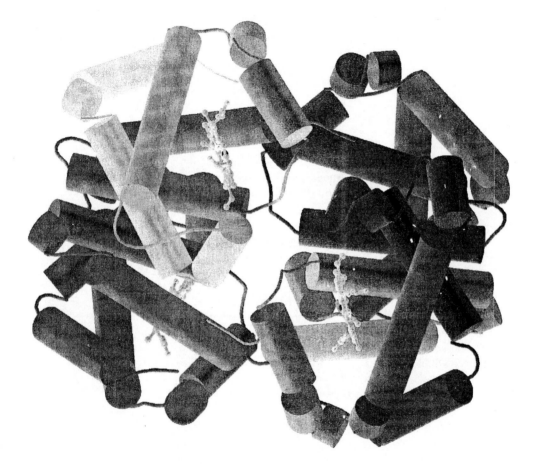

CHAPTER

Data Visualization

*When you are inspired by some great purpose, some extraordinary
project, all your thoughts break their bonds; Your mind transcends
limitations, your consciousness expands in every direction, and you
find yourself in a new, great and wonderful world.*
— *Patanjali*

We evolved as visual creatures, highly dependent for our survival on our
virtually instantaneous, visual pattern-recognition skills. When faced
with predator or prey, our ancestors who were able to assess the situation
quickly and take the appropriate action survived. Day-to-day survival favored
the quickest pattern recognizers.

In the modern, digital society, when it comes to communicating or understanding complex concepts and vast amounts of data quickly, the optical cor-
tex is still the best processor going. The rise of TV as a universal portal for
disseminating image-intensive news and entertainment, joined recently by the
multimedia-rich Web, is a testament to our ability to immediately evaluate
graphical content without conscious, focused mental processing.

Although there are exceptions, it's often difficult for even highly trained
professionals to intuitively evaluate strings of text or tables of data so that they

can act on them quickly. This is especially true when we are inundated throughout the day with data from a variety of sources, each source competing for attention. Everyone from aircraft pilots, drivers, anesthesiologists, and nuclear power plant operators to molecular biologists rely on graphical displays to operate equipment and communicate findings to others.

Consider that the typical physician understands or is at least familiar with the concepts of statistical sensitivity and specificity as applied to the interpretation of routine laboratory test results. However, when asked to apply these concepts to their everyday practice of reviewing tables of numerical laboratory test values, most cannot calculate when a test result is far enough from normal to warrant further investigation. For this reason, many laboratories report laboratory results to physicians in a tabular, numeric form in which each value is accompanied by a normal range and a simple graphic to show how it relates to what is generally accepted as the normal range.

The list of blood values for a male patient shown in Figure 5-1 is representative of how simple graphics are used at many hospitals and clinics to allow physicians to quickly visualize significantly abnormal results. In this example, the fasting blood glucose and hematocrit levels are outside of their normal ranges. The degree of abnormality can be calculated by looking at the range of normal values. However, because of the difference in ranges, it isn't immediately clear that the fasting blood glucose level is significantly out of normal range and that the hematocrit is just outside of normal. The advantage of the graphic is that the data ranges are normalized so that the distance outside of the normal range brackets has the same relative significance across all laboratory results.

Although the hemoglobin level is outside of its normal range, it may be acceptable clinically. It may be temporarily elevated if the patient is dehydrated, for example. Making this clinical decision is the physician's responsibility, based on her experience. However, before the physician can make this assessment, she must be able to quickly identify values that are significantly out of normal range—which is where visualization aids are most valuable.

The value of using graphical representations of data to provide added meaning and context is also evident in the field of neuroscience, where 3D visualization technologies such as functional magnetic resonance imaging (fMRI) have supplanted the squiggly lines of the electroencephalograph (EEG). Functional MRI, which is based on the nuclear magnetic resonance of protons to produce proton density maps, empowers researchers to observe activity in the brain—as a 3D color image of the gross brain—when the patient is asked to perform different mental tasks. Particular patterns of activity are also associated with personality traits, from aggression and risk-aversion to depression.

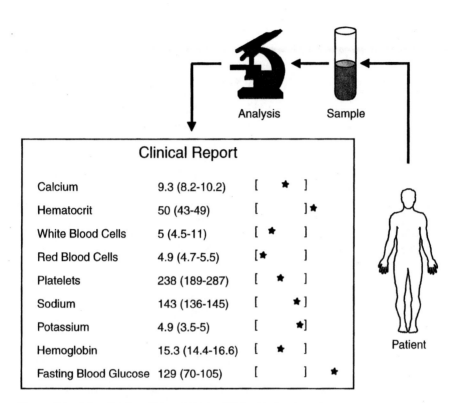

Analysis   Sample

Clinical Report

Calcium	9.3 (8.2-10.2)	[*]
Hematocrit	50 (43-49)	[ ]*
White Blood Cells	5 (4.5-11)	[*]
Red Blood Cells	4.9 (4.7-5.5)	[*]
Platelets	238 (189-287)	[*]
Sodium	143 (136-145)	[*]
Potassium	4.9 (3.5-5)	[*]
Hemoglobin	15.3 (14.4-16.6)	[*]
Fasting Blood Glucose	129 (70-105)	[ ] *

Patient

Figure 5-1   Visualization Aids to Tabular Clinical Laboratory Data.

Although these and other data have been available in the form of EEGs, before such advanced visualization technologies as fMRI, these patterns were not readily discernable, even to researchers who spent most of their time interpreting EEGs. Thanks to fMRI, researchers and clinicians with only minimal knowledge of neuroanatomy and neurophysiology can see changes in patterns of color on the brain surface and correlate the patterns with a patient's mental activity.

A major challenge in molecular biology has long been making sense of an abundance of potentially confusing data—even prior to the start of automated nucleotide sequencing of the human genome. Perhaps for this reason, some of the most influential advances in the field have been based on highly visual research. For example, in performing the basic research that formed the basis for his laws of inheritance, Mendel focused on readily visible, obvious traits of pea plants that he could definitively recognize and categorize. He and his attendants could unequivocally determine whether the peas were round or wrinkled, if the plants were tall or short, and whether the flowers were white or purple. He avoided measuring non-visual parameters such as weight days to flowering. Perhaps Mendel's findings would have been noticed by his contemporaries if he had included graphics in his publication similar to the type currently used in textbooks to describe his experiments. Similarly, Thomas Morgan decided to use *Drosophilae melanogaster* to understand genetics, evolution, and development, in part because he could easily observe visual changes in the flies, such as eye color. It also helped that he could house thousands of experimental subjects in a few jars.

In bioinformatics, the majority of data is in an abstract form that needs visualization technologies to enhance user understanding. This need is most pronounced in the areas of sequence visualization, user interface development, protein structure visualization, and as a complement to numerical analyses, especially statistical analysis. In each application area, the rationale for using graphics instead of tables or strings of data is to shift the user's mental processing from reading and mathematical, logical interpretation to faster pattern recognition.

A common activity in protein structure prediction is comparing the predicted structure with one experimentally determined by X-ray crystallography and the same Nuclear Magnetic Resonance Imaging (NMR, also referred to as MRI or Magnetic Resonance Imaging) technology used in clinical medicine. The degree of similarity is often expressed as a Root Mean Squared Deviation (RMSD) figure, which represents the distance between the corresponding atoms in each molecule. Similar structures typically have an RMSD in the 1–3 Angstrom range, with larger RMSD values corresponding to greater deviations in similarity. However, as the size of the protein increases, the minimum RMSD to qualify for what is considered a good fit increases. Whereas an RMSD of 10 Angstroms would be considered a poor fit for a small protein, it might be considered excellent for a longer protein with several hundred amino acids.

Consider the challenge of comparing the protein structures depicted in Figure 5-2. Although the RMSD value provides a quantitative measure of closeness of fit, visualizing the overlap of structure pairs is more intuitive. In addition to being more intuitive than simple RMSD values, the visualization provides additional information—just as the graphics in Figure 5-1 add value to a simple tabular listing of clinical data. Even though the RMSD values for the four pairs of structures is identical, there is clearly a difference in what the value represents in each case.

The difference between the experimental and predicted structures in (A) is uniformly distributed. However, in (B), most of the molecules match exactly. The single point of deviation is responsible for the majority of the RMSD score. In (C), there is considerable mismatch in structure, but because of the small number of atoms involved in the calculation, the RMSD score seems to indicate a good match. For example, even though the larger molecules in (D) have the same RMSD score, the overlap is much tighter along the entire length of the proteins.

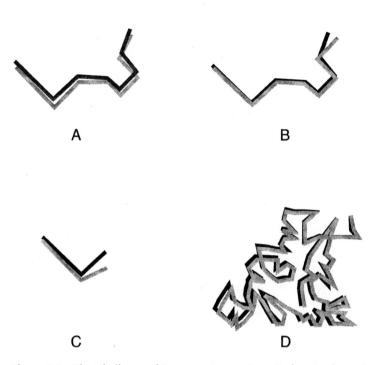

Figure 5-2 The Challenge of Structure Comparison. Each pair of protein backbones has the same RMSD value, but different relative amounts of structure similarity. Visualization, together with the RMSD value, provides the best indicator of structure similarity. A—Uniformly Distributed Difference; B—Localized Difference; C—Significant Difference with Few Atoms; D—Small Difference with Many Atoms.

Regardless of the visualization technologies used, the underlying assumption is that, for most researchers, the perceptual clues in graphical displays can enhance immediate understanding of the data being presented. Visualization technologies can provide an intuitive representation of the relationships among large groups of objects or data points that could otherwise be incomprehensible, while providing context and indications of relative importance.

This chapter explores data visualization techniques applicable to bioinformatics, from methods of generating 3D renderings of protein structures to creating maps of the physical location of genes on the chromosomes. The "Sequence Visualization" and "Structure Visualization" sections explore the technologies available to help researchers visualize nucleotide sequence data and protein structure data, respectively. The remainder of the chapter deals with the underlying technologies. For example, the "User Interface" section looks at how visualization techniques can make bioinformatics applications more easily understood and learned. "Animation Versus Simulation" explores difference between the two technologies, as applied to visualization. The "General Purpose" section explores the use of general-purpose software and hardware technologies that can be applied to bioinformatics. The "On the Horizon" and "Endnote" sections consider the prospects of practical virtual reality and other near-future visualization technologies.

SEQUENCE VISUALIZATION

Working with strings that represent nucleotide sequences is like programming in machine code. Although it's humanly possible to program a computer with strings of 0s and 1s, it's an arduous, error-prone, time-consuming process that doesn't lend itself to efficiency or easy maintenance and one that requires extensive program documentation. A step up from machine code is Assembly language, which allows programmers to use mnemonics such as "CLR" to clear a buffer and "ADD" to add two values. However, the programmer is still forced to think in terms of low-level CPU instructions. As a result, the programmer is constantly switching between a high-level problem such as how to best rotate a molecule in 3D space and a low-level problem, such as whether to use integer or floating-point math in the rotation algorithm.

Further up the programming hierarchy are languages such as C++, BASIC, and HTML that insulate programmers from the underlying computational hardware infrastructure and allow them to work at a level nearer the application purpose. Higher still are the flow diagrams or storyboards—maps of sorts—that provide a graphic overview of the application that can be understood and critiqued by non-programmers. Returning to nucleotide sequence work, the parallel to these storyboards are gene maps—high-level graphic representations of where specific sequences reside on a chromosome.

Sequence Maps

When it comes to visualizing nucleotide sequences, the obvious organizational metaphors are the amino acids, proteins, chromosome segments, and genes. Just as flow diagrams can be used to provide content and a high-level description of how the various components of a program are organized and function, gene maps provide a high-level view of relative and absolute gene and nucleotide sequence location. The quintessential gene mapping application is NCBI's Web-based Map Viewer, shown in Figure 5-3.

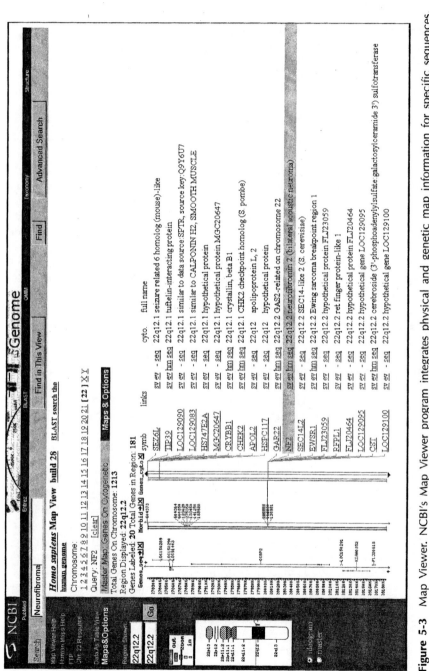

Figure 5-3 Map Viewer. NCBI's Map Viewer program integrates physical and genetic map information for specific sequences, proteins, and genes. This view shows the position of the gene associated with type 2 neurofibromatosis, located on chromosome 22.

The Web-based Map Viewer program, which is part of NCBI's Entrez integrated system, provides a composite interface to several of NCBI's online databases. Map Viewer enables users to identify a particular gene location with an organism's genome, the distance between genes, and the sequence data for a gene in a particular chromosomal region. Map Viewer illustrates how the main computational challenge in visualizing linear nucleotide sequences lies in integrating data from multiple databases. Map Viewer runs inside a Web-browser; all of the graphics processing and database integration is handled by NCBI.

Unlike working with three-dimensional protein structures, there is relatively little computational overhead involved in visualizing one-dimensional sequences. Sequences culled from NCBI's sequential databases are mapped onto the appropriate graphic and relevant links are provided to the corresponding databases that define the gene sequence and that are related to specific diseases.

Map Viewer provides a graphic depiction of nucleotide sequences through a composite of genetic, cytogenetic, physical, and radiation hybrid maps, each of which have their particular uses. Genetic maps show the relative position and order of genes and other sequences on a chromosome, and serve as high-level approximations of relative distances between sequences. Cytogenic maps provide a gross indication of the position of exons and entrons along a chromosome, based on optical microscope techniques. Physical maps show the actual physical location of sequences on a chromosome. Radiation hybrid maps link genetic and physical maps.

These different representations of a sequence along a chromosome have a variety of applications. For example, a cytogenic map is probably most appropriate for a researcher interested in quickly estimating the relative amount of DNA on a chromosome that is involved in coding. A physical map would be too detailed and difficult to work through, compared to a simple visual inspection of the relative percentage of exons to entrons across several chromosomes. Conversely, a researcher interested in the probability that the genes will separate during meiosis would be more interested in a genetic map, which shows distances between genes and markers (variations at a single genetic locus due to mutation or other alteration), measured in terms of recombination frequency. The recombination frequency figure reflects the tendency of genes located close together to be inherited together, while those that are far apart are more likely to be separated during meiosis. Markers include single nucleotide polymorphisms (SNPs), which are individual point mutations or substitutions of a single nucleotide anywhere in the genome.

The resolution provided by a physical map depends on the methodology used to create the map. The simplest form of physical mapping is cytogenic mapping, which is based on the banding of stained chromosomes that is visible through light microscopy. Generally more useful in bioinformatics work is high-resolution sequence-based physical mapping, which defines distances between markers and the intervening sequence in terms of base pairs. One of the most popular sequence-based physical mapping techniques uses sequence tagged sites (STSs), which are short, unique DNA sequences. A common source of STSs are expressed sequence tags (ESTs), which are short sequences derived from analysis of complementary DNA (cDNA). STSs can also be obtained by sequencing random pieces of cloned DNA.

Some of the most valuable mapping techniques provide connections between physical and genetic maps. The most common methods of identifying these connections involve radiation hybrid (RH) mapping and simple sequence length polymorphisms (SSLPs). Radiation hybrid mapping, which can be used to reveal the distance between genetic markers, is performed by exposing DNA to measured doses of radiation, which causes the DNA to break up. By varying the amount of radiation, the average distance between DNA sequence breaks can be modified. As a result, RH mapping can be used to localize virtually any genetic marker. Another approach to linking genetic and physical maps is based on SSLPs, which are arrays of repeat sequences that display length variations. Because SSLPs can serve as both a genetic marker and as the basis for sequence mapping—a Rosetta Stone of sorts—the technique is valuable in connecting physical and genetic maps.

The accuracy of the mapping process is highly dependent on computational methods used to manipulate the data acquired by experimentation or modeling. The typical mapping process, illustrated in Figure 5-4, involves an integration of several mapping approaches. Using link mapping, the chromosome is

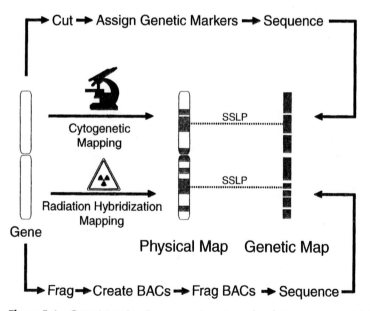

Figure 5-4 Gene Mapping Processes. A variety of techniques are available for creating physical and genetic maps.

cut into relatively large pieces, and markers are assigned in stages to make a more detailed map. Cytogenic mapping is used to create a first-pass, a low-resolution chromosome map that becomes more detailed as more marker data are collected and assigned to positions along the chromosome.

Sequence mapping involves first breaking up the chromosome at random into large fragments, which are then cloned with bacteria to make a bacterial artificial chromosome (BAC). These BACs are ordered in such a way as to maximize the contiguous regions while using the minimum number of BACs. Because BACs are too long to sequence, each one is broken at random into fragments that can be handled by a sequencing machine—less than around 500 nucleotides—and each fragment is sequenced. In this way the sequence of each BAC, and eventually of each contiguous region, are defined. The result is a physical map that may have a few gaps between contiguous regions.

STRUCTURE VISUALIZATION

One of the primary activities in proteomics R&D is determining and visualizing the 3D structure of proteins in order to find where drugs might modulate their activity. Other activities include identifying all of the proteins produced by a given cell or tissue and determining how these proteins interact. The current methods available for realizing these later activities include time-consuming protein purification and X-ray crystallography—both activities that take significant time, even with robotic automation. As such, it's generally understood by the molecular biology research community that the sequencing of the human genome, which will likely take several more years to complete, is relatively trivial compared to definitively characterizing the proteome.

Barring the introduction of some new technology, cataloging, interpreting, and dissecting the proteome will take many years. Unlike a nucleotide sequence, which is a relatively static structure, proteins are dynamic entities that change their shape and association with other molecules as a function of temperature, chemical interactions, pH, and other changes in the environment. Grasping the static structure of the approximately 30,000 proteins of the human proteome is difficult enough for many researchers, much less their potentially unlimited variation.

In contrast to visualizing the sequence of nucleotides on a strand of DNA, visualizing the primary structure of a protein adds little to the knowledge of protein function. More interesting and relevant are the higher-order structures. For example, understanding the docking of two proteins is greatly facilitated by visualizing the two 3D structures interacting in 3D space. Visualizing a protein's tertiary structure is valuable in comparing protein structure predictions.

Visualization Tools

The list of technologies in Table 5-1 only hints at the hundreds of available visualization tools that are either available or under development in bioinformatics. The vast majority of bioinformatics-specific tools are shareware utilities developed with government funding, supplemented with a few dozen commercial offerings. Many tools are hardware- or process-specific. For example, there are dozens of graphical interfaces or visualization tools made expressly for microarray devices and the data they generate. Some of these tools are written in low-level computer languages such as C++, and others are adaptations of high-level tools, such as the graphical user interface editors that ship with commercial database engines. In addition to these bioinformatics-centric tools, there are general-purpose visualization technologies that can be used in bioinformatics applications.

Table 5-1 Visualization Technologies. Visualization tools leverage the pattern-recognition capabilities of the viewer's visual apparatus as opposed to the logical, intellectual capabilities that can be more easily saturated.

Visualization Tool	Examples
Nucleotide Location	Map Viewer
Protein Structure	SWISS-PDBViewer, WebMol, RasMol, Protein Explorer, Cn3D, VMD, MolMol, MidasPlus, Pymol, Chime, Chimera
User Interface	Third-Party Browsers, VRML, Java Applets, C++
General-Purpose Software	Microsoft Excel, Strata Vision 3D, Max3D, 3D-Studio, Ray Dream Studio, StatView, SAS/Insight, Minitab, Matlab
General-Purpose Hardware	Stereo Goggles, Data gloves, 3D (Stereo) Displays, Haptic Devices

Rendering Tools

Most of the imaging work in bioinformatics involves data from the Protein Data Bank (PDB) or the Molecular Modeling Database (MMDB). Searching for a structure is typically through protein name or ID. For example, data in the PDB is accessible by name or four-letter identifier. As illustrated Figure 5-5, the identifier for Glutamine Synthetase is 1FPY. Note from the summary information in PDB that the Glutamine Synthetase molecule is represented by almost 46,000 atoms, which explains in part why rendering the data is so computationally expensive. The resolution listed for the data—the RMSD—is 2.89 Angstroms.

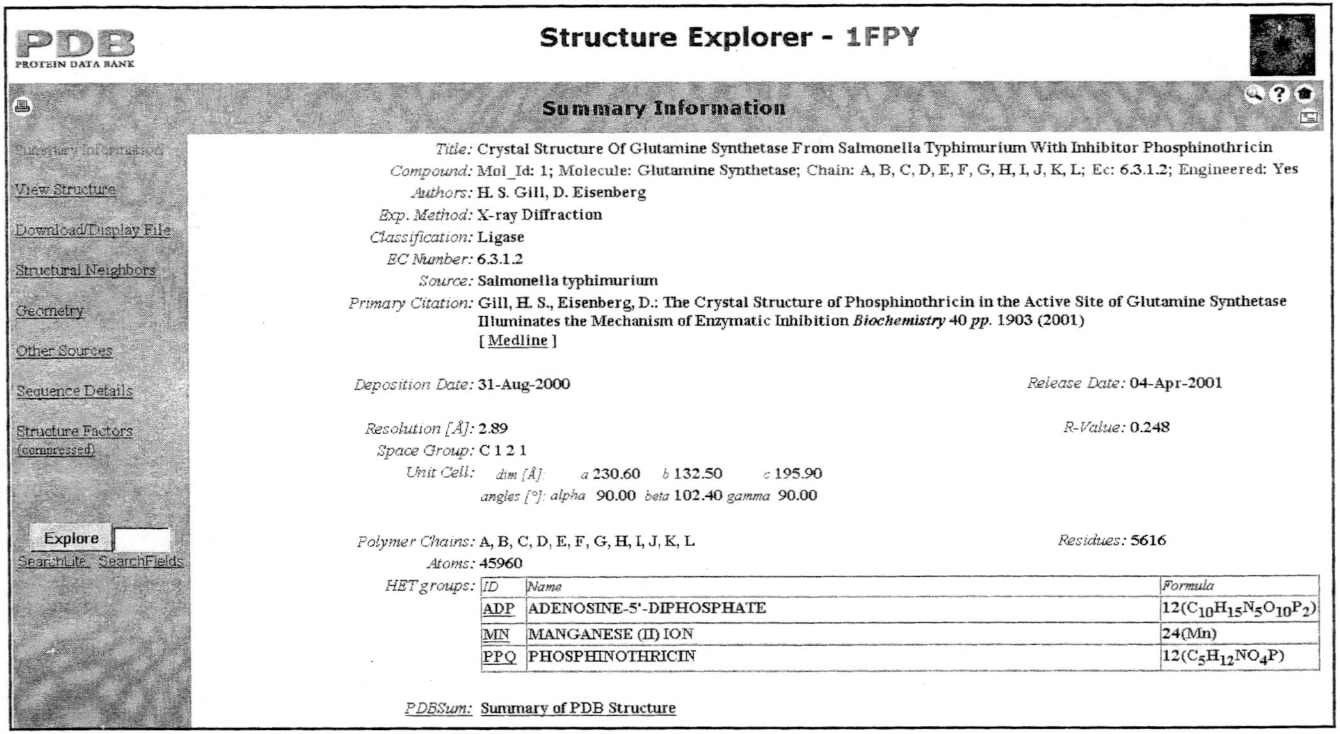

Figure 5-5   The Protein Data Bank (PDB). Here, the PDB shows summary data for Glutamine Synthetase, and the four-letter code for the protein, 1FPY. Note that there are almost 46,000 atoms and over 5,600 residues in the structure.

Representative protein structure rendering programs available as free downloads from the Internet include RasMol, Cn3D, PyMol, SWISS-PDBViewer, and Chimera. A summary of the features of these programs appears in Table 5-2.

Table 5-2 Application Feature Summary. Some of the more popular protein structure rendering programs are summarized here. All of these programs are available from the Internet at no cost for non-commercial users.

Feature	RasMol	Cn3D	PyMol	SWISS-PDBViewer	Chimera
Architecture	Stand-alone	Plug-in	Web-enabled	Web-enabled	Web-enabled
Manipulation Power	Low	High	High	High	High
Hardware Requirements	Low/Moderate	High	High	Moderate	High
Ease of Use	High; command-line language	Moderate	Moderate	High	Moderate; command-line language and GUI
Special Features	Small size; very easy to install and use; established user base; highly portable	Powerful; GUI	Powerful; GUI; ray-tracing option	Powerful; GUI	Powerful; GUI; built-in extensions for collaboration
Output Quality	Moderate	Very high	High	High	Very high
Documentation	Good	Good	Limited	Good	Very good
Support	Online and users groups	Online and users groups	Online and users groups	Online and users groups	Online and users groups
Speed	High	Moderate	Moderate	Moderate	Moderate/Slow
OpenGL Support	Yes	Yes	Yes	Yes	Yes

Table 5-2 Application Feature Summary. Some of the more popular protein structure rendering programs are summarized here. All of these programs are available from the Internet at no cost for non-commercial users. *(continued)*

Feature	RasMol	Cn3D	PyMol	SWISS-PDBViewer	Chimera
Extensibility	No	No	Yes; supports Python	No	Highly extensible; supports Python
Operating Systems	Universal	Universal	Universal	Universal	Universal

The selection of a protein structure rendering program should be a function of ease of use, power, speed, special features, cost, hardware requirements, documentation and support, and overall functionality. For example, rendering 3D protein structures can be extremely computationally intensive. The more complex the rendering output, the greater the computational load, and the more time required to render each image. Often, time and performance limitations dictate the use of a simple, fast rendering package such as RasMol (see Figure 5-6) for day-to-day rendering, and one of the higher-end packages, such as Chimera, for publication-quality output.

The minimum functionality of the open-source (source code is available for free or low-cost non-commercial) rendering programs available on the Web includes the selective viewing and manipulation of subsets of atoms, wireframe, ball-and-stick, or ribbon renditions of a protein. Each representation emphasizes different protein properties. For example, the ball-and-stick PyMol rendering of Glutamine Synthetase in Figure 5-7 emphasizes atoms and bonds. Wireframe views, such as the PyMol renderings in Figures 5-8 and 5-9, emphasize the molecular bonds. Ribbon diagrams, such as the Chimera rendering of Glutamine Synthetase shown in Figure 5-10, emphasize the protein's secondary structure, whereas the Van der Waals surface diagram of Deoxy Hemoglobin in Figure 5-11 rendered in SWISS-PDBViewer emphasizes the atomic volumes. Another popular format is the backbone, which shows the overall molecule structure (see Figure 5-12).

RasMol, placed in the public domain in 1993 by Roger Sayle and maintained today by the University of Massachusetts, Amherst, is the easiest-to-use molecular rendering program available on the Internet. Although this stand-alone program has been supplanted in functionality by a host of derivative programs, such as Chime and Protein Explorer, RasMol remains one of the standard tools in bioinformatics visualization. RasMol is limited in functionality compared to programs introduced in the past decade. However, it has a small footprint of less than a megabyte, runs on a standard laptop computer, and is computationally efficient.

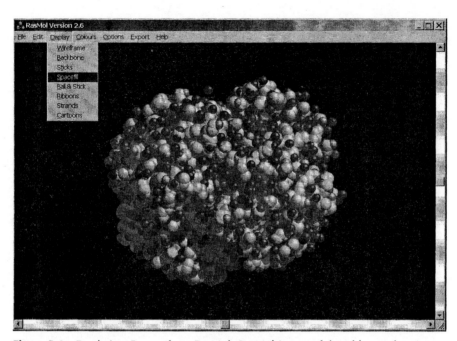

Figure 5-6   Rendering Output from RasMol. RasMol is one of the oldest and easiest to use molecular rendering programs available for bioinformatics work. This example shows the basic display options available. The molecule is Deoxy Hemoglobin.

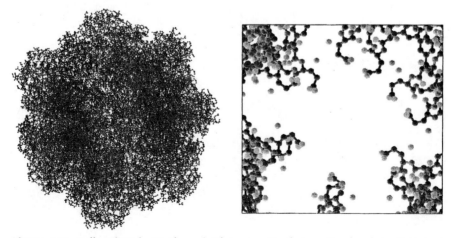

Figure 5-7   Ball-and-Stick Display of Glutamine Synthetase Rendered in PyMol. A close-up of the center of the molecule is shown on the right. The ball-and-stick format emphasizes atoms and bonds.

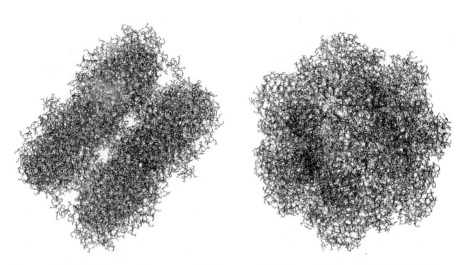

Figure 5-8 Wireframe Diagram of Glutamine Synthetase Rendered in PyMol. The wireframe view, shown here rendered edge-on (left) and face-on (right), emphasizes the atomic bonds. Compare with Figure 5-9.

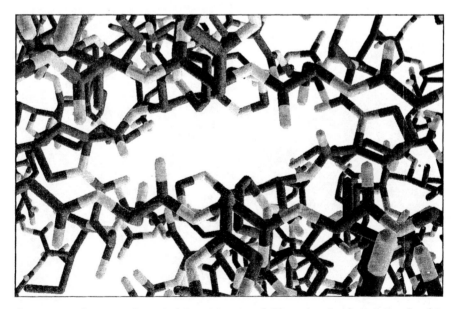

Figure 5-9 Close-Up of a Wireframe Diagram of Glutamine Synthetase Rendered in PyMol. In this view, bonds are highlighted without being obstructed by atoms.

Cn3D, which is closely linked with NCBI's MMDB, is a browser plug-in that supports interactive viewing of 3D protein structures in a Web browser environment. In addition to standard features such as selective coloring of subsets of the protein structure to emphasize certain regions of interest, Cn3D can correlate structure and sequence data to locate residues in a crystal structure that correspond to known disease mutations and can display structure-structure alignment. Cn3D can also export images in a variety of formats for publications and for use in other rendering engines, including high-end commercial rendering programs.

PyMol is a Web-enabled rendering program that emphasizes power and functionality over ease of use. PyMol is often used to produce graphics for publication, in part because of its built-in ray-tracing function. Ray tracing is a computationally challenging method of rendering an image so that shadows, highlights, and other photo-realistic features appear in the final image. The technique involves calculating the color and intensity of each pixel in an image by tracing single rays of light backward and determining how they were affected on their way from the light source illuminating the molecular structures in the image. In addition, PyMol supports the Python scripting language (hence the name), allowing automated processing of images.

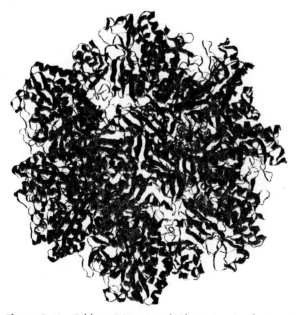

Figure 5-10   Ribbon Diagram of Glutamine Synthetase Rendered in Chimera. Ribbon diagrams emphasize the protein's secondary structure.

Figure 5-11   Van der Waals Surface Diagram of Deoxy Hemoglobin Rendered in SWISS-PDBViewer. This view emphasizes atomic volume.

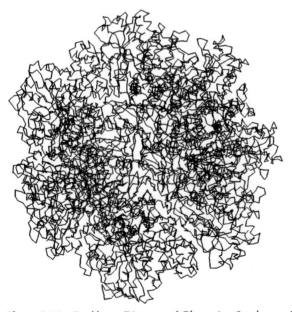

Figure 5-12   Backbone Diagram of Glutamine Synthetase Rendered in RasMol. This view emphasizes the protein's overall structure.

SWISS-PDBViewer was acquired by GlaxoSmithKline and then made available to non-commercial users at no cost. Like RasMol, SWISS-PDBViewer emphasizes ease of use over power and functionality. Even so, as illustrated in Figure 5-13, SWISS-PDBViewer is feature-laden. In terms of functionality, it's somewhere between RasMol and Pymol. As such, computer hardware requirements are moderate. Like RasMol, it's capable of reasonable performance on a low-end desktop or a laptop computer. The graphical user interface provides access to a variety of features. Unlike Pymol, however, there is no scripting language, which limits extensibility of the program.

Chimera is a high-end, highly extensible rendering program from the Computer Graphics Laboratory, University of California, San Francisco. Of the programs reviewed here, Chimera is clearly the most powerful, most feature-packed, and most demanding application. Features include multiple view tools, labeling of amino acids by a variety of criteria, alignment of molecules, and the ability to mix multiple renderings, such as transparent surfaces with ball-and-stick views. In addition to extensive online user documentation,

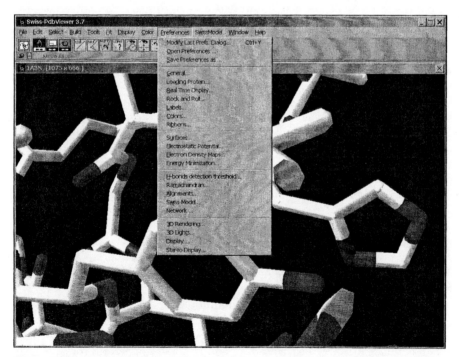

Figure 5-13 SWISS-PDBViewer. The Preferences menu hints at the extensive rendering capabilities of the program. The image in the background is a wireframe view of Deoxy Hemoglobin.

there is an online programmer's guide that describes how the plug-in can be integrated with custom applications. The prices for this functionality are a relatively steep learning curve and the need for a high-end workstation for productive work. For example, the download is over 27 MB, and the developers recommend a 1 GHz Pentium with high-end video hardware. One of the downsides of Chimera is that it is still under development, so some of the features may not be fully implemented. Chimera is the successor to the popular UCSF Midas and MidasPlus programs.

In addition to Cn3D, RasMol, PyMol, SWISS-PDBViewer, and Chimera, there are dozens of alternative free and commercial rendering systems available. Most of these programs tend to be predecessors of more functional programs either under development or recently released. Even though many of these programs overlap each other and the programs discussed here in functionality, they are typically very good at a particular function and require less hardware power than the latest do-everything packages. For example, MolMol supports the display of electrostatic potentials across a protein molecule. MidasPlus, a predecessor to Chimera, has a sequence editing feature that allows the user to define a point mutation—substitute one amino acid for another—and visualize the result on the protein structure. MolSript, Ligplot, and Dimplot are specifically designed to create images for print publication, in that they support fine control over the output formatting. Ligplot additionally generates 2D schematic drawings of bonds and structure, and Dimplot, a variant of Ligplot, renders interactions among multiple protein chains.

General-purpose rendering systems can be used to obtain images that fulfill special criteria, such as extra high-resolution images for publication, enhanced color or transparency options to emphasize specific regions on the protein, and other, custom applications. For example, a general-purpose 3D rendering engine such as Strata3D Pro, Bryce, Max3D, or LightWave can render molecules within the context of cell wall or other structure as part of an illustration for print or film production. Similarly, a fly-through of protein structure can be rendered in one of these programs for teaching purposes. Aside from cost, which can range from a few hundred dollars to several thousand dollars, the downside of using one of these commercial, general-purpose rendering programs is that setup time may be dozens of hours per molecule. Most of this time is typically spent translating data from PDB or MMDB into a format supported by the rendering engine.

One of the challenges of working with multiple rendering engines is that the expected file format and contents may vary from one system to the next. Most rendering applications, including RasMol, are compatible with the PDB format, which contains a simple description of amino acid sequences. Programs that use the PDB format are required to use rules—which may vary from one program to the next—to construct the protein structure, based on sequence data alone. That is, these programs not only render the image, but perform modeling of the underlying data as well.

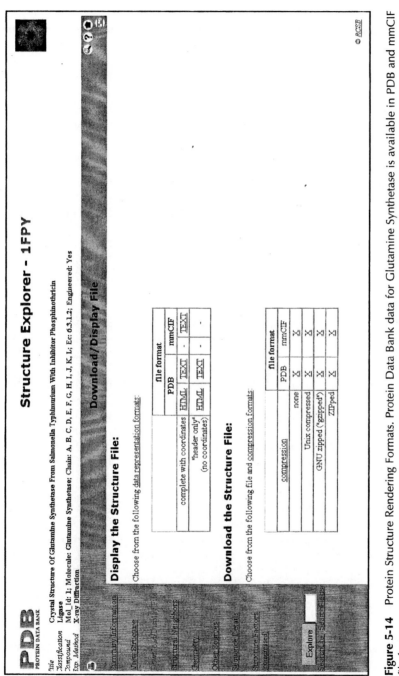

Figure 5-14 Protein Structure Rendering Formats. Protein Data Bank data for Glutamine Synthetase is available in PDB and mmCIF file formats.

The result is potentially wide variations between displays of rendering systems using the same PDB data. In contrast, the MMDB contains data on the molecular bonds in the protein structure in ANS.1 (Abstract Syntax Notation number One) format. Because the data on molecular bonds is provided, and not generated by the rendering engine, programs that render ANS.1 data tend to produce results that are highly consistent with each other. This doesn't necessarily translate to greater accuracy in the rendered image, however.

In addition to the PDB and ANS.1 formats, another common format for protein structure rendering engines is mmCIF (Macromolecular Crystallographic Information Format). Note that the PDB supports both PDB and mmCIF formats, as shown in Figure 5-14. Because reading in data in the mmCIF relational format is so extensive, it generally requires too much in computational resources for continual use. As such, it's much better used as an archival format. In contrast, data in the hierarchical ANS.1 format loads quickly, which is one reason why the ANS.1 format supported by the MMDB is preferable for viewing applications designed for browsing 3D protein structures.

USER INTERFACE

The user interface is the veneer that hides the intricacies of the computer hardware and software and presents users with images, sounds, and graphics that they can interact with on a cognitive level. Properly constructed, the user interface focuses the computer user's attention on what's being presented—a protein structure, for example—not on the image-rendering software or the display hardware. Every computer application and every workstation has a user interface defined by hardware and software. Whether the workstation is running a computer operating system such as Microsoft Windows, a Web browser extension designed to draw 3D protein structures, such as WebMol, or a Web-based nucleotide sequence viewer, such as Map Viewer, it's the user interface that defines the usability and usefulness of the underlying application and accessibility of the associated data.

The user interface determines the density of information that can be presented to the user, as defined by Information Theory, for which the user interface is the medium through which the data flow. As shown in Figure 5-15, the application—a 3D protein visualization tool, for example—is the information source, and the data created by the application is the message. The computer interface hardware, including the video card and monitor, is the transmitter. The user interface, including the buttons and other graphics rendered on the computer monitor, serves as the medium. In this model, the irrelevant data includes components of the system that interfere with the message generated by the application, such as superfluous graphics, distracting colors, and other irrelevant data that appear on the computer monitor, which only serves to confuse the user.

One purpose of the user interface is to simplify and focus the user's attention—superfluous data detracts from this purpose. The receiver in the Information Theory model is the user's perceptual apparatus, including eyes for visual content, ears for audio content, and proprioceptors for tactile or haptic content. Finally, the message, now containing relevant and irrelevant data, reaches the ultimate destination—the user's awareness.

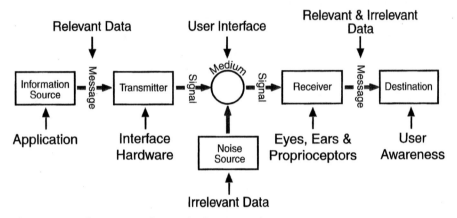

Figure 5-15   The User Interface and Information Theory.

The user interface is the medium and therefore a major bandwidth-limiting element in the delivery of data from the application to the user; everything that affects the effectiveness of the user interface affects delivery of data. Regardless of the complexity and technical marvel of the underlying molecular biology database and any related visualization tools, users see and interact with the user interface. This interaction with the user interface defines the utility of the 3D molecular models and other data displayed on the screen. Designing an interface to support bioinformatics, or any niche area for that matter, involves more than simply deciding on the layout for buttons and check boxes on a display.

User Interface Components

Even the simplest user interface can be viewed as a complex, multi-tiered structure that supports a dialogue or a communications channel between the user and the computer and between the user and the concepts presented by the software executing on the computer. The user interface minimally consists of a physical interface between the user and the computer. The user interface may also include graphical, logical, emotional, or intelligent interface components, as illustrated in Figure 5-16.

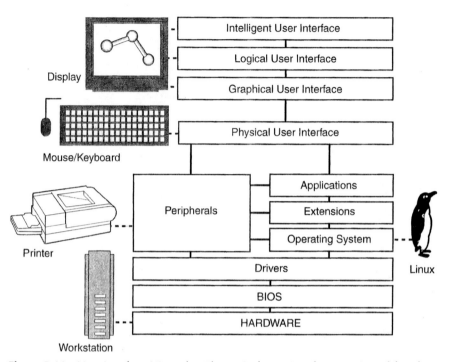

Figure 5-16   User Interface Hierarchy. The typical user interface consists of four basic components: the physical, graphical, logical, and intelligent interfaces. Higher-level components may be intentionally left out of the user interface in some systems.

This hierarchical model is especially relevant when discussing multimedia interfaces, which may incorporate graphics, video, and tactile feedback. A user interface may support sound, but sound has limited applicability in making molecular biology data more understandable. The model reflects our heavy reliance on visual information for communications, and most user interface work is graphical in nature. The hierarchical interface model also highlights the tactical aspects of human-computer interfaces, which may be critical in virtual reality presentation of data. Many concepts, such as energy wells, Van der Waals forces, and structural stability can be perceived more naturally through haptic devices, negating the need for the user to interpret graphics and colors used to represent physical forces.

The low-level interface layer, the physical layer, is concerned with the physical input and, more relevant as a component of visualization, physical output. With virtual reality visualization systems, this layer includes data gloves and other devices to manipulate synthetic 3D molecules or other objects. The physical layer also includes monitors of all types, haptic controls, speech synthesizers, and complex mechanisms such as robotic arms.

A major component of the physical interface is the monitor. Traditional cathode ray tube (CRT) monitors and LCD panels limit the quality of graphics and text that can be displayed. Although LCD monitors are more space- and energy-efficient, higher-end CRT monitors are considered superior for extended use because of their higher maximum refresh rate, and greater maximum resolution, brightness, and contrast. LCD monitors are clearly superior as head-mounted displays because of their lighter weight and the safety afforded by their lower operating voltage. The most promising display technology for virtual reality applications in bioinformatics uses a low-powered laser to paint an image directly on the wearer's retina. The result is a virtual, wide-screen display in which protein molecules or other objects appear to float in space directly in front of the wearer.

One of the more intriguing physical interface components is the haptic controller, which is a specially constructed electromechanical mouse, or joystick, or other controller that provides the computer user with computer-mediated tactile sensations (see Figure 5-17). Haptic devices use electric motors to provide variable resistance to the movement of the controlling device, allowing users to experience the elasticity, the viscosity, the texture of surfaces, and vibrations. In bioinformatics, the major use of haptics is in manipulating and testing protein binding sites in a virtual reality environment, with the amount of force provided by the interface used to provide an indication of the ease or difficulty in manipulating the quaternary structure of a protein introducing a molecule at a particular binding site.

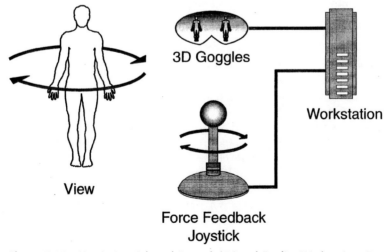

Figure 5-17 Haptic Joystick and Part of a Virtual Reality Workstation. Force feedback joysticks and 3D (stereo) goggles can be used to create virtual reality workstations in which proteins and other molecules exhibit attraction and repulsion as they are manipulated like physical objects.

Moving up the user interface hierarchy, the graphical user interface represents everything displayed on the computer display. Good graphical interface design is an art that's difficult to master. For example, even subtle differences in the relative size of objects displayed on the screen can profoundly affect how they are perceived. The graphical user interface typically makes use of mental models, which are the metaphors that give a graphical interface meaning. The desktop metaphor, with its desktop, trashcan, documents, and file folders, exemplifies how a metaphor can be used to provide a large number of users who have diverse backgrounds with a conceptual model of how and where information in a computer operating system fits together. Graphical interface designers have to make assumptions about the previous experiences of the typical user for an interface to work. The level of graphic complexity most appropriate for a graphical interface balances the need to focus a user's attention on a 3D model or other data, with hardware limitations, and the resources necessary to create a graphical interface.

The logical interface level is about rules, guidelines, and standards of interface behavior, such as how an interface should display the image of a molecule. A well-designed logical interface layer, like a properly executed graphical interface layer, allows users to focus on the problem at hand, such as identifying the location of a specific gene on a physical map, rather than on the mechanics of operating the interface. Logical interface design relies heavily on the concept of information design, which deals with the organization, presentation, clarity, and complexity of information. Information design focuses on communications and on developing a framework for expressing information, not aesthetics. The primary metric for assessing the degree to which an interface supports a logical model is commonly referred to as cognitive ergonomics.

Intelligent interfaces rely on a variety of pattern-recognition techniques to adapt to the user's behavior. Ideally, an intelligent interface learns user preferences by monitoring the user's responses to certain situations, tailoring the experience to the user's current interests, and never demands that users explicitly state their preferences. The inner workings of an intelligent interface may be very complex and rely on an elaborate knowledge base coupled to an expert system or statistical analysis program. Intelligent interfaces share many properties in common with intelligent agents, which are independent programs capable of completing complex assignments without intervention, as opposed to tools that must be directly manipulated by a user. By monitoring a user's activity on a Web site or within an application, an intelligent interface may learn, for example, user preferences for the color of a protein's acute region or the responsiveness of the protein rotation to mouse or joystick movement.

Alternative Metaphors

Visualization, whether as part of the user interface or as a means of presenting structure or sequence data, is largely about creating and supporting metaphors, which transform the data into a form that means something to the user. The pie chart is a useful metaphor only to the extent that users understand the difference between the slices of the pie and how that translates to relative quantities. The pie chart works for most of us because we intuitively understand the metaphor. However, the pie chart, like the Windows desktop metaphor, isn't very data-dense and doesn't lend itself to communicating advanced biotechnology concepts, such as tertiary protein structures. As a result, visual metaphors for user interfaces intended to present molecular biology data are necessarily more sophisticated than ordinary business graphics, especially when the challenge is to present large volumes of complex data.

One of the challenges of creating a suitable metaphor for bioinformatics work is the variety of potential users of the applications and their level of expertise. For example, bioinformatics researchers, high-school and college students studying molecular biology, research fellows, clinicians, and even the marketing departments of international pharmaceutical companies may use a given suite of applications. Devising a reasonable interface metaphor is therefore a compromise between information density, ease of use, and power—the ability to quickly and easily manipulate data communicated through the interface.

Bioinformatics is pushing the metaphor component of visualization technology to new levels. For example, even though the desktop, folder, and trashcan user interface—introduced by the Xerox Star, popularized by the Apple Lisa and Macintosh, and fully exploited and commercialized by Microsoft—is the dominant metaphor on desktop computers, it fails to reflect the needs of bioinformatics. Many researchers in bioinformatics contend that a new user interface is in order, one not based on folders and trashcans, but on molecular biology metaphors such as the Central Dogma, where chromosomes and genes provide organizational hierarchies in which form and function are mapped.

Work on interface design in clinical medicine provides one model for how a niche-specific interface can become the de facto standard. In clinical medicine, the metaphor of a paper medical record is pervasive. Many clinicians interact with a patient's electronic medical record through the metaphor of a paper medical chart in which the data are arranged by the patient's chief complaint, medical history, review of systems, physical exam, and laboratory results and never see or interact directly with the underlying operating system. Whether a bioinformatics-centric user interface evolves out of academic or commercial molecular biology laboratories depends on the creativity and resources of those in the field.

Developing a completely new user interface from scratch is a formidable task. It's easier to extend current interfaces through commercial utilities or by writing browser extensions, than to specify a new interface. For example, eXtensible Markup Language (XML), Virtual Reality Modeling Language (VRML), PHP: Hypertext Processing (PHP), and similar high-level languages can be used to extend browser functionality to work with manipulating 3D images and to create a new interface metaphor.

Another option is to select from commercial or shareware alternative front ends to desktop and Web-based applications that use alternative metaphors. TheBrain Technologies, illustrated in Figure 5-18, is but one of many alternatives to the business-oriented desktop metaphor. It uses the metaphor of a non-hierarchical mesh of linked associations, in which concepts are related to each other through logical association. For example, a mesh of associations based on the Central Dogma can be established in which nucleotide sequences are associated with protein structures through an intermediary link that associates proteins with both 3D structures and with genes that code for the specific protein.

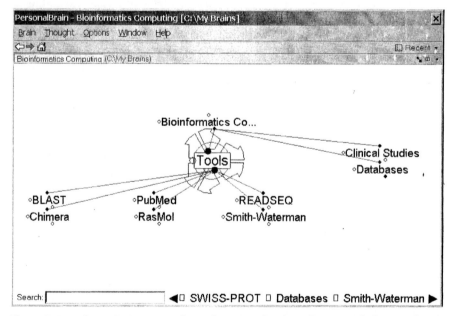

Figure 5-18   Alternative User Interface. This example of an alternative desktop and Web browser, TheBrain Technologies Corporation's PersonalBrain, illustrates how an alternative metaphor can be used to provide access to computer and Web-based bioinformatics applications and data.

Often the task defines the most appropriate user interface. For example, if the data are from a DNA microarray device, then an interface that mirrors the array of florescent markers may be the most appropriate, especially if the user is the same person who works directly with the microarray equipment. However, if the user is removed from the device and works more closely with the binding sites, then an interface based on a metaphor of nucleotide sequences may be more effective in support of his work.

Display Architecture

The user interface is defined and limited by the overall system architecture, especially as it relates to how the data and interface are communicated to the workstation and its display. As illustrated in Figure 5-19, system architectures range from standard Web-browser–based systems based on native Web browsers to stand-alone systems that use the Internet only as an asynchronous data source.

In the native browser model (A), the user interface is defined by the application running on the server, within the constraints of the browser environment. The user interface to the application—a graphic sequence display, for example—can range from a simple, static line art display to an interactive, graphically rich environment with color graphics and links to numerous web-based resources. Furthermore, since the program actually executes on the server, the responsiveness of the application is a function of the server performance and the bandwidth of the communications link to the Internet.

In the model in which a Java applet is employed (B), the server sends Java script to the workstation browser environment, which interprets and executes the script locally. This approach, typified by the Chime plug-in, provides potentially greater interactivity and responsiveness because the code runs locally and can take advantage of local workstation's processing power. In addition, the bandwidth limitation of the Internet isn't normally an issue nor is the degree of interactivity possible because only data and Java strings are communicated from server to the workstation. The primary downside of this architecture is that the user must periodically download the latest version of the applet or plug-in.

In example (C), a Web-enabled application interactively makes use of data over the Internet, but the application runs locally and extends the browser environment. As exemplified by PyMol, high levels of user interactivity are possible with this approach, and performance isn't affected by the potentially slow-speed Internet connection. The application can use any metaphor, input devices, and user interfaces within the limits of the operating system, local hardware, programming language, and the designer's skill and imagination. The other major approach to system architecture (D) is a stand-alone application, such as RasMol, that uses data from a local database. These data may be downloaded from local experiments or downloaded asynchronously from the public databases on the Internet.

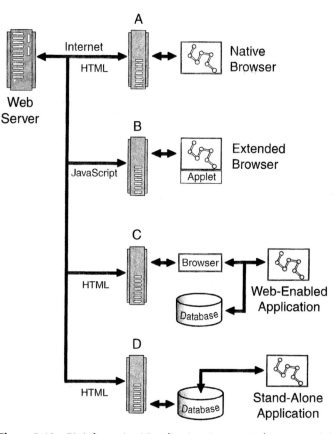

Figure 5-19 Bioinformatics Visualization System Architectures. (A) Native browser; (B) Extended browser; (C) Web-enabled application; (D) Stand-alone application.

Given this range of possible architectures, what remains to be defined are the implementation-specific capabilities that support visualization of data, such as nucleotide sequence or protein structures, and the format of the results of data analysis. Due to the wide range of open-source tools available, the new tools under development, and the additions being made to existing tools, selecting the best tool for a particular application generally begins with exploring the bioinformatics Web sites.

A summary of the characteristics of the four basic architectures is provided in Table 5-3. Note that a native browser application, such as Map Viewer, generally has high marks for portability and ease of maintenance. Portability is not a concern because virtually every computer platform is compatible with Netscape Navigator and/or Internet Explorer. In addition, because the graphics-rendering program sits on the server, there is nothing to update on the workstation running Map Viewer—with the possible exception of the Web browser if an application requires a later version than is installed on the workstation. The downside of this third-part maintenance of the application is that the user interface is limited to whatever the original designers defined; there isn't an easy way to alter how data are displayed in the Map Viewer program, for example. Similarly, the performance of Map Viewer is limited to that of the server, so there is little in the way that be done on the workstation to increase performance other than assuring a high-speed connection.

Table 5-3 Visualization Program Architecture Characteristics.

Architecture	Portability	Performance	User Interface Flexibility	Ease of Maintenance
Native Browser	X			X
Extended Browser	X	X	X	
Web-Enabled		X	X	
Stand-Alone		X		

The extended browser model gets high marks for portability, performance, and user interface flexibility, and, compared to a native browser application, less than stellar marks for ease of maintenance. Most, but not all, plug-ins are compatible with every platform that supports a Web browser. Some plug-ins are optimized for Netscape Navigator and don't perform well or at all with Microsoft's Internet Explorer. The Chime plug-in, for example, requires a Netscape browser. Moving from a native browser environment to a plug-in that executes on the local workstation means that local hardware can be used to improve program performance.

Most of this performance increase is due to support for high-performance OpenGL-compatible graphics cards. OpenGL is a cross-platform standard (Windows, MacOS 9 and X, Linux, and UNIX) for 3D rendering and hardware acceleration. The underlying architecture of an OpenGL-compatible video card is usually some variation of that depicted in Figure 5-20. An application communicates through the workstation bus to the controller hardware in the video card that drives a monitor.

OpenGL-compatible video cards are designed to accelerate specific graphics procedures. These cards have their own high-performance microprocessor, high-speed video RAM, and support programs stored in firmware that can be accessed through software drivers. Image data communicated to the video

Video Card

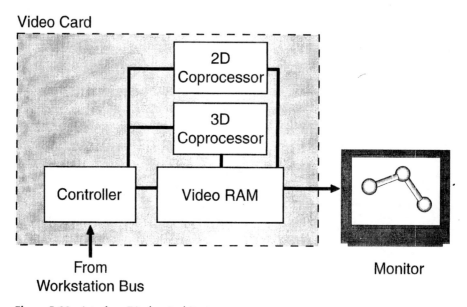

From
Workstation Bus

Monitor

Figure 5-20   Interface Display Architecture.

card from the workstation through the main bus are buffered and processed according to the type of content. Content such as windows, buttons, and icons common to the Windows interface is sent to the 2D graphics coprocessor that contains instructions in firmware optimized for rendering these objects. These and other graphical interface elements are rendered to the Video RAM, which is configured as a frame buffer. In this way, the processor can be rendering the next frame or image while simultaneously driving the monitor with the current image, allowing a high-speed refresh rate that eliminates flicker.

In a similar way, 3D structures are rendered at high-speed by the dedicated 3D graphics coprocessor. The processor is optimized for making the many calculations required for rendering 3D images—including smoothing image edges, shading, applying texture maps to objects, providing perspective corrections, and mapping polygons over wireframe skeletons—thereby freeing the computer's main CPU(s) to do other tasks. High-end, specialized workstations from Sun, Silicon Graphics, DEC, and other manufacturers often use proprietary graphic support hardware that may not be OpenGL-compatible. Programs that work on these computers must use special video driver software in order to take full advantage of proprietary high-performance hardware.

Returning to the discussion of visualization program architectures, both Web-enabled and stand-alone applications receive high marks for performance, for the same reasons cited for extend browser applications.

Web-enabled programs such as PyMol and stand-alone applications such as RasMol are designed to take advantage of local RAM and CPU power, as well as OpenGL-compatible video cards. Because updates to programs must be downloaded from the Web, maintenance is an issue, and it's up to the user to maintain the latest version of the program and keep associated drivers up-to-date. Portability is also an issue for Web-enabled and stand-alone programs because they have to be installed on every workstation that may be used for rendering. In addition, stand-alone applications tend to have a fixed user interface that can't be easily modified. In contrast, others, such as Chimera from the Computer Graphics Laboratory, University of California, San Francisco, can be heavily modified and integrated into other programs.

ANIMATION VERSUS SIMULATION

Visualization tools can be grouped into three major categories: simulation, animation, and static graphics. Simulation involves the dynamic, computationally intensive interaction of the user with a program that reevaluates the underlying data and renders the results. Animation, in contrast, involves the display of pre-computed data that can be accessed and analyzed as needed to illustrate certain findings or relationships. The data in the PDB, for example, serves as the data for a rendering program such as SWISS-PDBViewer that can be used to create animations of rendered molecules from various perspectives. Rotating a protein structure, as in Figure 5-21, doesn't result in a change in the underlying data. Static graphics, like animations, use fixed data. As in animations, viewing an image from different perspectives doesn't modify the underlying data.

Some of the rendering packages provide limited simulation capabilities. For example, SWISS-PDBViewer allows the user to create point mutations along a molecule and then visualize the results. This is a limited form of simulation, in that a more powerful system can compute the 3D interaction of multiple proteins as well as alter underlying sequences.

GENERAL-PURPOSE TECHNOLOGIES

The bioinformatics research community is characterized by cooperation in the sharing of data and in application development. Thanks to the efforts of thousands of researchers in laboratories around the world, there are libraries of bioinformatics-specific applications that are freely shared among members of the community. Many of these applications deal with visualization, given the overwhelming need to have an intuitive means of manipulating the vast amounts of molecular biology data being generated daily worldwide.

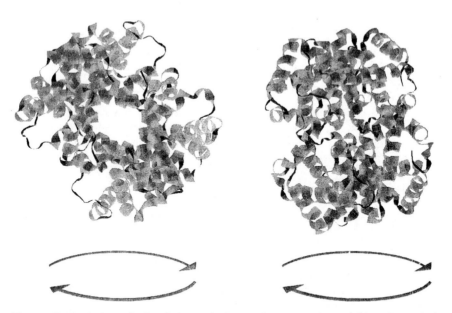

Figure 5-21 Animated Rendering of Deoxy Human Hemoglobin Created by SWISS-PDBViewer. Rotating structures doesn't result in a recomputation of the underlying data, but only affects the visualization of the data previously computed. This figure illustrates two separate frames captured from the spinning animation.

Many general-purpose data-analysis programs provide reasonable visualization capabilities that can be used in bioinformatics work. The challenge is identifying a proprietary or open-source software package that either accepts standard bioinformatics data formats or that uses a utility to convert bioinformatics data into a format suitable for the package.

When it comes to hardware, few laboratories can afford high-end, dedicated visualization workstations from Silicon Graphics and other manufacturers, much less develop custom hardware to supplement their visualization needs. The problem with high-end commercial visualization hardware—from 3D or stereo goggles, data gloves, 3D displays, and haptic devices—is a lack of standards. A visualization system designed around a particular model of stereo goggles likely won't work with other hardware because the proprietary software drivers may require a specific operating system and the display drivers may be incompatible with displays from other manufactures. As a result, sharing research findings with others is more difficult. The more standard the general-purpose hardware and software used to support visualization in a laboratory, the more easily the system can be shared with others. In addition, using a general-purpose tool shifts the maintenance and standards challenge to the hardware vendors, allowing R&D teams to focus on their own work.

A common approach taken by software developers in aiding the visualization of complex molecules is to create a stereo pair that can be printed or viewed on a computer screen. This low-tech alternative to stereo goggles, most of which work by opening and closing an LCD shutter on either of the two lenses in concert with the display, is based on the cross-eyed technique. If you hold this book a comfortable reading distance from your face and stare at the point between the two proteins while crossing your eyes, you should be able to mentally fuse the two images, differing in only a few degrees of perspective into one single 3D structure. For example, the stereo pair in Figure 5-22 illustrates a cross-eyed stereo pair of Deoxy Hemoglobin. Because the computational load of stereoscopic rendering is approximately twice that of a single image, rendering times can be painfully long.

The degree to which visualization can be supported by a generic workstation is a function of the workstation's overall system performance, specific hardware characteristics, the standards supported by the system, and their affect on overall performance, including the availability of software drivers and other interface technologies that may affect researcher's use or system performance. Visualization is one of the most computationally intensive processing challenges for workstation-based applications. Dedicated rendering workstations typically have the multiple, highest-speed processors commercially available, a gigabyte or more of RAM, and at least one fast hard drive for maximum image throughput. Special hardware or firmware graphics accelerators

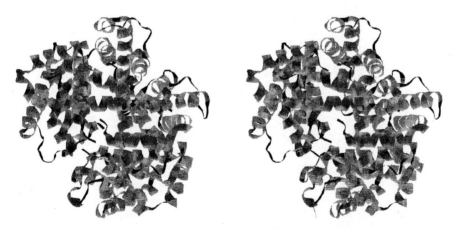

Figure 5-22   Cross-Eyed Stereo Pair of Deoxy Hemoglobin Created with RasMol. To view the molecule in stereo, with the image about 10 inches from your face, stare at the area between the two molecules and cross your eyes until a third image forms in the center of the two original molecules. The original images will remain visible, but will be located in the periphery of the visual field.

are typically used to handle operations such as providing perspective, shading of figures, and refreshing the screen quickly between redraws of images being manipulated in hardware that would otherwise have to be communicated through the computer bus, executed on the main CPU, and then communicated to the video card.

Software also profoundly affects the range of possibilities for visualizing simple graphics or complex 3D models. A visualization package written in Assembler by an accomplished programmer may outperform a poorly written application even when the later is running on higher-performance hardware. For example, if the application doesn't recognize the hardware graphics accelerator or make up for the maximum amount of RAM available, the visualization application won't deliver as much performance as possible. Similarly, the operating system may enhance or limit the performance of the visualization application. Support for OpenGL-compatible graphics accelerators and multiple processors is a basic requirement. Compatibility with industry-standard drivers, storage media, and networking protocols is also essential.

When it comes to visualization on generic hardware, standards are a double-edged sword. The high performance that is possible with specific graphics accelerators and software drivers and applications may make the workstation virtually incompatible with any other applications, even other visualization applications. The creation of a dedicated, high-speed visualization workstation by adding coprocessor boards and special drivers on an otherwise generic workstation may be a viable option if the enhanced performance and time savings is worth the additional expense and resources required to maintain an additional system.

ON THE HORIZON

Virtual reality—the use of computers to immerse the user in a multimedia environment that's rich enough in synthetic cues to make the simulated environment seem real—has great potential in bioinformatics R&D. In the general marketplace, the commercial uses of virtual reality technology include virtual prototyping, museum displays, design evaluation, architecture, trade show displays, engineering, aerospace simulation, collaborative engineering, game development, and education. Most of these applications of the technology translate directly to bioinformatics applications. For example, the virtual prototyping of the functionality of running shoes or tractors isn't conceptually different from prototyping drugs and their effects on different human protein binding sites. Just as many of the traditional museums have been placed online to allow access to those who don't have museums in their communities, so virtual tours of protein molecules allow researchers and students access to data in a form that they couldn't otherwise access.

Design evaluation, which involves illustrating how a device or apparatus will look, can also be applied to protein structures. Virtual reality visualization methods can illustrate, for example, the different shapes that a protein molecule might assume with changes in local pH or temperature. Similarly, just as virtual architecture applications allow potential clients to experience the finished product before it's built, a virtual reality model of a protein structure allows researchers to work with 3D images of molecules before they're actually synthesized. The advantage of this approach is that it allows potential problems to be identified before resources are invested in developing the molecule.

To date, the greatest commercial use of virtual reality in molecular biology is in the form of booth attractions at trade shows. The pharmaceutical industry spends several hundred-million dollars annually on the marketing of drugs at major medical conferences, and virtual reality and other forms of visualization technology are commonly used to attract future prescribers to their booths and to quickly communicate the mechanism of action and relative efficacy of their drugs.

Similarly, in the aerospace industry, the practical application of virtual reality includes everything from turbine design to flight simulation training for pilots and support personnel. Much of this is in the form of collaborative engineering, where engineers share models and interact online. Collaborative engineering has been used for years in the automotive and aerospace industries to design subsystems and test their functionality before actually creating them. The result is that ineffective designs are disposed of before they make it to the prototyping stage, saving the companies time and money.

Closely related to virtual reality entertainment systems in which combatants donning virtual reality helmets immerse themselves in battle situations is the use of virtual reality in education. Several medical boards have invested heavily in virtual patient encounter systems in which physicians interact with animated, talking 3D patient simulations. These virtual reality systems allow medical students, residents, and physicians to develop their clinical pattern-recognition skills before interacting with patients suffering from the conditions being studied.

These and other applications of virtual reality have obvious application in molecular biology and bioinformatics research. For example, in the area of education, there is a significant gulf in what traditionally educated health care professionals and researchers understand about the bioinformatics arena. Similarly, virtual reality technologies can be used to enable students, researchers, and professionals in other fields to understand and help address the challenges in bioinformatics.

ENDNOTE

Visualization is one of the most active areas of R&D in bioinformatics. One reason that visualization technology is so advanced today is the huge investment over the past several decades in the area by the military establishment. Consider that the development of the first bitmapped screens were supported by the military because the screens could track the trajectory of missiles more precisely than a simple grid of "Xs" on a character-oriented screen. Another reason for the rapid advances in the field is the parallel work in visualization being conducted in fields as diverse as the military, medicine, and weather forecasting. For example, based on the interfaces developed for use in clinical medicine, such as fMRI, the next generation of user interfaces used in bioinformatics will likely inherit some of this higher-level biological focus.

Bioinformatics visualization requirements, especially those related to 3D rendering of protein structures and modeling protein-protein interactions in real time, will certainly drive development in high-end computing, including supercomputer and grid computing. The challenge for the bioinformatics community is to devise visualization techniques and related technologies that are easily shared, capable of being supported in the long-term, and ones that provide developers of next-generation hardware and software with a viable target to support.

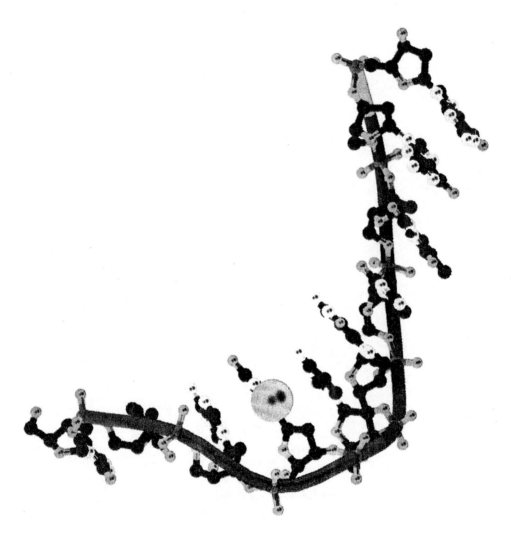

➤ X-ray structure of a DNA decamer containing 7,8-dihydro-8-oxoguanine. PDB entry183D. Image produced with PDB Structure Explorer.

CHAPTER

Statistics

*A mathematician is a blind man in a dark room
looking for a black cat which isn't there.*
— Charles Darwin

Although Gregor Mendel is often credited with quantifying biology, in reality the ancient Babylonians created tabulations of agricultural yields and related transactions several millennia earlier. Even earlier civilizations tracked the population of herds using pictographs on the walls of caves. However, not much changed in the way that population data were recorded for several decades after Mendel's death. For example, the 1870 and 1880 U.S. censuses were tabulated by hand—a process requiring about as much time as it took to sequence the human genome. As a result, the analysis of census data was not available until just before the next census was started. Things changed in 1890 when Herman Hollerith's tabulating machine was used to analyze the census—and they changed within about a year. Buoyed by this success, the Tabulating Machine Company evolved to service other areas, and eventually became known as IBM.

The U.S. Census Bureau collected samples from the U.S. population in the 1940 census, a modern statistical technique, instead of collecting data from every citizen. Because even this task was daunting using manual methods, the census bureau commissioned the UNIVAC Division of Remington Rand to build the first commercial non-military digital computer in the U.S., a UNIVAC model, in the late 1940s. Today, many molecular biologists routinely work with data sets that are considerably larger than those produced by the latest U.S. census, and they use a variety of advanced statistical techniques to do so.

This chapter explores the practical considerations involved in applying statistical techniques to modern bioinformatics challenges. It illustrates the range and complexity of issues that arise in controlling for the variability (which, in this discussion, encompasses errors) associated with microarray experiments and other bioinformatics work. "Statistical Concepts" introduces the underlying concepts of randomness and variability, while the "Microarrays" section provides an overview of the microarray experimental process. The "Imperfect Data" section reveals the numerous potential sources of variability in microarray experiments.

The "Basics" section relates microarray experiments to fundamental statistical concepts, while "Quantifying Randomness" discusses how randomness and variability are assigned to devices and processes. "Data Analysis" discusses how experimental output data are evaluated, and "Tool Selection" examines the criteria for statistical analysis tool selection. The "Statistics of Alignment" and "Clustering and Classification" sections illustrate the practical application of statistical concepts. "On the Horizon" introduces the technological innovations that bioinformatics is pushing forward, often ahead of the theoretical statistical underpinnings. "Endnote" addresses the implication of succumbing to the pressure to treat statistics as a black box solution to modern research challenges.

This chapter, like any book on statistical methods, should be considered a roadmap to potential issues to consider in discussing the selection of statistical methods with an expert statistician familiar with bioinformatics issues.

STATISTICAL CONCEPTS

Given the breadth of bioinformatics, the statistical concepts relevant to the field could easily fill a bookcase, much less a single chapter. As listed in Table 6-1, typical applications of statistics in bioinformatics range from clinical diagnosis and descriptive summaries to gene hunting and nucleotide alignment. Many of these applications are far removed from the traditional definition of a statistic, which is simply a value calculated from a sample. For example, consider that clinicians dealing with the efficacy of specific therapy in treating a genetic disease typically focus on disease prevalence (the number of cases of an illness or condition that exists at a particular time in a defined population). They also assess clinical and genetic tests for the probability of a negative result, given that the condition under consideration is absent (their specificity), and for the probability of a positive result, given that the condition under consideration is present (their sensitivity), and for the predictive value (the probability that a condition is present, based on the results of a test). The process of diagnosing patients potentially suffering from genetic disorders typically encompasses quantifying uncertainty and using statistical methods to predict long-term outcomes.

In most cases, statistics are gathered in order to estimate population characteristics or parameters. Furthermore, these parameters are typically unknown and unknowable. Further still, because a statistic is an estimate of a parameter, it is likely in error, and much of statistical work is devoted to quantifying the magnitude of this error.

Table 6-1 Applications of Statistics in Bioinformatics.

Clinical Diagnosis
Descriptive Summaries
Equipment Calibration
Experimental Data Analysis
Gene Expression Prediction
Gene Hunting
Gene Prediction
Genetic Linkage Analysis
Laboratory Automation
Nucleotide Alignment
Population Studies
Protein Function Prediction
Protein Structure Prediction
Quantifying Uncertainty
Quality Control
Sequence Similarity

At this point in the discussion of statistics, it's important to consider the basic concepts of randomness and probability as they relate to bioinformatics. Biological systems are inherently random, meaning that they involve variables that have undetermined value but definite probability. The first fruit fly to escape from a container of 50,000 flies when the container lid is opened may be male or female, for example. Even though the sex is a random event, the probability is 0.5 that the sex of the fly is male—assuming no external forces have been at work to affect the natural balance of fruit fly sex. Probability, the likelihood that an event will occur, is expressed as the ratio of the number of favorable outcomes in the set of outcomes divided by the total number of possible outcomes. Similarly, a stochastic system involves or shows random behavior.

Despite the apparent randomness at the organism level, when the same events are viewed at the population and ecosystem levels, they often appear as deterministic behaviors. That is, they have an outcome that can be predicted because all of its causes are either known or are the same as those of previous events. The concepts of evolution and chaos theory describe patterns in apparently random events that appear systematic and predictable over several generations. Chaos theory describes the unpredictability inherent in every system, in which apparently random changes occur because of a system's extreme sensitivity to small differences in initial conditions. A small increase in the earth's average temperature may drastically alter life on earth over several centuries, for example.

Mutations, chance mating, random environmental pressures, and the relative contribution of parents to the genotype of their offspring all lend themselves to statistical interpretation. An important distinction in biological systems is that some processes or measurements are either present or absent (discrete), while others are variable within some range (continuous). For example, a particular nucleotide is either at a location within a sequence or it isn't, just as a pea from one of Mendel's sweet pea plants either was round or wrinkled. In contrast, the expression of a gene, as measured by the fluorescence of a spot on a microarray slide, may range from absent to weak or pronounced. For example, consider a patient genetically predisposed to adult onset or Type II Diabetes. In many cases, by altering their behavior to include a low-calorie diet and regular exercise, a patient can control the symptoms of the disease—and presumably the expression of some genes. As such, bioinformatics methods encompass not only traditional statistics, but probability and stochastic processes, with both continuous and discrete variables.

Progress

Many advances in statistics were rooted in anecdotal observations that predated the development of formal mathematical proofs or models. For example, the first model of Mendel's work, Punnet Squares (see Figure 6-1), was developed about 50 years after Mendel's original observations. R.C. Punnet developed the model to illustrate the range of possible allele pairings, and to calculate the probability of each pairing. Using Mendel's mating of pea plants with round and wrinkled peas, Punnet's model predicts that the offspring will have four genotypes and a probability ratio of:

1 RR : 2 Rr : 1 rr

with a phenotype of:

3 round : 1 wrinkled

Punnet's model was soon extended by others, including his associate G.H. Hardy, to a more generalizeable form. For example, the Hardy-Weinberg Principle, proposed in 1908, states that, in the absence of forces that change gene ratios in populations, when random mating is permitted, the frequencies of each allele will tend to remain constant throughout the following generations. Work by subsequent scientists, such as the British statistician Ronald Fisher, further quantified the observations of Mendel, Punnet, Hardy, and others.

When Fisher applied his statistical methods to Mendel's work in the 1930s, he showed that Mendel's figures were too perfect. With the small sample size

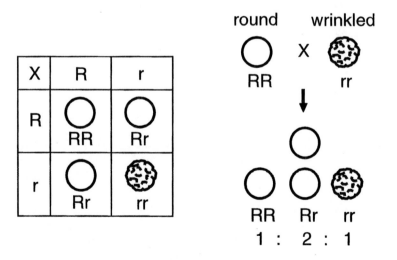

Figure 6-1 Probability and Punnet Squares. The model illustrates how the relative probability of a genotype relates to a given genotype mating.

used by Mendel, his findings, which agree with the ratios predicted by Punnet's squares, would be unlikely to be observed. Whether this apparently intentional error was the result of Mendel's manipulation of the data or, as some historians assert, due to incorrect reporting by his support staff, is unknown.

In terms of complexity, Mendelian genetics, while a milestone in the development of our understanding of genetics, pales in comparison to many of the statistical challenges of modern molecular biology. Even though many researchers work with statistics through the special function keys on their calculators or a dedicated statistical analysis program, the application of statistics is much more than simple data analysis. For example, statistical methods provide the basis for modern genomic and proteomic laboratory automation. Automating manual operations like pipetting not only saves time but, properly implemented, automation can eliminate or minimize many sources of variability and provide for a more robust experimental procedure. The rapid advances in bioinformatics, such as sequencing most of the human genome, have been possible because of the availability of statistical methods that compare and manipulate data representative of nucleotide sequences and computer-enabled laboratory automation. Machines—perhaps more appropriately referred to as robots—have been used to automate error-prone, manual procedures such as micro-pipetting to the point that computer-based tools can quickly analyze the data they produce in the time that it would have taken to simply set up a manual experiment.

Moving to the wet lab, sequencing machines generate data on thousands of base pairs per hour, and microarray experiments can collect data on the expression of tens of thousands of genes in a few hours. There are numerous potential sources of variability in the microarray experimental process and consequently a concomitant need for statistical processing. For these reasons, an examination of microarray technology represents a reasonable avenue to introducing many of the practical statistical concepts relevant to bioinformatics.

MICROARRAYS

Microarrays offer an efficient method of gathering data that can be used to determine the expression patterns of tens of thousands of genes in only a few hours. Microarray methods allow researchers to examine the mRNA from different tissues in normal and disease states to determine which genes and environmental conditions can lead to disease. Similarly, microarray methods can be used to determine which genes are expressed in which tissues and at which times during embryonic development. Spotting, the first widely used method of gene expression analysis using microarrays, is described by the process flow diagram in Figure 6-2 and depicted graphically in Figure 6-3. In preparation for a traditional spotting microarray experiment, several microarrays are created on a membrane, in a gel matrix, or, most often, on a scrupulously clean microscope slide made of low-fluorescence glass. When glass slides are used as a substrate, they are coated with a non-fluorescing compound to which known DNA sequences can easily adhere. Next, a solution containing expressed genes is applied to (spotted on) the treated face of each slide. This spotting is performed by mechanical robot controlled by micro pens or sprayers at a density of tens of thousands of spots per square inch. After the spotting process, the slides are heated and dried.

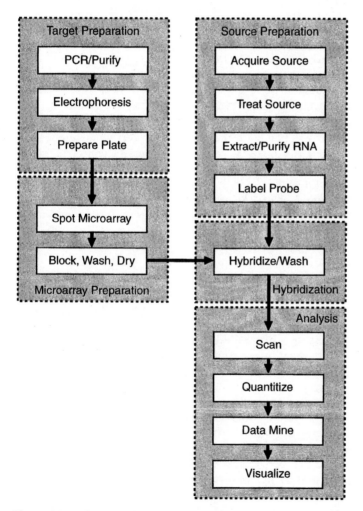

Figure 6-2   Microarray Spotting Process Flow.

Because loosely attached DNA can migrate from one spot to another during an experiment, the next step in processing involves removing loosely attached DNA from the microarrays by washing each slide in alcohol and then immersing them in boiling water for several minutes. A control is then run on one microarray with a known cDNA probe to verify that the reagents are active and on the microarrays in sufficient density to run additional experiments. With the prepared microarrays in hand, the next step is to create an experimental sample or probe.

To create a probe, a tissue sample is harvested by laser capture microdissection or other comparable method. Next, the mRNA from a few cells is isolated, purified, amplified, processed, and labeled with fluorescent nucleotides, eventually yielding fluorescent (typically red) cDNA. The sample is then incubated with a similarly processed cDNA reference (typically green). The labeled probe and reference are then mixed and applied to the surface of one of the prepared DNA microarrays, allowing fluorescent sequences in the probe-reference mix to attach to the cDNA adherent to the glass slide.

The attraction of labeled cDNA from the probe and reference for a particular spot on the microarray depends on the extent to which the sequences in the mix complement the DNA affixed to the slide. A perfect complement, in which a nucleotide sequence in a strand of cDNA exactly complements a DNA sequence affixed to the slide, will attach more strongly (hybridize) to the DNA sequence than will a strand of cDNA in which alignment isn't perfect. The strength of adherence, as well as the success in competing for a spot on the slide, is directly proportional to the degree to which the cDNA and DNA sequences complement each other.

The populated microarray is then excited by a laser and the resultant fluorescence at each spot in the microarray is measured. If neither the experimental nor the reference samples hybridize with the genes at a given spot on the slide—indicating that there are no sequences in either the probe or the reference that are complementary to the DNA on the slide—the spot won't fluoresce. However, if hybridization is predominantly with the probe, the spot will be red. Conversely, if hybridization is primarily between the reference and the DNA affixed to the slide, the spot will fluoresce green. If cDNA from the probe and reference samples hybridize equally at a given spot—indicating that they share the same number of complementary nucleotides in the appropriate sequence—the spot will be yellow. Similarly, various ratios of probe-to-reference hybridization with the slide-mounted DNA result in colors somewhere in the spectrum between red and green. An analysis of the location, extent, and exact proportions of red-to-green fluorescence provides a semi-quantitative measure of gene expression in the tissue sample. That is, even though the fluorescence is digitized and read by computer, the relative value of the ratios is more exactly determined than is the absolute fluorescence value, in part because of the variability in the quantity and quality of DNA that is affixed to the slide during microarray preparation.

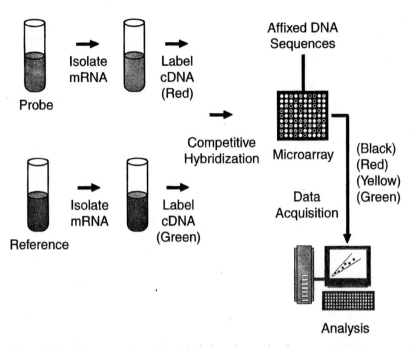

Figure 6-3 Microarray Spotting. Labeled probe and reference cDNA is competitively hybridized on a microarray prepared with known DNA sequences. Hybridization may not occur (no fluorescence or black), may be solely from the reference (green fluorescence), solely from the probe (red fluorescence), or a mixture of reference and probe (yellow). Other ratios of probe-to-reference mixtures result in colors between green and red in the spectrum.

An obvious point for the application of statistical methods is at the final stage of the experiment, where tens of thousands of data points, each indicating relative gene activity, may need to be analyzed. However, the random variability associated with every stage of the process has to be considered before the final data can be analyzed in a meaningful way.

A quick check for data validity is to create a scatter plot of fluorescence data from two identically treated microarrays. As shown in Figure 6-4, the ideal condition is when gene expressions as measured by the microarrays are identical, as indicated by data on the 45-degree ID line, as in (A). If the amplitude of gene expression on one microarray is greater than the other, data fall off the ID line, as in (B) and (C). The scatter plot also provides a measure of gene expression amplitude, in that the greater the distance from the origin, the greater the expression amplitude. For example, the gene plotted at position (C) has a greater expression amplitude than the gene at position (A).

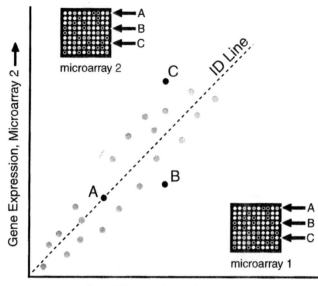

Figure 6-4 Microarray Results Analysis. Scatter plot illustrating inter-microarray variability in two identically treated microarrays, Microarray 1 and Microarray 2. Ideally, all data points fall on the ID line, as illustrated by data point (A).

The common reasons for variability in spotting, as reflected by deviation from the ID line, are listed in Table 6-2. Reasons for variability in spotting results include variability in the microarray surface chemistry, inaccuracies in the various instruments used to prepare the reagents and monitor the environment, and fluctuations in the temperature, humidity, and other hybridization conditions. Variations in the degree of DNA attachment to the slide, in the volume of cDNA applied during the spotting process, and in the location of spots on the microarray slide are often caused by the robot and other mechanical equipment.

Assuming a microarray passes scatter plot analysis, the microarray data are typically arranged in the form of an expression matrix. Whereas data on the microarray don't necessarily follow a particular pattern, the standard expression matrix is arranged by gene and experimental condition, as illustrated in Figure 6-5. Conditions may indicate elapsed time since some event, such as the activation of another gene, or local environmental changes, such as an increase in temperature, or the start of drug therapy. Although four experimental conditions are shown for each gene in this illustration, there is no inherent limitation in the relative number of conditions or genes that can be represented in the expression matrix, within the total capacity of the microarray. For example, there may be seven experimental conditions applied to one gene and three to another.

Table 6-2 Sources of Variability in Spotting.

Binding of cDNA to Microarray
cDNA Volume Deposited
Digitization of Spot Intensities
Environmental Conditions
Experimental Design
Hybridization of RNA to DNA
Instrument Error
Locating Spotted Areas
Microarray Surface Chemistry
Quality of Spotted Genes on Array
Reagent Preparation
Spot Placement (Robot Arm Accuracy)

The expression matrix format is a more human-readable form than a reproduction of arbitrarily arranged microarray data. A color version of an expression matrix is more useful in publications and for quick visual inspection of experimental results than is a table of relative red and green fluorescence amplitude values. The standard expression matrix format also means that it's possible to spot a microarray with an arbitrary pattern of genes-condition cDNA without regard to how the data will eventually be displayed. Note that the data used for analysis is actually based on the digitized (numerical) value of the relative red and green fluorescence of the spots on the microarray.

In many respects, the spotting process, which was developed at Stanford University, has many parallels with the early digital electronic computers. The first commercially successful digital computers, such as the UNIVAC line, used discrete components and mechanical means—including punched paper cards—to work with the system. Individual components were soldered by hand to create the thousands of circuits. Because of variability in the tubes and components, the circuits had to be tuned by hand. There were often failures of individual components because of device failure or because the solder joints of components and cables eventually failed. Because construction was done by hand and because every computer was built with thousands of components—each of which varied somewhat from their ideal values

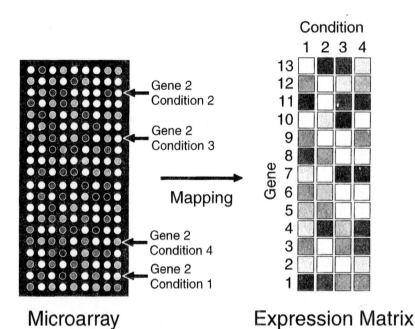

Figure 6-5 Mapping Microarray Data to an Expression Matrix. Note the lack of correlation between physical experimental position on the microarray and the mapping of data in the expression matrix. Although shown here in grayscale, the individual squares in the gene expression matrix are normally represented by the fluorescence color of the corresponding microarray spot.

and performance—it took a month or more to produce a computer system. This investment in time was well worth it. Compared to earlier computational methods, the early digital electronic computers shaved countless hours off the time required to compile a census or compute the trajectory of a projectile.

Even though the first discrete-component electronic digital computers worked well, because of the time required to create and test each computer, customers were limited to large corporations, the military, and the government. The situation changed with the introduction of the integrated circuit (IC). Not only did the development of the IC allow for much smaller computers, but component count and variability dropped precipitously. As a result, reliability increased, prices dropped, and computers became affordable to a mass market.

The process used to make ICs is based on photolithography. Instead of soldering discrete components by hand or with mechanical jigs, transistors, diodes, resistors, and capacitors are formed by a process in which multiple layers of semiconductor material are alternatively laid down on a ceramic or silicon substrate. Masks or barriers block the light used to sensitize the surface, allowing it to accept the next layer of semiconductor, insulator, or resistive material. As a result, tens of thousands of ICs can be produced in days. Furthermore, because most of the process is performed with high-tolerance, mostly non-mechanical methods, failure rates are low and performance is consistent from one IC to the next.

The approach used in IC fabrication has been applied to microarray preparation and analysis. For example, the process of microarray preparation based on photolithography and solid-phase chemistry commercialized by Affymetrix® is illustrated in Figures 6-6 and 6-7. The overall process depicted in Figure 6-6 illustrates how commercial process begins with a 5-inch square quartz wafer, similar to the quartz discs used to create ICs. The wafer is washed and then placed in a silane bath that forms a matrix of covalently linked molecules on the surface of the wafer. Linker molecules on the silane matrix provide a surface that may be light-activated.

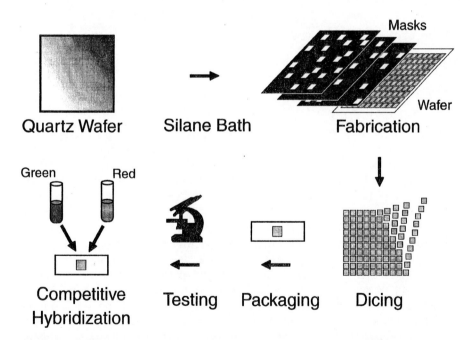

Figure 6-6   Affymetrix Microarray Preparation Process. The process parallels that used in the microcomputer industry used to create ICs. The technology offers much higher capacity and more quantitative results compared to microarray spotting.

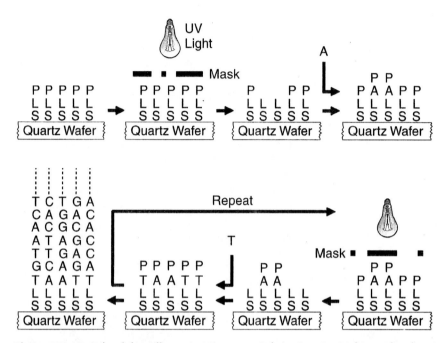

Figure 6-7 Details of the Affymetrix Microarray Fabrication. L—Linker molecules. S—Silane matrix. P—Protective layer. The process is repeated until the oligonucleotides are around 20 nucleotides long.

In the photolithography process, illustrated in Figure 6-7, fenestrated masks are placed over the coated wafer and exposed to UV light. The UV light exposes linkers, which are then available for nucleotide coupling. A solution containing a single type of deoxynucleotide (A, T, C, or G) is flushed over the surface, where the nucleotide attaches to the exposed linkers. The process is repeated with additional masks until the oligonucleotides on the surface of the wafer are 20–25 nucleotides in length.

Each wafer can produce between about 50 to 400 individual microarrays, each of which can hold up to 500,000 probes, depending on the yield of the process. In comparison, each glass slide in the spotting process can hold perhaps 30,000 spots. The quartz wafer is diced and each of the individual arrays is packaged for use, just as the semiconductor wafers are diced and the individual components are mounted in a plastic or ceramic housing. A sample of the packaged microarrays is tested by running control hybridizations. A quantitative test of hybridization is run using standardized control probes before the microarrays are available for use in competitive hybridization experiments. The hybridization process is essentially identical to that used in the spotting process outlined in Figure 6-3.

A comparison of spotting and the Affymetrix process, summarized in Table 6-3, reveals that spotting is associated with quicker setup and modification times. What's more, the spotting process results in more variability and lower density because it relies on mainly mechanical means. The Affymetrix process excels at providing absolute, quantitative results instead of qualitative results, in part because the oligonucleotides are of a fixed length and known quantity. A discussion of the variability of the spotting technique, in terms of statistical concepts, follows.

Table 6-3 Microarray Fabrication Comparison. Spotting is more variable than the Affymetrix process.

Factor	Spotting	Affymetrix
Source of Variability	Mechanical Pin Positioning Bonding of cDNA to Slide Reagent Purity Environment	Mask Positioning Mask Fenestrations Reagent Purity Environment
Repeatability	Moderate/Low	High
Layout Design Time	Low	High
Analysis Possible	Qualitative	Quantitative
Inter-Array Variability	High	Low
Modification Time	Low	High
Intellectual Property	Public Domain	Proprietary

IMPERFECT DATA

As in every other physical system, the data generated by a microarray experiment are imperfect. Determining the magnitude and pervasiveness of these imperfections is one reason for employing statistical techniques. One way to conceptualize these imperfections is as noise in the communications channel. This noise is due to limitations of the equipment, reagents, tissue samples, and deficiencies in the overall process. Some of this noise is unavoidable, and can at best only be reduced. For example, microarrays are commonly created on glass slides. However, the glass, like the coating that allows DNA to adhere to the slides, fluoresces slightly when it is excited by the laser light used to read spots on the microarray.

Similarly, the background noise level is directly proportional to the ambient temperature, in that all conductors operated above absolute zero produce thermal or Johnson noise. It's possible to operate the image sensors and amplifiers associated with reading fluorescence signals from microarrays close to absolute zero, and thereby significantly reduce the noise level contributed by the electronics equipment associated with the experiment. However, for most bioinformatics applications this approach to noise reduction isn't practical.

Variations in the preparation of a microarray can make the accuracy of results questionable. For example, in preparing a glass slide for spotting, slight variations in the volume of substrate deposited on the slide, or variations in the chemistry of the substrate, can severely compromise subsequent analysis. Although some applications of microarray expression data, like genetic mapping, are associated with binary measurements (either present or absent), most applications benefit from consistent volumes of materials deposited precisely on the microarray so that at least rudimentary qualitative measurements can be made.

Sources of variability in microarray spot analysis include the stability of the spotting technology used to create the microarray and the stability of the environmental conditions. For example, the reproducibility and accuracy of the robotic assembly that determines the location and volume of DNA material deposited at each spot are critical factors. Furthermore, the environment, including humidity, temperature, and amount of particulate matter in the air, can add additional variables that must be considered. For example, if the relative humidity is too high, then the samples in the microarray may not evaporate as fast as expected. Because of unavoidable variability in the spotting process, active areas on microarrays are commonly printed in triplicate to provide an internal control.

Variability in microarray experimental results is also a function of the methods used in the data acquisition phase of a microarray experiment. For example, the two most popular methods of capturing data from a microarray are scanning and spotting. In scanning, a laser illuminates each point in the microarray separately. Variability in the data is commonly due to inaccuracies in positioning the laser over each area where a spot is expected, as illustrated in Figure 6-8. In addition, there is a tradeoff between the diameter of the excitatory laser beam and the relevance of the fluorescence data. A beam that is only slightly larger than the expected spot size (high specificity) theoretically provides the least amount of extraneous fluorescence noise, assuming that the spot in the microarray is in the expected location, with the reading laser superimposed over the spot. A wider excitatory beam will control for variability in spot location, at a cost of more chances of fluoresce from contamination, slide coating, and the underlying glass contributing to the fluorescence signal.

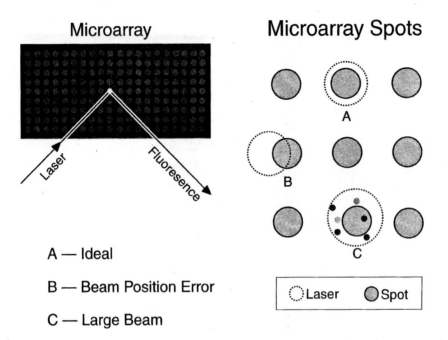

Microarray   # Microarray Spots

A — Ideal

B — Beam Position Error

C — Large Beam

⟨ Laser   ⬤ Spot

Figure 6-8 Sources of Variability in Reading Microarray Spots Through Spotting. The ideal situation (A) is when the excitatory laser beam is tightly focused on a single microarray spot. However, achieving this level of perfection requires accurate positioning of both the spot and the reading equipment. If beam position is off the mark (B), gene expression data will be underrepresented. Using a larger beam than absolutely necessary (C) incorporates a full spot in the analysis, even if the spot placement isn't ideal.

In the starring approach to gene expression analysis, a large swath of laser light excites many spots in the microarray at a time (see Figure 6-9), producing a fluorescence pattern resembling a field of stars—hence the name. The fluorescence pattern is captured by a photo detector, processed, and analyzed. In starring, the major sources of variability are non-uniformity in illumination intensity and differences in the sensitivity of the image-detection circuitry over the area of the microarray being read. For example, because the intensity of the florescence signal is a function of the power of the reading laser, if the power of the laser beam falls off significantly near the edges of a field, then the level of gene expression represented by those spots will be underrepresented. Similarly, the expression of genes represented by spots excited by the center of the beam will be overrepresented. Even if the excitation intensity is uniform across the area of the microarray being read, the characteristics of the image capture optics and associated circuitry can introduce artifacts in the fluorescence signal strength because of non-uniform sensitivity to light across the area being measured. For example, the sensitivity of the detector may vary from one edge of the detector to the next. As a result, unless these effects are addressed in the final analysis, the gene expression figures will be invalid.

Microarray

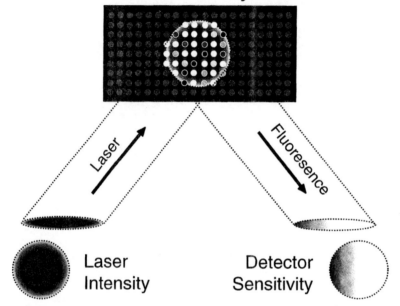

Laser

Fluoresence

Laser
Intensity

Detector
Sensitivity

Figure 6-9 Sources of Variability in the Starring Method of Reading a Microarray. Not only may the laser intensity be nonlinear across the area of the microarray that is excited by the swath of laser light, but the photodetector may exhibit variations in sensitivity across the detector aperture as well.

Even if the starring and scanning processes are tightly controlled, the data they produce may be highly variable because of limitations of the microarray preparation process. Figure 6-10 illustrates several sources of variability associated with microarray preparation, including variations in relative spot location (A), variations in spot density (B), variations in spot shape (C), and contamination (D).

The first source of variability to consider—a shift in relative location of a spot in the microarray—is problematic for several reasons. First is that when a microarray is scanned by a laser, a displaced spot won't read as strongly as it would otherwise because part of the spot may be outside of the field of the exciting laser beam. This type of variability can be addressed somewhat if starring is used to read the microarray because image-recognition technology can be used to identify spot location on the captured image. Image-recognition software can search the immediate vicinity where a spot is expected and appropriately adjust the location of the image pixels that are read.

Variations in spot density due to uneven adherence of cDNA to the slide during the spotting process may result in erroneous output signal interpretation, depending on the statistical method used to analyze spot intensity. Variations in spot shape and deviations from expected spot location result in errors in intensity reading of spot fluorescence. Starring and scanning are both susceptible to variations in spot shape. In starring, a mask is used to limit the extent of the area read on the captured image, even though the excitatory laser beam covers many spots at once. The opposite is true of scanning, in that the image capture device is receptive to fluorescence signals from anywhere on the microarray. However, only a small area of the array is excited at a time. As a result, a misshapen spot may not contribute fully to its expected fluorescence intensity.

Contamination of the microarray, whether from dust or extraneous organic material in the slide coating, is another source of variability that is difficult to counteract. Contamination can interfere with automated spot-locating technologies used with starring and partially obscure spots in the microarray so that they can't be properly scanned. Contamination can also give false positive indications of the level of gene expression when it is highly fluorescent and falls on spots that would otherwise not fluoresce.

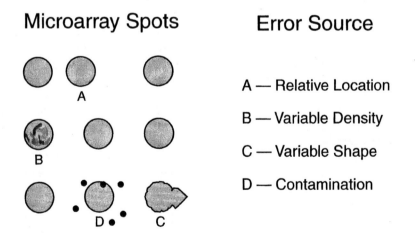

Microarray Spots

Error Source

A — Relative Location

B — Variable Density

C — Variable Shape

D — Contamination

Figure 6-10 Common Sources of Variability Associated with Microarray Preparation. These sources of error affect both the spotting and starring methods of microarray reading.

At a higher level is variability due to the overall system operation and processes. Sources of process variability include photobleaching, in which the exciting laser or other light bleaches the fluorescing dye, rendering the scanned spots useless for subsequent analysis. Photobleaching, which is a function of laser intensity and the time the laser dwells on each spot, is problematic when the microarray reading process is interrupted mid-way through a reading cycle and re-started. The previously excited area on the microarray may be faded relative to the unread area in the microarray. This may be problematic when gene activity corresponding to dual or multiple excitations is compared with areas of single excitation.

In addition to process variation, there is also variability due to the particular equipment used in the microarray system. Some of this variability or noise may be due to improper design or because of overwhelming noise level in the environment. For example, data acquisition devices are subject to noise from magnetic fields from nearby wiring and devices. There are also short-term errors due to equipment warm-up, and long-term drift with time because of aging of the electronic components.

Variation can be introduced by instrument loading and perturbation of the system under study, or by crosstalk. Crosstalk occurs when, for example, light from one channel or florescent color bleeds over to a detector intended for another signal. Using emission filters that block potential interfering light signals can minimize it. Variability can be introduced by noise in the power supply, by memory effects (image persistence) on the image sensors due to previous exposures, and by drift of sensor sensitivity and amplifier gain with time. Simply using the measuring equipment as it's intended to be used can demonstrate susceptibility to errors. For example, there is the issue of instrument loading, in that following Heisenberg's Uncertainty Principle, it's generally impossible to measure something with absolute accuracy without changing its value to some degree. For example, because of photobleaching by the laser, the process of reading a microarray also erases data from the microarray, making subsequent readings less accurate.

Imperfections in measuring equipment can introduce variation in the data. For example, because insulation used on wires is imperfect, there is current leakage and equipment noise. In addition, spurious signals can be induced by mechanical stress on wires and electronic components (the Piezoelectric effect), by friction, such as when materials rub together (the Triboelectric effect), or when insulation quality changes due to high humidity or because of surface contamination. Noise can also be induced by current-carrying cables and wires located near the measuring equipment.

Deciding on components to use in constructing a microarray system or other complex measuring system is a compromise between price, performance, and the intended use. For example, ceramic insulators have a high volume resistance but compared to cheaper polyvinyl chloride (PVC) insulators, they are a source of noise at high humidity and when subject to physical stress. Noise can also be produced by electrochemical effects on the circuit board and through thermoelectric potentials induced by conductors of different composition touching each other. Although these and other sources of low-level noise may not be relevant in typical bioinformatics work, it's important to realize the spectrum of possible sources of variation that, taken together, can affect the data produced by microarray experiments.

BASICS

The overview of a typical microarray experiment underscores the dependence of bioinformatics work on an awareness of error sources and variability so that statistical methods can be used to control for their effects on experimental results.

Randomness

One of the key statistical concepts highlighted by the microarray experiment is that data are inherently noisy and that randomness is inherent in any sampling process. Furthermore, randomness is inherent in, and a necessary component of, biological systems. Whereas the randomness in mechanical systems and electronic circuitry is often minimized as much as is economically possible, randomness is an integral component of the workings of biological systems. Mutations and the distribution of maternal and paternal genetic material during meiosis are biological processes that reflect the dependence of biodiversity on the randomness of biological processes.

Every measurement system introduces noise—random variability—into the desired signal. This noise can be minimized by controlling the external environment (for example, by reducing the ambient temperature in a system designed to make very low-level measurements), or, more often, by reducing the bandwidth of the system, using statistical techniques. For example, by reducing the bandwidth of acceptable (good) data, it can be more readily differentiated from bad data and made more apparent and available. Even though statistical techniques can be used to filter data during the final analysis of a gene expression experiment, reliance on statistical analysis of the final results alone isn't optimal. For example, although analysis of intra-array spot fluorescence intensity can be used to control for contamination and other sources of variability, a better approach is to minimize variability in the overall process. As a result, there will be more experimental data, and less need to run controls that add to the experimental overhead without contributing directly to gene expression discovery.

The microarray experiment also illustrates how conventional mechanical systems are more variable than their electronic counterparts. Compared to computers and other so-called finite-state machines defined in silicon and software, conventional mechanical systems such as robotic arms and micro-pipettes are much more variable in their operation. One of the greatest potential sources of variability in the placement of cDNA solution on a prepared glass slide microarray is the robotic assembly that performs the spotting of the microarray. What's more, the amount of cDNA that actually adheres to the slide can vary widely as well, as a function of the slide coating, the ambient environmental conditions, and the presence of contaminants. Estimating the variability contributed by the mechanical and biochemical systems—through computer modeling or direct measurement—provides an indication of the expected value of the data. Nanotechnology may eventually reduce the variability of computer-enabled mechanical systems to the point that it is comparable to that of digital electronic circuitry.

Variability Is Cumulative

Regardless of whether the source is mechanical, biological, or electronic, variability is cumulative, in that noise introduced in the early stages of a system propagates and is amplified by later activity in the system. For example, extraneous genetic material commingled with the cDNA used to create a microarray will add to the fluoresce activity measured from each spot. This not only adds to the noise level of the system and decreases the effective dynamic range of the experiment, but the fluoresce activity at otherwise quiescent locations in the microarray will be amplified by the PMT or CCD-based system and digitized. Unless the variability can be quantified through control experiments, the gene expression conclusions suggested by the data analysis will be incorrect.

Controlling variability is a key component of process management. Managing the chain of processes in the microarray experiment involves controlling variability through computer-enabled statistical controls. For example, correlating gene expression of microarray runs in a timely manner is impractical without computer-based statistical analysis and visualization tools. One reason is that noise and variability are dynamic; most complex systems get noisier and accumulate variability with time—hence the need for timely recalibration.

Approximation

The microarray experiment also illustrates that statistical summaries, probability-based predictions, and estimates of variability introduced by various processes are at best approximations. For example, Punnet's square allows a researcher to predict, with some degree of certainty, the outcome of mating pea plants with specific characteristics. The degree to which the predictions hold is based on sample size and the extent to which the explicit and implicit assumptions of the model are upheld. That is, sample size, external variables that may affect pea plant phenotype, the method of recording and analyzing data, and the basic design of the model all affect the accuracy of results.

Interface Noise

Much of bioinformatics work involves interfacing mechanical, biological, and electronic systems, each of which has its own non-linearities, variability, and noise sources. Furthermore, each interface introduces noise and variability in the overall process. For example, translating analog fluorescence intensity to a digital signal introduces noise, decreases overall system dynamic range, and adds non-linearities and variability to the gene expression data. Similarly, the mechanical and optical-to-digital interfaces in a nucleotide sequencing machine contribute noise, errors, and random variability to sequence data.

Assumptions

Most statistical methods assume basic premises that hold regardless of the specific application in bioinformatics. For example, one of the most popular statistical pattern classification methods is Bayes' Theorem, developed by the clergyman Thomas Bayes in the 18th Century. His theorem, applied to such problems as determining the probability that disease is present given that a gene is shown to be expressed in a microarray experiment, combines the prior probabilities of outcomes together with the conditional probabilities of various input features in order to reach a conclusion. Using the odds-likelihood form of Bayes' Theorem, the probability that a patient has a particular disease can be calculated from three parameters: the pretest probability of the patient having the disease, the probability that the test is positive in diseased people, and the probability that the test is positive in non-diseased people.

For example, given that probability (p) and odds are related as follows:

$$odds = \frac{p}{1-p}$$

$$p = \frac{odds}{1+odds}$$

In addition, the relationship between pretest and post-test odds is:

Post-test odds = pretest odds × likelihood ratio

Expressed in the odds-likelihood form of Bayes' Theorem, this relationship appears as:

$$\frac{p[D \mid R]}{p[-D \mid R]} = \frac{p[D]}{p[-D]} \times \frac{p[R \mid D]}{p[R \mid -D]}$$

Using this equation, assume that the pretest odds of a patient having a particular genetic disease is 0.50, and that it's known that the probability that a gene expression test is positive in people with the genetic disease is 0.65 and that the probability that the same gene expression test is positive in people without the disease is 0.20. The post-test odds that the patient has the disease given a positive gene expression test result is calculated as:

Post-test odds = pretest odds × likelihood ratio

$$Pretest\ odds = \frac{0.50}{1 - 0.50} = \frac{0.50}{0.50} = 1$$

$$Likelihood\ ratio = \frac{0.65}{0.20} = 3.25$$

$$Post\text{-}test\ odds = 1 \times 3.25 = 3.25 : 1$$

Converting odds to probability:

$$p = \frac{odds}{1 + odds} = \frac{3.25}{1 + 3.25} = 0.77$$

That is, the post-test odds that the patient is suffering from the disease is 0.77, up from even odds prior to the gene expression test results. A better test—one with a greater likelihood ratio—would have provided a greater increase in post-test odds that the patient has the disease.

The most significant limitation of Bayes' Theorem is that the input features must not only be independent of each other, but they must be either present or absent. Furthermore, the possible outcomes must be mutually exclusive, and there can be only one outcome.

A basic assumption in many statistical analyses is that the sample mean tends to approach the population mean, given a large enough sample size or enough smaller samples. Descriptive statistics such as mean, mode, median, and variance—a measure of how dispersed the values are around the distribution mean—are measures of this central tendency. For example, the Punnet Square accurately predicts the expected probability of genotypes and phenotypes, but only for sufficiently large sample sizes. A single, random sample of only four plants might reveal all wrinkled peas, despite the expected result of one wrinkled to three smooth offspring.

Sampling and Distributions

Much of statistics deals with obtaining as much information as possible from small samples. The question is how large a sample is large enough considering it's usually unrealistic to measure every data element, even if they are generated by a sequence machine or other automatic device. We estimate population mean and variance by sampling population data and drawing inferences from the sample data, based in part on assumptions of how the data are distributed in the population.

Popular distributions used in statistical analysis of discrete random variables include the Binomial, Hypergeometric, and Poisson distributions. The more well-known Normal distribution is used for analysis of continuous random variables. A special case of the Normal distribution is the z-distribution, which is normally distributed data with a mean of zero and a standard deviation of one (see Figure 6-11). The distinction between distributions of continuous and discrete variables is important because many statistical methods are valid only when used with data drawn from populations with specific distributions. For example, the analysis of discrete random variables, such as the position of a nucleotide on a given sequence, may use techniques based on a binomial distribution, but may not use techniques that assume a normal distribution. If assumptions of distribution aren't valid, then the relevance of the analysis should be downplayed accordingly.

Returning to the starring method of capturing fluorescence intensity data, the response characteristics of the image-capture electronics results in a skewed distribution (see Figure 6-12). Aberrations in the exciting laser and fluorescence intensity detector in a microarray experiment result in a peaked and skewed distribution, compared to the ideal (dotted line) distribution that is flat across the area excited by the laser.

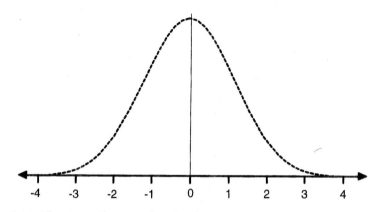

Figure 6-11   The Z-Distribution. This distribution is a special case of the Normal distribution, with mean of zero and a standard deviation of one.

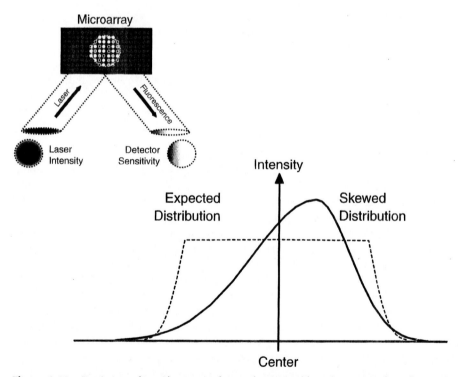

Figure 6-12   Deviations from the Normal Distribution. Although statistical analysis of continuous random variables assumes a normal distribution, many distributions are not normal, as illustrated by the skewed and expected distributions.

Hypothesis Testing

Hypothesis testing, in which a hypothesis (often termed the "null hypothesis" because it is a negatively stated hypothesis that a researcher suspects is incorrect) is assumed to hold unless there is enough evidence to reject it, is another basic statistical method. In microarray work, a typical hypothesis is that two microarrays that have been subjected to the same spotting and hybridization process will produce identical gene expression fluorescence results. The degree to which this hypothesis is true can be estimated by examining the gene expression scatter plots created from data gleaned from each microarray and correlating the values mathematically.

QUANTIFYING RANDOMNESS

From the earlier discussion, it should be clear that randomness—which refers not to the data, but how they are obtained—is inherent in every measuring device. In general, the lower the randomness, the better. Randomness is commonly quantified in the equipment's published specifications document, which characterizes the equipment's performance in terms of accuracy, resolution (precision), repeatability, stability, and sensitivity.

Accuracy—the degree to which a data value being measured is correct—is usually expressed as plus or minus a percentage of the reading, as "± (0.2%)". The accuracy of digital systems is further defined in terms of the number of counts of the least significant digit, such as "± (0.2% + 1 count)". Resolution, sometimes referred to as precision, is the ability of an instrument to resolve small differences. In a digital system, resolution is often expressed in terms of the number of bits available to represent a signal. For example, in a 4-bit digital device, there are 2^4 or 16 discrete steps.

Consider an analog-to-digital (A-to-D) converter, a device that converts continuously variable analog signals, such as the intensity of fluorescence emitted by a spot in a microarray, to digital values. If a 4-bit A-to-D converter has full-scale capacity of 16 volts, then the resolution is one volt. Signals are rounded to the nearest integer, so that 0.5, 1.2, and 3.6 volts are represented as 1, 1, and 4 volts, respectively. In general, the higher the resolution, the greater the accuracy of a device.

Sensitivity—the ability of a device to detect low-level signals—is a function of the resolution and the amount of noise in the system. For example, continuing with the example of the 4-bit A-to-D converter with a 16-volt full-scale capacity, the maximum sensitivity would be 0.5 volts, assuming a perfect, noiseless system. However, as noise is added to the system, the sensitivity decreases as a function of the amplitude and time distribution of the noise.

That is, the higher the signal-to-noise ratio, the higher the effective sensitivity of the device.

Repeatability is the ability of an instrument or system to provide consistent results. For example, the initial intensity of a spot's fluorescence, as measured with a photomultiplier tube, should ideally agree with a subsequent measurement. Repeatability is related to stability, which is the ability of an instrument or device to provide repeatable results over time, assuming certain environmental conditions, such as ambient temperature, are maintained within a certain range and the process of photo bleaching is consistent. Repeatability is also affected by any changes in the data source caused by the measurement process.

An instrument may provide highly repeatable results, but the results may be inaccurate unless the instrument is properly calibrated. All instruments are subject to changes in accuracy over time, whether or not they are operating. For example, an ordinary mercury thermometer is subject to a change in accuracy because of changes in the glass housing, which crystallizes and contracts over several years. Accuracy specifications are therefore stated in terms of time, such as within one year of calibration. The accuracy of a calibration standard limits the maximum accuracy of the equipment being calibrated.

In assessing the capabilities of a microarray experiment system, one measure of overall system performance is the dynamic range of the system—the ratio of the maximum signal level to the minimum signal level that can be measured or represented. The dynamic range of a microarray system, which is typically expressed in terms of orders of magnitude, is a function of the scanner electronics, the chemical dynamic range of the chemicals used, and the biological dynamic range of the system under investigation. All else being equal, a system with a greater dynamic range is capable of greater precision and accuracy in quantifying the relative gene expression. Furthermore, the dynamic range of the system is limited by the element in the signal chain with the smallest dynamic range.

Although the biological dynamic range is usually an unchangeable parameter, there is some latitude in selecting reagents with the greatest dynamic range and even more choice in the microarray electronics. Consider that the detector used in the image-acquisition component of a microarray system is commonly either a solid-state charge-coupled-device (CCD) or a glass and vacuum photomultiplier tube (PMT). The choice of one device over the other involves a tradeoff between cost, sensitivity, complexity, and dynamic range. A PMT is larger and much more fragile than a solid-state CCD and requires a more complex power supply because of the PMT's much higher operating voltage. In addition, a PMT is also more easily damaged than a CCD. However, a PMT provides superior sensitivity and dynamic range compared to a CCD.

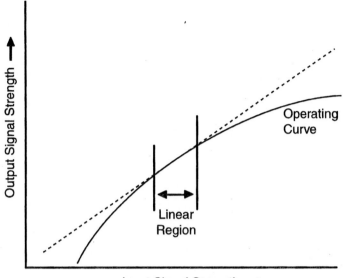

Output Signal Strength

Operating
Curve

Linear
Region

Input Signal Strength ➡

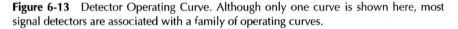

Figure 6-13 Detector Operating Curve. Although only one curve is shown here, most signal detectors are associated with a family of operating curves.

Both CCD and PMT components exhibit non-linearities outside of their optimal operating ranges. For example, both devices saturate at some input level, so that increases in signal strength aren't matched with corresponding increases in output, as illustrated in Figure 6-13. In general, there is a tradeoff between the amplification possible and the extent of the linear region. For example, operating a PMT at the highest voltage and gain that the device will tolerate may produce phenomenal signal gain, but at the expense of a severely compressed linear operating region. This non-linearity has the effect of compressing the dynamic range of the device.

DATA ANALYSIS

Once a fluorescence signal is detected, it has to be quantitized or digitized before it can be manipulated statistically. The digitization or A-to-D conversion is performed at a fixed sampling frequency, with a converter rated at a certain dynamic range, as measured in bit depth (see Figure 6-14). For example, a 16-bit A-to-D converter can process a signal into one of (2^{16}) or 65,636 levels, a dynamic range of over 4 orders of magnitude—which is generally

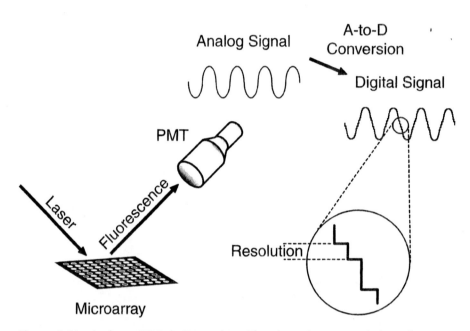

Figure 6-14 Analog-to-Digital Conversion. The dynamic range of the microarray experiment is limited by the resolution or bit depth of the A-to-D conversion process, as illustrated by the magnified view of the digital signal.

considered the minimum for gene expression applications. The output of the digitizer, typically a 16-bit TIFF (.tif) file, is fed to the workstation for analysis and visualization. One reason that the TIFF format is used over the more common and space-efficient JPEG (.jpg) format, is that JPEG format uses lossy compression. If data from the image digitizer are discarded in the compression process, the result is a compressed dynamic range of the overall system.

Analysis of the fluorescence data includes a check for microarray-to-microarray variability using a scatter plot, as illustrated earlier in Figure 6-4. However, assuring microarray-to-microarray agreement in gene expression levels first assumes that the fluorescence associated with each spot can be adequately quantified. The most common methods of accomplishing this is to rely on simple descriptive statistics, such as mean, mode, and median.

The mean is the average pixel density over a spot, corresponding to the average fluorescence intensity (see Figure 6-15). The advantage of using the mean intensity level is that it decreases error due to variance in DNA deposition during microarray preparation. The mode is the most likely intensity value, represented by the highest peak in the fluorescence plot. The mode is

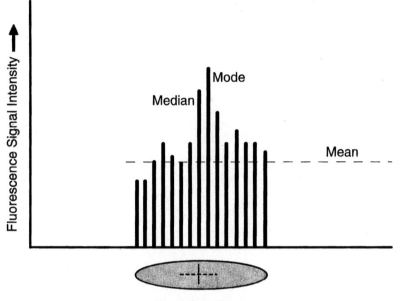

Figure 6-15   Microarray Fluorescence Statistical Analysis.

resistant to outlier values, but the measure is unstable when the intensity plot is bimodal (has two major peaks). The median, the mid-point in the intensity plot, is also resistant to outliers.

Other measures of assessing spot intensity include the total pixel intensity—the sum of all pixels corresponding to fluorescence in an area. However, the total intensity value is sensitive to the amount of DNA deposited on a spot in the microarray. The volume measure is the sum of signal intensity above background noise for each pixel. Although there are several additional means of quantifying spot fluorescence, the most common measure is the mean, followed by the mode and median descriptive statistics.

Possible fluorescence intensity distributions associated with common spotting errors are illustrated in Figure 6-16. Notice that each distribution results in a different mean and median intensity reading, even though the gene expression in each case is identical. The role of statistical analysis in reading the intensity value associated with each spot is to control for variability—a challenge that isn't always possible. For example, when a microarray is contaminated, simple statistical analysis on individual spots offers little in the way of reducing variability or noise. However, inter- and intra-microarray comparisons can be used to identify contamination and other sources of variability.

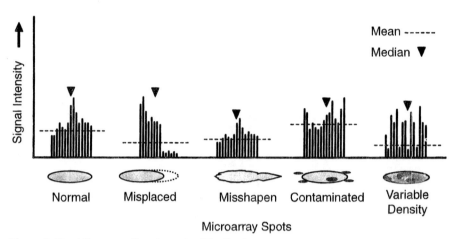

Figure 6-16   Microarray Spot Intensity Distributions.

Intra-microarray comparisons, in which spotting is duplicated within the same microarray, allow the statistical analysis to control for variability in the spotting process at the expense of fewer gene expression experiments per microarray. If three spots are used per expression experiment, then one of the three spots that are contaminated can be identified through statistical analysis of the relative intensities (see Figure 6-17).

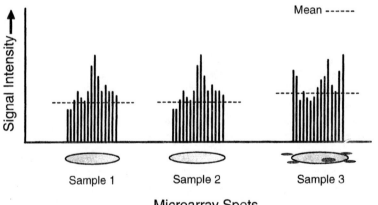

Figure 6-17   Intra-Microarray Intensity Comparisons. Statistical analysis of the means of relative fluorescence intensity can be used to programmatically identify a contaminated sample (far right) that can be discarded from the final gene expression analysis, thereby reducing variability in the experiment.

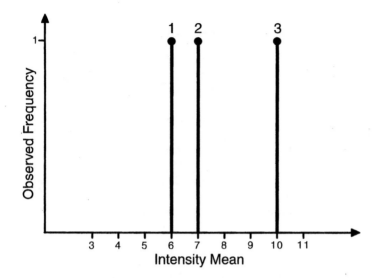

Figure 6-18 Observed Frequency of Differences Between Means. The intensity values associated with sample 3 appears to be different from the values derived from samples 1 and 2. The scale of intensity mean values is arbitrary.

Although the mean intensity of fluorescence from Sample 3 in Figure 6-17 is, by visual inspection, obviously different from the means of Samples 1 and 2, the issue is whether this difference is statistically significant—that is, if the difference can't be explained by chance alone. Whether or not the differences in mean values (depicted in a frequency plot in Figure 6-18) are significant depends on the cutoff criteria.

Mathematically, the mean intensity value is computed as:

$$\bar{X} = \frac{\sum\limits_{i=1}^{n} X_i}{i} = \frac{6+7+10}{3} = 7.67$$

The standard deviation (s), a measure of variability in the sampled data, is computed as:

$$s^2 = \frac{1}{n-1} \sum\limits_{i=1}^{n} (X_i - \bar{X})^2 = \frac{1}{2}[(6-10)^2 + (7-10)^2 + (10-10)^2]$$

$$s^2 = \frac{1}{2}[(-4)^2 + (-3)^2 + (0)^2] = \frac{1}{2}(16 + 9) = 12.5$$

$$s = \sqrt{12.5} = 3.54$$

The standard deviation is useful in defining the distribution of data in terms of z-scores, which are measures that represent the deviation of a specific observation from the mean divided by the standard deviation. Given a standard deviation (s) of 3.54, the mean intensity levels of the three samples are all within about one standard deviation of the mean—much better than the typical criterion for inclusion of within the typical four z-scores (four standard deviations from the mean), as illustrated in Figure 6-19.

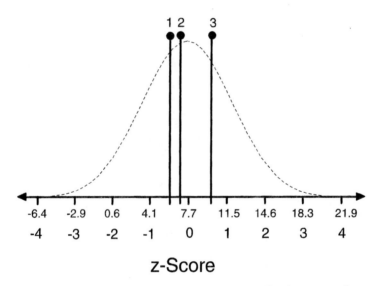

Figure 6-19   Z-Scores of Mean Intensity Values. All values are within one z-score (one standard deviation from the mean).

TOOL SELECTION

An arbitrary decision to use median spot fluorescence intensity instead of a mean or mode measurement, for example, can drastically alter gene expression analysis. Ideally, the selection of a statistical method reflects the researcher's knowledge of the underlying biological principles as well as the inherent limitations of the statistical methods used to analyze the data. Researchers typically consider the statistical methods used when determining whether the data from a particular experiment is valuable to them.

With the proliferation of multifunction calculators, dedicated statistical analysis software packages (see Table 6-4), and statistical analysis available through general-purpose database and spreadsheet programs, it's all too easy to statistically analyze research data without considering the underlying assumptions of the statistical tools used. For example, many of the descriptive statistics assume that the population data—the parameters—follow a known and definable distribution, even though the distribution may be unknown. Similarly, even though Bayes' Theorem assumes independence of variables, it's often used to estimate probabilities of co-occurring events that may be linked in some way. In addition, it's possible to spend months on an experimental design and end up with worthless data because the sample size or composition of the experimental groups is insufficient to address the question at hand. In the vernacular of statisticians, the experimental design has insufficient power to reject the null hypothesis.

Table 6-4 Statistical Analysis Tools. This sample is representative of the thousands of tools available on the market for statistical analysis.

Type of Tool	Examples
Dedicated, General-Purpose	SAS, Minitab, Matlab, Decision Pro, MVSP, SimStat, NCSS, PASS, SISA, Statistica, S-Plus, R, Splus, SPSS, Perl, SigmaStat, Statview, Prism, Mathematica, ProStat
Ancillary, General-Purpose	Microsoft Excel
Bioinformatics-Specific	BLAST, VAST, BioConductor
Excel Add-Ons	Analyse-it, XLStat, XLStatistics

Selecting the statistical methods and tools most appropriate for a problem requires an understanding of the assumptions of the available statistical methods, the underlying biology, the data requirements, the validity of the overall experimental design, and computational requirements. One way of assessing the performance of a set of statistical tools is to determine its sensitivity and specificity. Given a criterion for when to call a test abnormal, sensitivity is the percentage of actual positives that are counted as positive, whereas specificity is the percentage of actual negatives that are rejected.

Expressed another way, sensitivity is the number of true positives divided by the sum of true positives and false negatives, as illustrated in Figure 6-20. Similarly, specificity is the number of true negatives divided by the sum of false positives and true negatives.

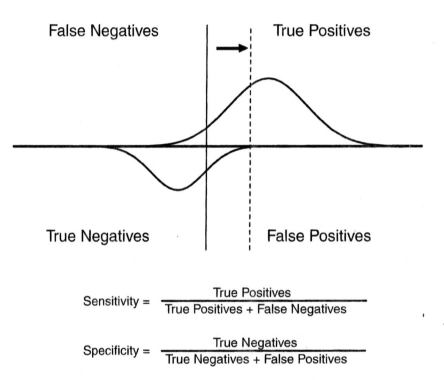

$$\text{Sensitivity} = \frac{\text{True Positives}}{\text{True Positives} + \text{False Negatives}}$$

$$\text{Specificity} = \frac{\text{True Negatives}}{\text{True Negatives} + \text{False Positives}}$$

Figure 6-20 Sensitivity and Specificity. Both are a function of the number of true and false positives and negatives. Moving the cutoff value (vertical bar) to the right (dotted line) results in almost no false positives at the expense of fewer true positives.

Another way to evaluate the sensitivity and specificity of a statistical test is to determine its receiver operating characteristic (ROC) curve, as in Figure 6-21. The ROC curve is a plot of a test's sensitivity versus 1 – specificity, or true-positive rate versus false-positive rate. The higher the curve of a test, the greater its discriminative ability. Every point along an ROC curve corresponds to test sensitivity and specificity at a given threshold of abnormal. All else being equal, a test with the greatest discriminative ability (Test A) is superior to a test with lower discriminative ability (Test B).

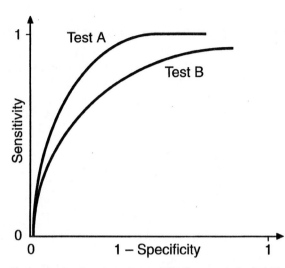

Figure 6-21 Receiver Operating Characteristic (ROC) Curves For the two tests shown here, Test A provides superior discrimination over Test B.

STATISTICS OF ALIGNMENT

Given that much of the day-to-day statistical work in bioinformatics involves using tools that utilize statistical principles to explore nucleotide and protein sequences, a review of some of the principles related to the statistics of alignment are in order. Because good alignment of nucleotide sequences can occur by chance alone, statistical methods, often combined with heuristics, are used to help determine the significance of an alignment. For example, the BLAST algorithm computes the expected frequency of matching sequences that should occur in an alignment search in order to conduct a more efficient search.

In calculating an alignment score (S), the underlying question is usually "is the alignment score high enough to suggest homology?" The first part of the answer is to determine how high a score could occur by chance alone. However, the challenge here is no mathematical theory adequately describes statistics of the scores that can be expected for global alignments. In lieu of an underlying mathematical basis for computing the significance of global alignments, ad-hoc methods have been devised for comparing alignment scores with scores of random sequences that seem to align, using sequences the same length and composition as those under study.

The situation is different for local alignment, because extreme value distribution adequately describes the expected distribution of random local alignment scores. By relating the observed direct score to the expected distribution, the statistical significance of alignment can be assessed.

A statistic commonly used in alignment searches is the z-score, which is a measure of the distance from the mean, measured in standard deviation units. If each sequence to be aligned is randomized and an optimal alignment is made, the result is a series of scores (S) for the alignment of two sequences, with a mean (μ) and standard deviation (δ). In this scenario, the z-score (z) is computed as:

$$z = \frac{S - \mu}{\delta}$$

The advantage of a z-score over a simple percentage score is that it corrects for compositional biases in the sequence and accounts for the varying length of sequences. The problem with using a z-score to assess whether an alignment occurred by chance is that a z-score assumes a normal distribution. However, alignment data don't follow a normal distribution. As a result, a higher z-score should be taken as a threshold of significance.

Distributions have different uses in bioinformatics statistical works. Binomial distributions are used for spotting stretches of DNA with unusual nucleotide sequences and pair-wise sequence comparisons. Normal distributions are used for modeling continuous random variables, with applications such as the statistical significance of pairwise sequence comparison. Multinomial distributions are used for spotting stretches of DNA with unusual content, distinguishing tests for introns by composition, and quantifying relative codon frequency.

Relying solely on purely mathematical methods for statistical analysis without incorporating heuristics or knowledge of the underlying biology can often lead to incorrect conclusions. For example, a run of pure C-G sequences in a sequence to be aligned will likely match many C-G–rich regions in a sequence database. Based on this knowledge, masks can be used to hide these regions from the database search, allowing the search algorithm to ignore these regions during the search process.

CLUSTERING AND CLASSIFICATION

Two statistical operations commonly applied to microarray data are clustering and classification. Clustering is a purely data-driven activity that uses only data from the study or experiment to group together measurements. Classification, in contrast, uses additional data, including heuristics, to assign measurements to groups.

Two of the most common methods of clustering gene expression data are hierarchical clustering (see Figure 6-22) and k-means clustering (see Figure 6-23). Mathematically, hierarchical clustering involves computing a matrix of all distances for each expression measurement in the study, merging and averaging the values of the closest nodes, and repeating the process until all nodes are merged into a single node. One of the many options of computing the matrix of distances involves evaluating the relative ranking of the measures of red and green fluorescence intensities taken from the expression matrix associated with a given microarray study.

K-means clustering involves generating cluster centers (squares in Figure 6-23) in n-dimensions and computing the distance of each data point to each of the cluster centers. Data points are assigned to the closest cluster center. A new cluster position is then computed by averaging the data points assigned to cluster center. The process is repeated until the positions of the cluster centers stabilize.

Clustering microarray gene expression data is useful because it may provide insight into gene function. For example, if two genes are expressed in the same way, they may be functionally related. In addition, if a gene's function is

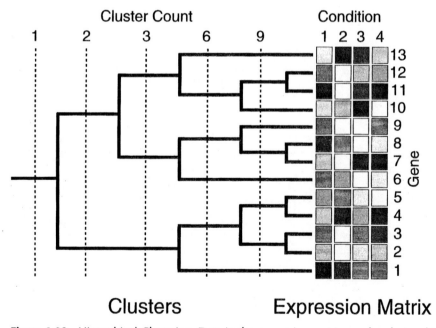

Figure 6-22 Hierarchical Clustering. Data in the expression matrix can be clustered to an arbitrary depth.

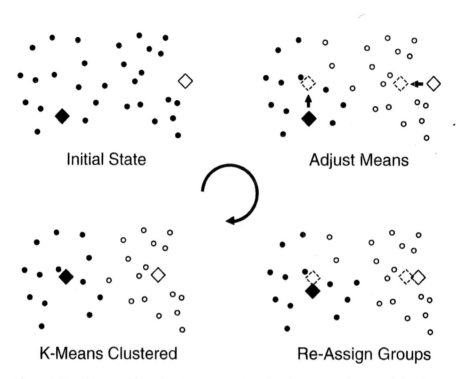

Figure 6-23   K-Means Clustering. Items are assigned to the nearest cluster and the cluster centers (squares) are recalculated. This process is repeated until the cluster centers don't change significantly. In the end, there are two clusters, one with filled circles and one with empty circles.

unknown, but it is clustered with genes of known function, the gene may share functionality with the genes of known function. Similarly, if the activity of genes in one cluster consistently precedes activity in a second cluster, the genes in the two may be functionally related. For example, genes in the first cluster may regulate activity of genes in the second cluster.

Common classification methods applied to gene expression data include the use of linear models, logistic regression, Bayes' Theorem, decision trees, and support vector machines. For example, consider using Bayes' Theorem to classify microarray data into one of two groups, illustrated graphically in Figure 6-24.

Using Bayes' Theorem to determine whether given a data point should be classified as a member of, for example, the open-circle group, the following equation applies:

$$p(OpenCircles \mid X_i Y_i) = p(OpenCircles \mid X_i) \times p(OpenCircles \mid Y_i)$$

For the data point A ($x = 7, y = 3$), B ($x = 10, y = 5$), and C ($x = 14, y = 3$) the equations take the form:

$$p(OpenCircles \mid X_aY_a) = p(OpenCircles \mid 7) \times p(OpenCircles \mid 3)$$

$$p(OpenCircles \mid X_bY_b) = p(OpenCircles \mid 10) \times p(OpenCircles \mid 5)$$

$$p(OpenCircles \mid X_cY_c) = p(OpenCircles \mid 14) \times p(OpenCircles \mid 3)$$

Visually, the data point C in Figure 6-24 can reasonably be classified as a member of the open-circle group. Conversely, the probability that data point A is a member of the open-circle group is high. The main issue surrounds the cutoff probability for evaluating the equations. If the probability must be high in order to accept the hypothesis that a given data point is a member of the open-circle group, then data point B may not be able to be classified in the open-circle group, and may best be assigned to another group.

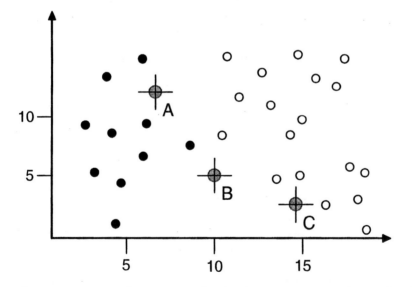

Figure 6-24 Bayes' Theorem Example. The data points A, B, and C can be classified using Bayes' Theorem.

ON THE HORIZON

For decades, statistical analysis has been recognized as a necessary component of scientific R&D. Since the work of Ronald Fisher and others in the 1930s, statistical methods have been applied to everything from process control in automobile factories to predicting the results of presidential elections to estimating crop yields. Many computer-aided statistical methods, such as Monte Carlo methods, were first applied in nuclear physics and migrated soon thereafter to research and engineering. Today, the desktop microcomputer has made it possible for every researcher, student, and layperson to explore statistical principles. With the ever-decreasing cost of computation, this trend of moving statistical concepts out of the laboratory and into the public domain is expected to continue.

Consider that, since the introduction of genetically modified crops in the mid-1990s, a great deal of public attention has been focused on the likelihood that these crops could either contaminate traditional crops or have an adverse effect on consumers. Statistical methods have been embraced by politicians, scientists, and farmers in the EU and elsewhere to back their particular perspective on the issues. For example, the British government has established buffer zones to separate organic and genetically modified crops, based on statistical models. For example, genetically modified maize can't be planted within 200 meters of organic crops, thereby preventing the genetically modified maize from cross-fertilizing organic maize. With the various special interest groups involved, each using statistical analyses to back their positions on genetically modified foods, it's likely that statistical methods could easily hold the key to whether at least one end-product of bioinformatics R&D survives.

ENDNOTE

Modern bioinformatics methods are considerably more complicated than simple Mendelian genetics. Advanced methods, such as BLAST, are based on statistical methods that aren't completely understood by the average researcher. With the thrust into post-genomic bioinformatics, it's likely that many more statistical methods will be created to solve practical problems—long before researchers fully grasp their theoretical foundations and limitations. Because of the number of variables and underlying assumptions involved in experimental design and the even relatively trivial statistical analysis, unless you're well versed in statistical methods, the best approach is to consult with a statistician before investing time and resources in a research project.

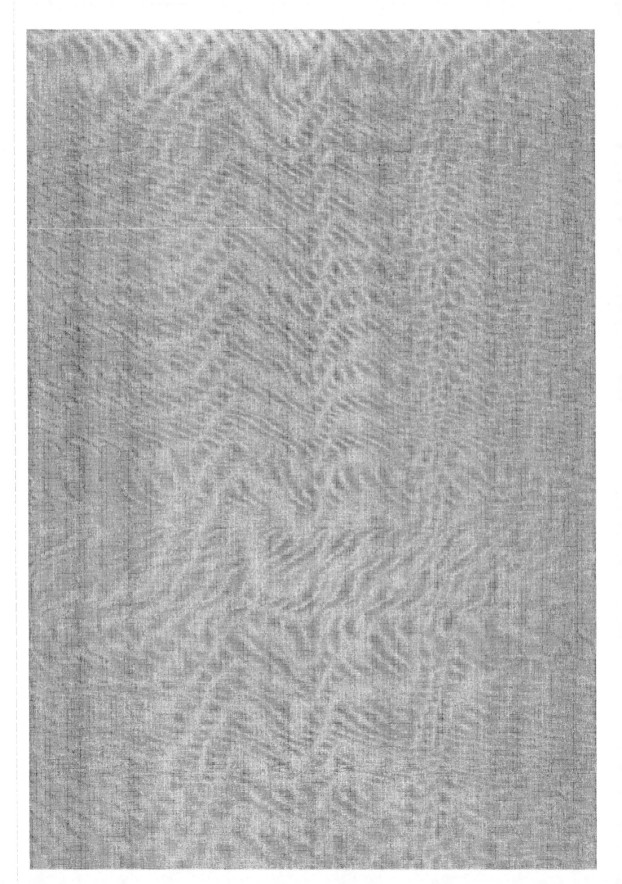

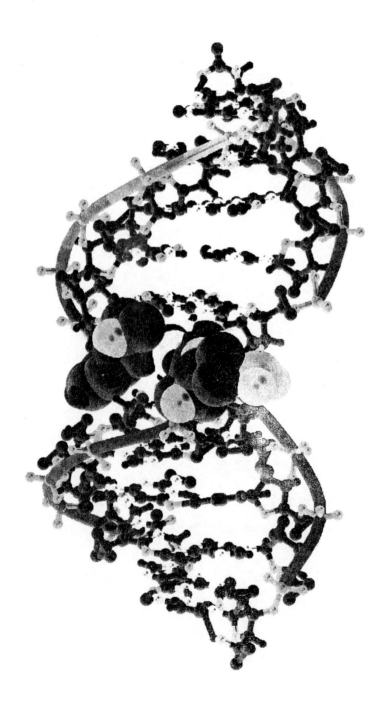

> Structure of the reduced form of Merp, the periplasmic protein from the Bacterial Mercury Detoxification System. PDB entry 1AFI. Image produced with PDB Structure Explorer.

CHAPTER

Data Mining

Where is the knowledge we have lost in information?
Where is the wisdom we have lost in knowledge?
— T.S. Elliot, "The Rock"

Getting at the hard-won sequence and structure data in molecular biology databases and the functional data in the online biomedical literature is complicated by the size and complexity of the databases. Often, it's assumed—sometimes incorrectly—that certain data are contained in a database. However, exhaustively searching for the raw data and performing the transformation and manipulations on the data through manual operations is often impractical. Similarly, in cases where it isn't certain what relationships can be garnered from searching through a database, the odds of finding every biologically relevant relationship through manually authored query statements are low. When it's known in general what resides in a database and there is a need to extract it, the challenge is more of a translation problem. Conversely, when very little is known about what resides in the database, the work is primarily data discovery. In either case, the time and computational resources required to locate and manipulate the data are limiting factors.

Camouflaged by the size and complexity of a database, the millions of data points from genomic or proteomic studies are of little value. Only when these data are categorized according to a meaningful theme are they useful in furthering our understanding of sequence, structure, or function. Regardless of whether this categorization is at the base pair, chromosome, or gene level, an organizing theme is critical because it simplifies and reduces the complexity of what could otherwise be a flood of incomprehensible data. For example, the individual databases managed by the NCBI represent generally recognizable organizational themes that facilitate use of their contents. At a higher level, our understanding of health and disease is facilitated by the organization of clinical research data by organ system, pathogen, genetic aberration, or site of trauma.

Ideally, the creator and the users of the database share an understanding of the underlying organizational theme. These themes, and the tools used to support them, determine how easily databases created for one purpose can be used for other purposes. For example, in a relational database of gene sequences, the data may be arranged in tables, and the user may need to construct Structured Query Language (SQL) statements to search for and retrieve data. However, if inherited diseases organize the relational database, it may not readily support an efficient search by protein sequence.

The challenge for researchers looking in the exponentially increasing quantities of microbiology data for assumed and unknown relationships can be formidable, even if the number of data elements and dimensionality are relatively small. For example, a relational database with a few hundred records (rows) and a small number of fields per record (low dimensionality) can probably be searched manually for new interrelationships in the data. However, the task may involve creating relatively complicated, computationally intensive joins in order to create views that support a given hypothesis of how data are related. In addition, even within a relatively small database, it may be practically impossible to specify a relationship query exactly. At issue is how best to support the formulation of a hypothesis-based query. In addition, even if the technology is available that allows a researcher to specify any hypothetical query, the potential for discovering new relationships in data is a function of the insights and biases imposed by the researcher. While these limitations may be problematic in relatively small databases, they may be intolerable in databases with billions of interrelated data elements.

To avoid the computational constraints imposed by these large molecular biology databases, researchers frequently turn to biological heuristics to avoid exhaustive searches or processes with a low likelihood of success. For example, in hunting for new genes, a good place to start, from a statistical perspective, is near sequences that tend to be found between introns and exons. However, even with heuristics, user-directed discovery is inherently limited by the time required to manually search for new data.

An alternative to manual searching—and one that has had considerable success in the travel, banking, and telecommunications industries—is to use computer-mediated data mining, the process of automatically extracting meaningful patterns from usually very large quantities of seemingly unrelated data. Unlike human-directed exploration of databases, data mining can initiate queries that aren't limited to the user's fluency in authoring effective database queries. This isn't to say that data mining reduces the need for the researcher to establish a strategy or to evaluate the results of a data-mining session. When used in conjunction with the appropriate visualization tools, data mining allows the researcher to use her highly advanced pattern-recognition skills and knowledge of molecular biology to determine which results warrant further study. For example, mining the millions of data points from a series of microarray experiments might reveal several clusters of data, as visualized in a 3D cluster display. The researcher could then select data belonging to one or more of the clusters and use a variety of tools to determine the parameters that distinguish it from the other data.

Given the ever-increasing store of sequence and protein data from several worldwide genome projects, data mining the sequences has become a major research focus in bioinformatics. This is in part because molecular biologists can now conduct basic bioinformatics research from their desktop workstation, without the overhead of establishing a wet lab. The aim of this chapter is to explore data-mining techniques as an automated means of reducing the complexity of data in large bioinformatics databases and of discovering meaningful, useful patterns and relationships in data. The "Methods" section explores data mining from the perspective of the process of knowledge discovery. "Technology Overview" reviews the underlying computer infrastructure and algorithms that make data mining a practical endeavor. "Infrastructure" reviews the hardware and software requirements of an efficient data-mining operation. "Pattern Recognition and Discovery" explores the basic pattern-recognition process and how it can be extended to pattern discovery.

The "Machine Learning" section reviews the numerous technologies that can be applied to support data mining, from neural networks to Hidden Markov Models. "Text Mining" focuses on the importance of mining the biomedical literature for data on functions to complement the sequence and structure data mined from nucleotide and protein databases. The "Tools" section introduces some of the practical general-purpose and bioinformatics-specific tools available for data mining. The "On the Horizon" section looks at the leading-edge data-mining technologies, especially real-time transaction monitoring that promises to decrease the infrastructure requirements. The "Endnote" section explores the long-term role of machine learning versus human-directed data-mining efforts.

METHODS

Data mining isn't an endpoint, but is one stage in an overall knowledge-discovery process. It is an iterative process in which preceding processes are modified to support new hypotheses suggested by the data.

As illustrated in Figure 7-1, given a data warehouse or separate databases, the knowledge-discovery process involves:

1. Selection and sampling of the appropriate data from the database(s)
2. Preprocessing and cleaning of the data to remove redundancies, errors, and conflicts
3. Transforming and reducing data to a format more suitable for the data mining
4. Data mining
5. Evaluation of the mined data
6. Visualization of the evaluation results
7. Designing new data queries to test new hypotheses and returning to step 1

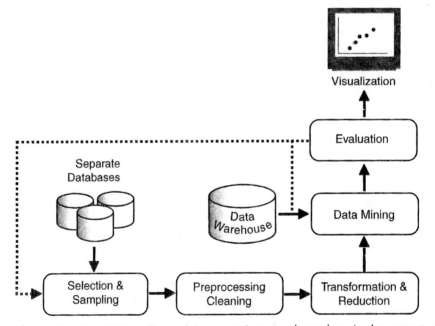

Figure 7-1 Data Mining. Data mining operations are shown here in the context of a larger knowledge-discovery process.

The relative timing of sequences in the knowledge-discovery process depends on whether the source of data is a data warehouse or one or more separate databases. A data warehouse is a central database in which data have been combined from a variety of non-compatible sources, such as sequencing machines, clinical systems, textual bibliographic databases, or national genomic databases. In the process of combining data from disparate sources, the data are selected, cleaned, and transformed to support user-driven analytical and data-driven mining tools.

Whereas a data warehouse is a ready store of data to be mined at any time, using separate databases requires much more work on an as-needed basis. The processing up to the point of data mining may take hours or weeks, depending on the complexity and size of the databases involved in the process.

The advantage of using a data warehouse approach to data mining is time-savings. Assuming that everything needed for data mining is available in the data warehouse, a typical mining operation may be able to be completed in a matter of hours, depending on the processing power available, the size of the data warehouse, and the complexity of the mining operation.

However, this ability to begin mining operations at any time comes at a cost. A data warehouse that is capable of efficiently supporting data mining is significantly larger and the associated data processing takes much longer than in a simple database, one designed to provide a central, unified data repository that can be accessed through a single user interface. The reason for the increased data warehouse size and increase in complexity of associated processing is the increasingly fine-grained data required for data-mining support, as well as the need to incorporate contextual or metadata to support the data-mining process. For example, data mining requires a controlled vocabulary, usually implemented as part of a data dictionary, so that a single word can be used to express a given concept. Similarly, the extra attention to cleaning the data and other processing is necessary to maximize the odds that the conclusions based on data mining are valid.

What's more, there is no guarantee that the data in the data warehouse will be sufficient to support the desired data-mining activities. Additional data may be needed from the source databases, which then must also be cleaned, transformed, and stored, activities that obviate the time advantage of the data warehouse. One approach to guarding against this eventuality is to incorporate more data into the data warehouse when it is built, at the cost of increased complexity and size, with no guarantee that any of the additional data in the warehouse will ever be used in mining activities.

The primary advantage of using a database approach to data mining is that resources are used on an as-needed basis. Only those data from the separate databases that are involved with a specific data-mining operation are processed. Although it may take days or weeks in order to arrange for the appropriate processing in preparation for data mining, the resources required for just-in-time data mining are generally much less than those associated with data warehousing.

Regardless of the data source, knowledge discovery is an iterative process that involves feedback at each stage, as illustrated in Figure 7-1. This feedback can be used programmatically or can serve as the basis for human decision-making. For example, if the preprocessing and cleaning of data from a data warehouse results in an insufficient quantity of cleaned data, or inappropriate data altogether, then the researcher may redefine the selection and sampling criteria to include more or different data.

Although the methodology seems straightforward, data mining and the overall knowledge-discovery process involve much more than the simple statistical analysis of data. For example, difficult-to-describe metrics, such as novelty, interestingness, and understandability, are often used to define data-mining parameters for data discovery. Similarly, each phase of the knowledge-discovery process has associated challenges, as outlined here.

Selection and Sampling

Because of practical computational limitations and a priori knowledge, data mining isn't simply about searching for every possible relationship in a database. In a large database or data warehouse, there may be hundreds or thousands of valueless relationships. For example, a researcher interested in the relationship of SNPs with clinical findings can reasonably ignore the zip code of the tissue donors or the dates that the tissue samples were obtained. There are exceptions, of course, such as if there is a concentration of a specific ethnicity in a geographical area defined by a zip code.

Because there may be millions of records involved and thousands of variables, initial data mining is typically restricted to computationally tenable samples of the holding in an entire data warehouse. The evaluation of the relationships that are revealed in these samples can be used to determine which relationships in the data should be mined further using the complete data warehouse. With large, complex databases, even with sampling, the computational resource requirements associated with non-directed data mining may be excessive. In this situation, researchers generally rely on their knowledge of biology to identify potentially valuable relationships and they limit sampling based on these heuristics.

Preprocessing and Cleaning

The bulk of work associated with knowledge discovery is preparing the data for the actual analysis associated with data mining. The major preparatory activities, listed in Table 7-1, are normally performed to some extent in the creation of a data warehouse. However, data mining may be performed on one or more independent databases, or the data in the warehouse may not have been cleaned initially, at least to the degree necessary for optimum data-mining results. In either case, these activities need to be performed as part of the preprocessing and cleaning phase of the overall knowledge-discovery process.

Table 7-1 Data Mining Preparatory Activities.

Data Characterization
Consistency Analysis
Domain Analysis
Data Enrichment
Frequency and Distribution Analysis
Normalization
Missing Value Analysis

Data characterization involves creating a high-level description of the nature and the content of the data to be mined. This stage in the knowledge-discovery process is primarily for the programmers and other staff involved in a data-mining project. It provides a form of documentation that can be referred to by those who may not be familiar with the underlying biology represented by the data.

Consistency analysis is the process of determining the variability in the data, independent of the domain. Consistency analysis is primarily a statistical assessment of data, based solely on data values. Outliers and values determined to be significantly different from other data may be automatically excluded from the knowledge-discovery process, based on predefined statistical constraints. For example, data associated with a given parameter that is more than three standard deviations from the mean might be excluded from the mining operation.

Domain analysis involves validating the data values in the larger context of the biology. That is, domain analysis goes beyond simply verifying that a data value is a text string or an integer, or that it's statistically consistent with other data on the same parameter, to ensure that it makes sense in the context of the biology. For example, values for physiological parameters can be validated to the extent that they are within physiologically possible ranges consistent with life. A blood pH of 13, a body temperature of 45 degrees Celsius, a protein with molecular weight of 20 milligrams, and a patient age of 120 would be flagged as invalid values that should be excluded from the knowledge-discovery process. Domain analysis requires that someone familiar with the biology create the heuristics that can be applied to the data.

Data enrichment involves drawing from multiple data sources to minimize the limitations of a single data source. For example, two databases on inherited diseases might each be sparsely populated in terms of proteins that are associated with particular diseases. This deficit could be addressed by incorporating data from both databases, assuming only a moderate degree of overlap in the content of the two databases. Data enrichment may be tied to consistency analysis, so that outliers that would skew knowledge-discovery results aren't included in the final analysis.

Frequency and distribution analysis places weights on values as a function of their frequency of occurrence. The effect is to maximize the contribution of common findings while minimizing the effect of rare occurrences on the conclusions made from the data-mining output. For example, a clinical database of genetic diseases might contain 500 entries for one disease and only 1 entry for another, based on the number of patients with each disease who were admitted to a given hospital or clinic. Ignoring the relative frequency of each disease in the database could lead a researcher to conclude that the odds of patients expressing either disease is the same.

The normalization process involves transforming data values from one representation to another, using a predefined range of final values. For example, qualitative values, such as "high" and "low," and qualitative values from multiple sources regarding a particular parameter might be normalized to a numerical score from 1 to 10.

The major issues in normalization are range, granularity, accuracy, precision, scale, and units. Range is the difference between the highest and lowest values that are represented, whereas granularity is a static property of the scale. For example, length might be measured with a granularity of either nanometers or millimeters. Accuracy is a measure of how close measurements come to actual values, and precision is a measure of the repeatability of the measurements.

The most common scales used in the normalization process are listed in Table 7-2. Absolute scales are based on quantities, such as the number of amino acids in a protein. Nominal scales are based on unique identifiers, such as names and descriptions. Categorical scales assign data to numerical or textual categories. Ordinal scales put things in order, according to some organizational theme. For example, proteins can be ordered according to molecular weight. Rank scales are like ordinal scales with the addition of a natural ranking, such as "more stable" and "less stable" protein configurations. Interval scales have a natural ordering, such as time. Ratio scales are expressed as a multiple or a fraction of a unit or interval, such as micrometers and milligrams.

Table 7-2   Scales Used in Normalization.

Scale	Example
Absolute	Count (3 amino acids)
Nominal	List of Protein Names (Lysine, Arginine, Tyrosine)
Ordinal	Process Phase (first, second, third)
Categorical	Types of Amino Acids (essential, non-essential)
Rank	Protein folding (primary, secondary, tertiary)
Interval	Time (seconds)
Ratio	Weight (micrograms)

With the exception of absolute scales, these scales can be converted to another scale if they are the same type and measure the same attribute. When data are defined with the same scale, the normalization process depends on the type of data. For example, nominal scales are converted to other nominal scales by a mapping function. However, mapping can introduce errors when there is a one-to-many mapping or many-to-one mapping between the two nominal scales. For example, the name of an amino acid can be mapped to a triplet of base pairs, but if there are multiple possible base pairs that code for a given amino acid, then the alternative base pair sequences are lost in the translation.

Both ordinal and rank order scales are translated by a function that maintains their relative order. As in the mapping of nominal scales, errors of omission are introduced by the conversion process when there isn't a one-to-one mapping between the two scales. Interval scales are converted to other interval scales through linear functions that preserve the ordering but shift the relative values, as in the conversion of degrees Fahrenheit to degrees Celsius. Ratio scales are converted to another ratio scale by a constant multiplier. For example, a ratio scale of 0 to 2 meters could be multiplied by a factor of 100 to provide a scale of 0 to 200 centimeters.

The units used in the process of normalization may be primary, such as seconds of time or micrograms of mass, or derived, such as density (grams per cubic centimeter) or volume (cubic millimeters). The standard Systeme International (SI) measurement units for primary units include meter for length, kilogram for mass, second for time, ampere for electrical current, degree Kelvin for temperature, and the mole for molecules.

The final preprocessing and cleaning activity, missing-value analysis, involves detecting, characterizing, and dealing with missing data values. One way of dealing with missing data values is to substitute the mean, mode, or median value of the relevant data that are available.

Transformation and Reduction

In the transformation and reduction phase of the knowledge-discovery process, data sets are reduced to the minimum size possible through sampling or summary statistics. For example, tables of data may be replaced by descriptive statistics, such as mean and standard deviation.

Transformation involves translating one type of data to another through mathematical or mapping operations that, for example, map numerical data onto textual data (or vice versa). Transformation differs from the normalization process in the preprocess and cleaning phase of knowledge discovery in that the purpose of the transformation isn't to allow the combination of data from multiple sources, but rather to directly support the data-mining and knowledge-discovery process. For example, normalized data may be transformed from floating-point (such as 3.14) to integer data to increase computer processor performance.

Data-Mining Methods

The process of data mining is concerned with extracting patterns from the data, typically using classification, regression, link analysis, segmentation, or deviation detection (see Figure 7-2). Classification involves mapping data into one of several predefined or newly discovered classes. In the former case, a set of predefined examples is used to develop a model that can be used to classify data culled from the data warehouse or database. In the latter case, the system develops its own models that it uses to classify data according to analysis of the data. In the illustration, there are three groups or classes of data, (A), (B), and (C). The classification rule may specify minimum proximity to the center of a particular group, as defined by numerical range or statistical spread, for example.

Data mining based on regression methods involves assigning data a continuous numerical variable based on statistical methods. One goal in using regression methods is to extrapolate trends from a few samples of the data. In the example in Figure 7-2, the extrapolation formula is a simple linear function of the form:

$$y = mx + b$$

where x and y are coordinates on the plot, m is the slope of the line, and b is a constant. In practice, more complex extrapolation formulas are used to describe data trends.

Link analysis evaluates apparent connections or links between data in the database or data warehouse. Link analysis highlights correlations in data that can suggest linkage, but not causality. In the illustration, the two pairs of data points are apparently linked, in that the value of one data element in the pair can be predicted by the value of the other data point in the pair.

Deviation detection identifies data values that are outside of the norm, as defined by existing models or by evaluating the ordering of observations. The outlier in the illustration is an example of a data value outside of the expected spread of data in a sample. The data may represent a particular sequence of amino acids or the molecular weight of a protein, or a vital sign, for example.

Segmentation-based data mining identifies classes or groups of data that behave similarly, according to some metric. Segmentation is akin to link analysis applied to groups of data instead of individual data points. In the figure, groups (A) and (C) behave similarly.

These methods of data mining are typically used in combination with each other, either in parallel or as part of a sequential operation. For example, segmentation requires classes to be defined through a classification process. Similarly, link analysis assumes that statistical analysis, including correlation coefficients, are available. Likewise, deviation detection assumes that the data have been properly classified and evaluated statistically to define the "normal" model. As described later in this chapter, there are a variety of technologies available to support these methods.

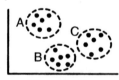
Classification

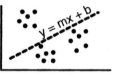
Regression

Link Analysis

Deviation Detection

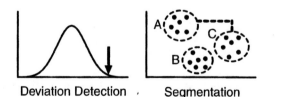
Segmentation

Figure 7-2 Data Mining Methods. Classification—Mapping to a class or group. Regression—Statistical analysis. Link Analysis—Correlation of data. Deviation Detection—Difference from the norm. Segmentation—Similarity function.

Evaluation

In the evaluation phase of knowledge discovery, the patterns identified by the data-mining analysis are interpreted. Typical evaluation ranges from simple statistical analysis and complex numerical analysis of sequences and structures to determining the clinical relevance of the findings.

Visualization

Visualization of evaluation results is an optional stage in the knowledge-discovery process, but one that typically adds considerable value to the overall system. Visualization can range from converting tabular listings of data summaries to pie charts and similar business graphics, to using real-time data to create 3D virtual reality displays that can be manipulated by haptic controllers.

Designing New Queries

Data mining is an iterative continual activity, in that there are always new hypotheses to test. Sometimes the new hypotheses are suggested by the data returned by the mining process, and other times the hypotheses originate from other research. In either case, testing the new hypotheses requires formulating new queries and revisiting the selection and sampling stage of the data-mining process.

TECHNOLOGY OVERVIEW

The remainder of this chapter provides an overview of the key technologies that can be applied to data mining, especially those capable of supporting the basic data-mining methods outlined earlier. As a prelude to this discussion, it's important to note that an efficient and effective data-mining system requires, above all, an experimental design that reflects the biology of the data being mined. In this regard, technology is an empowering agent that provides leverage to facilitate a well-designed data-mining initiative—technology isn't a solution in itself. Simply connecting a black box to a database with hopes of it turning up fruitful information on previously hidden relationships in the data is unlikely at best.

Given this caveat, data mining requires a hardware and software infrastructure capable of supporting high-throughput data processing and a network capable of supporting data communications from the database to the visualization workstation. With a robust hardware and software infrastructure in place, processes such as machine learning can be used to automatically manage and refine the knowledge-discovery and data-mining processes. This work can be performed with minimal user interaction once a knowledgeable researcher has established the basic design of the system.

The core technologies that actually perform the work of data mining, whether under computer control or directed by users, provide a means of simplifying the complexity and reducing the effective size of the databases. This focus isn't limited to genome sequences and protein structures, but extends to the wealth of data hidden in the online literature. Advanced text-mining methods are used to identify textual data and place them in the proper context.

Finally, as discussed later in this chapter, although data mining was once relegated to internal research groups, the technology is readily available today through a variety of commercial and academic shareware tools. These tools range from shrink-wrapped, general-purpose software tools to bioinformatics-specific commercial and academic systems designed for highly specific data-mining applications.

INFRASTRUCTURE

At first glance, data mining can be performed with little more than a laptop and a connection to the Internet. Although it's possible to work with such a system, serious data-mining work typically requires much more in terms of infrastructure. As illustrated in Figure 7-3, a typical laboratory data-mining infrastructure includes high-speed Internet and intranet connectivity, a data warehouse with a data dictionary that defines a standard vocabulary and data format, several databases, and high-performance computer hardware. Not shown are the software tools, including the database management system (DBMS) software that supports queries and searching and ensures data integrity and the data mining software.

In the example in Figure 7-3, the data-mining operations take place on a workstation with a high-speed connection to the data warehouse. However, this centralized data-mining infrastructure is only one of several configurations possible. For example, a competing infrastructure involves distributing the data-mining operation to process-specific workstations, as illustrated in Figure 7-4. In this configuration, a server doles out data in a format appropriate to the process performed by a particular workstation. In this way, greater overall throughput can be achieved, using inexpensive desktop hardware that is configured with the appropriate hardware and software tools to support a specific process. A distributed architecture also supports parallel processing, so that intermediate results from one workstation can be fed to another workstation. For example, link analysis performed on one workstation can be fed the regression analysis results from another workstation.

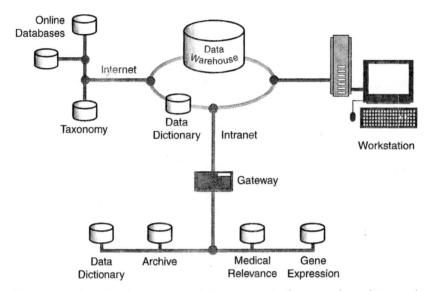

Figure 7-3 Centralized Data-Mining Infrastructure. In this example, a data warehouse, data dictionary, high-bandwidth access to data on the Internet, and a high-performance workstation form the basis for an effective data-mining operation.

The trend of distributed data mining using relatively inexpensive desktop hardware is largely a reflection of the economics of modern computing. Not only is the price-performance ratio of desktop hardware superior to that of mainframe computers, but the cost of desktop software licenses is typically several orders of magnitude less than that for mainframe computer systems. Of course, if time is the primary issue, then a mainframe computer optimized for data mining can provide superior performance compared to small networks of desktop computers.

PATTERN RECOGNITION AND DISCOVERY

Data mining is the process of identifying patterns and relationships in data that often are not obvious in large, complex data sets. As such, data mining involves pattern recognition and, by extension, pattern discovery. In bioinformatics, pattern recognition is most often concerned with the automatic classification of character sequences representative of the nucleotide bases or molecular structures, and of 3D protein structures.

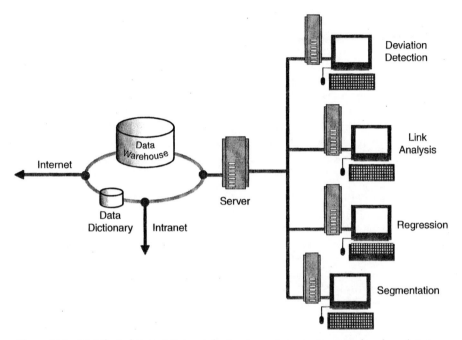

Figure 7-4 Distributed Data-Mining Infrastructure. A server to specialized workstations distributes data from a central data warehouse or single database. The distribution refers to the processing, not the data source.

As illustrated in Figure 7-5, the pattern-recognition process starts with an unknown pattern, such as a potential protein structure, and ends with a label for the pattern. From an information-processing perspective, pattern recognition can be viewed as a data simplification process that filters extraneous data from consideration and labels the remaining data according to a classification scheme.

The major steps in the pattern recognition and discovery process are:

■ **Feature Selection.** Given a pattern, the first step in pattern recognition is to select a set of features or attributes from the universe of available features that will be used to classify the pattern. When pattern recognition is directed at known patterns, the researcher defines a priori the features that will be used to distinguish the pattern from other data. Feature selection often takes the form of exemplars or representative examples of the features that will be measured, such as the tertiary geometry of a protein. In pattern discovery, which is more complex than simple pattern recognition, feature selection is under program control. Instead of an a priori definition of pattern attributes defining a class or group of data that are similar or equivalent in some way, samples are classified programmatically into empirically established groups, based on groups or clusters in the unlabeled collection of samples. That is, simple pattern recognition is assumption-driven, in that a hypothesis is developed and tested against the data. In pattern discovery, the extracted data serve as the seed of a new hypothesis. Clustering techniques are used to group samples that are more similar to each other than to other groups, and that have a low internal cluster variability or scatter.

■ **Measurement.** The measurement phase of the pattern-recognition and discovery process involves converting the original pattern into a representation that can be easily manipulated programmatically. For example, a 3D vector image of a protein might be represented as a series of 2D matrices. Similarly, a nucleotide sequence may be represented by a series of integers (for example, A = 1, T = 2, C = 3, and G = 4), depending on the underlying technology used to perform the pattern-matching operation.

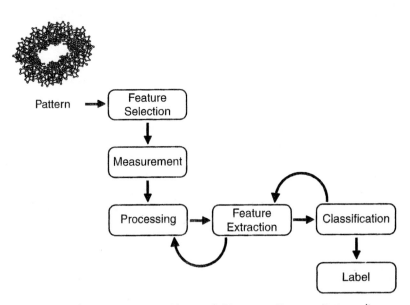

Figure 7-5 The Pattern-Recognition and Discovery Process. Pattern discovery differs from pattern recognition in that feature selection is determined empirically under program control.

- **Processing.** After the measurement process, the data are processed to remove noise and prepare for feature extraction. Processing typically involves executing a variety of error checking and correction routines, as well as specialized processes that depend on the nature of the data. For example, images may undergo edge enhancement and transformation to correct for size and orientation variations (normalization) in order to facilitate feature extraction.
- **Feature Extraction.** Feature extraction involves searching for global and local features in the data that are defined as relevant to pattern matching during feature selection. Clustering techniques, in which similar data are grouped together, often form the basis of feature extraction.
- **Classification and Discovery.** In the classification phase of pattern recognition and discovery, data are classified based on measurements of similarity with other patterns. These measurements of similarity are commonly based on either a statistical or a structural approach. In the statistical approach, exemplar patterns are represented by points in a multidimensional space that is partitioned into regions associated with a classification. In the structural approach, the structures of the exemplar patterns are explicitly defined. In either case, the similarity of the data to be classified is compared with the exemplar data to assess closeness of association.
- **Labeling.** The pattern-recognition process ends when a label is assigned to the data, based on its membership in a class.

As illustrated in Figure 7-5, the pattern-recognition process isn't unidirectional, but is iterative to the extent that failures at the classification and feature-extraction stages can be corrected by reevaluating the preceding phase. For example, if the feature-extraction phase fails to identify relevant data, then the processing of the original image may need to be modified by removing extraneous data from consideration and by taking other, more relevant data, into consideration.

Feature extraction and classification and discovery, which represent the core of the pattern-recognition and discovery process, are performed by using some combination of classification, regression, segmentation, link analysis, and deviation detection methods, depending on the nature of the data. Similarly, these methods are supported by a variety of technologies and approaches, collectively referred to as machine learning, as described here.

MACHINE LEARNING

The pattern-matching and pattern discovery components of data mining are often performed by machine learning techniques. Machine learning isn't a single technology or approach, but encompasses a variety of methods that represent the convergence of several disciplines, including statistics, biological modeling, adaptive control theory, psychology, and artificial intelligence (AI). Although many computer scientists consider the entire field of machine learning to be an outgrowth of traditional statistical methods, biological modeling is clearly a source of several machine learning approaches. These include genetic algorithms and neural networks. Similarly, adaptive control theory, in which system parameters change dynamically to meet the current conditions, and psychological theories, especially those regarding positive and negative reinforcement learning, heavily influence machine learning methods. AI techniques, such as pattern matching through inductive logic programming, are designed to derive general rules from specific examples. As illustrated in Table 7-3, the spectrum of machine learning technologies applicable to data mining includes inductive logic programming, genetic algorithms, neural networks, statistical methods, Bayesian methods, decision trees, and Hidden Markov Models.

Table 7-3   Machine Learning Technologies and Their Applicability to Data-Mining Methods.

Machine Learning Technologies	Data-Mining Methods				
	Classification	Regression	Segmentation	Link Analysis	Deviation Detection
Inductive Logic Programming	X	X			
Genetic Algorithms	X	X	X		
Neural Networks	X	X	X		
Statistical Methods	X	X	X	X	X
Decision Trees	X		X		
Hidden Markov Models	X				

Regardless of the underlying technology, most machine learning follows the general process outlined in Figure 7-6. Input data are fed to a comparison engine that compares the data with an underlying model. The results of the comparison engine then direct a software actor to initiate some type of change. This output, whether it takes the form of a change in data or a modification of the underlying model, is evaluated by an evaluation engine, which uses the underlying goals of the system as a point of reference. Feedback from the actor and the evaluation engine direct changes in the model. In this scenario, the goals can be standard patterns that are known to be associated with the input data. Alternatively, the goals can be states, such as minimal change in output compared with the system's previous encounter with the same data.

The feedback loops and a mechanism capable of responding to feedback enable two types of machine learning: supervised and unsupervised. In supervised learning, the system is trained with a set of examples, called the training set. The goals are specific outputs that are associated with each input. For example, a specific amino acid sequence on the input can be associated with the name of a protein on the output. The performance of a supervised learning system can be evaluated by presenting the system with a known testing set that is similar to the training set.

In unsupervised learning, there is no specific output associated with a given input, and the system must invent new categories and ways to classify the input data. In machine learning systems based on unsupervised learning, it isn't known a priori whether the input data contains a biologically significant pattern, where it is, or even what it looks like.

One of the key issues in supervised learning is that the training set must be sufficiently large relative to the number of categories or different outputs provided by the machine learning system. When there are too many categories or recognized patterns that are consistent with the input data, the training data is said to be overfitted. That is, overfitting is the process of assigning undue importance to random variations in the data.

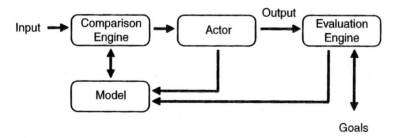

Figure 7-6   The Machine Learning Process.

Whether supervised or unsupervised, the machine learning process requires bias. It isn't enough to simply open a database up to a machine learning algorithm and sit back while it automatically discovers all of the interrelationships in the data. Bias is created in a machine learning system by placing constraints on the data that can be examined, by using different underlying models, and by altering the machine learning system goals. Bias can increase the efficiency of the machine language process and provide more meaningful results. For example, the process can probably ignore a correlation between the time of day a sample was evaluated and gene expression in a microarray. In practice, the bias can be a single heuristic, such as preferring the single, simplest rule that explains the data to a more complex solution. This "simplest solution" bias is often used with machine learning approaches to mining nucleotide sequence data.

Inductive Logic Programming

Inductive logic programming uses a set of rules or heuristics to categorize data. A common heuristic is to use change in entropy to iteratively choose an attribute of the data that will subset the data according to the attribute. That is, an entropy-based classification system based on an induction algorithm works by incrementally dividing the data into the largest possible spaces until all data has been assigned to a collection.

Consider the scenario depicted in Figure 7-7, in which the data to be classified includes 20 circles and 10 squares, 16 of which are white and 14 of which are black. With two dimensions to compare—shape and color—an entropy-based inductive classifier bifurcates the space first according to color because it provides the maximum change in entropy, resulting in one group of 14 black circles and squares and one group of 16 white circles and squares. After dividing the space by color, it's further subdivided by shape, as shown in the figure.

The alternative, bifurcating the circles and squares initially by shape would have resulted in a split of 10 to 20, which is less than the spread (increase in entropy) associated with a 14-to-16 split. In a typical bioinfomatics data-mining problem, there may be 10 or more attributes to consider, according to entropy change or some other driving heuristic.

Genetic Algorithms

Genetic algorithms are based on evolutionary principles wherein a particular function or definition that best fits the constraints of an environment survives to the next generation, and the other functions are eliminated. This iterative process continues indefinitely, allowing the algorithm to adapt dynamically to the environment as needed. Genetic algorithms evaluate a large number of

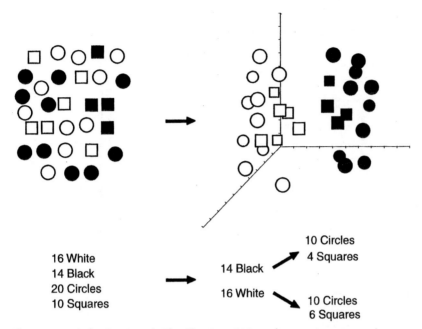

Figure 7-7 Induction-Based Classification. Using changes in entropy (a measure of disorder) as an organizational heuristic, the induction algorithm divides the unorganized data (top left) first by color and then by shape.

solutions to a problem that are generated at random. The members of the solution population with the highest fitness scores are allowed to "mate" with crossovers and mutations, creating the next generation.

Figure 7-8 illustrates the typical operation of a genetic operation. In this example, the possible solutions to a problem defined by the fitness function are represented by bit strings. Each bit represents the presence or absence of some quality that is mapped to the real-world solution. If there is a need to represent gradations of quantities, then integers or floating-point variables could be used instead of bit strings. However, in this example, 12 bits are used to represent the problem matrix.

When the algorithm is initialized, a population of bit strings is generated, using a random number generator. Although only four bit strings are shown here in the initial population, a typical population may include hundreds or even thousands of patterns. The larger the initial population, the more likely a high-scoring or "fit" solution will emerge, at the expense of computation time. From this initial population, two children are selected, based on the two high-est-scoring patterns. All other bit strings are discarded. These children are then allowed to "mate" with crossovers (bottom, left) and point mutations (bottom, right).

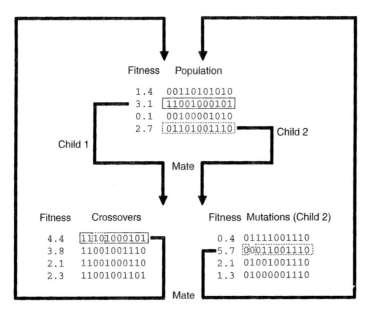

Figure 7-8 Genetic Algorithm Operation.

As in the initial population, there are hundreds or even thousands of crossovers and mutations created, and each resulting bit string is ranked by the fitness function to identify two new children. There are various combinations of crossover and mutations possible. For example, the fittest two children from the crossover population can each be subject to point mutations at each position in their strings, and the fittest children with mutations can be mated with the highest-ranking crossover children or with the parents. In this way, the string with the highest score from the fitness function is iteratively generated. The process can continue indefinitely or, as is normally done, terminated after a set number of generations.

Both the encoding of bit strings and the fitness function are domain-specific. For example, the first position in the bit string might represent the presence of a particular amino acid in a protein, the presence of a start codon in a nucleotide sequence, or the presence of a hydrogen bond at a position on an alpha helix. Similarly, the fitness function can be as simple as positive and negative weightings for each of the 12 bits (for example, 1s at odd positions are weighted with –1, and 1s at even positions are weighted with +1) for a sequence analysis problem or as a complex trigonometric function for a structure prediction problem.

Neural Networks

Neural networks are simulations loosely patterned after biological neurons. They are said to learn, or be trainable. In molecular biology, they learn to associate input patterns with output patterns in a way that allows them to categorize new patterns and to extrapolate trends from data. In operation, a neural network is presented with a pattern on its input nodes and the network produces an output pattern, based on this learning.

The power of neural networks is that they can apply this learning to new input patterns. For this reason, neural networks, like genetic algorithms, are often referred to as a form of "soft" or "fuzzy" computing because the answers or pattern matching provided by these methods represent best guesses, based on the data available for analysis. Neural networks always produce an output pattern when presented with an input pattern. However, the resultant categorization isn't necessarily the best answer. The best answer, computed using traditional algorithms, may require weeks of computing time on a desktop workstation. In comparison, a neural network may be able to categorize the data in a few seconds using the same hardware.

The inner workings of a neural network are independent of the problem domain, in that the same neural network configuration (with different training) can be used to recognize a nucleotide triplet, or a critical pattern on a patient's EKG tracing, or a potential mid-air collision when used with radar data. It's up to the researcher to determine what the input and output patterns represent. That said, neural networks, like other fuzzy systems, work best in a narrowly defined domain in which input patterns are likely to follow the same progression or logic. As the number and complexity of the possible input patterns increases, the ability of a neural network to classify input patterns deteriorates. For example, a neural network that works well classifying proteins within a given protein family will likely fail to classify the universe of known proteins, despite additional training.

An increase in the number and complexity of input patterns typically requires reconfiguring or rewriting a neural network with more layers and different interconnections. For example, the simple three-layer neural network shown in Figure 7-9 may have to be replaced by a four-layer neural network with double the number of interconnections. As a result, training time—the time required for a neural network to consistently associate an input pattern with an output pattern correctly—may be extended from a few minutes to several hours, even on high-performance hardware. Recognition time should be relatively unaffected.

The challenge of using a neural network to recognize and categorize data, especially novel data that haven't been presented to the system before, is that of validating the results and of communicating the rationale behind the results

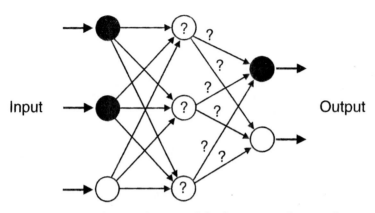

Figure 7-9   Neural Network. One of the limitations of a neural network is that the significance of the strength of the internal interconnections is unknown. As a result, as a pattern recognizer or categorizer, the neural network can be treated as a black box.

to the user. The greatest drawback of neural networks is that it's practically impossible to assess the significance of what's happening inside of a complex network. Even though the "wiring" of the nodes may be known, the relevance of changes in the strength of the connections is difficult to assess, even when the strengths are known. As a result, the inner workings of a neural network are difficult to validate.

Because a pure neural network presents such a formidable validation challenge, many neural network data-mining systems are used in conjunction with rule-based expert systems that contain human-readable rules in the form:

IF condition THEN outcome

These hybrid systems can categorize novel patterns and provide researchers with insight into the operation of the biological system. The challenge in creating hybrid classification systems is integrating the neural networks and rule-based expert systems in a way that doesn't compromise classification performance while providing enough information on internal operation to allow the user to assess the validity of the classification results. One approach to maximizing performance is to develop a neural network and then use a tool that converts the network into a rule base that can be compiled in C++ or Assembly language.

Statistical Methods

The statistical methods used to support data mining are generally some form of feature extraction, classification, or clustering. Statistical feature extraction is concerned with recovering the defining data attributes that may be obscured by imperfect measurement, improper data processing, or noise in the data.

A variety of statistical pattern-classification methods may be applied to data mining. For example, probabilistic classifiers are based on the principle that a pattern should be assigned to the class that is most probable. Bayesian techniques that estimate the joint probability of distributions can also be used to assess this probability. Although this method of classification generally provides excellent results, it has a major drawback of requiring more complete data than other methods.

Geometric classifiers are based on template matching in which the observed pattern is compared to a geometric template that represents data in each category. The nearness of the mined data to the template can be assessed in terms of the number of features in the observed data that match the template. Conceptual classifiers rely on biological heuristics to define categories, and fuzzy logic techniques can be used to assign data to a class by degree. Similarity measures may also weight certain features more than others, according to some measure of separateness. For example, if the distribution of data is spherical, the data mean may be used.

Statistical data-mining methods based on structural pattern recognition attempt to describe complex patterns in terms of simpler patterns. They extract features from the data and represent the structural features as vectors that are used with statistically determined discriminant functions. They use a rule base to define structural features in a given class, or transform the data into a descriptive language based on pattern primitives. The descriptions are then analyzed syntactically to provide the classification.

Predictive modeling, which uses data within a database to predict other missing data, can be based on continuous numerical variables (regression) or, more frequently, on categorical data (classification). The major challenge in predictive modeling is to select the input criteria that are most influential in defining missing data and in identifying the most appropriate transformation. With continuous numerical variables, nonlinear transformations on the input data are often used. With categorical data, feature extraction serves the same purpose.

Cluster analysis, also known as data segmentation, groups data into subsets that are similar to each other. Cluster analysis is a technique that can take a large amount of data about a number of objects and construct a simple, unique tree diagram that expresses those objects' similarities and differences. Cluster analysis involves sorting data so that members of the same cluster are most alike and members of different clusters are least alike. In this way, each cluster describes the class to which its members belong.

The results of cluster analysis are commonly reported in human-readable form as a dendogram, illustrated in Figure 7-10. In this dendogram, groups (D) and (E) are the most alike, as indicated by the shortest bracket. The next level of similarity is between (F) and the (D)-(E) complex. In addition, Groups (A) and (B) are similar. Group (G) shares the least similarity with the other groups.

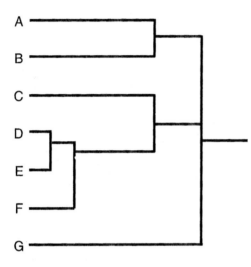

Figure 7-10 Dendogram Showing the Results of a Cluster Analysis. Groups (D) and (E) show the greatest similarity, whereas Group (G) shows the greatest differences between groups, based on cluster analysis criteria.

Cluster analysis may reveal associations and structure in data that, though not previously evident, are sensible and useful once found. The results of cluster analysis may contribute to the definition of a formal classification scheme, such as a taxonomy for related bacteria. It may suggest statistical models with which to describe populations, or indicate rules for assigning new cases to classes for identification and diagnostic purposes.

Cluster analysis includes metric-, model-, and partition-based methods (see Figure 7-11). In metric-based clustering, the data are partitioned so that they are closer to the centroid or center of mass than they are to other data in the cluster. In model-based clustering, a hypothetical model for each cluster is defined and the data that best fit the model are considered part of that cluster. A problem with model-based approaches is overfitting—by chance, a model may fit data that is irrelevant to it. Partition-based methods, which are general cases of metric- and model-based methods, use an ad hoc method of dividing the data space.

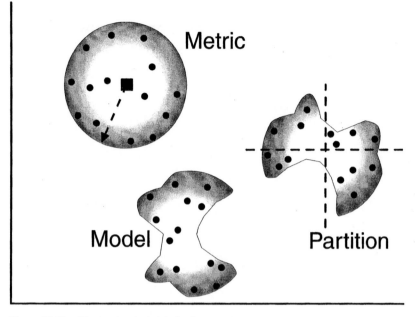

Figure 7-11   Cluster Analysis Methods.

Decision Trees

Decision trees are hierarchically arranged questions and answers that lead to classification. As shown in Figure 7-12, decision trees are formed by input nodes and tests on input data and whose leaf nodes are categories of those data. In the decision tree in the figure, the tests (Test 1–Test 8) result in textual categories (categories (A)–(H)), but they can also result in numerical categories. An advantage of using decision trees in data mining is that they can be easily read and modified by humans. For example, the results of Test 1 may lead to Test 2, 3, or 4. Once Test 2 is selected, the only options are to characterize the input as belonging to category (A), or to select Test 7. Category (A) can represent a particular family of proteins, for example. The only options from Test 7 are to place the data into category (A) or category (F).

The tests can be binary (yes/no) as in Test 2, or multi-variant (high, medium, low) as in Test 1. For example, in operation, a decision tree can be used to categorize a protein based on a combination of molecular weight, length, and configuration. As illustrated in the figure, the terminal or leaf nodes needn't result in mutually exclusive categorization of the input data. Both Test 2 and Test 7 classify the input into category (A), for example.

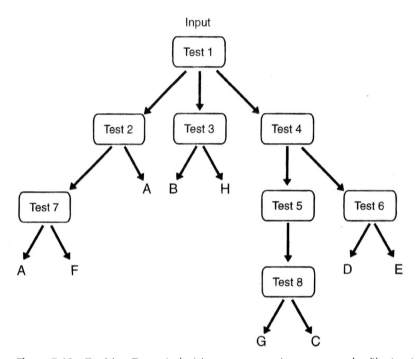

Figure 7-12　Decision Trees. A decision tree categorizes a pattern by filtering it down through the tests in a tree.

A potential limitation of using decision trees is related to their inability to represent relative occurrence frequencies. For example, with a very small training set, it's likely that the terminal leaves of a complex tree are defined by chance alone. Consider the typical evolutionary tree that represents the speciation over the past several hundred-million years. A single fossil may be responsible for a bifurcation in the tree, even though the fossil may represent a relatively small, insignificant mutation in a much larger population. However, in the tree representation, the populations have equal weights.

In some cases, this inability to represent the relative frequency of occurrence can be used to advantage. For example, in classifying globins from a variety of species, multiple samples from the same or closely related species may skew the relative abundance of some properties over others. However, if these properties are represented as a decision tree, then the skew due to sample anomalies can be avoided.

Hidden Markov Models

A powerful statistical approach to constructing classifiers that deserves a separate discussion is the use of Hidden Markov Modeling. A Hidden Markov Model (HMM) is a statistical model for an ordered sequence of symbols, acting as a stochastic state machine that generates a symbol each time a transition is made from one state to the next. Transitions between states are specified by transition probabilities. A Markov process is a process that moves from state to state depending on the previous n states. The process is called an *order n* model where n is the number of states affecting the choice of the next state. The Markov process considered here is a first order, in that the probability of a state is dependent only on the directly preceding state.

In order to understand HMMs, consider the concept of a Markov Chain, which is a process that can be in one of a number of states at any given time (see Figure 7-13). Each state generates an observation, from which the state sequence can be inferred. A Markov Chain is defined by the probabilities for each transition in state occurring, given the current state. That is, a Markov Chain is a non-deterministic system in which it is assumed that the probability of moving from one state to another doesn't vary with time. A HMM is a variation of a Markov Chain in which the states in the chain are hidden.

Like a neural network classifier, a HMM must be trained before it can be used. Training establishes the transition probabilities for each state in the Markov Chain. When presented with data in the database, the HMM provides a measure of how close the data patterns—sequence data, for example—resemble the data used to train the model. HMM-based classifiers are considered approximations because of the often unrealistic assumptions that a state is dependent only on predecessors and that this dependence is time-independent.

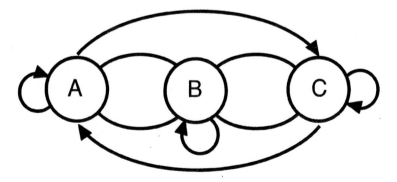

Figure 7-13 Markov Chain. (A), (B), and (C) represent states, and the arrows connecting the states represent transitions.

TEXT MINING

For mankind to benefit from bioinformatics research, the sequence and structure of proteins and other molecules must be linked to functional genomics and proteomics. The primary store of functional data that links clinical medicine, pharmacology, sequence data, and structure data is in the form of biomedicine documents in online bibliographic databases such as PubMed (see Figure 7-14). Mining these databases is expected to reveal the relationships between structure and function at the molecular level and their relationship to pharmacology and clinical medicine.

Text mining—automatically extracting this data from documents, which is´ published in the form of unstructured free text, often in several languages—is a non-trivial task. Although computer languages such as LISt Processing (LISP) have been developed expressly for handling free text, working with free text remains one of the most challenging areas of computer science. This is primarily because, unlike the analysis of the sequence of amino acids in a protein, natural language is ambiguous and often references data not contained in the document under study. For example, a research article on the expression of a particular gene in PubMed may contain numerous synonyms, acronyms, and abbreviations. Furthermore, despite editing to constrain the sentences to proper English (or other language), the syntax—the ordering of words and their relationships to other elements in phrases and sentences—is typically author-specific. The article may also reference an experimental method that isn't defined because it's assumed as common knowledge in the intended readership. In addition, text mining is complicated because of the variability of how data are represented in a typical text document. Data on a particular topic may appear in the main body of text, in a footnote, in a table, or imbedded in a graphic illustration.

Natural Language Processing

The most promising approaches to text mining online documents rely on natural language processing (NLP), a technology that encompasses a variety of computational methods ranging from simple keyword extraction to semantic analysis (see Figure 7-15). The simplest NLP systems work by parsing documents and identifying the documents with recognized keywords such as "protein" or "amino acid." The contents of the tagged documents can then be copied to a local database and later reviewed.

More elaborate NLP systems use statistical methods to recognize not only relevant keywords, but their distribution within a document. In this way, it's possible to infer context. For example, an NLP system can identify documents with

Figure 7-14 PubMed Home Page. This source of biomedicine literature contains over 11 million citations, and has an annual growth of about 3 percent.

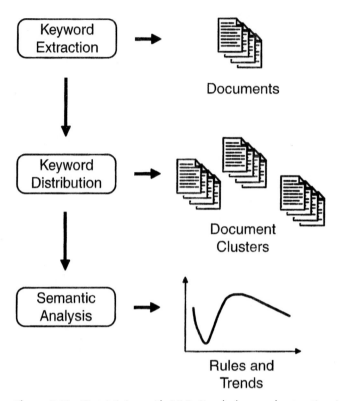

Documents

Document
Clusters

Rules and
Trends

Figure 7-15   Text Mining with NLP. Simple keyword extraction is useful in identifying documents, analysis of keyword distribution identifies document clusters, and semantic analysis can reveal rules and trends.

the keywords "amino acid", "neurofibromatosis", and "clinical outcome" in the same paragraph. The result of this more advanced analysis is document clusters, each of which represents data on a specific topic in a particular context.

This capability of identifying documents or document clusters is used by the typical Web search engines, such as Google or Yahoo!, or the native PubMed interface. This approach is also used in commercial bibliographic database systems, such as EndNote®, ProCite®, and Reference Manager®, which create a local subset of PubMed data by capturing the native field definitions, such as author name, publication title, and MESH keywords. However, these products don't support the automatic integration of structure and sequence data with functional data. Their support for text mining of the data within a document is limited to simple user-directed keyword search.

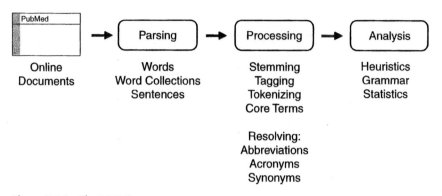

Figure 7-16   The NLP Process.

The most advanced NLP systems work at the semantic level—the analysis of how meaning is created by the use and interrelationships of words, phrases, and sentences in a sentence. Unlike a typical search engine, these advanced systems attempt to automatically populate a database with, for example, functional genomic and proteomic data relevant to a specific gene, protein, or disease, including rules and trends not explicitly stated or defined in the documents. These systems, which represent the leading edge of NLP R&D, are less reliable than systems based on keyword extraction and distribution techniques in that they sometimes formulate incorrect rules and trends, resulting in erroneous search results.

Regardless of the level of NLP, most systems follow the basic process outlined in Figure 7-16. Online documents are first parsed into words, word collections, or sentences, depending on the NLP method used. The simplest systems simply look at individual words, whereas systems that support mining of document clusters focus on word collections to establish context. The most advanced NLP systems, which attempt to extract meaning from words and word order, parse the documents at the sentence level.

The processing phase of NLP involves one or more of a variety of the following techniques:

- **Stemming**—Identifying the stem of each word. For example, "hybridized", "hybridizing", and "hybridization" would be stemmed to "hybrid". As a result, the analysis phase of the NLP process has to deal with only the stem of each word, and not every possible permutation.

- **Tagging**—Identifying the part of speech represented by each word, such as noun, verb, or adjective.

- **Tokenizing**—Segmenting sentences into words and phrases. This process determines which words should be retained as phrases, and which ones should be segmented into individual words. For example, "Type II Diabetes" should be retained as a word phrase, whereas "A patient with diabetes" would be segmented into four separate words.
- **Core Terms**—Significant terms, such as protein names and experimental method names, are identified, based on a dictionary of core terms. A related process is ignoring insignificant words, such as "the", "and", and "a".
- **Resolving Abbreviations, Acronyms, and Synonyms**—Replacing abbreviations with the words they represent, and resolving acronyms and synonyms to a controlled vocabulary. For example, "DM" and "Diabetes Mellitus" could be resolved to "Type II Diabetes", depending on the controlled vocabulary.

The analysis phase of NLP typically involves the use of heuristics, grammar, or statistical methods. Heuristic approaches rely on a knowledge base of rules that are applied to the processed text. Grammar-based methods use language models to extract information from the processed text. Statistical methods use mathematical models to derive context and meaning from words. Often these methods are combined in the same system. For example, grammar-based methods and statistical methods are frequently used in NLP systems to improve the performance of what could be accomplished by using either approach alone.

Heuristic or rule-based analysis uses IF-THEN rules on the processed words and sentences to infer association or meaning. Consider the following rule:

IF <protein name>
 AND <experimental method name> are in the same sentence
THEN the <experimental method name> refers to the <protein name>

This rule states that if a protein name, such as "hemoglobin", is in the same sentences as an experimental method, such as "microarray spotting", then microarray spotting refers to hemoglobin. One obvious problem with heuristic methods is that there are exceptions to most rules. For example, using the preceding rule on a sentence starting with "Microarray spotting was not used on the hemoglobin molecule because..." would improperly evaluate the sentence.

Grammar-based methods use language models that serve as templates for the sentence- and phrase-level analysis. These templates tend to be domain-specific. For example, a typical patient case report submitted by a clinician might read:

"The patient was a 45-year-old white male with a chief complaint of abdominal pain for three days."

A template that would be compatible with the sentence is:

<patient> <patient age> <race> <sex> <chief complaint><complaint duration>

Templates tend to work better in clinical publications than they do in basic research publications because much of physician education involves learning a strict method of reporting clinical findings. However, scientists involved in basic research tend to have less indoctrination in a particular way of revealing their findings, and so the statement of findings doesn't follow a syntactic formula.

Most statistical approaches to the analysis phase of NLP include an assessment word frequency at the sentence, paragraph, and document level. Word frequency is relevant because words with the lowest frequency of occurrence tend to have the greatest meaning and significance in a document. Conversely, words with the highest frequency of occurrence, such as "and", "the", and "a", have relatively little meaning.

In one statistical approach based on word frequency, a document is represented as a vector of word frequency, with the individual words or phrases forming the axes of the multi-dimensional space. This vector can be compared to a library of standard vectors, each of which represents a particular concept. Because the closeness of the two vectors represents similarity in concepts or at least content, this method can be used to automatically classify the contents of the document under analysis. For example, in Figure 7-17, a document represented by a vector is compared with a vector that represents the use of microarray spotting of the hemoglobin extracted from patients with sickle-cell anemia. Similarly, documents dealing with other proteins and experimental processes can be identified by comparing their vectors with a library of vectors representing other concepts.

Text Summarization

In addition to NLP, text mining is facilitated by text summarization, a process that takes a page or more of text as its input and generates a summary paragraph as the output. Because each summary paragraph represents a sample of the source document, analysis of the summaries can be used as an initial screen for data on a particular topic described in documents or document clusters. In effect, text summarization utilities, such as the "AutoSummarize" feature within Microsoft Word, are useful in creating a rough abstract of a document when none has been provided by the author. Like semantic-level NLP, text summarization is an imperfect, evolving technology that works well in niche areas, but not universally.

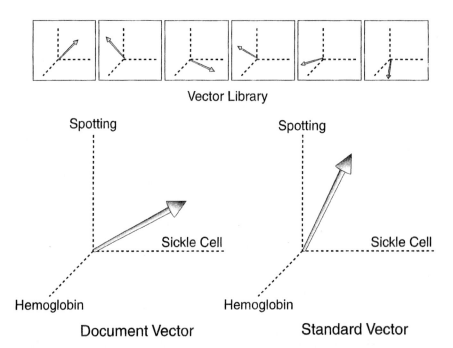

Figure 7-17 Documents Represented as Word Frequency Vectors. The vector of a document under analysis (left) is compared to the standard vector (right) that represents spotting of hemoglobin from patients suffering from sickle-cell anemia. A vector library (top) contains vectors representing a variety of concepts relevant to the researcher.

TOOLS

For most applications, data mining needn't involve writing neural networks or genetic algorithms in a traditional programming language. Instead, it can make use of a variety of general-purpose and bioinformatics-specific tools, as well as several high-level languages (see Table 7-4).

The most common languages used to perform data mining in bioinformatics are Perl, Python, and SQL. Perl and Python are scripting languages that are useful for implementing custom character- and string-based data mining for textual and sequence data. As true programming languages, they are flexible and powerful. The greatest limitation of Perl and Python is that they are interpreted scripting languages. That is, unlike C++ or other high-performance languages, the scripts are not compiled, but instead execute at runtime in an interpreter. As a result, data mining with Python or Perl is slower than using a well-written program using the same algorithms in C++. The time penalty associated with Python is considerably less that that associated with Perl, however, because it is based primarily on modules written in C++. Using either Perl or Python, a script defining a data-mining routine can be modified and executed within a few seconds without taking the time to compile source code. This advantage often outweighs the runtime speed penalty of using an interpreted language. In addition, Python and Perl are open-source, free programs.

Table 7-4 Examples of Data Mining Tools.

Tool	Examples
Languages	Perl, Python, SQL, XML
General-Purpose	Angoss, Clustran, Cross-Graph, Cross-z, Daisy, Data Distilleries, Database Marksman, DataMind, GVA, IBM Intelligent, Miner, Insightful Miner, Integral Solutions, KXEN, Magnify, MatLab, NeoVista Solutions, Oracle Darwin, Quadstone, SAS, Spotfire, SPSS Clementine, StatPac, Syllogic, ThinkAnalytics, Thinking Machines, Weka
Bioinformatics-Specific	MEME, PIMA, Pratt, PrattWWW, SPEXS

SQL is also an interpreted language. However, SQL lacks the flexibility of Perl or Python, in that it's useful only for querying a relational database. This specificity results in high performance, even as an interpreted language. In addition, SQL isn't a stand-alone application, but is normally part of a vendor-specific DBMS. The advantage of using SQL is that the language is portable from one relational database system to the next, independent of the vendor, allowing a researcher to query different database systems without having to learn a new query language. The SQL commands are identical, regardless of whether the database is manufactured by Oracle, Microsoft, or IBM. Although SQL statements can be manually submitted in real-time, they are frequently embedded in another language, such as Perl, so that the other language can perform operations on the returned data, such as writing the data to a new database, plotting the data, or translating it to a new format.

XML is a data format that's the current darling of online database development because of its extensibility and use of tags that can provide contextual clues helpful in data mining. A database or data warehouse built around XML can more readily support data mining than one that only supports standard relational tables and SQL database queries. A major disadvantage of XML is the lack of constraints on how it can be extended. Unless external standards are used, databases written by different programmers using XML may bear little resemblance to each other.

In addition to programming languages, there are hundreds of general-purpose stand-alone and Web-based data-mining applications. Of the commercial data-mining applications, many of the more popular offerings are listed in Table 7-4. Some of these applications, such as Oracle Darwin, are tied to specific database products, whereas others, such as SAS, can be used with any major database system. Similarly, some of these applications, such as MatLab, support a wide variety of data-mining capabilities. MatLab is an example of a commercial application that can be extended through a variety of commercial and public-domain add-ons. If performance isn't a primary concern, then a researcher with knowledge of Perl or Python, SQL, and MatLab can probably handle any data-mining challenge.

A sampling of the many academic bioinformatics-specific data-mining tools available include MEME, Pratt, PIMA, and SPEXS. MEME (Multiple Em for Motif Elicitation) is a motif discovery tool. Pratt, a stand-alone pattern discovery tool, is designed to uncover patterns conserved in sets of unaligned protein sequences. The user can specify what kind of patterns should be searched for, and how many sequences should match a pattern to be reported. The Web-based version of Pratt, PrattWWW, includes a visualization tool written as a Java applet to display patterns discovered in different sequences. PIMA (Pattern-Induced Multi-sequence Alignment program) can be used to perform a multi-sequence alignment of a set of sequences. All pairwise comparisons between sequences in the set are performed and the resulting scores clustered into one or more families. SPEXS (Sequence Pattern EXhaustive Search) is a sequence pattern discovery tool.

Because most of the other bioinformatics-specific data-mining tools tend to be optimized for a specific data-mining application, they tend to be very efficient. The downside of using these specific tools is the need to learn several different packages if data mining extends from nucleotide sequences to protein structures.

ON THE HORIZON

Real-time data mining, sometimes referred to as transaction monitoring, is rapidly gaining in popularity because of its increased value over the traditional mining of a data warehouse or database. In many industries, just-in-time analysis of data is much more valuable than analysis of data dredged up from the past—even if the past is only an hour or two removed from the present. For example, transaction monitoring is used by the credit card industry to detect fraud. As soon as a questionable transaction—a major purchase from a vendor not frequented by the legitimate card holder, for example—is detected, the system flags the point-of-sale system and the retailer has to call the credit card company for authorization. Mining the data even 30 seconds after the transaction is complete is of relatively little value, especially if the thief disposes of the card after the purchase.

In clinical medicine, real-time data mining is being used to detect potential drug-drug interactions, allergic reactions, and other side effects at the time a prescription is ordered. In some instances, a drug already in the body can potentiate another drug, causing the patient to overdose on the second drug, even though the dosage would be therapeutic without the other drug in the body. An overdose may result, for example, because both drugs are eliminated by the same pathway in the liver, and one drug completely saturates the metabolic pathway for drug elimination. Obviously, data on possible interactions is pertinent only before a patient is accidentally given the wrong drug or wrong dose of the appropriate drug.

The same technology can be extended to provide real-time analysis of drugs against a patient's genome, enabling the just-in-time delivery of custom drugs or as a means of detecting likely side effects of standard drugs on a given patient. In the bioinformatics laboratory, real-time data mining of results as they are generated by a sequencing machine or microarray reader can provide researchers with indicators as to the value of the data, error rate, and relatedness of the data to previous studies.

Three technologies that support real-time data mining are real-time capture, message-oriented middleware, and rule-based systems. Real-time data capture intercepts data from the source, before it is written to the database or data warehouse. This allows comparison of data to be made without a time-consuming data extraction process. Similarly, message-oriented middleware captures transactions, takes them off-line in batches, and stores the data in high-speed RAM (see Figure 7-18). While in RAM, the data are mined using a high-performance database manager with powerful RAM-based data handling

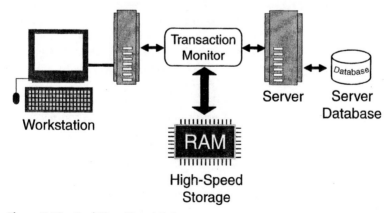

Figure 7-18   Real-Time Data Mining.

features. The third technology, rule-based systems, can be used to create filters that intercept only those real-time transactions fitting a profile defined in easily edited rules. The data selected by the filter can then be rapidly mined using conventional processors or RAM-based technologies, as dictated by the performance limitations of the system.

Each of these technologies supports different levels of data mining and has unique architectural limitations, such as the maximum number of transactions that can be monitored per minute. Overcoming these limitations at a reasonable cost is the focus of many computer scientists and corporations involved in data mining R&D.

ENDNOTE

The technologies and methodologies associated with data mining and knowledge discovery, while mature in areas such as fraud detection in credit card use, are not yet fully developed for bioinformatics applications. One issue is that, while fraud can be defined on an intuitive basis—sudden expenditure for luxury goods, transactions through vendors not frequented in the past, out-of-state transactions, and the like—much of the nature of genetic material under scrutiny is unknown.

Because researchers provide the final filtering in the knowledge-discovery process, it's likely that unfamiliar concepts—truly new discoveries—will more likely be attributed to chance clustering than to some underlying process. What's more, labels such as "junk DNA," for example, influences the amount of time and energy that a researcher will invest in applying data-mining tools to the non-coding regions of a genome, in favor of areas more likely to provide meaningful results. Similarly, for years scientists took for granted that there were only 20 genetically coded amino acids. When additional amino acids were discovered, they were first verified by arduous wet-lab work that required several years of work. For example, it took scientists over two years to crystallize and determine the structure of pyrrolysine, the 22nd amino acid. Given the existence of an additional amino acid, however, searching through a database for occurrences ignored in the past is comparatively trivial.

Despite the effects of bias, humans are an indispensable part of the data-mining process. One reason for their continued inclusion in what would otherwise be an automated process is that current technologies assume uniform and relatively simple data structures. Very large, complex databases, replete with multiple potential relationships present scalability issues that may require significant computational time on powerful computer systems. In addition, many of the traditional data-mining methods were developed for homogenous numerical data. However, bioinformatics databases increasingly hold text sequences, protein structure, and other data sets that are anything but homogeneous.

The technical challenges associated with data mining are compounded by the lack of statistical methods that can adequately assess the significance of figures calculated from very large database sets. Similarly, because few bioinformatics databases are static, but are growing exponentially with time, the statistical concept of a fixed population from which samples are drawn is violated. As a result, a statistical analysis of a particular relationship at one point in time may provide a different result a month or two later. These and similar challenges remain for those in the bioinformatics arena to solve.

➤ Human Transthyretin (Prealbumin), PDB entry 1BMZ. Image produced with PDB Structure Explorer.

CHAPTER

Pattern
Matching

Do not be desirous of having things done quickly. Do not look at
small advantages. Desiring to have things done quickly prevents
their being done thoroughly. Looking at small advantages prevents
great affairs from being accomplished.
— Confucius

Automated pattern matching—the ability of a program to compare novel
and known patterns and determine the degree of similarity—forms the
basis for automated sequence analysis, modeling of protein structures, locating homologous genes, data mining, Internet search engines, and dozens of
other activities in bioinformatics. Some of the key bioinformatics applications
of pattern recognition and matching—often referred to as simply pattern
matching—are listed in Table 8-1. For example, as explored in Chapter 7,
"Data Mining," data mining relies on heuristic and algorithmic pattern matching to locate patterns in online and local databases, using a variety of technologies, from simple keyword matching to rule-based expert systems and
artificial neural networks.

Table 8-1   Pattern-Matching Applications in Bioinformatics.

Constructing Controlled Vocabularies
Data Mining
Functional Genomics
Functional Proteomics
Genome Sequencing
Homologous Gene Identification
Homologous Protein Identification
Natural Language Processing
Neural Network–Based Structure Classifiers
Nucleotide Sequence Alignment
Protein Sequence Alignment
Protein Structure Prediction
Rule-Based Structure Classifiers

One of the major challenges associated with using pattern matching in bioinformatics is that, in most cases, the task isn't simply one of finding a match for a given pattern, but finding one or more matches quickly from large databases using affordable and readily available hardware. In addition, the task is often complicated by the need to identify patterns that are "similar" to a target pattern, but the concept of similarity isn't well-defined from a programmatic and biological sense. Not only is the degree of similarity defined in part by the technology underlying a particular software tool, but the relationship of a technology based on mathematical principles to the biological reality is often unclear. This ambiguity is common in the bioinformatics literature in the confusion of homology with similarity, for example.

This challenge of relating computational methods in pattern matching to our knowledge of the real world isn't limited to bioinformatics. For example, it's been a major focus of Artificial Intelligence (AI) research for several decades. Consider the illusion in Figure 8-1. We can quickly decide that this picture could not denote a real object because of our knowledge of what constitutes the fundamental physical properties of objects. Even so, it has taken decades to formulate this knowledge into algorithms that confer the same

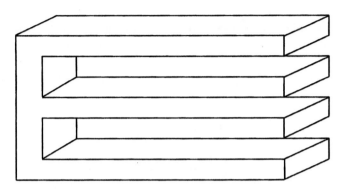

Figure 8-1   Three- or Four-Prong Illusion. Endowing computational pattern-recognition systems with knowledge of physical reality remains a challenge in AI and in other fields that rely on pattern-recognition methods.

capabilities on computer-based pattern-matching devices. Now, consider the challenges of extending this example to a complex protein-protein interaction, in which physical principles that act at an atomic level must be considered in systems designed to automatically classify proteins and other complex molecular structures. Despite these and other hurdles, pattern matching has been applied with varying degrees of success in areas as diverse as voice, image, and optical character recognition, as well as the monumental task of sequencing the human genome.

This chapter explores the application and methodology behind pattern matching, with a focus on nucleotide and protein sequence alignment. The "Fundamentals" section explores the challenges of sequence alignment, and the following five sections, from "Dot Matrix Analysis" to "Bayesian Methods" review the key pairwise sequence alignment approaches. "Multiple Sequence Alignment" extends the discussion to more challenging multiple sequence alignment tasks. The "Tools" section examines the more popular of the Web-based tools available for sequence alignment. "On the Horizon" explores the future of pattern matching, given the surge in proteomic research, and "Endnote" considers the ultimate fate of user-directed pattern recognition, given the move to intelligent agents and other technologies.

FUNDAMENTALS

Sequence alignment is fundamental to inferring homology (common ancestry) and function. For example, it's generally accepted that if two sequences are in alignment—part or all of the pattern of nucleotides or polypeptides match—

then they are similar and may be homologous. Another heuristic is that if the sequence of a protein or other molecule significantly matches the sequence of a protein with a known structure and function, then the molecules may share structure and function. The issues related to single pairwise sequence alignment, global versus local alignment, and multiple sequence alignment are introduced here.

Pairwise Sequence Alignment

Pairwise sequence alignment involves the matching of two sequences, one pair of elements at a time. The challenge in pairwise sequence alignment is to find the optimum alignment of two sequences with some degree of similarity. This optimum condition is typically based on a score that reflects the number of paired characters in the two sequences and the number and length of gaps required to adjust the sequences so that the maximum number of characters are in alignment. For example, consider the ideal case of two identical nucleotide sequences, (A) and (B):

A)   **ATTCGGCATTCAGTGCTAGA**
B)   **ATTCGGCATTCAGTGCTAGA**

Assuming that the alignment scoring algorithm counts one point per pair of aligned characters (shown in bold type), then the score is one point for each of the 20 pairs, or 20 points. Now, consider the case when several of the character pairs aren't aligned:

C)   **ATTCGGCATT**CAGTG**CTAGA**
D)   **ATTCGGCATT**GCTA**GA**

In this case, the score would be 11, because only 11 pairs of characters in sequences (C) and (D) are aligned. However, by examining the end of the sequences, it can be seen that the sequence of the last six characters are identical. By moving these last six characters ahead in sequence (D) by adding four spacers or gaps, the sequences become:

E)   **ATTCGGCATT**CAGT**GCTAGA**
F)   **ATTCGGCATT**----**GCTAGA**

Now the score, based on the original algorithm of character pairings, is 16. However, because the score would have been 11 without the inserted gaps, a penalty should be extracted for each gap inserted into the sequence to favor alignments that can be made with as few gaps as possible. Assuming a gap penalty of –0.5 per gap, the alignment score becomes 10 + 6 + (4 × –0.5) or 14.

A more likely scenario is one in which the areas of similarity and difference are not obvious. Consider the sequences (G) and (H):

G) **ATTCGG**CATT**CAGAGCGAGA**

H) **ATTCGA**CATT**GCTAGTGGTA**

Unlike the previous cases, there are no relatively long runs of character pairings, and the matching pairs are separated by unaligned characters. The alignment score is 1 point per aligned pair, or 13. One attempt at visual alignment by adding four gaps into sequence (H) results in:

G) **ATTCGG**CATT**CAGAGCTAGA**

I) **ATTCGA**CATT----**GCTAG**TGGTA

This alignment results in a score of 12, or 14 alignments minus 2 points for the 4 gaps introduced into sequence (H), transforming it to sequence (I). In addition, a penalty of –0.5 per character pair is scored for an inexact match. In the case of sequences (G) and (I), there are 6 inexact matches, for a penalty of (6 × –0.5 = –3). Using this new alignment-scoring algorithm, and ignoring the length difference between the two sequences, the alignment score for the (G)-(I) alignment becomes:

$$Alignment\ Score = 14\ alignments + 4\ gaps + 6\ inexact\ matches$$
$$= 14 + (4 \times -0.5) + (6 \times -0.5)$$
$$= 14 - 2 - 3$$
$$= 9$$

In this example, adding gaps results in a lower alignment score, illustrating how the relative worth of exact matches, inexact matches, and gaps determines the eventual alignment of two sequences. For example, if gaps are penalized heavily and inexact matches are minimally counted, then sequences will have few gaps.

Although a simple gap penalty of –0.5 point per gap has been used to illustrate the role of alignment scores on sequence alignment, gap penalty is typically calculated as:

$$Penalty_{gap} = Cost_{opening} + Cost_{extension} \times Length_{gap}$$

In this formula, $Penalty_{gap}$ is the total gap penalty, $Cost_{opening}$ is the cost of opening a gap in a sequence, $Cost_{extension}$ is the cost of extending an existing gap by one character, and $Length_{gap}$ is the length of the gap in characters. The minimum value of $Length_{gap}$ is one. Returning to sequence pair (E)-(F), assuming that $Cost_{opening}$ is (–0.5) and $Cost_{extension}$ is (–0.5), the gap penalty becomes:

$$Penalty_{gap} = Cost_{opening} + Cost_{extension} \times Length_{gap}$$
$$= -0.5 + (-0.5 \times 4)$$
$$= -2.5$$

With the expanded method of computing gap penalty, the score becomes 10 + 6 – 2.5 = 13.5 points. The gap penalty formula can be extended to include a penalty for alignments for the gaps at the end of a sequence to make the sequences of equal length. However, if the sequences are of very different lengths, then it probably doesn't make sense to penalize for these end gaps.

It's important to realize that picking arbitrary gap opening and extension costs typically has no real relationship to the underlying biology of the protein or DNA involved. One solution is to use gap penalty values that relate to biologically relevant data, as described in the "Substitution Matrices" section later in this chapter.

Local Versus Global Alignment

Sequence pair (E)-(F) is an example of a global alignment—that is, an attempt to line up the two sequences matching as many characters as possible, for the entire length of each segment. Global alignment considers all characters in a sequence, and bases alignment on the total score, even at the expense of stretches in the sequence that share obvious similarity (see Figure 8-2, top). Global alignment is used to help determine whether two protein sequences are in the same family, for example.

There are several methods of performing local sequence alignment, each of which has particular uses, advantages, and computational overhead. For example, the Smith-Waterman dynamic programming method, which uses a scoring system that penalizes the total score for a mismatch, is a computationally intensive sequence alignment method that favors local over global alignment.

Multiple Sequence Alignment

Multiple sequence alignment, in which three or more sequences must be aligned, is useful in finding conserved regulatory patterns in nucleotide sequences and for identifying structural and functional domains in protein

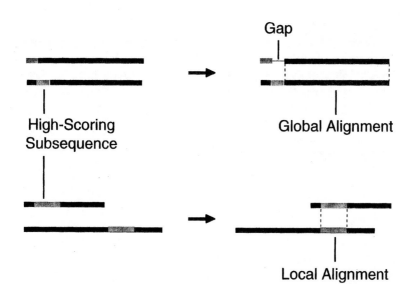

Figure 8-2 Local (top) versus Global (bottom) Alignment. In local alignment, the alignment of local, high-scoring sequences takes precedence over the overall alignment. In global alignment, the best overall alignment is sought, regardless of whether local, high-scoring subsequences are in alignment or not.

families. Unfortunately, multiple sequence alignment is much more challenging than single pairwise alignment. For nucleotide sequences, the problem appears as:

J) TCAGAGCGAGA
K) ATCCGGCCCGGCAGCGAGA
L) CAAAATTCAGAGCGAGA
M) ATCCGCAGAGCCCGGGGAGA
N) CCCGGCAGCGAGA
O) ATCCGTTTTTTTTTTGAGA

Instead of simply considering gaps, inexact matches, and global-versus-local alignment for a pair of sequences, multiple sequences must be considered—in this example, six sequences. Of course, in an actual multiple sequence alignment, each sequence may consist of several hundred characters, making manual gap insertions and other non-computational methods infeasible. Although most of the following discussion deals with single pairwise alignment, multiple alignment is an area of active research in bioinformatics because of the computational challenges involved.

Computational Methods

Fortunately, a variety of computational methods is available for sequence alignment, whether single, multiple, global, or local. A sampling of major computational approaches to pattern matching and sequence alignment is listed in Table 8-2.

Table 8-2   Computational Methods of Sequence Alignment.

Bayesian Methods
Dot Matrix
Dynamic Programming
Genetic Algorithms
Hidden Markov Models
Neural Networks
Scoring Matrices
Word-Based Techniques

Of the methods listed in Table 8-2, word-based techniques, followed by dynamic programming methods, are used most often. The popularity of word-based techniques is in part because of the ready availability of Web-based tools that use these methods, such as Fast Alignment (FASTA) and Basic Local Alignment and Search Tool (BLAST). Similarly, dynamic programming techniques, such as the Smith-Waterman algorithm, while computationally expensive, are also popular because of free access to Web-based tools. Dot matrix methods, once a mainstay of manual and computer-enabled sequence alignment, have become less popular since the advent of BLAST and its derivatives. However, dot matrix methods are still studied because of the insight they provide into other techniques, including dynamic programming.

Many of the other approaches to sequence alignment, such as the use of artificial neural networks, genetic algorithms, Bayesian approaches, and Hidden Markov Models (HMMs), are either experimental or combined with dynamic programming or word-based methods to provide users with practical tools. Similarly, many adjunct technologies, such as scoring matrices, have become integral to the operation of the major sequence alignment methods.

DOT MATRIX ANALYSIS

Because alignment by visual inspection of linear sequences hundreds of characters or more in length was impractical, researchers developed a more visually intuitive method of pattern detection called the dot matrix method. This method of sequence alignment, which was first performed manually and then computerized, makes the similarities in patterns more obvious to visual inspection. Using this method, one sequence appears along the top, and one along the side of the matrix, and a dot is placed at the intersection of matching character pairs. Contiguous diagonal rows of dots indicate sequences of matching pairs, as in the dot matrix plot of sequences (G) and (H) in Figure 8-3.

The dot matrix pattern for a pair of perfectly matching sequences would include a contiguous sequence of dots running down the center diagonal of the matrix. However, this pattern is rarely seen in practice. Most often, the diagonal patterns are difficult to discern without additional processing. In addition to the use of color and other methods of highlighting matching sequences, a variety of filters are often applied to the data. For example, a common filter is

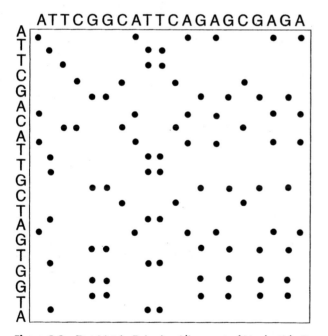

Figure 8-3   Dot Matrix Pairwise Alignment of Nucleotide Sequences (G—top) and (H—side). Diagonal sequences of dots indicate areas of contiguous sequences of aligned pairs. In a typical plot, there may be hundreds of characters in each sequence.

a combination of window and stringency. The window refers to the number of data points examined at a time, while the stringency is the minimum number of matches required within each window.

With a filter in which the window size is set to 2 and the stringency to 1, a dot is printed at a matrix position only if 1 out of the next 2 positions is identified, as in Figure 8-4. Similarly, with a window size of 6 and a stringency of 3, a dot would be printed at a matrix position only if 3 of the next 6 positions in the sequences are identified. A typical window-stringency combination is 15/10 for nucleotide sequences and much narrower combinations for polypeptide sequences, such as 1/1 or 3/2.

Dot matrix analysis is especially useful in identifying repeats—repeating characters or short sequences—within a sequence, as in mapping the repeated regions of whole chromosomes. Repeats of the same character, as in sequence (P), create alignments with artificially high scores and make sequence alignment more difficult. Dot matrix methods are most applicable to single pairwise alignment problems, especially those with relative high degrees of similarity. Sequences with lower degrees of similarity as well as multiple sequence alignment require methods that are more powerful.

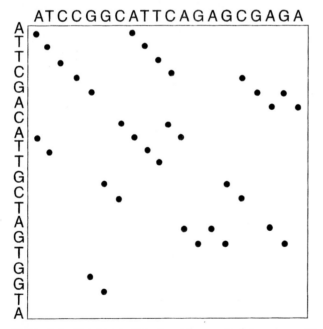

Figure 8-4 Dot Matrix Pairwise Alignment of Sequences (G—top) and (H—side). The filter, with a window of 2 and stringency of 1, emphasizes contiguous aligned sequence pairs.

Although window-stringency values are often established heuristically, they may also be based on dynamic averages, scores based on the occurrence of matches in aligned protein families, or on various methods of scoring the similarity of amino acids. For example, scoring matrices provide scores for alignment based on their statistical occurrence in aligned protein families. Using these matrices, described in the following section, a sliding window feature can be implemented, in which only dots above a certain average score can appear in the matrix.

SUBSTITUTION MATRICES

Protein structure and function are surprisingly resistant to polypeptide substitution, to the degree that the substitutions don't alter the chemistry of the protein. Substitutions are common over large expanses of time and from one species to the next. In many cases, the substitution of polypeptides through evolution can be predicted. In this way, a matrix of likely polypeptide substitutions can be constructed. As in a dot matrix analysis, the amino acids are listed across the top and side of a matrix, typically using the amino acid code letters listed in Table 8-3. At each intersection, the matrix is filled with a score that reflects how often one polypeptide would have been paired with the other in an alignment of related protein sequences. An underlying assumption is that this association is symmetrical, in that either polypeptide can be substituted for the other.

Two popular substitution matrices are Percent Accepted Mutation (PAM) and Blocks Amino Acid Substitution Matrix (Blosum), examples of which are shown in Figures 8-5 and 8-6, respectively. Unlike dot matrix analysis, these matrices are static. Furthermore, these matrices aren't mere mathematical constructs designed simply to facilitate computational sequence alignment, but they reflect the biology of the molecules represented by the sequences. For example, each PAM matrix in the series is named after the level of change assumed by the matrix. For example, the commonly used PAM-250, shown in Figure 8-5, assumes a 250-percent change in the probability matrix.

The figures used to populate the matrices are based on the formula:

$$MatrixValue = \log\left[\frac{frequency_{Observed}}{frequency_{Expected}}\right]$$

A matrix value of "0" signifies that a substitution typically occurs at a random base rate, whereas a negative matrix value infers that the substitution is less likely than by chance alone. A positive matrix value means that

Table 8-3   Amino Acid Code Letters. Courtesy NCBI.

Code	Meaning
A	Alanine
B	Aspartate or Asparagine
C	Cysteine
D	Aspartate
E	Glutamic Acid
F	Phenylalanine
G	Glycine
H	Histidine
I	Isoleucine
K	Lysine
L	Leucine
M	Methionine
N	Asparagine
P	Proline
Q	Glutamine
R	Arginine
S	Serine
T	Threonine
V	Valine
W	Tryptophan
X	Unknown
Y	Tyrosine
Z	Glutamate or Glutamine

the substitution occurs more often than suggested by chance. For example, in the PAM-250 matrix, A and N (Alanine and Asparagine) substitute for each other at a rate (0) that is expected by chance alone. Conversely, A and W (Alanine and Tryptophan) substitute for each other at a rate (–6) much lower than expected for a random substitution.

From the perspective of supporting sequence alignment, the main diagonal reveals the relative value of maintaining matches in the pairwise sequence alignment process. For example, in the PAM-250 substitution matrix, given a choice of shifting a sequence by adding gaps or other means that affect either an A-A (Alanine-Alanine) alignment or a C-C (Cysteine-Cysteine) alignment, the C-C alignment should not be disturbed. This is because the C-C alignment is rated at 12, compared to only 2 for the A-A alignment.

PAM-250 SUBSTITUTION MATRIX																						
	A	R	N	D	C	Q	E	G	H	I	L	K	M	F	P	S	T	W	Y	V	B	Z	X
A	2																						
R	-2	6																					
N	0	0	2																				
D	0	-1	2	4																			
C	-2	-4	-4	-5	12																		
Q	0	1	1	2	-5	4																	
E	0	-1	1	3	-5	2	4																
G	1	-3	0	1	-3	-1	0	5															
H	-1	2	2	1	-3	3	1	-2	6														
I	-1	-2	-2	-2	-2	-2	-2	-3	-2	5													
L	-2	-3	-3	-4	-6	-2	-3	-4	-2	2	6												
K	-1	3	1	0	-5	1	0	-2	0	-2	-3	5											
M	-1	0	-2	-3	-5	-1	-2	-3	-2	2	4	0	6										
F	-4	-4	-4	-6	-4	-5	-5	-5	-2	1	2	-5	0	9									
P	1	0	-1	-1	-3	0	-1	-1	0	-2	-3	-1	-2	-5	6								
S	1	0	1	0	0	-1	0	1	-1	-1	-3	0	-2	-3	1	2							
T	1	-1	0	0	-2	-1	0	0	-1	0	-2	0	-1	-3	0	1	3						
W	-6	2	-4	-7	-8	-5	-7	-7	-3	-5	-2	-3	-4	0	-6	-2	-5	17					
Y	-3	-4	-2	-4	0	-4	-4	-5	0	-1	-1	-4	-2	7	-5	-3	-3	0	10				
V	0	-2	-2	-2	-2	-2	-2	-1	-2	4	2	-2	2	-1	-1	-1	0	-6	-2	4			
B	0	-1	2	3	-4	1	2	0	1	-2	-3	1	-2	-5	-1	0	0	-5	-3	-2	2		
Z	0	0	1	3	-5	3	3	-1	2	-2	-3	0	-2	-5	0	0	-1	-6	-4	-2	2	3	
X	0	0	0	0	0	0	0	0	0	0	0	0	0	0	0	0	0	0	0	0	0	0	0

Figure 8-5 The Percent Accepted Mutation Substitution Matrix 250 (PAM-250).

Although the values in the Blosum matrix mean the same as in a PAM matrix, the Blosum matrices incorporate substitution scores that encompass a range of evolutionary periods and in some cases provide greater sensitivity over PAM matrices. Blosum takes its name from the blocks—areas of conserved amino acids—used to define substitution patterns. Unlike PAM, which is based on a relatively small set of closely related proteins, Blosum is based on a large-scale analysis of over 500 families of related proteins. Similarly, Blosum doesn't explicitly consider evolutionary factors.

Matrices aren't necessarily symmetric or based on the same alphabet. For example, it's possible to relate polypeptides to experimental or environmental conditions. Furthermore, although this discussion of matrices has centered on polypeptides, they can also be designed for use with nucleic acids. The matrix values of these matrices are necessarily different from those used with polypeptides.

BLOSUM62 SUBSTITUTION MATRIX

	A	R	N	D	C	Q	E	G	H	I	L	K	M	F	P	S	T	W	Y	V	B	Z	X
A	4																						
R	-1	5																					
N	-2	0	6																				
D	-2	-2	1	6																			
C	0	-3	-3	-3	9																		
Q	-1	1	0	0	-3	5																	
E	-1	0	0	2	-4	2	5																
G	0	-2	0	-1	-3	-2	-2	6															
H	-2	0	1	-1	-3	0	0	-2	8														
I	-1	-3	-3	-3	-1	-3	-3	-4	-3	4													
L	-1	-2	-3	-4	-1	-2	-3	-4	-3	2	4												
K	-1	2	0	-1	-3	1	1	-2	-1	-3	-2	5											
M	-1	-1	-2	-3	-1	0	-2	-3	-2	1	2	-1	5										
F	-2	-3	-3	-3	-2	-3	-3	-3	-1	0	0	-3	0	6									
P	-1	-2	-2	-1	-3	-1	-1	-2	-2	-3	-3	-1	-2	-4	7								
S	1	-1	1	0	-1	0	0	0	-1	-2	-2	0	-1	-2	-1	4							
T	0	-1	0	-1	-1	-1	-1	-2	-2	-1	-1	-1	-1	-2	-1	1	5						
W	-3	-3	-4	-4	-2	-2	-3	-2	-2	-3	-2	-3	-1	1	-4	-3	-2	11					
Y	-2	-2	-2	-3	-2	-1	-2	-3	2	-1	-1	-2	-1	3	-3	-2	-2	2	7				
V	0	-3	-3	-3	-1	-2	-2	-3	-3	3	1	-2	1	-1	-2	-2	0	-3	-1	4			
B	-2	-1	3	4	-3	0	1	-1	0	-3	-4	0	-3	-3	-2	0	-1	-4	-3	-3	4		
Z	-1	0	0	1	-3	3	4	-2	0	-3	-3	1	-1	-3	-1	0	-1	-3	-2	-2	1	4	
X	0	-1	-1	-1	-2	-1	-1	-1	-1	-1	-1	-1	-1	-1	-2	0	0	-2	-1	-1	-1	-1	-1

Figure 8-6 The Blocks Amino Acid Substitution Matrix 62 (Blosum62).

As noted in the earlier discussion of gap penalties, arbitrarily selecting opening and extension costs so that the output "looks nice" from a mathematical perspective likely has no relevance to the actual biology of the protein under study. It's commonly assumed that a better approach is to assign gap extension and opening costs relative to the substitution matrix used for a given protein. If the gap penalty figures are too high relative to the matrix scores, the gap penalty figures will override the matrix scores, and gaps will never appear in the sequence alignment. Conversely, if gap penalty figures are too low relative to the matrix scores, gaps will be used wherever possible in order to align the sequences. That is, simply because a substitution matrix is used doesn't guarantee biologically relevant results. The matrices and related calculations must be used appropriately, and in consideration of the underlying biology.

DYNAMIC PROGRAMMING

One way to be certain that the solution to a sequence alignment is the best alignment possible is to try every possible alignment, introducing one or more gaps at every position, and computing an alignment score based on aligned character pairs and inexact matches. However, the computational overhead of evaluating all possible alignments of one sequence against another grows exponentially with the length of the two sequences. For reasonable length sequences of several hundred characters each, an exhaustive evaluation of potential alignments could take days of computer time without using specific algorithms developed for sequence alignment, such as dynamic programming.

Dynamic programming is a form of recursion in which intermediate results are saved in a matrix where they can be referred to later by the program. The comparison can be likened to solving a series of complex mathematical equations, with the results of one equation feeding the input of another, with and without the benefit of pen and paper or other temporary storage and retrieval mechanism. With pen and paper (as with dynamic programming), the intermediate results can be recorded and the next equation can be solved without regard to the previous or following equation. Without the pen and paper, it may be impossible for some people to solve the series of equations. Dynamic programming is processor- and RAM-intensive, but the technique of storing intermediate values in a matrix can transform an otherwise intractable problem requiring immense computational capabilities into one that is computationally feasible.

To illustrate the value of dynamic programming in sequence alignment, consider the function:

$$MaxValue = f(A_i, B_j)$$

In this equation, $MaxValue$ is some function of variables A_i and B_j, where i and j are indices to the variables defined in the tree structure illustrated in Figure 8-7. That is, the possible values of A_i are represented by A_1 through A_5, and the possible values of B are represented by B_1 through B_{11}. The best solution to $MaxValue$ depends on the equation that defines $MaxValue$. For example, consider the following possible definition of $MaxValue$:

$$MaxValue = (A_i \times B_j)$$

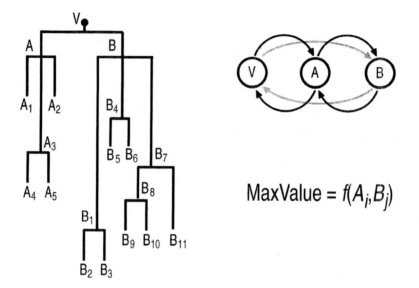

$$MaxValue = f(A_i, B_j)$$

Figure 8-7   Dynamic Programming Problem. Values for A and B are defined in the tree structure. Maximizing *MaxValue* requires evaluating the equation for every combination of *i* and *j*.

In this example, the solution is simply the largest value of *A* and the largest value of *B*. However, consider the following definition of *MaxValue*:

$$MaxValue = \sqrt[3]{14 \times A^2 \Big/ \log\left(A^2 + B^2\right)}$$

In this example, the solution to *MaxValue* is less obvious and much more computationally intensive.

The brute-force method of solving for *MaxValue* is to recursively walk down each of the trees and try the various combinations of *A* and *B* in the *MaxValue* equation. However, as illustrated in the upper-right of Figure 8-7, evaluating every value of *B* in the *MaxValue* equation entails evaluating every value of *A*. For example, assume that the values for A_i and B_j are defined as:

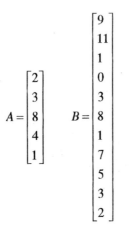

$$A = \begin{bmatrix} 2 \\ 3 \\ 8 \\ 4 \\ 1 \end{bmatrix} \qquad B = \begin{bmatrix} 9 \\ 11 \\ 1 \\ 0 \\ 3 \\ 8 \\ 1 \\ 7 \\ 5 \\ 3 \\ 2 \end{bmatrix}$$

Solving for the first value of A_i ($A_1 = 2$) and ignoring the specific equation for *MaxValue* for clarity:

$$MaxValue_{1,1} = f(A_1, B_1) = f(2, 9) = 5$$
$$MaxValue_{1,2} = f(A_1, B_2) = f(2, 11) = 3$$
$$MaxValue_{1,3} = f(A_1, B_3) = f(2, 1) = 0$$
$$MaxValue_{1,4} = f(A_1, B_4) = f(2, 0) = 2$$
$$MaxValue_{1,5} = f(A_1, B_5) = f(2, 3) = 8$$
$$MaxValue_{1,6} = f(A_1, B_6) = f(2, 8) = 0$$
$$MaxValue_{1,7} = f(A_1, B_7) = f(2, 1) = -2$$
$$MaxValue_{1,8} = f(A_1, B_8) = f(2, 7) = 1$$
$$MaxValue_{1,9} = f(A_1, B_9) = f(2, 5) = 2$$
$$MaxValue_{1,10} = f(A_1, B_{10}) = f(2, 3) = 8$$
$$MaxValue_{1,11} = f(A_1, B_{11}) = f(2, 2) = 4$$

If the branches of A and B have hundreds of sub-branches, representing hundreds of values, then the problem is likely computationally infeasible. This is especially true if the *MaxValue* function, which must be evaluated for each combination of variables, is also computationally intensive.

Dynamic programming can address this computational and time dilemma by creating a matrix to store the values for A_i, B_j, and *MaxValue* for each combination of i and j. Instead of solving one complex CPU- and RAM-intensive problem, the task is decomposed into hundreds or even thousands of easily and quickly solved problems. For example, consider the solution matrix for *MaxValue* in Figure 8-8. The solution set to *MaxValue* computed earlier for A_1

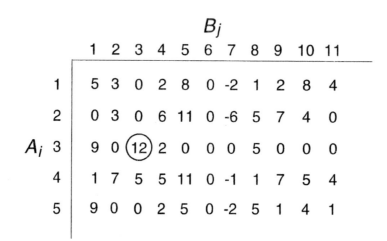

Figure 8-8 Solution Matrix for *MaxValue* for A_i and B_j. The solution to *MaxValue* is A_3 and B_3 with *MaxValue* = 12.

appears in the first row of the matrix. Examining only this first row, it can be seen that there are two solutions to *MaxValue*, B_5 and B_{10}, each of which results in a value of 8.

With the completed solution matrix available for examination, it's a trivial matter to locate the best values for i and j, second-best, and so on. The same approach can be extended to any number of dimensions. For example, consider adding a third variable, as in Figure 8-9. The equation for *MaxValue* now takes the form:

$$MaxValue = f(A_i, B_j, C_k)$$

In this new equation, *MaxValue* is some function of variables A_i, B_j, and C_k, where $i, j,$ and k are indices to the variables defined in the tree structure illustrated in Figure 8-9. The best solution to *MaxValue* is in the form $[i = 3, j = 3, k = 2]$, for example. As in the simpler 2D problem, a matrix of solutions can be constructed. However, the matrix of solutions is now much larger, and is better represented as a 3D structure, as in Figure 8-10.

Even though there are now many more solutions to consider, the process of evaluating *MaxValue* for three variables and saving intermediary results in the 3D matrix is the same as in the previous 2D example. Adding additional dimensions, although computationally intensive, makes it possible to evaluate all possible ways of aligning the three sequences against each other in a reasonable time, even though the number of such possible alignments grows exponentially with the length of the two sequences. Similarly, just as adding a dimension to the problem doesn't fundamentally change the evaluation process, the alignment of multiple strings can be evaluated using this process as well.

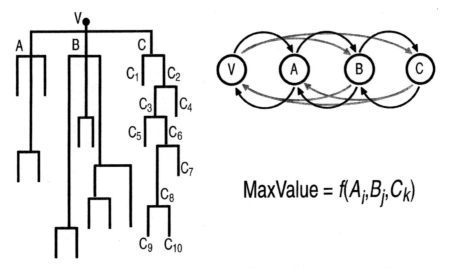

$$MaxValue = f(A_i, B_j, C_k)$$

Figure 8-9 Dynamic Programming Problem with Added Dimensionality. Values for A_i, B_j, and C_k are contained in the tree structure (left). The exhaustive solution to *MaxValue* involves evaluating every combination of *i, j,* and *k*.

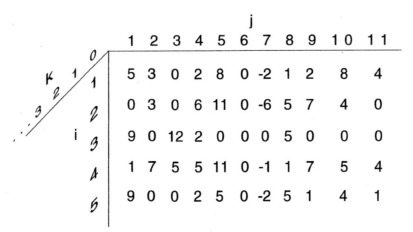

	j										
i	1	2	3	4	5	6	7	8	9	10	11
1	5	3	0	2	8	0	-2	1	2	8	4
2	0	3	0	6	11	0	-6	5	7	4	0
3	9	0	12	2	0	0	0	5	0	0	0
4	1	7	5	5	11	0	-1	1	7	5	4
5	9	0	0	2	5	0	-2	5	1	4	1

Figure 8-10 Solution Matrix for *MaxValue* = $f(A_i, B_j, C_k)$. Only one value for k ($k = 0$) is shown here for clarity.

To bring the power of dynamic programming into the realm of pairwise sequence alignment, consider *MaxValue* to be the alignment score for pairwise alignment of two sequences. *MaxValue* takes into account gap penalties, correct alignments, and imperfect alignments. After the matrix is filled in using the alignment score to determine *MaxValue*, the highest scoring path is followed back to the beginning of the alignment to define the best alignment of elements in the sequence, including gaps.

Graphically, this approach to the local alignment of two sequences is illustrated in Figure 8-11. The starting point is the best score in the matrix, the C-C alignment with a value of 11. Working backwards to the row and column to the upper left, step (1), the best score is for the G-G alignment, with a score of 10. Because the value is on the diagonal immediately adjacent to the value for the C-C alignment, there is no gap penalty. Now, moving to step (2), the highest score, 8, is also immediately adjacent and therefore free of a gap penalty. In step (3), there are three high scores, each of which has a gap penalty. The minimum gap penalty is associated with the closest alignment with a score of 5, the A-A alignment. Continuing to step (4), there are two competing high scores. Because there is no penalty for the C-C alignment that is diagonally adjacent to the A-A alignment, with a value of 6, the process continues to the G-G bond with a value of 8, to completing the local alignment. That is, the local alignment appears as:

Q)   ATCGA**GCA–GCATG**...
R)   -----**GCATGCT**...

In this example, sequence (Q) appears across the top and sequence (R) is listed across the side of Figure 8-11. The characters involved in the local alignment appear in bold.

Mathematically, the algorithm for this form of local alignment, known as the Smith-Waterman algorithm, is defined as:

$$H_{ij} = \max \begin{cases} H_{i-1,j-1} + s(A_i B_j) \\ \max(H_{i-x,j} - w_x, \\ x \geq 1 \\ \max(H_{i,j-y} - w_y, \\ y \geq 1 \\ 0 \end{cases}$$

Where A_i and B_j are the two sequences to be aligned; H_{ij} is the score at position A_i, B_j; $s(A_i B_j)$ is the score for aligning the characters at positions i and j; w_x is the penalty of a gap of length x in sequence A, and w_y is the penalty for a gap of length of y in sequence B.

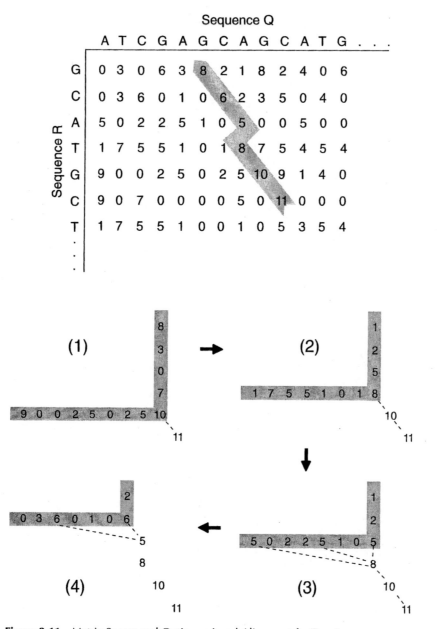

Figure 8-11   Matrix Scores and Optimum Local Alignment for Two Sequences.

The three special provisions of this algorithm that favors local alignments are:

- Negative numbers are not allowed in the scoring matrix.
- Inexact matches are penalized.
- The best score is sought anywhere in the matrix, and not simply in the last column or row.

Even though dynamic programming guarantees to find the best local or global alignment because the technique considers all possible alignments, the technique is computationally intensive. Short pairwise comparisons using the Smith-Waterman algorithm can require several hours of workstation processing. High-end parallel processing hardware, such as the UCSC Kestrel server, which provides the equivalent of 40 times the processing power of a desktop workstation, requires several minutes for pairwise alignment using the Smith-Waterman algorithm. Given the computational overhead of dynamic programming, a variety of first-pass, heuristic-based methods have been developed to support alignment on the desktop workstation. These techniques, often referred to as word methods, include the ubiquitous FASTA and BLAST algorithms, as described in the next section.

WORD METHODS

BLAST and FASTA are called word methods of sequence alignment because these algorithms work at the level of words—multiple polypeptides or nucleic acids—instead of with individual polypeptides or nucleic acids. Both methods of sequence alignment are fast enough to support searching for alignments of query sequences against entire nucleotide or protein databases.

The high-level flow of the FASTA algorithm, which predates BLAST, is shown in Figure 8-12. The first step in the FASTA algorithm is to create a hash table of words from the query sequence. Hashing is a function that maps words to integers to get a smaller set of values so that the search space is minimized, for example. A hash table, such as the one in Figure 8-13, maps words to array positions, based on the hash function. For proteins, word length is typically one or two amino acids long. For nucleic acid sequences, the word length is usually from four to six characters. In either case, the longer the word length, the more rapid and the less thorough the search.

Next, the characters are compared to those in the database, which has previously been processed into words of the same length. FASTA uses the Blosum50 substitution matrix to score the top-10 alignments (without gaps) that contain the most similar words. These words are then merged into a gapped alignment, which is scored, producing an "optimized score." FASTA

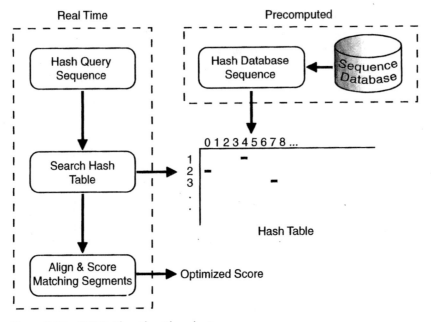

Figure 8-12   FASTA Algorithm Flowchart.

produces an expectation score, E, which represents the expected number of random alignments with z-scores greater than or equal to the value observed, thereby providing an estimate of the statistical significance of the results.

Although FASTA was the first widely used program for sequence alignment against genome-length sequences, and is still actively supported in both Web and workstation versions, BLAST is by far the more popular of the word-based algorithms for sequence alignment. Like FASTA, BLAST is a heuristic approach to sequence alignment that provides speed through a hashing technique. BLAST also differs from FASTA in that words are typically 3 characters long for proteins and 11 characters in length for nucleotide sequences.

Like FASTA, BLAST also searches a pre-computed hash table of sequences in the protein or DNA database. However, where BLAST excels is that the matching words are then extended to the maximum length possible, as indicated by an alignment score. The top-scoring alignments in a sequence, called maximal-scoring pairs (MSPs), are combined if possible into local alignments. The latest version of BLAST can attempt gapped alignment. However, this tends to extend computational time significantly, compared to ungapped alignments. One of the major issues of both BLAST and FASTA results is how to interpret the significance of results. An individual score depends on a number of variables, including the lengths of the sequences being aligned, the gap penalties, and the alignment scoring system used.

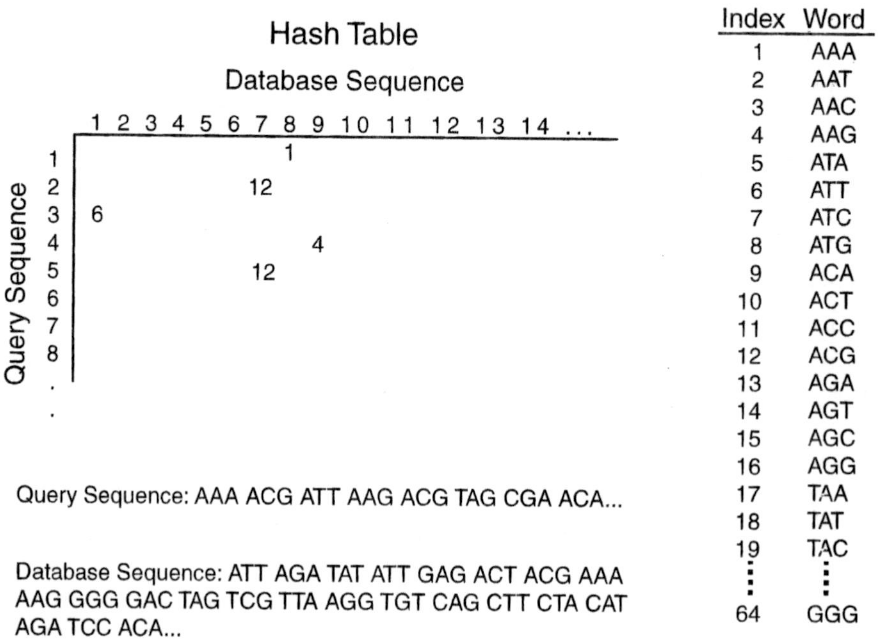

Figure 8-13 Hash Table for FASTA. The possible words are keyed to index numbers (right), which are used to represent words in the hash table.

BAYESIAN METHODS

Although not considered mainstream by many researchers in the bioinformatics field, Bayesian statistical methods can be used to determine pairwise sequence alignment and to estimate the evoiutionary distance between DNA sequences. Bayesian methods involve examining the probabilities of all possible alignments, gap scores, and substitution matrix values (the prior probabilities) to assess the probability of an alignment (the posterior probability). Proponents of the Bayesian approach to sequence alignment cite as advantages over the limitations of dynamic program the method's ability to fully and exactly describe uncertainty, derive exact significance measures, and eliminate the need to specify all parameters.

In practice, Bayesian-based tools, such as the Bayes Block Aligner, a workstation-based tool available from the Center for Bioinformatics at Rensselaer and Wadsworth Center of the New York Department of Health, performs better than dynamic programming in some cases, and not as well in others. The Block Aligner manipulates two sequences to find the highest-scoring contiguous regions (blocks), which are then joined in various combinations to form alignments. Unlike a dynamic programming or word-based approach, the Bayes Block Aligner, which works with both DNA and protein sequences, doesn't require the user to specify a particular substitution matrix or gap scoring system. Instead, it bases the posterior probability distributions of alignments on the number of blocks expected in an alignment and a range of substitution matrices. A Web-based Bayesian analysis tool, the Bayesian Algorithm for Local Sequence Alignment (BALSA) is also available from the center. BALSA is described in the "Tools" section later in this chapter.

MULTIPLE SEQUENCE ALIGNMENT

Applications of multiple sequence alignment—aligning three or more sequences—range from suggesting homologous relationships between several proteins to predicting probes for other members of the same family of similar sequences in a proteome. Although multiple sequence alignment can be performed on nucleotide sequences, it's more often performed on polypeptide sequences, and draws upon many of the techniques used for single pairwise sequence alignment. In addition, several novel methods have been devised to deal with the challenge of aligning multiple sequences. An overview of several key multiple sequence alignment technologies follows.

Dynamic Programming

Dynamic programming methods used for pairwise sequence alignment are easily extended to encompass multiple sequences, at least in theory. Algorithmically, there is little difference between a two- or three-dimensional alignment problem, as discussed earlier. However, the computational requirements for 10 or more relatively short polypeptide sequences are beyond the reach of most research laboratories. Three- or four-sequence alignment is the limit for workstation-class hardware. As a result, for desktop work in multiple sequence alignment, several heuristic methods have been developed that provide results in reasonable time, even though it's usually impossible to prove that the results achieved through these methods are the best attainable.

Progressive Strategies

Progressive strategies take the salami-slice approach to multiple sequence alignment. Instead of addressing the multidimensional problem head-on, progressive strategies break the multiple sequence alignment challenge into a series of pairwise alignment problems. The first pair of sequences is aligned, and then that result is aligned with the third sequence, and so on, aligning each subsequent search with the previous alignment. Alternatively, the first pair of sequences can serve as the basis for aligning all subsequent sequences, which are then combined at the end of the process. Other alignment schemes are possible as well.

For example, the approach used by the PILEUP program is to start with pairwise alignments that score the similarity between every possible pair of sequences. These similarity scores are used to define the order of alignment. That is, PILEUP first aligns the two most-related sequences to each other in order to produce the first alignment. It then aligns the next most-related sequence to this alignment or the next two most-related sequences to each other in order to produce another alignment. A series of such pairwise alignments that includes increasingly dissimilar sequences and alignments of sequences at each iteration eventually creates the final alignment.

The problem with progressive methods is that the validity of the result varies greatly as a function of the order in which pairs of sequences are aligned. Errors in the earlier alignments are propagated to the later alignments. In addition, progressive strategies are a heuristic approach in that they don't necessarily return best possible alignment. In addition to PILEUP, programs that use a progressive strategy are CLUSTALW, CLUSTALX, MSA, and PRALINE.

Iterative Strategies

Because of the limitation of progressive strategies due to sensitivity to errors introduced by early alignments, iterative methods have been developed that correct for the problem by repeatedly realigning subgroups of sequences. Iterative methods include the use of genetic algorithms and HMMs.

Approaches based on genetic algorithms generally start with a random definition of gap insertions and deletions and use the alignment score as the fitness function. The pattern that defines the gaps and the relative position of each sequence is allowed to mutate and mate with other patterns. Offspring of these original patterns that maximize the alignment score are in turn allowed to mate and mutate, creating other patterns. In this way, *an* optimal—but not *the* optimal—multiple alignment solution is obtained.

Multiple alignment methods based on HMMs have been incorporated into a variety of tools. As introduced in Chapter 7, "Data Mining," a HMM is a statistical model for an ordered sequence of symbols, acting as a stochastic state machine that generates a symbol each time a transition is made from one state to the next. A limitation of a HMM approach is that the model must be trained before it can be used. As such, HMMs tend to be problem-specific, albeit powerful.

Other Strategies

There are dozens of approaches to multiple sequence alignment, some relegated to specific laboratories, and others vying for use as a standard in the bioinformatics arena. Many of these methods are highly specialized at solving specific types of multiple sequence alignment problems. For example, the eMOTIF Method is optimized for identifying motifs in protein sequences. Profile analysis is used for localized alignments in multiple sequence analysis. BLOCK analysis is used for working with conserved regions (blocks) in a multiple sequence alignment. Expectation Maximization (EM) is used to perform local multiple sequence alignment (as in Multiple EM for Motif Elicitation or MEME). These and other approaches are constantly evolving, thanks to feedback and support from the worldwide bioinformatics user community.

TOOLS

Although general-purpose pattern-matching tools can be used in search engines and data-mining applications, nucleotide and polypeptide sequence alignment applications generally dictate the use of bioinformatics-specific tools. As illustrated in Table 8-4, in addition to the sequence alignment tools designed for nucleotide and polypeptide pattern alignment, there are support utilities for format conversion, sequence editors, and protein and nucleotide databases.

Table 8-4 Sequence Alignment Tools. These examples typify the dozens of pattern-matching tools available to the bioinformatics community.

Tool	Examples
Nucleotide Pattern Alignment	BLASTN, BLASTX, TBLASTX, DotLet, BALSA
Polypeptide Pattern Alignment	BLASTP, PHI-BLAST, PSI-BLAST, Smith-Waterman, ScanPROSITE, ExPASy, DotLet, BALSA
Utilities	READSEQ, Text Editors
Protein Sequence Databases	SWISS-PROT, TrEMBL, PROSITE, BLOCKS
Nucleotide Sequence Databases	GenBank, Entrez Nucleotide Database
Sequence Editor	CINEMA, GeneDoc, MACAW

Nucleotide Pattern Matching

BLAST

The best known and most used nucleotide pattern-matching programs are the original Nucleotide-Nucleotide BLAST—sometimes referred to as BLASTN—and its derivatives. In addition to the most recent version of BLAST, two popular derivatives are BLASTX (Nucleotide Query BLAST) and TBLASTX (Nucleotide Query–Translated Database). Figure 8-14 shows the Web interface to NCBI's BLASTN, developed for nucleotide-nucleotide pattern matching.

Executing a BLAST search for a pattern match involves simply filling out the template depicted in Figure 8-14. The search string representing the nucleotide sequence to be searched for is entered, in FASTA format, in the "Search" field. The entire string can be used in the search, or only a subset of the string. To use a subset, the researcher enters the subset sequence locations in the "From" and "To" fields of the "Set subsequence" area. For example, to limit matches to the region in the search string from nucleotide 10 to nucleotide 20, the researcher would enter "From" = 10 and "To" = 20. The default search includes the entire search string.

The only other parameter that must be defined for a basic BLAST search is the database to use for the search. Database options available through a pull-down menu include, among others, "nr" (all GenBank, EMBL, DDBJ, and PDB sequences), "est" (GenBank, EMBL, and DDBJ sequences from EST Divisions), "pat" (nucleotides from the Patent division of GenBank), "pdb" (sequences derived from the 3D structures in the Protein Data Bank), and "month" (all new or revised GenBank, EMBL, DDBJ, and PDB sequences released in the last 30 days).

Options are also available for advanced searches, as shown in the bottom half of Figure 8-14. The "Limit by entrez query" option allows BLAST searches to be limited to the results of an Entrez query against the selected database. Because Entrez supports a powerful query engine, the search can be significantly narrowed through an Entrez query. Alternatively, the search can be limited to one of several dozen organisms from a pull-down menu.

The "Choose filter" option enables masks for low compositional complexity, human repeats, lookup table, and lowercase characters in the search sequence; all or none of these options can be selected. The low complexity filter masks off the regions of the query sequence (the sequence entered in the "Search" field) that have low compositional complexity. Areas of low complexity, such as those composed of only a few characters repeated, are not likely to be biologically interesting. The "Human repeats" option masks repeating sequences, speeding the search, especially against databases containing sequences with large numbers of repeats. The "Mask for lookup table only"

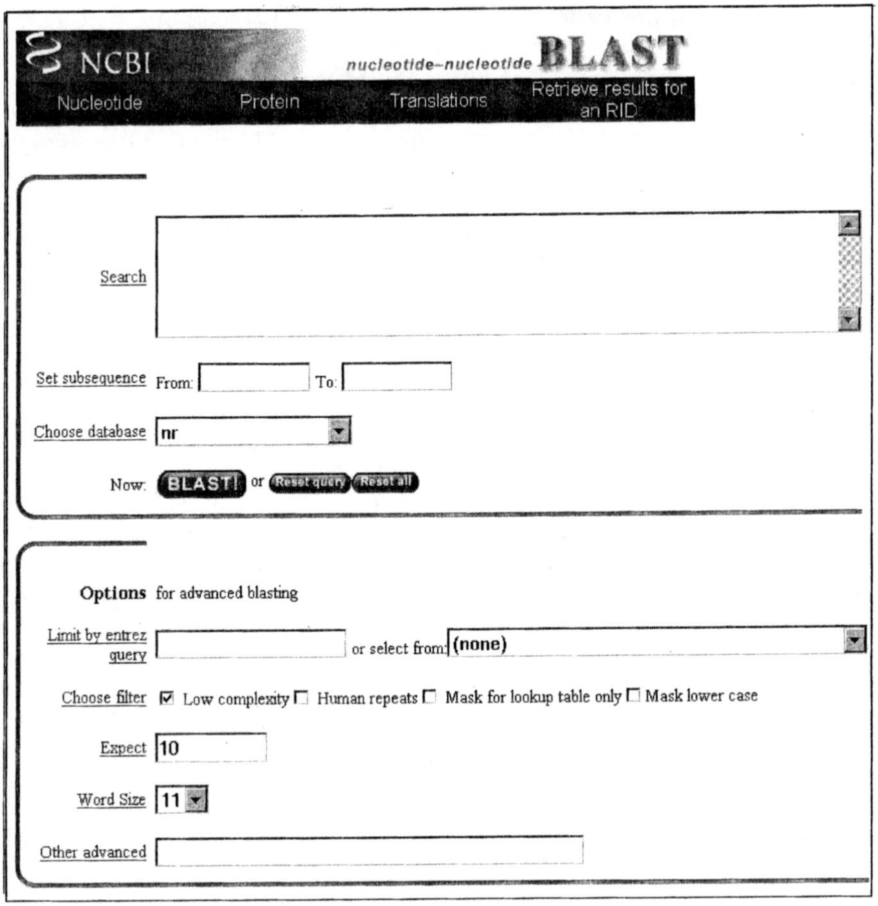

Figure 8-14 NCBI's Nucleotide-Nucleotide BLAST (BLASTN) Web Interface.

option is an experimental mask that eliminates hits based on low-complexity sequences. The "Mask lower case" option causes only the uppercase sequences in the "Search" field to be executed.

The "Expect" field represents the statistical significance threshold for reporting matches against database sequences. The lower the threshold, the more stringent the alignment criteria, resulting in fewer chance matches being reported. The default value is "10," meaning that of the reported match values, 10 will occur by chance alone. In comparison, a search with an "Expect" value of "1" would likely return only 1 result by chance alone. Too small a value in the "Expect" field will result in too few search results. "Word Size" can be set to 7, 11, or 15 nucleotides through a pull-down menu.

In addition to the pull-down menu and checkbox options, the "Other advanced" field accepts command-line entry of advanced options, including the cost to open and extend gaps, the specification of penalties for nucleotide mismatch, the reward for a match, and the ability to adjust output formatting. The "Other advanced" field can also be used to override many of the program default settings. For example, the command "-W12" sets the word size to 12, an option not available through the pull-down menus.

The other major options of BLAST deal with formatting the output. Formatting options range from color graphics in which the colors represent alignment scores to page formatting. Perhaps the most useful output utility is a Database Linkout feature, which provides reference links from the BLAST Results to various NCBI databases and other resources.

BALSA

The BALSA tool, from the Center for Bioinformatics at Rensselaer and Wadsworth Center of the New York Department of Health, provides Web-based access to Bayesian-based sequence alignment (see Figure 8-15). A virtually identical tool, BALSA Database Query, is available for database queries using either the PDB or the Structural Classification of Proteins (SCOP) databases.

BALSA determines the probability that a given pair of sequences should be aligned by sampling alignments in proportion to their joint posterior probability. Probabilities are based on alignments produced by specific combinations of substitution matrix, gap penalty, and gap extension. In operation, the two sequences to be aligned are entered in FASTA format. BALSA supports copy-paste as well as local file retrieval to populate the query and comparison sequences.

Up to four sets of scoring matrix, gap penalty, and gap extension penalty combinations can be specified. The PAM-250 as well as Blosum30 to Blosum80 scoring matrices are available. Output, which consists of the posterior probability for each scoring matrix/gap penalty/gap extension combination, is sent to the e-mail address entered on the form. A separate output is provided for each matrix-gap entry specified.

Polypeptide Pattern Matching

BLASTP

Protein-Protein BLAST (BLASTP) shares many of the features and options of BLASTN, with a focus on polypeptide sequences instead of nucleotide sequences. The BLASTP interface is similar to the interface used with BLASTN, as illustrated in Figure 8-16. The major differences are in the databases available and in the advanced options available in BLASTP. For example, the peptide parallels to the nucleotide sequence databases are available to

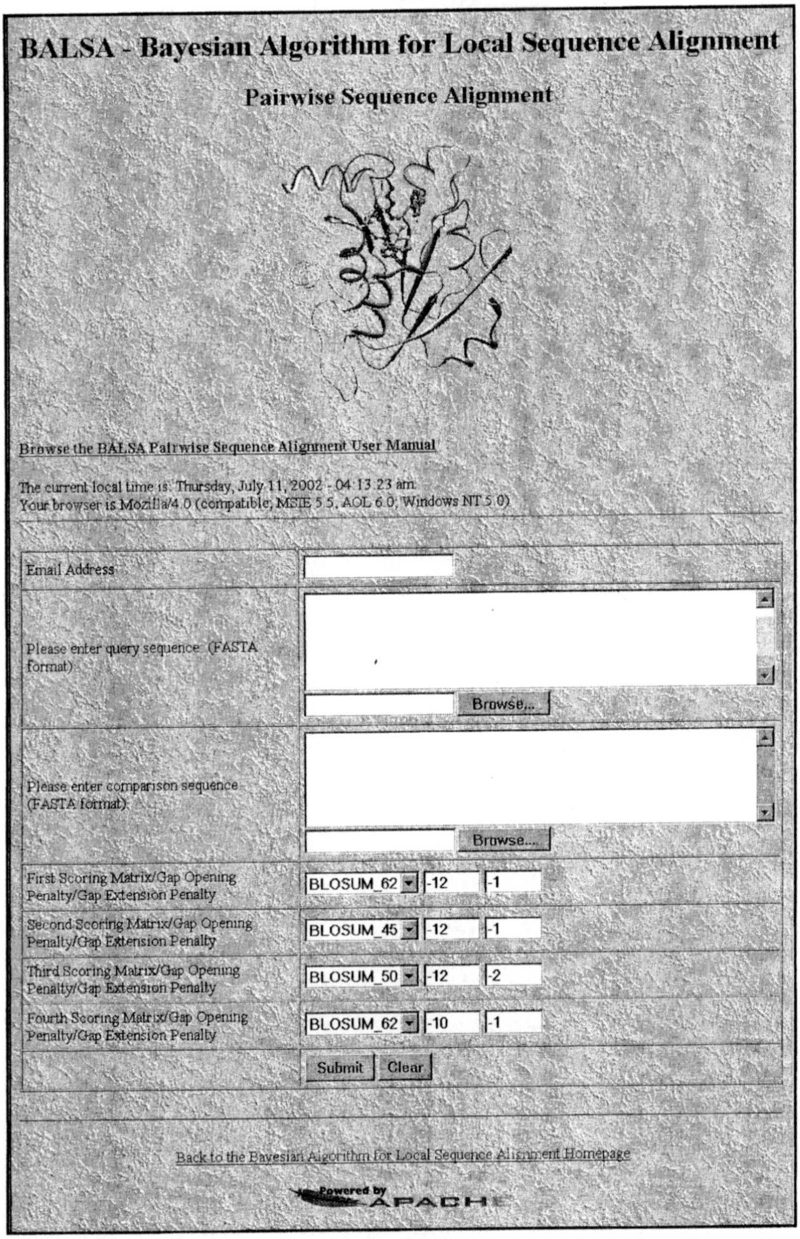

BALSA - Bayesian Algorithm for Local Sequence Alignment

Pairwise Sequence Alignment

Browse the BALSA Pairwise Sequence Alignment User Manual

The current local time is: Thursday, July 11, 2002 - 04:13:23 am.
Your browser is Mozilla/4.0 (compatible; MSIE 5.5; AOL 6.0; Windows NT 5.0)

Email Address	
Please enter query sequence (FASTA format)	
	Browse...
Please enter comparison sequence (FASTA format)	
	Browse...
First Scoring Matrix/Gap Opening Penalty/Gap Extension Penalty	BLOSUM_62 ▾ -12 -1
Second Scoring Matrix/Gap Opening Penalty/Gap Extension Penalty	BLOSUM_45 ▾ -12 -1
Third Scoring Matrix/Gap Opening Penalty/Gap Extension Penalty	BLOSUM_50 ▾ -12 -2
Fourth Scoring Matrix/Gap Opening Penalty/Gap Extension Penalty	BLOSUM_62 ▾ -10 -1
	Submit Clear

Back to the Bayesian Algorithm for Local Sequence Alignment Homepage

Powered by APACHE

Figure 8-15 BALSA Pairwise Sequence Alignment Tool. This Web-based tool is provided by the Center for Bioinformatics at Rensselaer and Wadsworth Center of the New York Department of Health.

BLASTP, including "nr" (non-redundant GenBank CDS translations, PDB, SWISS-PROT, PIR, and PRF), "swissprot" (SWISS-PROT protein sequence database), and "month" (the GenBank CDS translation, PDB, SWISS-PROT, PIR, and PRF data released in the last 30 days).

A feature in the basic BLASTP search is the "Do CD-Search" option, which is checked to compare protein sequences to the conserved domain (CD) database maintained by NCBI. The "Do CD-Search" option may be used to identify the conserved domains (modules with distinct evolutionary origin and function) present in a protein sequence.

Advanced options include the ability to specify a substitution matrix and gap costs. The substitution matrix is used to assign a score for aligning residue pairs, and should reflect the types of sequences being searched. The default matrix is BLOSUM62, which assigns a probability score for each position in an alignment that is based on the frequency with which that substitution is known to occur among related proteins. The "Gap Costs" field allows the penalties to be specified for opening and extending a gap. Increasing the gap costs results in alignments with fewer gaps.

The PSSM field holds the matrix automatically computed by PSI-BLAST (Position-Specific Iterative BLAST). A Position-Specific Scoring Matrix (PSSM) is a matrix of scores representing a locally conserved region of a sequence of motif. A PSSM is used in the scoring of multiple alignments with sequences. A PSSM plots the probability score for the occurrence of each amino acid along the length of a motif.

PSI-BLAST, which is based on the BLAST algorithm, is enhanced to be more sensitive than BLASTP. This sensitivity comes from the use of a profile of the position-specific scores for every position in the alignment that is constructed from a multiple alignment of the highest-scoring hits in the initial BLAST search. The profile or matrix created by PSI-BLAST can be formatted, saved, and then pasted into the PSSM field of BLASTP.

A feature recently added to BLASTP is the ability to specify a PHI pattern, which is used by PHI-BLAST (Pattern Hit Initiated BLAST) to search for similarities that are presumably also homologues. PHI-BLAST, which expects as input a protein query sequence and a pattern contained in that sequence, searches the current database for other protein sequences that also contain the input pattern and have significant similarity to the query sequence in the vicinity of the pattern occurrences. PHI-BLAST filters out cases where the pattern occurrence is probably random and not indicative of homology.

Smith-Waterman

The Smith-Waterman dynamic programming algorithm is available on the UCSC Kestrel Server, which is an experimental, high-performance, 512-processor system. As shown in Figure 8-17, compared to the BLASTP interface

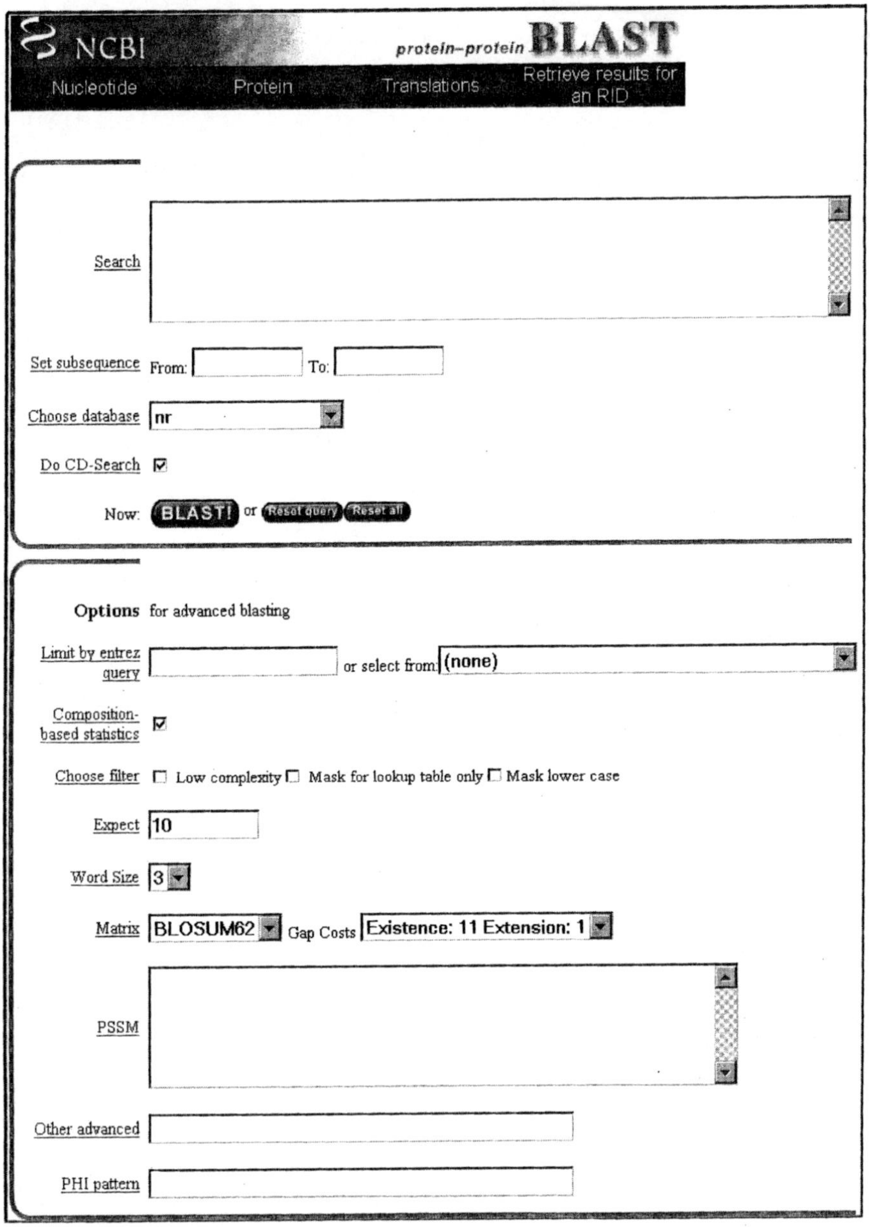

Figure 8-16   NCBI's Protein-Protein BLAST (BLASTP) Web Interface.

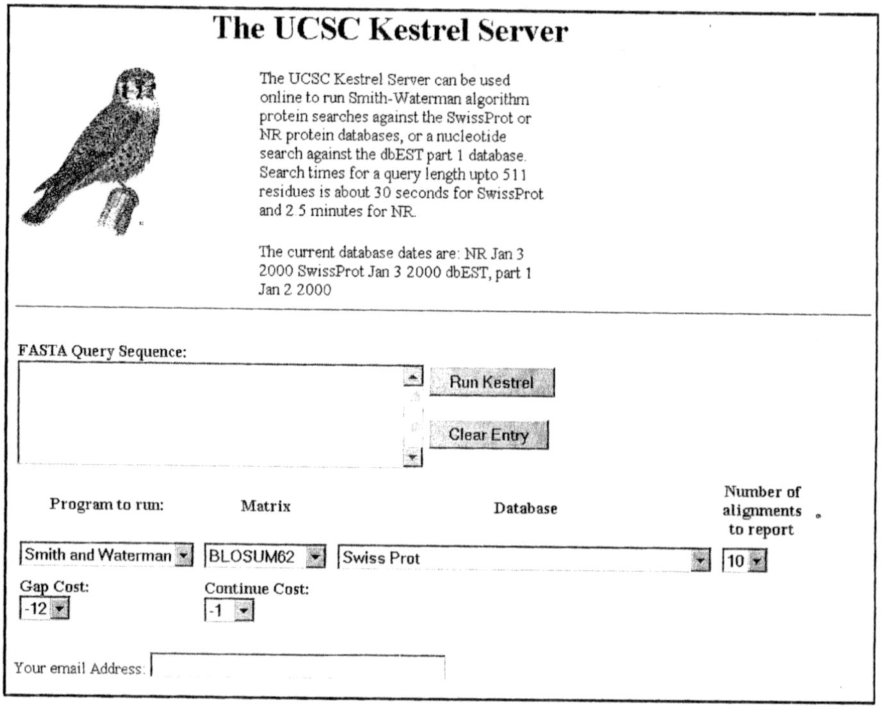

Figure 8-17 Smith-Waterman on the High-Performance UCSC Kestrel Server.

with its array of options, the interface presented by the Kestrel Server appears somewhat limited. The parameters are simply costs to open and extend gaps, the substitution matrix, the database to search, and the number of alignments to report.

The Kestrel implementation of Smith-Waterman supports the use of PAM-10 through PAM-500 and BLOSUM30 through BLOSUM100 substitution matrices against the SWISS-PROT or NR protein databases, or a nucleotide search against the dbEST part 1 database. A maximum of 40 alignments can be e-mailed to the address specified in the query form.

DotLet

The DotLet dot matrix analysis program, available on the Expert Protein Analysis System (ExPASy) server, is one of the most popular of the Web-based dot matrix analysis programs. As shown in Figure 8-18, the program—a Java applet—supports the pairwise analysis of nucleotide or polypeptide sequences that are pasted into the pop-up input fields accessed by the "input" button.

DotLet also supports a variety of matrices (Blosum30 to Blosum100 and PAM-30 to PAM-250), sliding window size (1 to 15), and zoom (1:1 to 1:8) through pull-down menus along the top of the screen.

Each pixel in the main display (center, left) corresponds to a residue in the horizontal and vertical sequences, with the darker pixels representing higher scores. The histogram window to the right of the main display window supports the interactive adjustment of the display. The height of the histogram peak indicates the quality of data, in that the higher the peak, the greater the signal-to-noise ratio. The alignment panel along the bottom of the figure shows the actual sequence alignment and supports interactive manipulation of the sequence positions.

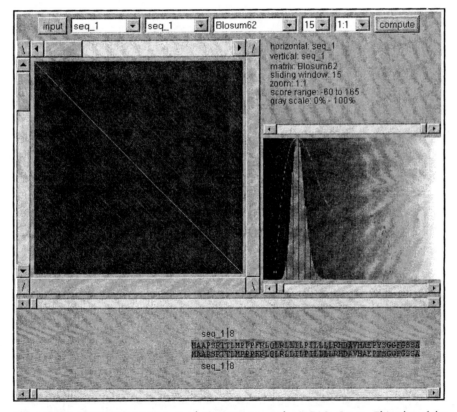

Figure 8-18   DotLet Dot Matrix Analysis Program on the ExPASy Server. This plot of the *Drosophila melanogaster* SLIT protein, plotted against itself, illustrates perfect alignment of two polypeptide sequences. At lower magnification, patterns of repeated protein domains are visible.

Utilities

Most pattern-matching programs accept data in the FASTA format. Format conversion can be performed manually with a text editor or a sequence editing utility such as READSEQ. A Web-based version of READSEQ (see Figure 8-19) is available through the Bioinformatics & Molecular Analysis Section (BIMAS) of the National Institutes of Health.

READSEQ accepts and automatically recognizes 16 different input formats, including IG/Stanford, GenBank/GB, NBRF, EMBL, Plain/Raw, Fitch, and Pearson/FASTA. Output formats include support for the major formats, including ASN.1, EMBL, PAUP/NEXUS, DNAStrider, GenBank/GB, Phylip, and IG/Stanford. READSEQ, like most file translation utilities, doesn't handle every format conversion. This is in part due to the hundreds of application-specific file formats used in bioinformatics work.

Sequence Databases

The key protein sequence databases used for sequence alignment are SWISS-PROT, TrEMBL, and PROSITE. These and other databases and tools are available through the ExPASy server of the Swiss Institute of Bioinformatics.

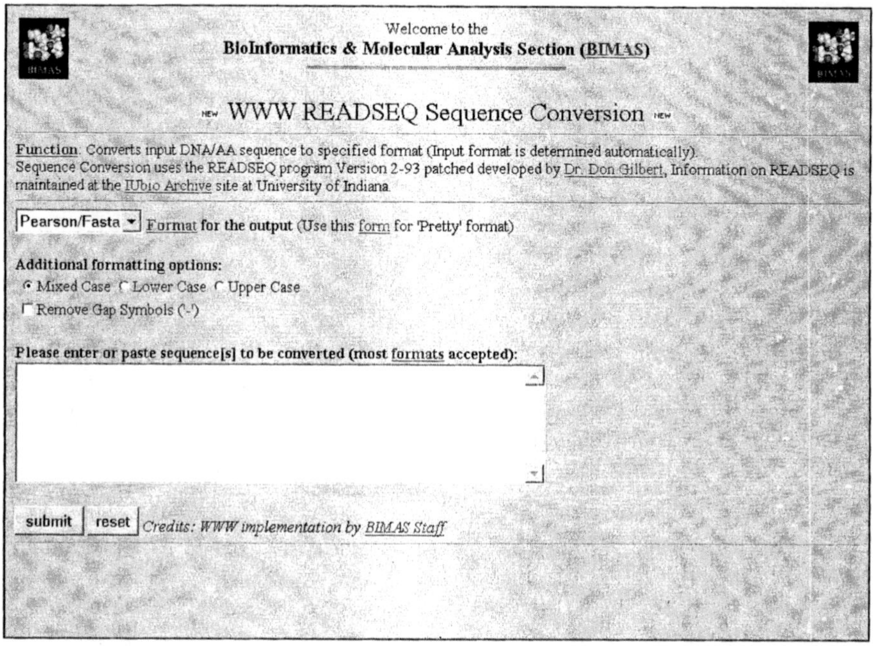

Figure 8-19   WWW READSEQ Format Conversion Utility (courtesy of BIMAS).

SWISS-PROT is a highly annotated protein sequence database that is highly integrated with other databases in the ExPASy system. The TrEMBL database is a supplement of SWISS-PROT that also contains translations of the EMBL nucleotide database that have not yet been integrated into the latest official release of SWISS-PROT. PROSITE is a database of protein families and domains that contains high-level profiles such as categories of toxins, inhibitors, chaperone proteins, and hormones. The major source of nucleotide sequence data for alignment research is NCBI's integrated Entrez system, which contains data from GenBank, RefSeq, and PDB. BLOCKS is a database of ungapped multiple protein sequence alignments. Finally, SCOP, which incorporates all PDB entries, is a structural classification database expressly designed for the investigation of protein sequences and structures.

ON THE HORIZON

The latest version of BLAST available from the NCBI illustrates movement toward integration of methodologies within the same toolset. As in other areas of computing, the hundreds of bioinformatics methods and tools have grown out of niche areas to address specific needs of investigators. However, as the field of bioinformatics matures and methodologies are extended out from their original niche areas, researchers are clustering around standards and a small subset of the many tools that have been developed, and rely less and less on translation utilities such as READSEQ. Similarly, whether traditional methods, such as dot matrix analysis and still-experimental methods, such as genetic algorithms, survive into the next generation of tools depends on how these techniques can be adapted to support current challenges in a computationally robust and user-friendly manner.

Web portals, such as Entrez and, to a lesser extent, ExPASy, represent the first level of integration of bioinformatics data, methodologies, and tools. They also illustrate the central role that funding from the government and academic institutions plays in the continued development and maintenance of tools to support the bioinformatics community.

ENDNOTE

The pattern-matching approaches using scores for gaps and inexact matching or black-box neural network technology discussed here are statistically valid for assessing the degree of string similarity. However, in selecting gaps and other methods to make the matches "look good," it's important to remember that these techniques don't necessarily relate to the biology of the nucleotide or polypeptide chains represented by the symbols manipulated by BLAST or other algorithms. It's easy to rationalize the need for gaps because of the computational infeasibility of solving long string comparisons without the provision for gaps. However, even a short gap in a polypeptide sequence can disrupt the secondary and tertiary structures of a protein, and probably alter its function as well.

Heuristic approaches, such as match matrices, attempt to add some sense of biological relevance to the mathematical equations that define the relative similarity of nucleotide and polypeptide sequences. It's up to individual researchers to consider the biological implications of the techniques and assumptions they make in simply filling out a form on a Web page during the course of their daily work.

CHAPTER

Modeling and Simulation

*The formulation of a problem is far more often essential
than its solution, which may be merely a matter of
mathematical or experimental skill.*
— Albert Einstein

Experimental molecular biology research is often a painstakingly slow process that typically involves a long sequence of carefully performed experiments, using a variety of equipment and laboratory specialists. For example, positively identifying a protein by structure may take years of work. The protein must be isolated, purified, crystallized, and then imaged. Because each step may involve dozens of failed attempts, many scientists not primarily interested in the experimental methods, but simply needing the structure data, look to other non-experimental methods.

In determining protein structure, the primary alternative to experimental or wet-lab techniques is bioinformatics. Although computational methods may be able to deliver a solution to a molecular biology problem such as structure determination in days or weeks instead of months or years, the solution is only as good as the formulation of the problem. In the case of protein structure determination or prediction, formulating the problem entails creating a model of the molecule and the major environmental factors that may influence its structure. With a valid model definition, arriving at a solution—that is, using the model to drive a simulation of the molecule's behavior and structure—is simply a matter of executing a program and then evaluating the results.

In order to appreciate the significance of modeling and simulation in bioinformatics, consider that the first "killer app" on the desktop microcomputer—the one application that raised the status of the technology from a hobbyist's plaything to a "must have" in business and in the laboratory—was the now-defunct electronic spreadsheet, VisiCalc. This spreadsheet enabled accountants, engineers, and physicists to interactively run a variety of what-if scenarios or implicit attempts at problem formulation to predict the outcomes of virtually any activity that they could express mathematically. VisiCalc's initial success was due largely to its easy-to-understand user interface of rows and columns of cells interrelated by position and formulas and a powerful back-end that interpreted the formulas and graphed the output. Working with Microsoft Excel, Lotus 1-2-3, or other modern electronic spreadsheets involves creating or using a pre-defined model—a logical, simplified description of how a real-world system performs. With a valid model—that is, one that adequately describes relationships in the real world—the spreadsheet provides an environment in which the model can be brought to life, simulating the activity of the real-world system over time or in response to specific events. For example, an accountant might look at the expected profits from a business, given a spreadsheet model that describes sales and business expenses over the course of a year. An engineer might use a model of a steel beam to explore its dynamic stability when used as a supporting structure in a bridge. Similarly, a biologist might examine the population dynamics in a closed ecosystem of various strains of bacteria, based on a model that describes the relationships between population, food supply, and the environment. A spreadsheet model is a set of linear equations relating the values of several variables (cells).

Equipped with a spreadsheet and a few equations, a molecular biologist, might define a model of a neural network that can learn to recognize amino acid sequences and assign protein structures to certain sequences, as in Figure 9-1. The model of a single neuron in the artificial neural network defines the output of the neuron as the weighted sum of inputs to the neuron, including feedback from the output: The model of the entire neural network additionally specifies the interconnection of the individual neuron models. Mathematically, the model of an individual neuron that can accept four outputs (o) with their associated fixed weights (w) can be expressed as:

$$Output = \sum_{i=0}^{4} o_i w_i$$

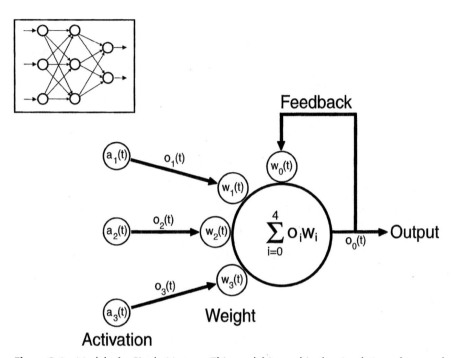

Figure 9-1   Model of a Single Neuron. This model is used in the simulation of a neural network (inset) that can be used to classify patterns, such as protein structures associated with specific amino acid sequences. The model and associated simulation can be created in a general-purpose spreadsheet or in a computational environment specifically designed for the simulation of neural networks.

Note that this model for an individual neuron is a greatly simplified representation of the function of an actual neuron in the human nervous system. For example, neurons in the brain are regularly bathed in substances—from naturally produced endorphins to drugs such as seratonin release inhibitors—that dynamically alter the strength of connections, represented by the *fixed* weights (w) in the neuron model. The advantage of ignoring the intricacies of the actual nervous system is computational efficiency and lower overhead associated with developing a model. A simpler model is also easier to develop and maintain compared to developing and maintaining a more complex model. The challenge is defining a model that is simple enough computationally and yet is rich enough to accurately define the behavior of the system.

Although spreadsheets are still used for modeling and simulation applications in business, science, and engineering, all but the simplest modeling is performed with software optimized for particular domains. For example, nuclear physicists use custom modeling and simulation programs running on supercomputers to simulate the power of nuclear explosions. Similarly, life scientists use a variety of microcomputer-based simulations to explore everything from population dynamics to the docking of proteins.

The downside of using a general-purpose spreadsheet as a platform for modeling and simulation is related to performance, flexibility, visualization capabilities, standards, and startup time. A general-purpose spreadsheet, like a general-purpose language such as eXtensible Markup Language (XML) or C++, is designed to solve a variety of problems. As such, it represents a compromise between flexibility and performance. Although a spreadsheet can be used to prototype virtually any type of simulation, the simulation will likely run several orders of magnitudes slower than a simulation developed in an environment designed for modeling and simulation.

Similarly, coding a simulation in C++ may result in a system with a higher performance than can be obtained with a dedicated simulation system. However, the startup time associated with a domain-specific simulation will likely be several orders of magnitude lower that that associated with the general-purpose language. For example, classification systems based on a neural network simulation are typically outperformed by classification systems developed in C++ or some other compiled language. However, creating a classification system with a neural network system may take only minutes. Neural network systems typically provide a library of predefined models that the user can incorporate in a neural network by connecting icons graphically instead of making extensive use of mathematical equations. Like using a high-level programming language, there is no need to develop or even fully understand low-level neuron model operation in these systems to create functional classifiers.

Even if a general-purpose language is used to develop a simulation, there are numerous reasons for going through the time and hassle of developing a model of a real-world system. Simulations allow conditions in the real world to be evaluated in compressed or expanded time and under a variety of conditions that would be too dangerous, too time-consuming, occur too infrequently, or that would otherwise be impractical in the real world. Instead of taking days or weeks to set up and run a series of biological experiments on the population dynamics of yeast under a variety of environmental conditions, the effect of, for example, an increase in temperature, can be explored in a few minutes through a simulation.

Common uses of modeling and simulation include predicting the course and results of certain actions, and exploring the changes in outcome that result when actions are modified. Several bioinformatics R&D groups are focused on developing simulation-based systems to determine, for example, if a candidate molecule for a new drug will exhibit toxicity in patients before money is invested in actually synthesizing the drug. In this regard, simulation is a means of identifying problem areas and verifying that all variables are known before construction of the drug development facility is begun. As an analysis tool, simulations help explain why certain events occur, where there are inefficiencies, and whether specific modifications in the system will compensate for or remove these inefficiencies.

As listed in Table 9-1, the range of possible applications of modeling and simulation in bioinformatics is extensive. These applications range from understanding basic metabolic pathways to exploring genetic drift. One of the most promising application areas of modeling and simulation in bioinformatics—and the most heavily funded—is as a facilitator of drug discovery, which in turn depends on modeling and simulating protein structure and function. Given the exponentially increasing rate at which models of proteins are being added to the Protein Data Bank (PDB), modeling and simulation of proteins and their interaction with other molecules are the most promising means in our lifetimes of linking protein sequence, structure, function, and expression, with the clinical relevance of the proteome.

Table 9-1   A Sample of the Applications of Modeling and Simulation in Bioinformatics.

Clinical What-If Analysis
Drug Discovery and Development
Experimental Toxicology
Exploring Genetic Drift
Exploring Molecular Mechanisms of Action
Personal Health Prediction
Drug Efficacy Prediction
Drug Side-Effects Prediction
Gene Expression Prediction
Protein Folding Prediction
Protein Function Prediction
Protein Structure Prediction
Metabolic Pathway Visualization
Pharmacokinetic Visualization

This chapter provides an overview of the usual modeling and simulation techniques used in bioinformatics. The "Drug Discovery" section introduces many of the concepts of modeling and simulation in the context of the drug discovery process. "Fundamentals" examines the fundamentals of modeling and simulation techniques, including the numerical processes associated with modeling and simulation. The "Protein Structure" section explores the most popular application of modeling and simulation in bioinformatics. The "Systems Biology" section provides an overview of modeling and simulation designed to operate at the cellular and organ levels. The "Tools" section provides a survey of general-purpose and bioinformatics-specific modeling and simulation hardware and software tools. "On the Horizon" looks at the future of modeling and simulation in bioinformatics, and "Endnote" considers the relative merit of human-based heuristic approaches in the face of increased reliance on computer-based methods of using modeling and simulation to predict protein structure.

DRUG DISCOVERY

Pharma, the primary backer of bioinformatics R&D worldwide, is keenly interested in automating and speeding the drug discovery and development process. The typical drug discovery and development process, shown in Figure 9-2, involves an often arduous series of events that starts with perhaps 5,000 candidate drug molecules and ends with a single product that can be brought to market.

Because any technology that can shorten the discovery and development process has the potential to save the industry billions of dollars, there is considerable R&D involved in replacing or supplementing the drug discovery process with modeling and simulation. A better understanding of the underlying metabolism of a particular disease or condition can suggest which molecules will be most effective for treatment, and which ones may cause toxic reactions in a patient. Similarly, assuming that protein molecules with similar structure also have similar function, modeling protein structure and comparing it with known drugs can potentially serve as a more effective screener for candidate drugs, compared to wet-lab techniques.

Later in the drug discovery process, modeling and simulation of pharmacokinetics and of drug absorption can potentially be used to shorten clinical trials. Currently, each phase of the clinical trials takes a year or more. Phase I, involving about 100 subjects, deals with safety. Phase II, which involves about 200 subjects, deals with evidence for efficacy at various dosages. Phase III, involving up to about 5,000 subjects, deals with assessing the clinical value of

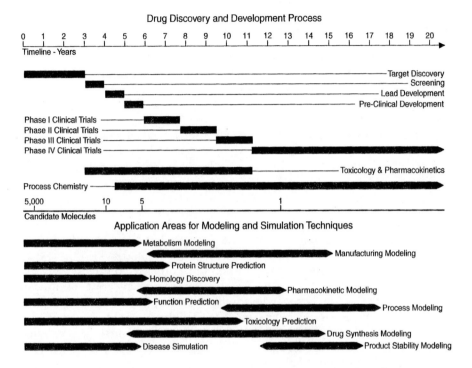

Figure 9-2   The Drug Discovery and Development Process (top) and Application Areas of Modeling and Simulation (bottom).

a molecule. Phase IV, which begins with the release of the drug, involves monitoring patients for adverse reactions. The FDA approves only about 1 molecule in 5 that makes it to Phase I clinical trials.

As illustrated in the bottom half of Figure 9-2, modeling and simulation techniques can also be applied to various aspects of the drug development process. For example, process modeling can be used, starting around year nine of the drug discovery and development process, to develop the most efficient and cost-effective development processes. Similarly, the manufacturing process can be modeled to determine the best use of materials, product stability, and best method of product synthesis—all without modifying the actual process. Before delving into one of the key modeling and simulation areas, protein structure determination and prediction, consider the following review of the fundamentals of modeling and simulation.

FUNDAMENTALS

The numerous potential applications of modeling and simulation in the drug discovery process illustrate that whether the intent is to predict the toxicity of a candidate drug or to streamline the screening process, the fundamental components and processes are identical. However, as described here, the drug discovery process also illustrates how there are also domain and implementation-specific issues, including numeric considerations, selecting the most optimum algorithms for a given problem, determining which simulation perspective best fits the problem, and hardware requirements.

Components

Every modeling and simulation system is composed of a model, a database, a simulation engine, and a visualization engine. The user and some form of feedback device, such as a computer monitor, are normally considered key elements as well. These components aren't necessarily separate entities as illustrated in Figure 9-3, but may be combined and integrated in various ways. For example, the model and data may be combined within the simulation engine, or the simulation engine and visualization engine may be combined. Regardless of how they are represented in a system, each component is necessary for operation of the simulation.

The components of a simulation system typically vary in form, complexity, and completeness, as a function of what is being modeled and the required fidelity of the simulation. For example, the model, which can be a mathematical equation, a logical description encoded as rules, or a group of algorithms that describes objects and their interrelationships in the real world, defines the underlying nature of the simulation.

The database may take the form of a few lines of data imbedded as statements within the model code, or consist of a separate text file that describes variables and constants that can be used with the underlying model. However, in most bioinformatics applications, the database consists of a large, complex system that contains libraries of data that can be applied to the underlying model. The contents of the database typically range from physical constants, such as the bond lengths of covalently bound atoms, to user-defined input, such as heuristics regarding situations in which the underlying model can be applied.

The simulation engine consists of functions that are evaluated over time, and triggered by time, events, or the value of intermediate simulation results. The simulation engine takes the model, data from the database, and direction from the user to create an output that corresponds to a condition in the real

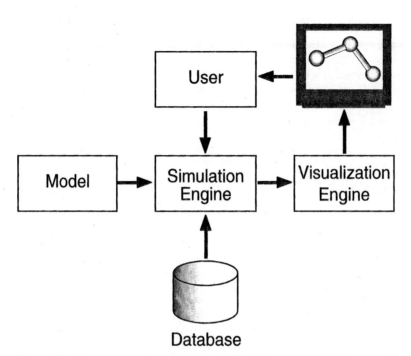

Figure 9-3   Components of a modeling and simulation system include a model, database, simulation engine, and visualization engine.

world, such as a description of the folding of a protein molecule in an aqueous solution. Finally, the visualization engine takes the output of the simulation engine and formats it into a more user-friendly form. For example, a string of digits can be formatted into a 3D rendition of a protein structure. The visualization engine may be little more than a text-formatting utility or it can take the form of a high-performance, real-time, high-resolution 3D rendering engine.

Process

The basic modeling and simulation process outlined in Figure 9-4 is applicable to most problems in bioinformatics. The first step is to define the problem space, such as predicting protein structure from amino acid sequence data— one application of modeling among the many depicted by Figure 9-4. Defining the problem space involves specifying the objectives and requirements of the simulation, including the required accuracy of results. This phase of the process also involves establishing how an observer in some experimental frame observes or interacts with some part of reality. The experimental frame defines the set of conditions under which a system will be observed, including initial states, terminal conditions, specifications for data collations, and observable variables and their magnitudes. The system represents a collection of objects, their relationships, and the behaviors that characterize them as some part of reality. The underlying assumption in defining the problem space is that the phenomenon or problem to be modeled can be positively identified and measured.

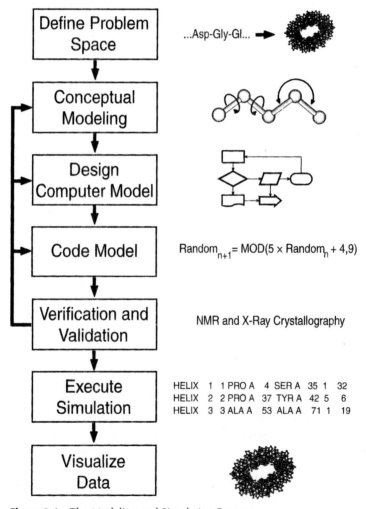

Figure 9-4 The Modeling and Simulation Process.

Once the problem space has been defined, the next phase in the modeling and simulation process is conceptual modeling, which involves mapping the systems objects, relationships, processes, and behaviors to some sort of organized structure. For example, in predicting protein structure from sequence data, the conceptual modeling might entail using ab initio methods—that is, working from first principles, such as bond lengths and angles—to construct the protein's secondary and tertiary structures.

Activities at this phase of the process also include documenting assumptions about the system so that the appropriate simulation methods can be selected. For example, if ab initio methods are going to be used to predict protein structure from sequence data, then an underlying assumption is that the data on amino acid sequence, bond length, bond angles, and related atomic-level data are not only available, but the data are accurate to some verifiable level.

Given the underlying data and a conceptual model, the next phase of the modeling and simulation process is translating the conceptual model into data structures and high-level descriptions of computational procedures. Designing the computer model involves extracting from the conceptual model only those characteristics of the original system that are deemed essential, as determined by the model's ultimate purpose. For example, the purpose of predicting protein structure from sequence data may be to allow the end-user to visualize the protein structure, so that a high degree of accuracy isn't that essential. In this example, the purpose of the model is to simplify and idealize, and the characteristics selected from the conceptual model should reflect this purpose.

Designing the computer model, like defining the problem space and conceptual modeling, is largely an art. Designing a simple model that adequately mimics the behavior of the system or process under study is a creative process that incorporates certain assumptions. The art of making good assumptions may well be the most challenging component of modeling, considering success depends as much on the domain experience of the modeler as it does on the nature of the system to be modeled. Biological systems are seldom presented in a quantitative manner, often requiring that the model designer derive or invent the needed mathematical formalisms or heuristics.

Coding of the computer model involves transferring the symbolic representations of the system into executable computer code. Model coding marks the transition of the modeling process from an artistic endeavor to a predominantly scientific one, defined by software engineering principles. Model coding may involve working with a low-level computer language, such as C++, or a high-level shell designed specifically for modeling and simulation.

Once a model is in the form of executable code, it should be subject to verification and validation. Verification is the process of determining that the model coded in software accurately reflects the conceptual model by testing the internal logic of a model to confirm that it is functioning as intended, for example. The simulation system and its underlying model are validated by assessing whether the operation of the software model is consistent with the real world, usually through comparison with data from the system being simulated. For example, in a system designed to predict protein structure, the validation process would include comparing model data with protein structure data from NMR and X-ray crystallography. Validating X-ray crystallography data might involve comparing it with the pattern resulting from bombarding the crystal lattice of a purified protein with X-rays. In contrast, validating NMR data might involve comparing it with actual data produced by scanning a pure protein in solution.

Validation also involves certifying that the output of the system as a whole is adequate for the intended purpose and is consistent with the presumptions of expert opinion. As such, validation is at least in part a subjective call. The validity of a model is a function of the objectives of the model designer and the context of its application. For example, the usefulness of a model of protein structure for a decision-making application is a function of the accuracy of prediction. There are no concepts such as "best" or "correct" in model validity assessment, considering that the degree to which a model needs to reflect or mimic a real-world system varies with each case. In addition, because verification is a check for internal consistency, it's possible for a model to be verifiable and yet fail validation because of errors in the conceptual model.

Executing the simulation ideally generates the output data that can illustrate or answer the problem initially identified in the problem space. Depending on the methods used, the amount of process and time required to generate the needed data may be extensive. For example, predicting protein structure using ab initio methods can involve thousands of iterations and take days of supercomputer time in order to arrive at statistically reliable results.

Visualizing the output data opens the simulator output to human inspection, especially if the output is in the form of 3D graphics that can be assessed qualitatively instead of in tables of textual data. For example, even though the structure of a protein may be described completely in a text file that follows the PDB format, the data take on more meaning when they can be visualized as a 3D structure that can be rotated in 3D space using a visualization program such as RasMol, Chimera, or SWISS-PDBViewer. Data are typically subject to numerical analysis as well as visualization, in order to provide a quantitative measure of accuracy and to determine whether the underlying model needs to be improved upon.

Documentation, although not represented as a formal step in Figure 9-4, is key to model validation, reuse, and communication with others. For example, the data format used by many molecular modeling systems follows the PDB format, which includes extensive documentation with each molecule described in the database. The partial listing of structure 1A3N from the PDB, shown in Figure 9-5, documents the geometry and stereochemistry of the Deoxy Human Hemoglobin molecule.

```
REMARK 500 GEOMETRY AND STEREOCHEMISTRY
REMARK 500 SUBTOPIC: CLOSE CONTACTS IN SAME ASYMMETRIC UNIT
REMARK 500
REMARK 500 THE FOLLOWING ATOMS ARE IN CLOSE CONTACT.
REMARK 500
REMARK 500  ATM1 RES C  SSEQI   ATM2 RES C  SSEQI         DISTANCE
REMARK 500   NZ  LYS B  66  -  O   HOH    394             0.958
REMARK 500
REMARK 500 GEOMETRY AND STEREOCHEMISTRY
REMARK 500 SUBTOPIC: COVALENT BOND LENGTHS
REMARK 500
REMARK 500 THE STEREOCHEMICAL PARAMETERS OF THE FOLLOWING RESIDUES
REMARK 500 HAVE VALUES WHICH DEVIATE FROM EXPECTED VALUES BY MORE
REMARK 500 THAN 4*RMSD AND BY MORE THAN 0.150 ANGSTROMS (M=MODEL
REMARK 500 NUMBER; RES=RESIDUE NAME; C=CHAIN IDENTIFIER; SSEQ=SEQUENCE
REMARK 500 NUMBER; I=INSERTION CODE).
REMARK 500
REMARK 500 EXPECTED VALUES: ENGH AND HUBER, 1991
REMARK 500
REMARK 500  M RES CSSEQI ATM1   RES CSSEQI ATM2   DEVIATION
REMARK 500
REMARK 500  0 LYS A  60   CG    LYS A  60   CD      0.621
REMARK 500  0 LYS A  90   CG    LYS A  90   CD      0.231
REMARK 500  0 LYS A  99   CG    LYS A  99   CD      0.195
REMARK 500  0 HIS B   2   CB    HIS B   2   CG      0.097
REMARK 500  0 GLU B   6   CB    GLU B   6   CA      0.153
REMARK 500  0 LYS B  66   CG    LYS B  66   CD      0.487
REMARK 500  0 LYS C  16   CD    LYS C  16   CE      0.480
REMARK 500  0 LYS C  60   CE    LYS C  60   NZ      0.199
REMARK 500  0 HIS D   2   CB    HIS D   2   CG      0.112
REMARK 500  0 LYS D 144   CD    LYS D 144   CE      0.405
```

Figure 9-5 Documentation of Data. Data documentation in the PDB is in the form of header data in each description of protein structure. This example, taken from Deoxy Human Hemoglobin (PDB ID 1A3N), describes factors relating to geometry and stereochemistry of the data described in the main body of the file.

Perspectives

During the design of a computer model, one of the major decisions is what perspective to use. The three basic simulation perspectives are continuous, discrete, and hybrid discrete/continuous. These perspectives, which differ in how the system states change with time and events, define the tools, methods, and algorithms that should be used in the model coding phase of the modeling and simulation process.

Continuous Simulation

The continuous simulation methods are most appropriate when what is of primary interest is the time-varying nature of objects or processes in some real-world system. The variables in a continuous model are assumed to vary continuously with advancing time. Because there is no instant of time when the system is not in flux, continuous simulations are said to be time-driven. Behavior patterns modeled as a mixture of differential and algebraic equations provide the basis for this simulation perspective.

A differential equation defines a relationship between a continuous variable and its own rate of change. To take an example from pharmacokinetics, consider the time-varying nature of the plasma level of a drug ingested. Given the initial concentration of the drug in the body, the time since the drug was ingested, and the rate at which the drug is absorbed in the gut, we can model the current concentration of drug in the body with the following relationship:

$$[Drug]_{plasma} = \frac{Dose}{Volume_{plasma}} \times e^{-KT}$$

In this equation, the fraction of the drug lost from the plasma per-unit time is represented by KT, where K is a constant and T is time. The elimination of constant K is a function of the type of drug administered, administration route, method of elimination or conversion, health of the patient, and renal function. Drugs with a large number for K will be eliminated faster from the body than those with a smaller number for K.

When this model of drug elimination is coded, the formula for drug plasma concentration becomes a DO LOOP in which the value for T is incremented by an appropriate value, dt, with each loop. Depending on what is being studied, dt might be 1 millisecond or 10 seconds. In pseudocode form, the solution to the preceding equation during the first 100 seconds after drug administration, assuming an initial dose of 1000 milligrams, a plasma volume of 6000 ml, an elimination constant of 0.4, and a dt of 0.1 seconds, appears as:

```
DOSE = 1000
PLASMA VOLUME = 6000
T = 0
K = 0.4
DT = 0.1

FOR INDEX = 1 TO 1000
DO
   CONCENTRATION = (DOSE/plasma volume) × EXP(–K × T)
     T = T + DT
LOOP
```

This differential equation is solved by advancing time in relatively small increments dt and recomputing the continuous variable *concentration* at each step. Larger steps may be taken to decrease computation time at the expense of greater approximation error. Termination of the program occurs after 1000 iterations of the DO LOOP. However, termination could also be linked to a maximum runtime, or a maximum or minimum concentration, or some combination of the two. The drug concentration, as described in the preceding differential equation, isn't limited to integer values, but is instead most accurately expressed in real values, such as 3.457 mg per ml. When run, the output of the simulation results in a plasma drug concentration that initially decreases rapidly and then more slowly as the concentration approaches zero.

Discrete Simulation

A discrete event simulation perspective lends itself to modeling systems in which an object or process arrives at a stage, waits in a queue until it receives attention, and then moves on to the next stage. Discrete event simulation is characterized by relatively large quantities of time during which the underlying system doesn't change. Advancing the simulation from one event to the next simulates time. Another characteristic of discrete methods is that the progress of objects or processes moving through the system are typically measured as integers.

Hybrid Simulation

Hybrid simulation methods are useful when the system to be modeled displays a variety of behaviors, some of which lend themselves to discrete event methods, and some of which are more easily solved through continuous simulation techniques. Consider the challenges faced by a modeler attempting to simulate a complex neuromuscular system involving individual packets of neurotransmitter substances, receptor sites, and resulting muscular contraction. Describing the release, transport, and subsequent absorption of neurotransmitter packets might be most easily mapped in a discrete event model. The resulting time-varying contraction, however, is likely to be most easily described in terms of differential equations within a continuous simulation model.

In general, any system can be simulated with models adhering to continuous, discrete, or hybrid perspectives. However, the perspective that most closely maps to the actual system characteristics will minimize development effort. The optimal modeling perspective is also a function of the characteristic of the system to be modeled. For example, a system can be modeled with discrete and continuous methods, with each method answering a different question. In addition, in extremely complex simulations, computation consideration may dictate the most appropriate perspective. For example, it's often more economical, in terms of computational time and hardware requirements, to approximate an event-driven system with a continuous simulation.

Numeric Considerations

The algorithms underlying a model necessarily reflect the scope and nature of the simulation. Depending on the simulation requirements, the algorithms used may vary from simple and approximate to very complex, computationally expensive, and as accurate as possible.

Errors

There is a limit to the degree of accuracy available in every simulation, as dictated by the software and hardware available. For example, all complex digital computations, especially those employing multiple operations on floating-point numbers, are prone to errors. Because of the way in which the two components of a floating-point number are handled, computations involving numbers in this format are not exact. Given enough iterations, the cumulative errors of multiple operations will become significant.

Floating-point relationships such as 2/3 (0.666666...) are represented in a digital computer system to only so many decimal places. Errors of this type, sometimes referred to as roundoff errors, can be minimized at the expense of computational speed by working the highest precision possible. For example, double-precision variables can be used for operators in computations. Rearranging the sequence of computational events so that significant figures aren't lost can also minimize round-off errors. In comparison, computations involving strictly integer numbers are exact as long as the results are within the range of the data type used. The primary benefit of using an integer over a floating-point number is speed.

Round-off errors are due to computer hardware limitations. They can be minimized by the judicious use of appropriate data types and algorithms. The other major type of error, *truncation error,* is independent of computer hardware, and is attributable instead to the algorithms used in the simulation. These errors occur when the algorithms use approximations to arrive at an answer. For example, instead of computing the sum of an infinite series, a practical algorithm might stop after a sufficient number of elements have been added. Truncation error can best be thought of as the difference between the actual answer and the answer obtained by way of a practical calculation. Unlike round-off errors, which are a function of the computer hardware, operating system, and programming language, truncation errors are a function of the algorithms used to solve a given problem.

Differential Equations and Integration

Solving differential equations and performing numerical integration are two common computational operations performed in continuous simulation. A differential equation defines a relationship between a continuous variable and its own rate of change. In general, the goal in solving a differential equation is to be able to predict the value of a function at any point in time. Differential equations involving one independent variable are said to be ordinary differential equations. Ordinary differential equations can be further classified as either initial value problems or boundary value problems depending on whether information about the problem is known at a particular value of the independent variable, or at two different values of the independent variable, respectively.

It's often the case that a problem to be modeled can't be solved by an ordinary differential equation such as described previously for drug concentration. Accurately determining the total amount of drug remaining in the plasma will require numerical integration techniques that are based on one or more differential equations. In many instances, it isn't possible to obtain an exact or analytical solution to a differential equation. In these situations, numerical solutions can be used to prove an approximation of the solution, within some degree of accuracy.

Numerical integration methods differ in accuracy, speed of execution, complexity, and the nature of the underlying assumptions that must be made for their use. In general, they work by evaluating a function at a finite number of points and performing a weighted sum of the function values. Eventually, the weighted sum should converge to the correct value of the integral. Some numerical integration methods use a constant time slice or step size (see Figure 9-6), while others change the step size as needed to increase computational efficiency.

Two of the most popular integration methods are the Euler and Runge-Kutta methods. The Euler method is simple to implement but the least elegant, with

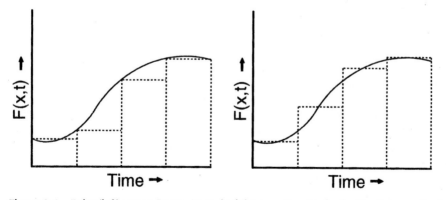

Figure 9-6   Euler (left) versus Runge-Kutta (right) Integration Methods. The Euler method is simpler to implement, but the Runge-Kutta method is more accurate and more efficient.

truncation errors inversely proportional to step size and round-off errors directly proportional to step size. A larger step size or time slice results in fewer round-off errors, which are cumulative, at the expense of increased truncation errors. In addition, because the Euler method ignores the underlying change in the equation, it becomes unstable with a relatively large step size.

The Runge-Kutta method of numerical integration is more elegant, more efficient, more stable, and more accurate than the Euler method. The basic Runge-Kutta method allows the use of a larger step size for a given round-off error, and so reduces computational time, even though the algorithm is more complex than that of the Euler method. A variation of the basic Runge-Kutta method, the Adaptive Runge-Kutta method, adjusts step size dynamically during program execution to reflect the rate of change in the equation. For example, it decreases step size with an increasing rate of change in the equation, and increases step size when the rate of change diminishes. As a result, while the Euler method might require 1,000 steps to evaluate an equation, the Runge-Kutta method might involve only 100 steps.

As illustrated in Figure 9-6, the Euler method of numerical integration involves repeatedly accumulating slices of area, of constant width, to determine the area under the curve defined by the differential equation. In contrast, the Runge-Kutta method considers the slope of the equation at multiple points along each time slice, resulting is better curve fit and less truncation error.

Random Numbers

Random numbers from a variety of distributions form the basis of many simulation techniques. At best, most digital methods produce nearly random numbers, typically through programs called pseudorandom number generators. Figure 9-7 shows that the output from the pseudorandom generator of a popular simulation package running under Windows on a Pentium III hardware platform isn't perfect. Ideally, the numbers would be evenly distributed throughout the range, with no significant peaks and no holes, such as the band of missing numbers around 22,000.

One of the most common methods of implementing a pseudorandom number generator is through the use of a Linear Congruential Generator (LCG) algorithm, which produces a series of numbers in which each successive term is computed from its predecessor. As such, the LCG produces a pseudorandom sequence because each number isn't independent of all earlier numbers.

The arbitrary starting point for the LCG algorithm is called the *seed*. Because an LCG algorithm computes successive terms from predecessor terms, including seed values, a new seed value results in a different random number sequence. Conversely, the same seed will result in the same pseudorandom

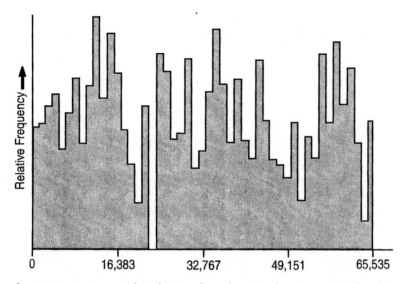

Figure 9-7 Frequency Plot of a Pseudorandom Number Generator. The plot represents the cumulative output of 20,000,000 iterations of the generator over the range of 0 to 65,535, using the same numerical starting point (seed).

sequence. As a result, one way to help ensure that the same pseudorandom sequence isn't generated at each run of a simulation is to use a new seed value.

Another limitation of pseudorandom number generators is that the series of random numbers repeats with a finite period. Furthermore, in some implementations of the LCG algorithm, the numbers between zero and the period aren't fully represented in the output of the generator. If the nature of the output of the system-supplied pseudonumber generator is unacceptable, there are a number of possible solutions. The simplest is to add a randomizing shuffle to the output of the LCG to alter the deterministic nature of the series. The effect of this shuffle is to randomize the output of the LCG. However, the simple shuffle can't overcome the problem of a sparse period, because a shuffle will not produce additional numbers, but instead alters only the sequence of the numbers produced. If a richer period is required, then a substitute for the LCG will have to be developed.

Algorithms

Modeling in bioinformatics is a multidisciplinary activity that borrows algorithms from statistics, mathematics, Artificial Intelligence (AI), and even robotics. For example, robotics algorithms are being used to explore the manipulation of proteins by chaperone molecules. Instead of defining a rotation or unfolding of a protein in 3D space, the space is split into n-dimensions. As a result, the movements of molecules can be described with simple linear functions that are much less computationally intensive than vector algebra. In addition to the esoteric algorithms that are useful in niche areas of bioinformatics, there are several algorithms that have general applicability in modeling and simulation, notably the Monte Carlo methods.

Monte Carlo Method

An approach developed through the collaboration of a computer scientist, physicist, and mathematician, the Monte Carlo method, forms the basis for much modeling and simulation activity in bioinformatics. The Monte Carlo method, named after the famous Monaco casino, involves running multiple repetitions of a model, gathering statistical data, and deriving behaviors of the real-world system based on these models. Each run of a model represents chance behaviors that cannot be modeled exactly, but only characterized statistically. Monte Carlo methods are particularly useful in modeling systems that have a large number of degrees of freedom and quantities of interest. The first uses of the method were in nuclear physics and various military applications. Today, Monte Carlo methods are used in bioinformatics for applications ranging from optimizing the drug discovery process to protein structure prediction.

Metropolis Algorithm

The most important variant of the basic Monte Carlo method used in bioinformatics work is the Metropolis Algorithm. The Metropolis Algorithm is useful in the minimization problems that are common in performing likelihood fits and optimization problems. For example, consider the function graphed in Figure 9-8. Within the boundaries defined by $x1$ and $x2$, A and B are local minima and C is the global minimum. The general problem is to find x so that it minimizes $f(x)$ with as few function calls as possible. The caveat is that the formula for solving $f(x)$ is non-trivial and may be computationally intractable using ordinary means. One of the pitfalls of solving for $f(x)$ through ordinary means is that the solution may be stuck at a local minima, such as A or B in the figure. That is, the algorithm determines that $f(x)$ increases to either side of a local minima, and therefore settles down in the local minima, ignoring the global minimum.

The value of using the Metropolis Algorithm is that it offers a means of maximizing the odds of jumping out of a local minima and into the global minimum—and staying there. In nature, molten materials, such as quartz, when allowed to cool slowly, find the global local minimum state—they crystallize. However, when the material is cooled quickly, the material ends up in local minima—an amorphous state.

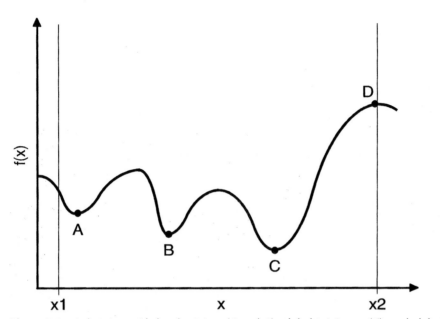

Figure 9-8 A function with local minima (*A* and *B*), global minimum (*C*), and global maximum (*D*) within the boundaries defined by *x*1 and *x*2.

Algorithmically, the probability that a system at temperature T is in a state of energy E (not at the global minimum) appears as:

$$p(E) \sim e^{-E/kT}$$

Assuming a temperature of T is assigned to the system, the probability of changing from state 1 to state 2 is:

$$p = \min(1, e^{-(E_2 - E_1)/kT})$$

The initial value of T should be great enough to allow all local minima and the global minimum to be evaluated. As long as T is greater than zero, there is a probability of a jump from a local to a global minimum. Consider the method graphically in Figure 9-9.

As the temperature is decreased, the maximum value of the function $f(x)$ decreases as well. $f(x)$ is represented by the black circle in Figure 9-9, which can be thought of as a particle with kinetic energy defined by the temperature.

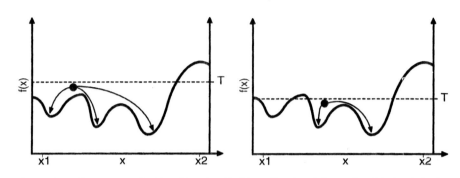

Figure 9-9 The Metropolis Algorithm Applied in a Simulated Annealing Method. As the temperature (*T*) of the system decreases, the number of local minima available to evaluate *f(x)* decreases. Whereas three minima are available at the initial temperature (left), at a lower temperature (right) only two minima are available.

As random values of x are evaluated by the annealing function, the function locates local minima and maxima by chance. Assuming enough iterations of evaluating $f(x)$ and lowering the system temperature T, the maximum function value will be trapped somewhere in the global minimum. A major issue in simulated annealing is the cooling schedule, because abruptly decreasing T may trap the function at a local minima. However, extending the cooling schedule may lengthen the time required for the algorithm to locate the global minimum unacceptably. Typical runs of the Metropolis Algorithm involve 100 to 1,000 iterations.

Execution time is often a significant issue in bioinformatics applications because many problems are multidimensional. That is, instead of simply locating the global minimum in one plane, the minimization problem is often one best represented in n-dimensional space, as in Figure 9-10. Because thousands of iterations in each dimension may be required to determine the global minimum, computational time becomes prohibitive with increasing n.

Hardware

Simulations, especially those involving tens of thousands of data points and relationships, such as those dealing with protein structure prediction, are extremely hardware-intensive. Many simulations are beyond the capabilities of all but the most powerful general-purpose desktop workstations operating at over 1 GHz with dual CPUs and several GB of RAM—and even these systems may take days of processing time per simulation. The most affordable general-purpose alternatives to mainframe hardware are to create a Linux cluster of affordable, modest-power workstations. A cluster of 20 or more workstations can provide the computational power approaching that of a mainframe at a fraction of the cost.

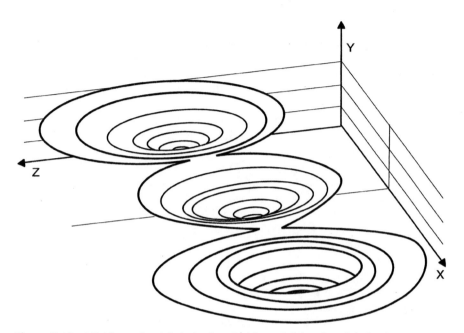

Figure 9-10 3D View of a Minimization Problem. Solving for global minimum in a multi-dimensional space is computationally expensive.

Depending on the nature of the simulation, specialized hardware may be available to make some modeling and simulation tenable on desktop systems. For example, there are graphics accelerator cards to enhance the rendering of molecules and other 3D structures. Similarly, for neural network–based simulations, there are cards designed to represent the individual nodes in hardware, speeding the lengthy learning process by several orders of magnitude.

True ab initio methods of predicting the structure of large protein molecules, which are based on modeling of atomic-level forces, are beyond the capabilities of even the fastest supercomputers. For all but the smallest protein molecules, true ab initio modeling will have to wait for affordable, higher-performance computing.

Issues

Two major concerns in modeling and simulation in bioinformatics are consistency and performance. Consistency is an issue in tasks such as protein structure prediction because different assumptions and simplifications result in different protein structures, even with the same source data. For example, if two different computer systems use the Metropolis Algorithm to solve for the global minimum of a function used to define protein structure, and one system provides a more random distribution without major holes in the distribution while the other system produces much more pseudorandom data, each system will produce different analytical results. As a result, two different tools designed to predict protein structure will likely predict two different structures, for example. The difference in the predicted structures may be significant, depending on how poorly the pseudorandom number generator on the inferior system performs, and how reliant the system is on the Metropolis Algorithm for predicting protein structure. As such, it's important for the user to determine the underlying assumptions and intended purpose of a simulation-based tool before blindly relying on it to provide credible results.

As noted in the discussion of hardware, performance is always an issue in modeling and simulation systems intended to work with large data sets exemplified by protein data. Many commercial programs claim significant performance advantages over the academic versions of the same program due to more efficient coding or the use of proprietary algorithms. Whether the expense of commercial systems is warranted depends the amount of modeling and simulation work routinely performed in the course of R&D, the available hardware, and cost considerations.

However, even with an unlimited hardware budget, it's currently impossible to simulate the interaction of each of the thousands of atoms in a large protein molecule with each of the hundreds of thousands of atoms in the surrounding aqueous environment. Assumptions and simplifications have to be made to realize reasonable performance, and these simplifications and assumptions will inevitably have an adverse affect on consistency.

PROTEIN STRUCTURE

Knowledge of protein structure is generally considered a prerequisite to understanding protein function and, by extension, a cornerstone of proteomics research. Because months and sometimes years are involved in verifying protein structure through experimental methods, computational methods of modeling and predicting protein structure are currently viewed as the only viable means of quickly determining the structure of a newly discovered protein. This section explores the role of modeling and simulation methods in determining protein structure.

Proteins, like genes, don't exist as linear sequences of molecules, but assume complex, compact 3D shapes. Protein shapes or configurations are characterized as secondary, tertiary, or quaternary. The primary protein configuration—the simple linear sequence of covalently bound amino acids—is functionally uninteresting. The secondary structure is the local geometry along the sequence, typically in the form of sheets, coils, loops, and helices.

Most proteins are composed of a combination of secondary structures. A protein's tertiary structure describes how the molecule folds in 3D space. Quaternary structure describes the complex configuration of a protein that is interacting with other molecules in 3D space.

There are two main computational alternatives to experimental methods of determining or predicting secondary and tertiary protein structures from sequence data. The first approach is based on ab initio methods, which involve reasoning from first principles. The second approach, often termed heuristic methods, is based on some form of pattern matching, using knowledge of existing protein structures. Ab initio methods rely on molecular physics, and ignore any relationship of the molecule with other proteins. Heuristic methods, in contrast, use information contained in known protein structures. Figure 9-11 shows a flowchart of the methods available for determining or predicting protein structure from protein sequence data.

The difference between the two approaches can be appreciated with parallel approaches in archaeology. When a fossilized skeleton of a small animal is discovered, one approach to reconstructing the physical structure of the animal

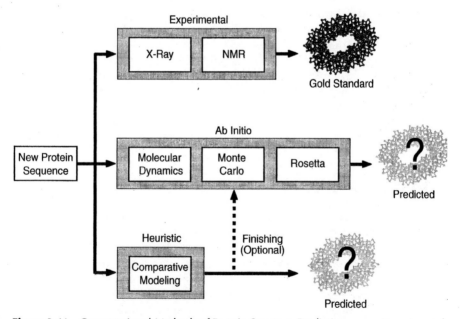

Figure 9-11 Computational Methods of Protein Structure Prediction versus Experimental Protein Structure Determination Methods. Ab initio and heuristic methods promise to provide less accurate but more timely results, compared to experimental methods that can require a year or more of research per molecule.

and its lifestyle is to reason from first principles, using the size, arrangement, thickness of the various bones, the size of the brain case, and other physical indicators, such as the bowing of the long bones (which indicate the amount of musculature present). Wear patterns on the teeth might suggest a diet rich in grains, and the presence of canines may suggest the animal was omnivorous.

The second approach to assessing the fossil of the extinct animal is to compare the skeleton with those of known animals. The leg and arm bones may approximate those of small modern monkey, for example. The teeth may approximate those of a modern primate, with large, flat molars and prominent canines. The relative size of the brain case, when compared to present-day monkeys, might give an indication of the relative intelligence and social lifestyle of the extinct animal, based on current primates.

Comparing fossilized skeletons of animals with those of modern animals is frequently practiced because it's easy, rapid, and to the best of our knowledge, fairly accurate. Reasoning from first principles is usually reserved for those cases where there is nothing resembling the newly discovered fossil in the current fossil record. In many cases, the methods overlap and complement each other. For example, first principles may be used to reconstruct the general body shape and stature of the extinct animal, but give no indication of the skin or hair coloring. However, by extrapolating current behavior and habitat knowledge of current species, a good guess can be made as to the composition and color of the skin, fur, or feathers.

Similarly, in bioinformatics, ab initio and heuristic methods of determining protein structure are commonly used in parallel or sequentially because of the accuracy limitations of either approach when used alone. For example, hand editing is commonly applied to ab initio data to improve the accuracy of the results. The primary methods used in the two basic approaches are reviewed here, with an emphasis on the underlying modeling and simulation techniques involved in each method.

Ab Initio Methods

Pure ab initio methods of determining protein structure are based on sequence data and the physics of molecular dynamics. Newtonian physics, atomic-level forces, and solving equations for the most stable (minimum free energy) conformation or structure form the basis for these methods. Reasoning from first principles assumes that the shape of a protein can be defined as a function of the amino acid sequence, the temperature, pressure, pH, and other local conditions without knowledge of the biology associated with the molecule. For example, the fact that a protein unfolds or becomes denatured at elevated temperatures and reverts to its normal, active, folded state can be modeled irrespective of the structure or function of the protein. However, unlike our knowledge of physics or other hard sciences, our understanding of the first principles of molecular biology is largely incomplete. As a result, attempts thus far at using first principles as the basis for determining protein structure have been successful primarily as a means of defining limited areas (finishing) of the global protein architecture. For example, with the overall protein structure approximately known, reasoning from first principles can be used to define a particular bend in the structure.

Because of the computational demands associated with ab initio methods, assumptions and simplifications are required for all but the smallest proteins. For example, just as the models of individual neurons discussed earlier are composed of simple equations, instead of considering the dozens of variables affecting each atom and bond in a real neuron, a common simplifying assumption is that protein structure can be computed from bond lengths, bond angles, and torsion (dihedral) angles (see Figure 9-12).

Additional assumptions are that bond lengths are constant, and that bond length is a function of the two atoms involved in the bond. Bond angles, which are a function of the relative position of three atoms, are also assumed to be constant. Bond angles, which are limited to the range of about 100 to 180 degrees, are a function of the type of atoms involved and the number of free electrons available for bonding.

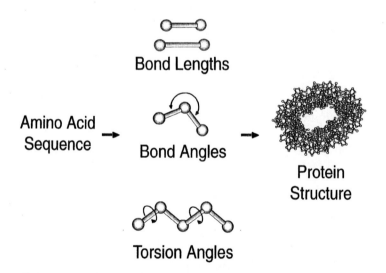

Figure 9-12 Ab Initio Protein Structure Determination. Based on the protein's amino acid sequence (primary structure), secondary and tertiary structures are computed. Tertiary structures typically takes the form of *xyz* coordinates for each atom in the protein molecule. Many ab initio methods assume that protein secondary and tertiary structures are a function of bond lengths, bond angles, and torsion angles.

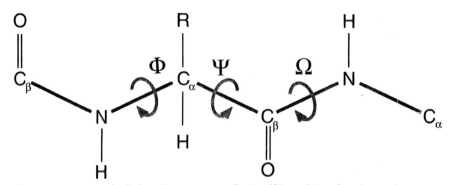

Figure 9-13 Key Dihedral Angles—Omega (Ω), Psi (Ψ), and Phi (Φ). The angles refer to the torsion about the two planes defined by the two atoms to either side of the labeled bond.

Torsion angles, which are a function of four atoms, are considered to be variable, and range from 0 to 360 degrees. The three principal dihedral angles are commonly referred to as omega (Ω), psi (Ψ), and phi (Φ), as illustrated in Figure 9-13. Together, they define the protein backbone for each amino acid in a polypeptide chain. Omega, the Cα-to-Cα torsion angle about Cβ and N, is assumed to be constant at 180 degrees. Psi, the N-to-N dihedral angle about Cα and Cβ, and Φ, the Cβ-to-Cβ torsion angle about the bond between the N and Cα, are restricted because of the interaction of residues attached to the backbone. Typical values for phi and psi are –57 and –47 for an alpha helix and –119 and 113 for a beta sheet, respectively.

A graph called the Ramachandran plot describes the allowed combinations of phi versus psi for a protein molecule (see Figure 9-14). One way to model a protein structure is to limit the values of psi and phi for a particular dihedral angle to those allowed by the Ramachandran plot. The Ramachandran plot is useful in constructing a model of a protein because the values for psi and phi used in the model must be in agreement with the allowed values shown in the plot.

A major consideration in defining bond and torsion angles is whether to use the traditional Cartesian coordinate system or internal coordinates. The Cartesian coordinate system, with origin 0 and three orthogonal axes, commonly labeled x, y, and z, is used by the major protein databases, including the PDB (see Figure 9-15). For example, the first atom in the sequence for Deoxy Human Hemoglobin, PDB entry 1A3N, contributes to the first amino acid in the sequence, Valine (VAL). The coordinates for the first atom, a Nitrogen atom (N), are 10.720 (x) 19.523 (y), and 6.163 (z). Also listed are the occupancy (21.36), the frequency with which the atom is present in the protein, and temperature (1.00), which is a measure of the uncertainty in the position

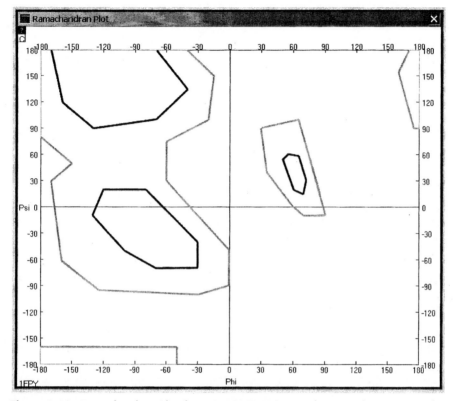

Figure 9-14 Ramachandran Plot from SWISS-PDBViewer Showing Phi versus Psi for Glutamine Synthetase.

of the atom in the crystalline protein. The listing also indicates the role of each atom in the sequence. For example, the second atom is an alpha carbon, while the fifth atom is a beta carbon.

Whereas the Cartesian coordinate system maps atoms involved in a protein structure relative to an absolute special geometry, internal coordinate schemes define all angles and positions relative to an arbitrary structure, such as the first bond in an amino acid sequence. The use of an internal coordinate scheme often provides a computational advantage over a Cartesian system, especially when thousands of atoms are involved. However, working with an internal coordinate system often makes it difficult to relate protein structures that are not connected, and it's difficult to determine absolute distances between molecules and atoms.

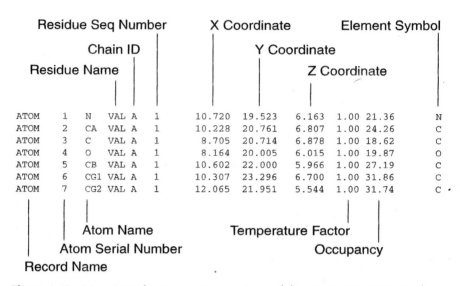

Residue Seq Number   X Coordinate   Element Symbol

Chain ID   Y Coordinate

Residue Name   Z Coordinate

ATOM	1	N	VAL A	1	10.720	19.523	6.163	1.00	21.36	N
ATOM	2	CA	VAL A	1	10.228	20.761	6.807	1.00	24.26	C
ATOM	3	C	VAL A	1	8.705	20.714	6.878	1.00	18.62	C
ATOM	4	O	VAL A	1	8.164	20.005	6.015	1.00	19.87	O
ATOM	5	CB	VAL A	1	10.602	22.000	5.966	1.00	27.19	C
ATOM	6	CG1	VAL A	1	10.307	23.296	6.700	1.00	31.86	C
ATOM	7	CG2	VAL A	1	12.065	21.951	5.544	1.00	31.74	C

Atom Name   Temperature Factor

Atom Serial Number   Occupancy

Record Name

Figure 9-15 PDB Entry for Deoxy Human Hemoglobin, PDB ID 1A3N. It shows Cartesian coordinates for the first amino acid (Valine) in the sequence.

The assumption that a protein's secondary structure can be completely defined as a function of bond lengths, bond angles, and torsion angles, while not always valid, greatly simplifies the computations involved. However, in some instances, even limiting consideration of protein structure to bond lengths, bond angles, and torsion angles is too computationally intensive. For example, modeling protein-protein interactions, with each protein molecule composed of perhaps several thousand atoms, in an aqueous environment with several hundred-thousand water molecules, is currently practically impossible on desktop hardware and may require days of supercomputer time. As a means of simplifying the computations, protein molecules are commonly simplified by representing certain chemical groups as points or ellipses that are either attracted to or repelled by surrounding water molecules.

The overall process of determining or predicting tertiary protein structure from a known primary structure or sequence is illustrated in Figure 9-16. Given a sequence of amino acids, the first step is to generate a reasonable secondary structure by using bond lengths, angles, and torsion angles. The next phase of the process, generating the tertiary structure, involves methods such as molecular dynamics and Monte Carlo methods to create a library of tertiary protein structure candidates.

Molecular dynamics involves using Newtonian physics to calculate the force on each atom and move that atom a distance in a small unit of time.

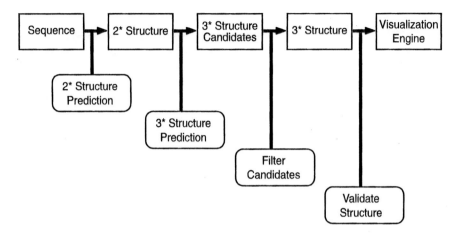

Figure 9-16   General Ab Initio Protein Structure Prediction Process.

The process is repeated until a pre-determined time limit is reached. The two major limitations of molecular dynamics in generating tertiary candidates are round-off error and computation overhead. With longer runs of the program, round-off errors tend to accumulate. This usually becomes apparent when the total energy of the protein under study begins to drift. Determining the tertiary structure of a protein based on physical principles alone is challenging because of the sheer number of possible folds.

Assuming that there are three possible conformations for a given amino acid—a helix, sheet, or coil—the number of folds is equal to 3^n, where n is the number of amino acids or residues in the protein. This relationship between the possible number of conformations and amino residue count is illustrated in Figure 9-17. Considering that a molecule with only 100 residues would have 3^{100} or 5.2×10^{47} folds, computationally examining every fold using Newtonian physics would take several lifetimes on the fastest supercomputer. Generating every possible tertiary structure candidate for a typical protein, such as Glutamine Synthetase, which has over 5,600 residues, is unlikely without the invention of fundamentally new form of computing. Currently, generating a 3D structural candidate with about 50 residues (with 3^{50} folds) requires several hours of high-end workstation time. Because the process may be repeated thousands of times in the creation of a library of candidates, months of computer time could be involved in the project.

Given a library of 3D structure candidates, the most promising structures are filtered from the less promising structures. A common method of filtering is to use the Metropolis Algorithm to identify the most stable molecular conformations. This method is based on the assumption that the native conformation of a protein is the conformation with the lowest free energy. This method

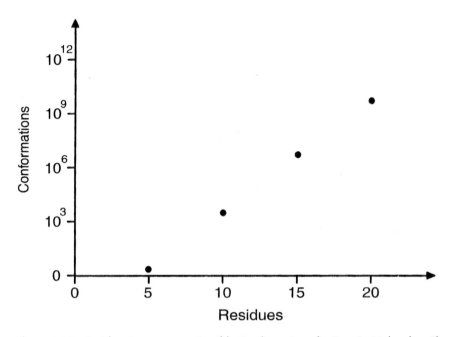

Figure 9-17   Residue Count versus Possible Conformations for Protein Molecules. The number of possible conformations for protein molecule with n residues is 3^n.

works for many proteins, but not others. For example, prions (proteinaceous infectious particles) are energetically unstable and are more stable in their disease-inducing state. Similarly, not all proteins go to a lowest energy state in nature. Some proteins fold independently, whereas other proteins require chaperones—molecules that act as catalysts—to fold.

Once the top protein structure candidate is identified, it is validated and visualized. Validation typically refers to comparing the predicted protein structure with a structure derived from NMR and X-ray crystallography experiments. That is, ab initio methods are still being perfected. Eventually, ab initio methods may provide enough accuracy and handle molecules large enough to supplant experimental methods. However, for now, validation involves assigning a figure of merit to the predicted structure, based on comparison to the gold standard. The most often-used figure of merit in protein structure comparison is the root mean squared deviation (RMSD). The calculation for RMSD, expressed in Angstroms, is shown in Figure 9-18.

Perfectly identical structures would have an RMSD of 0; matching short to moderate-length protein structures typically have RMSDs in the 1–3 Angstrom range. A problem with RMSD is that it doesn't take the size of the protein into

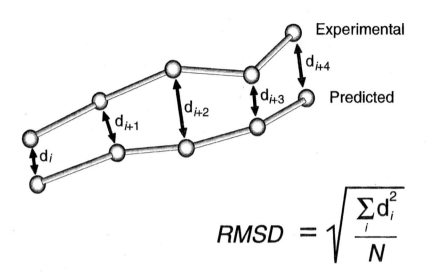

$$RMSD = \sqrt{\dfrac{\sum\limits_i d_i^2}{N}}$$

Figure 9-18   Root Mean Squared Deviation (RMSD) Calculation. N = number of atoms. D = the distance in Angstroms between corresponding atoms in the experimental and predicted protein structures.

account, and therefore the significance of the RMSD score can't be taken as an absolute measure across all proteins. An RMSD of 5 or 6 Angstroms may be intolerable in a molecule with only 50 residues, but perfectly acceptable in large protein molecules for applications such as searching structure databases for known protein structures. However, even as a relative measure, RMSD is valuable when working within a single family of proteins because the size of structures will be about the same.

In addition to the RMSD measure, a variety of visualization techniques are available to provide qualitative measures of similarity. Visualizing the protein structure is typically performed through the use of any number of freely available protein rendering engines on the Web, such as RasMol, Chimera, or SWISS-PDBViewer, as described in Chapter 5, "Data Visualization." An important note in the use of visualization software as an adjunct to validation is that many visualization engines incorporate embedded simulations in order to derive structure from simple bond angle data (see Figure 9-19) and may introduce uncertainty or bias in the output renderings. For example, visualization packages that work with the PDB data format create images of molecules based on rules and assumptions contained within the visualization package. Because rules and assumptions vary from one tool to another, there may be significant differences among the graphic output produced by these systems. In contrast, tools expecting ANS.1 format data don't rely on an embedded simulation to create the visual output, and their output is free of bias.

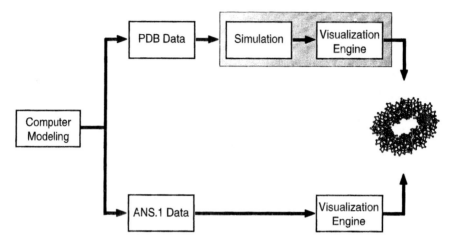

Figure 9-19 Embedded Simulation. Many visualization tools incorporate embedded simulation systems (top) in order to create the data necessary for visualization. Tools that expect data in the PDB data format are included in this category.

Before leaving the discussion of ab initio methods, the Rosetta method is worth mentioning because it is widely recognized as one of the most promising of the protein structure prediction methods. The Rosetta method typically involves breaking up a protein of unknown structure into words of three and nine amino acids in length. The fragment libraries that are used to limit the conformations of these segments are extracted from one of the online protein structure databases. Monte Carlo methods are used to identify conformation combinations with the lowest free energy. The sequential construction of protein structures is repeated thousands of times using independent simulations that start from different random number seeds. The resulting structures or candidates are clustered and a candidate from the centers of each of the largest clusters is selected as the predicted structure.

The Rosetta method is based on the assumption that the distribution of conformations sampled by a local amino acid sequence is taken as an approximation of the set of local conformations that a given sequence segment in a protein of unknown structure would have available during the folding process. Given the possible conformations that each segment can assume, the combination of local conformations with the lowest overall energy is taken as a candidate structure.

Although this method, which has been used with very good results with protein segments of up to about 90 residues in length, is often billed as form of ab initio protein structure prediction, it actually represents a hybrid method because it incorporates data from a library of protein structures.

Heuristic Methods

While ab initio methods of protein structure prediction can be used to identify novel structures from sequence data alone, they're too computationally intensive to work with all but the smallest proteins. For most proteins of unknown structure, short of X-ray crystallography and nuclear magnetic resonance (NMR) studies, heuristic methods offer the fastest, most accurate means of deriving structure from amino acid sequence data. Heuristic methods use a database of protein structures to make predictions about the structure of newly sequenced proteins. A basic premise of heuristic methods is that most newly sequenced proteins share structural similarities with proteins whose structures and sequences are known, and that these structures can serve as templates for new sequences. It's also assumed that because relatively substantial changes in amino acid sequence may not significantly alter the protein structure, similarity in sequences implies similarity in structure.

The primary limitation of a heuristic approach to protein structure prediction is that it can't model a novel structure. There must be a suitable template—meaning that the sequences of the template and the new protein can be aligned—available to work with as a starting point. For this reason, heuristic approaches often have difficulty with novel mutations that induce structural changes in the new (target) protein molecule. Within the constraints of these assumptions and limitations, the advantages of heuristic methods over ab initio methods are significant, and include improved accuracy and an ability to work with large protein molecules as opposed to protein fragments. In addition, the potential time savings of heuristic over experimental methods is a driving force for investment in heuristic methods from the pharmaceutical and private investment communities.

The main heuristic method of predicting protein structure from amino acid sequence data is comparative modeling—that is, finding similarities in amino acid sequence, independent of the molecule's lineage. Comparative modeling is sometimes confused with homology modeling. However, homology implies ancestral relationships, and assumes that proteins from the same families share folding motifs even if they don't share the same sequences. In contrast, comparative modeling assumes that proteins with similar amino acid sequences share the same basic 3D structure.

The basis for comparative modeling is typically the PDB, which contains descriptions of 3D structures of proteins and other molecules as determined by NMR and X-ray crystallography experiments. Another source of modeling data is the Molecular Modeling Database (MMDB), which combines PDB data with cross references to sequence, chemical, and structural data. It's important to note that the protein structures defined within PDM, MMDB, and virtually every other protein structure database are based on assumptions that may not be completely valid. For example, the common assumption that similar amino acid sequences result in similar protein structures is known to have exceptions.

Comparative modeling is an iterative, multi-phase process. As outlined in Figure 9-20, given protein sequence data, the main phases of the process are template selection, alignment, model building, and evaluation. 3D visualization is often performed as part of the evaluation phase. The key activities in each phase of the comparative modeling process are outlined here.

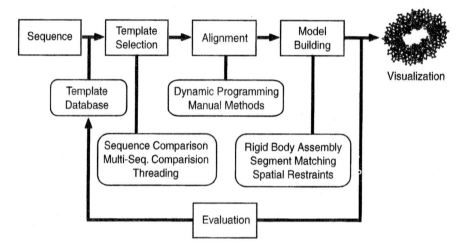

Figure 9-20 Comparative Modeling Process. Not illustrated is the optional use of ab initio methods at the end of the model building phase to reduce errors in the computed structure.

Template Selection

The first phase of the comparative modeling process, template selection, involves searching a template database for the closest match or matches to the new (target) molecule, based on the target's amino acid sequence. The goal of template selection is to discover a link between the target protein and a known protein structure. This usually involves the use of a protein structure template databases, such as the PDB. Selecting an appropriate group of database entries from the database to serve as structure templates is typically based on some form of sequence comparison or threading.

Pairwise sequence comparison involves searching sections of the template candidate for amino acid sequences that are similar to sequences in the target protein. A key decision in sequence comparison is how similar is similar enough. Multiple sequence comparison relies on an iterative algorithm that expands the template search to include all reasonable candidate templates from the template databases. As a result, multiple sequence comparison is more sensitive and more likely to find suitable templates in the template database.

Threading involves aligning the sequence of the target protein with the 3D structure of a template to determine whether the amino acid sequence is spatially and chemically similar to the template. Threading can be thought of as searching through a bin of factory-second gloves, looking for a glove that fits, where the hand is the target protein and the gloves represent templates. Some gloves may be able to accommodate only four fingers (no thumb), whereas others might have a channel for a sixth finger. These gloves represent templates that don't match the target protein. Gloves that, on visual inspection (the gloves aren't actually tried on—yet) can accommodate five fingers on the proper hand—assuming the hand is "normal"—are retained as potential templates. Similarly, templates that best fit the target protein are identified for use later in the comparative modeling process.

There are various forms of threading. For example, in contact potential threading, which is based on the analysis of the number and closeness of contacts between amino acids in the protein core, the idea is to position amino acids and compute empirical energies from the observed associations of amino acids. The most energetically stable conformation is the most likely protein structure. A more complex form of threading involves modeling energies from first principles. This method is based on dynamic programming techniques and is a recursive method of solving a problem that involves saving intermediate results in a matrix or table so that they can be used for future calculations. Regardless of the technology used, the goal is to find the template that best fits the target protein's structure. Template selection is complicated because not only do different sequences adopt the same fold, but many combinations of amino acids can fit into the same 3D conformation.

Alignment

The goal of the alignment phase of comparative modeling is to align the sequence of polypeptides in the target sequence with that of the template structure in order to position the target and template in the same 3D orientation. Continuing with the glove scenario, alignment involves placing the hand in the glove so that all of the fingers fill the appropriate sections of the glove. Many of the alignment procedures are based on dynamic programming techniques, often supplemented with manual methods based on visual inspection of the molecule.

Model Building

Once the libraries of templates that match the target protein have been identified, the actual model building or assembly can begin. Ideally, the structure of one of the templates will exactly fit the definition of the target protein, suggesting that the structure of that target is identical to that of the template. However, this almost never occurs. For any given target-template pair, there are likely to be several bends or kinks in the template backbone that don't align with the sequence in the target protein. Because a single change in only one bond angle can result in a major change in the conformation of a protein molecule, there is a better chance of identifying a fit if parts of the template are pieced together, one at a time. The issue in this approach is how big a piece of template structure to use.

One approach, rigid body assembly, uses large segments of the template that are dissected at natural folds and reassembled over the superimposed structure of the target molecule. The accuracy of model building through rigid body assembly can be increased if parts from several templates are available because there is an increased chance that a sub-assembly of the molecule—a rigid body—will be available that closely matches the sequence in a corresponding area in the target protein, as illustrated in Figure 9-21. The use of rigid bodies can be compared to building a house from pre-fabricated rooms, complete with walls, ceilings, closets, and windows.

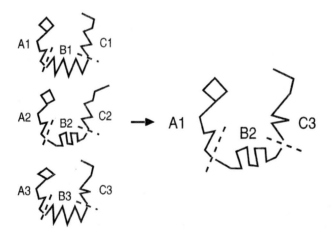

Figure 9-21 Rigid Body Assembly of Protein Structure. The target protein structure backbone (right) is defined by rigid bodies (large protein structure segments) from the three protein backbone templates (left).

Segment matching is a more flexible approach to model building, compared to rigid body assembly. The goal is to identify areas on structure templates that match areas in the target protein with similar sequences. These short matching segments in the template are used as guiding positions in the target molecule, as illustrated in Figure 9-22. Returning to the house-building metaphor, segment matching is like using prefabricated walls, floors, and ceilings. Compared to using prefabricated rooms, there are many more pieces to deal with, but it's more likely that the resulting structure will fit the architecture's plans (the sequence data) because of the flexibility allowed by the finer granularity of the available parts.

Modeling by satisfaction of spatial constraints is a technique that uses data from a variety of sources to constrain the physical configuration of the target protein molecule. Such techniques use data employed in ab initio modeling, such as data on bond lengths, bond angles, dihedral angles, and the free energy associated with various molecular geometries. Data from experimental studies, such as NMR and electron microscopy, can also be used to further constrain the allowable structure of the target protein. One of the advantages of constraint-based modeling is that the method is inherently extensible and capable of incorporating any new data or technology into the body of constraints.

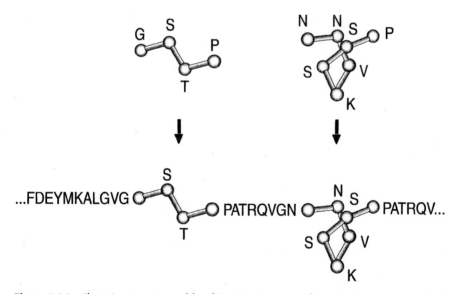

Figure 9-22 Short Segment Assembly of Protein Structure. Short structure segments (top) with sequences matching those of the target protein (bottom) are used to define the 3D structure of the protein, segment-by-segment.

Evaluation

In evaluating comparative modeling results, it's important to remember that heuristic modeling, like ab initio methods, is an experimental process, and that even the best methods rarely achieve accuracies approaching 70 percent. As such, the modeling-evaluation process is typically repeated dozens of times before a reasonable target structure is constructed. In this evaluation process, visualization is key as a first-pass screening tool used to validate gross measures, such as whether the model has the correct fold.

For a more quantitative evaluation, a measure of target-template similarity can be used. The greater the similarity of the model with the closest template, as measured by RMSD, the more likely the model is an accurate prediction of the actual structure. A target model that is radically different from any of the templates used to construct it isn't likely to be a valid structure. Comparative modeling isn't intended to model novel structures—an area where ab initio methods shine—but to build upon existing structure models. Returning to the archeology analogy, if the bones of a newly discovered early primate are found, the feet should be below the pelvis, and the arms attached to the shoulder joints, for example. A reconstruction in which the head faces backwards—like the model of a new protein—isn't likely to be a valid structure. It *could* be a new species with a backward-facing head, but a close examination of the cervical and thoracic vertebrae (reasoning from first principles or ab initio modeling) would likely suggest the head faces forward.

In comparative modeling, this inclusion of ab initio modeling to check the validity of bond lengths, bond angles, and torsion angles is termed finishing. An evaluation of free energy is sometimes used in the evaluation phase as well. The working assumption is that a correct protein structure has less free energy (is more stable) than a protein structure that is in an incorrect conformation.

In cataloging potential sources of errors, it's important to consider that the accuracy of protein structure modeling is inherently limited by the accuracy and purity of the NMR and X-ray crystallography data that form the basis of protein structure templates. Each experimental method is associated with specific artifacts that should be considered when the results of comparative modeling or ab initio predictions are evaluated. For example, both techniques produce erroneous data if there is lack of homogeneity in the protein samples. In the more time-intensive X-ray crystallography, these errors appear as a range of values instead of a single value for the distance between two atoms. In contrast, with NMR methods, the data returned for inter-atomic distances is often a single value that represents an average value. As such, errors in NMR data that result from populations of proteins in the sample may be more difficult to detect. However, in many instances, choosing NMR over X-ray crystallography or vice versa isn't possible, especially in niche areas. For example, NMR techniques are limited to small- and medium-sized protein molecules.

SYSTEMS BIOLOGY

Just as genomics research, which focuses on sequencing of human and other genomes, is being supplanted by proteomic research as the work of sequencing has become commonplace, proteomic research has a limited lifespan as well. Eventually, the dozens of computer-based methods of protein structure modeling and the numerous tools that support these methods will be replaced by one or two accepted methods, and the focus of the bioinformatics community will move up another level toward functional proteomics. Following this progression to its natural conclusion, the focus of bioinformatics will eventually converge with clinical medicine at the cellular and organ-system level—so-called systems biology.

A major challenge in modeling and simulating systems biology is integrating high- and low-level models so that a more accurate picture of the entire biological process can be obtained. Integrating models of protein structure and function with those of biochemical pathways promises to provide insight into disease processes and, by extension, the most efficacious designer drugs.

Although some researchers are working with systems biology today, for the most part they are limited by both data and computational methods and power. A single cell might contain tens of thousands of molecules, each interacting with each other in complex ways not yet understood. Furthermore, not only must researchers understand the function of normal cells, but they must be able to model and simulate cells involved in cancer or HIV, for example.

Today, the focus is on what can be practically accomplished with current technology and data, such as creating physiologically complete models and simulations of the heart, pancreas, and liver. Although very broad clinical simulations of these and other organs have been developed for teaching purposes, the kinds of models applicable to drug research are at a much greater level of detail and complexity and require Linux clusters or a mainframe to run them in real time. With time, these requirements will be more easily met, as affordable desktop computing power continues to increase in performance. What remains is for researchers to discover how to best apply this hardware toward solving the next generation of bioinformatics challenges.

TOOLS

Modeling and simulation are complex operations that tax even the most advanced hardware. Developing modeling and simulation systems de novo requires knowledge of advanced computing techniques, from Markov Modeling to network computing and numerical calculus. Fortunately, a wide variety of modeling simulation tools is available on the Web and from commercial vendors. As listed in Table 9-2, there are tools specifically designed to aid modeling and simulation in bioinformatics as well as tools for general-purpose modeling. For example, a tool such as Prospect (PROtein Structure Prediction and Evaluation Computer Toolkit), a threading-based protein structure prediction program, can be used as part of a comparative modeling process. A commercial system, such as Extend, can be used to determine the most cost-effective means of staffing the research lab, based on a model of individual researcher output and the overall protein structure modeling process.

Table 9-2   Modeling and Simulation Tools.

Tool	Examples
Databases	CATH, GenBank, GeneCensus, ModBase, PDB, Presage, SWISS-PROT+TrEMBL
Template Search	123D, BLAST, DALI, FastA, Matchmaker, PHD, PROFIT, Threader, UCLA-DOE FRSVR
Sequence Alignment	BCM Server, BLAST, Block Maker, CLUSTAL, FASTA3, Multalin
Modeling	Coposer, Congen, CPH Models, Dragon, ICM, InsightII, Modeller, Look, Quanta, Sybyl, Scwrl, Seisss-Mod, What If
Verification	Anolea, Aqua, Biotech, Errat, Procheck, ProCeryon, Prosall, PROVE, SQUID, VERIFY3D, WHATCHECK
Visualization	CHIMERA, SWISS-PDBViewer, RasMol, Pymol
Academic	SLAM III
Commercial	Extend, Crystal Ball, MedModel, ProModel, Simul8, Micro Saint, ACSL, Arena, GPSS/H, iThink, MAST, MODSIM III, Simprocess, Taylor II

In considering the tools in Table 9-2, it's important to consider that most of these are in flux—especially those developed for bioinformatics-specific roles. New releases of existing systems and new programs that replace current programs are a constant occurrence. In contrast, the commercial, general-purpose programs are more stable, in part because of demand from a variety of arenas that don't include bioinformatics. Of course, as discussed previously in the section on fundamentals, it's imperative to understand the assumptions made by the simulation system designer and then to decide if those assumptions are in agreement with your needs.

ON THE HORIZON

The availability of affordable, powerful computer hardware and software affects more than simply the throughput of modeling and simulation experiments in bioinformatics. A common finding in simulation-based R&D is that as more computer processing power becomes available, the time required to run a simulation doesn't decrease significantly. Instead, researchers tend to increase the complexity of the underlying models in order to provide higher-resolution—and presumably more realistic—simulations. This phenomenon is most obvious in the motion picture industry in which computer-animated figures, which are based on models of synthetic characters, have become virtually indistinguishable from real actors. For example, the T-1000 robot in *Terminator II*, the first use of a simulated actor in a major motion picture, is virtually indistinguishable from a human actor.

Similarly, in the life sciences, increased access to computing power is resulting in the development and use of more complex, higher-resolution models and simulation systems. This is critical, because inadequate resolution can lead to incorrect conclusions. For example, a model of protein-protein interaction that doesn't take temperature, pH, and the presence or absence of sugars and other molecules in the local environment into consideration may incorrectly predict a level of interaction that wouldn't be possible in reality.

Work is underway to develop increasingly complex modeling and simulation software that is designed to use the ever-present next-generation of desktop computer hardware and operating systems. There is also considerable activity in the areas of heuristic control of simulations, as well as advancing cluster, grid, and mainframe computing. This power is being directed at rapid computation and is enabling researchers to consider additional phenomena that are relevant to the structure and function of proteins, such as the role of functional glycomics, for example. Approaches to realizing more computational throughput includes making existing simulation code parallel so that it can make use of multiple processors, and of special, high-performance mainframe hardware architectures used by IBM's SP-2 Blue Gene, and similar machines.

ENDNOTE

For researchers who focus on modeling the 3D structure of proteins, the biannual meeting of the Critical Assessment of Techniques for Protein Structure Prediction (CASP) is a moment of truth. Participants, whose future funding often rests on the results of their efforts, are challenged with the task of using their computer algorithms to predict the precise 3D structure of an array of relatively small proteins. Results are judged by comparing predicted structures with those determined experimentally through NMR or X-ray crystallography methods. Before the competition was limited to fully automated means of structure prediction, one of the top performers at the conference wasn't an algorithm running on a supercomputer or Linux cluster, but a mere human—Alexey Murzin of the Medical Research Council's Laboratory of Molecular Biology in Cambridge, England.

Murzin's predictions of protein structure, which are based on biological heuristics, cast such a doubt over the need for computational methods that there was talk of cutting government funding to the computer laboratories involved in structure prediction. Even though Murzin is now barred from officially competing in the current CASP meetings, his heuristic methods consistently compare favorably with the best computational solutions.

The human-machine competition in bioinformatics, like the competition between Garry Kasparov and a chess-playing computer in 1997, is likely to eventually be won by the machine, if for no other reason than the lack of human experts to predict the structure of the thousands of proteins discovered every year. However, even as the price of computing power drops, Murzin's performance suggests that simply adding faster processors isn't the best solution, and that a combination of ab initio and heuristic methods will eventually provide the most accurate, consistent, and affordable predictions of protein structure.

> Crystal structure of Colicin E3 in complex with its immunity protein. PDB entry 1JCH. Image produced with PDB Structure Explorer.

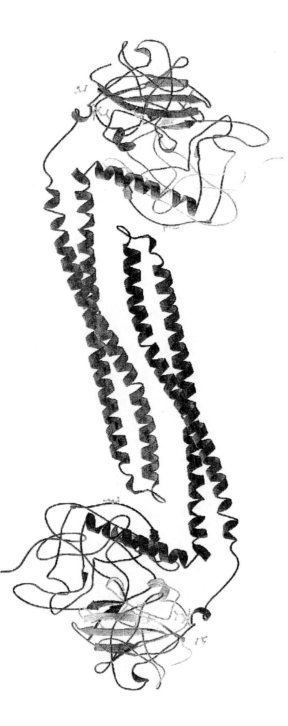

CHAPTER 10

Collaboration

*The chess board is the world, the pieces are the phenomena of
the universe, the rules of the game are what we call the laws of
Nature. The player on the other side is hidden from us. We
know that his play is always fair, just and patient. But we also
know, to our cost, that he never overlooks a mistake, or makes
the smallest allowance for ignorance.*
— *Thomas Henry Huxley*

The highly publicized fracas between the publicly sponsored Human
Genome Project and the commercial Celera Genomics often overshadows the remarkable fact that the former involved the collaboration of 20 laboratories in 6 countries. Although academics in the bioinformatics field struggle
for tenure, publications, and discoveries just as vehemently as researchers in
other fields of academia, bioinformatics is characterized by an unusually high
degree of collaboration among the researchers seeking to further the fields of
genomics and proteomics.

At least part of the reason for this level of cooperation is the reward system
established for sharing data. Virtually all molecular biology journals require
authors to submit the sequence or structure described in their manuscripts to

public databases prior to publication. What's more, unlike only a decade ago, many universities now consider software development as a type of publication worth consideration when the author is up for promotion or tenure. Another factor is that, unlike other fields such as nuclear physics, where the results of some multi-billion dollar experiment is put into the hands of perhaps a dozen scientists to evaluate, there is a flood of data that couldn't possibly be handled in a dozen scientist's lifetimes. Without the thousands of investigators developing tools and analyzing sequences and structures as they are generated, the field would be at a standstill. Perhaps everyone realizes that there's more than enough data and associated challenges to go around, and that it's only through cooperation and parallel exploration that the full potential of genomics and proteomics can be realized in our lifetimes.

This chapter explores the technologies and processes that can be used to facilitate collaboration in bioinformatics, starting with the "Collaboration and Communications" section, which distinguishes between communications and collaboration on the basis of technology, introduces many of the concepts underlying communications and collaboration, and focuses on real-time versus asynchronous methods. The remainder of the chapter deals with the issues underlying communications in bioinformatics. For example, the "Open Source" section looks at how the rise in popularity of open-source software has made a major impact on the development of bioinformatics programs. "Standards" explores the role of standards in bioinformatics, from file formats to operating systems, and their affect on day-to-day operations. Finally, the "On the Horizon" and "Endnote" sections consider the future of communications and the role of commercialization in making many of the dreams in bioinformatics research a reality.

COLLABORATION AND COMMUNICATIONS

When the Human Genome Project started in 1990, Web browsers hadn't been invented, cell phones were lunchkit-sized luxury items, the volume of e-mail was a distant fourth behind telephone, fax, and surface mail communications, and academic journal publishers expected printed manuscripts for submissions. Even the National Library of Congress didn't recognize electronic documents as copyrightable material.

Today, e-mail competes head-on with surface mail and the telephone as a means of communications in business and academia. Networks support real-time collaboration between researchers distributed around the globe, and academic publishing revolves around timely e-mail submissions. Cell phone and personal digital assistants (PDAs) are not only everyday business tools, but they're fashion items for high-school and college students. As another indicator of the shift in perception of the increased worth of electronic communications, the National Library of Congress changed its policy on electronic documents and accepted the first copyright application for an electronic book—this author's *The Hitchhikers' Guide to the Wireless Web*—in July of 2001.

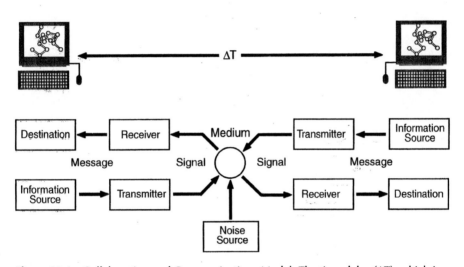

Figure 10-1 Collaboration and Communications Model. The time delay (ΔT), which is a function of the system design and bandwidth, defines the level of communications and collaboration possible.

Engineers commonly characterize electronic communications as either asynchronous or synchronous. Fax, e-mail, streaming video, online journals, bulletin boards, newsgroups, and voicemail are forms of asynchronous communications. Synchronous or real-time communications includes the use of the telephone, instant messaging, chat rooms, and videoconferencing. Regardless of whether it's synchronous or asynchronous, communications implies that there is a common language—or at least a common intermediary language—and that there is a communications channel between sender and receiver with a bandwidth that is compatible with the data transfer rate requirements. There is also an underlying assumption that the communication is of reasonable quality, in terms of signal-to-noise ratio, and that the data contained in the communication is valuable to the recipient. For example, computer-based real-time videoconferencing requires a relatively high-bandwidth communications channel, such as a connection to the Internet via DSL, cable modem, or Ethernet, and the computer hardware to support the transmission and reception of data with a reasonably short time delay (ΔT) of up to a few hundred milliseconds between the sender and the receiver.

Electronic communication is essential to most R&D activities in bioinformatics. However, collaboration is even more valuable. Collaboration—the act of working in a group to achieve a common goal—follows the basic model defined in Figure 10-1, but is much more focused and interactive than simple communications. As illustrated in Figure 10-2, collaboration builds upon a communications infrastructure. In order to achieve the common goal, there is a real or virtual place for collaborators to work and share perspectives, to view common work, and to interactively evaluate and critique each others' contributions to achieving the goal.

Communications and collaboration rely on a variety of technologies for the creation, modification, use, and transfer of data—activities that, taken together, constitute knowledge management. They include a variety of authoring tools for creating content and developing user interfaces, as well as database management systems (DBMSs) and controlled vocabularies for archiving data, plus software and hardware for creating a communications

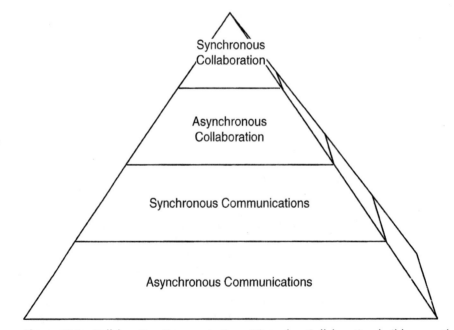

Figure 10-2 Collaboration-Communications Hierarchy. Collaboration builds upon the capabilities of a functional communications infrastructure.

infrastructure. In addition, there are visualization and analysis aids, including tools for creating graphics, animations, and simulations. As described in the following sections, the technology requirements increase as a function of the collaboration-communications hierarchy.

Asynchronous Communications

The most common form of asynchronous electronic communications in bioinformatics is e-mail and its derivatives, including bulletin boards and newsgroups, Web postings, online publications, streaming (pre-recorded) video, and fax. The real benefit of asynchronous communications—minimal disruption of workflow—is also its main limitation. The recipient of an asynchronous message, such as an e-mail, has the option of viewing the message in his or her own time, or simply ignoring it. On the other hand, the technical infrastructure requirements for asynchronous electronic communications are modest. A wireless, self-contained PDA is all that is needed to send and receive e-mail through the Internet or private network.

Synchronous Communications

Synchronous communication generally requires a more robust technical infrastructure than does asynchronous communication, especially in terms of bandwidth to support a higher level of interactivity. Video conferencing, instant messaging, and chat rooms are examples of synchronous communication that are useful in bioinformatics R&D. Although the telephone is the popular real-time communications device, real-time videoconferencing technology is increasingly popular because of its affordability and ability to minimize the time-consuming travel associated with face-to-face meetings.

The technology required to support real-time videoconferencing over the Internet or an intranet can involve little more than installing an inexpensive digital camera and software driver for each networked workstations that will be conferenced in. These systems are typically used for their video capabilities; the audio component of the communications is carried by a telephone. Although inexpensive videoconferencing systems produce somewhat jerky images up to a few hundred pixels in height and width on each workstation screen, they provide an enhanced level of communication over a traditional telephone conversation. Full-screen, high-resolution videoconferencing that can provide more than a talking head requires a much more expensive, high-bandwidth videoconferencing system. What's more, these systems, which can cost more than a high-end workstation, require several dedicated ISDN lines or other high-bandwidth connectivity to the Internet or other network for adequate performance.

Asynchronous Collaboration

Technologically, asynchronous collaboration can be supported by e-mail and voicemail communications exchanged according to a prearranged schedule or on an as-needed basis. That is, collaboration can be viewed as a layer of management or process control over a basic communications infrastructure. For example, one of the most significant formal asynchronous collaborations in bioinformatics is the submission of protein structures to the Protein Data Bank (PDB). Although collaborators could simply e-mail their results to PDB staff, quality control communications issues wouldn't be able to be properly addressed in a timely manner with manual methods. Instead, collaborators are required to use the Auto Dep Input Tool (ADIT) utility provided by the Research Collaboratory for Structural Bioinformatics (RCSB). ADIT accepts X-ray, NMR, and electron microscopy structure data, validates the data, and creates reports detailing the quality of the submission. A benefit of technologies that support asynchronous one-to-many collaborations like making submissions to the PDB is that significant collaborations can be established with minimal demands on the contributor's time and resources.

Synchronous Collaboration

Because the key technological issues in synchronous collaboration are time, reliability, and bandwidth, this type of collaboration requires a more robust synchronous communications infrastructure. Furthermore, the ideal system supports work-centered interactivity that supercedes what is possible through simple telephone communications, even if supplemented by desktop videoconferencing. As such, synchronous collaboration necessarily incorporates technologies that provide a virtual common workspace, such as an electronic whiteboard, and a means of working with applications and data interactively.

Synchronous collaboration draws upon many of the technologies and processes developed in the field of knowledge management. For example, the creation and acquisition of data benefit from technologies such as data mining, text summarizing, a variety of graphical tools, and a variety of information-retrieval methodologies. Similarly, archiving and access are facilitated by databases and database management tools. In addition, virtually all of these technologies require an infrastructure that is not only capable of supporting moderate to high-speed connectivity, but that provides privacy, security, and fault-tolerance as well.

As an example of the technologies supportive of synchronous collaboration, consider the options available for working with applications and data interactively. Three popular synchronous or real-time collaboration technologies are peer-to-peer screen sharing, commercial online conferencing services, and application-specific integrated collaboratories, as illustrated in Figure 10-3.

Each of these technologies allows collaborators to see and control, either directly or indirectly, an application running on a remote workstation.

Peer-to-peer screen sharing allows a user with the appropriate access privileges to connect to and take control of a remote workstation. This form of screen sharing is especially popular in training and troubleshooting situations, where a collaborator can demonstrate how to perform an operation in an application, and then watch as the collaborator performs the operation. PcAnywhere™ from Symantec is an example of several of the commercial peer-to-peer collaborative systems that supports two collaborators through a dedicated Microsoft Windows application that runs on the workstations involved in the collaboration.

Commercial online conferencing services extend the screen-sharing model by using a third-party Internet server that can support hundreds of simultaneous users without burdening the host machine. WebEx™ from WebEx Communications is an example of a browser-based, fee-for-use, multi-user collaborative system that enables collaborators to share presentations, documents, applications, voice, and video using Windows, MacOS, or Solaris operating systems.

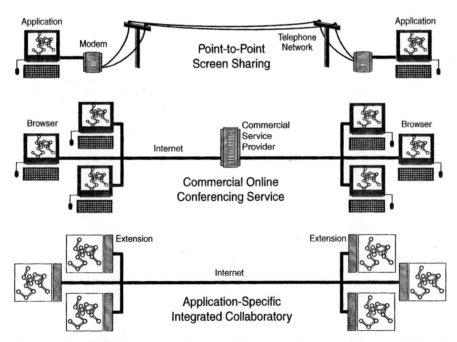

Figure 10-3 Collaborative Application Sharing Options. Popular methods of synchronous collaboration range from point-to-point screen sharing over the telephone network (top), to Internet-based commercial online conferencing services (middle) and application-specific integrated collaboratories (bottom).

Both peer-to-peer screen sharing and online conferencing services allow a remote collaborator to see and interact with a program running on another computer, using either dial-up or high-speed communications. However, even with a high-bandwidth communications medium, these technologies don't offer the degree of interaction and level of collaboration possible with an inherently shareable application. This is in part because screen-sharing programs don't support local video acceleration hardware to increase 3D rendering speed. In the case of peer-to-peer screen sharing, rendering speed on the remote workstation is limited by the capabilities of the host machine and the bandwidth of the connection. The same issues apply to browser-based multi-user systems, with the caveat that the demands on the host machine are minimized because it only has to communicate with the commercial server.

The most advanced form of application sharing is to use applications specifically designed as integrated collaboratories. An example of this level of application sharing is the Chimera molecular modeling system. The Chimera Collaboratory Extension of the program enables multiple collaborators to interactively model 3D protein structures in real-time. The Chimera Collaboratory, when combined with a high-bandwidth communications network, represents the next best thing to working on a molecule in the same room with collaborators.

The collaborative environments provided by applications such as Chimera are generally superior to peer-to-peer screen sharing and online conferencing services because of the collaboratory architecture. For example, each user of Chimera has a separate copy of the application running on their workstation, as well as a local copy of the modeling data. As a result, each workstation is responsible for its own rendering and database access, and isn't excessively burdened by having to send a screen image to a server or another workstation. In addition, Chimera supports the OpenGL graphics standard, which enables the application to take advantage of local graphics-acceleration hardware. To avoid chaos when a large number of collaborators are working together in Chimera, one collaborator is arbitrarily assigned the hub, which the other collaborators can join and leave at will. The collaborator controlling the hub can pass on authority of controlling a session to another collaborator at any time.

Application-specific integrated collaboratories are commonly referred to as groupware, which is typically defined as any software that enables group collaboration over a network. Groupware ranges from niche applications, such as molecular modeling, programming, and scheduling, to general-purpose utilities that can support a variety of collaborative activities. These utilities include electronic whiteboards, shared document libraries, authoring tools, videoconferencing tools, instant messaging, text forums, and screen sharing.

Electronic whiteboards, which are expressly designed for group collaboration, are virtual whiteboards that enable multiple collaborators to take turns authoring and modifying hand-drawn or computer-generated graphics, highlighting points of interest on digital images, or presenting a digitized slide as part of a presentation. Shared document-authoring tools are designed to enable multiple authors to create and edit a document online. Text forums are synchronous, text-based systems that allow group postings of responses to text messages. Most text forums are also asynchronous to the extent that they are self-archiving. A record of text interchanges is maintained as a database for review by other collaborators. Related utilities, such as instant messaging, that broadcast or exchange short text messages, may be used to extend collaboration to users with cell phones and wireless PDAs and laptops.

Videoconferencing—the real-time, one-to-one and one-to-many broadcasting of video and audio—is often configured to use the telephone lines for audio and the Internet or other network for the video channels. This is because brief interruptions in the packets of data passing through the Internet result in annoying dropouts in the audio signal, even though the interruption may not be noticeable with video because of the persistence of the image to the human eye. When there is ample network bandwidth available, videoconferencing may be extended to multimodal conferencing, that is some combination of electronic whiteboard, a text forum, audio communications, and multiple-channel videoconferencing—as a means of enabling real-time collaboration.

From a practical perspective, the limitations on the level of collaboration possible as a function of the bandwidth of the communications channel can best be appreciated by exploring the relationship between the level of interactivity versus the maximum number of simultaneous users that can be supported by a system. As illustrated in Figure 10-4, because e-mail is asynchronous, it can support a large number of users, but with little interactivity. Online text forums, which may involve real-time communications, offer more interactivity but can support fewer simultaneous users. As the user capacity of the text forum system is approached, interactivity will drop as a function of the available server resources.

Shared authoring tools, such as the Chimera Collaboratory Extension or a general-purpose shared document editor, offer highly interactive levels of collaboration, but can only support a relatively limited number of participants. Multimedia conferencing, which integrates applications such as video conferencing, electronic whiteboards, screen-sharing applications, and shared authoring tools, offers the greatest flexibility in collaboration and the highest potential level of interactivity. However, it also demands the most of the communications infrastructure, and typically supports the fewest number of collaborators. Groupware that enables multimedia conferencing is often limited more by the bandwidth of the underlying network than by any inherent limitations in the application software or workstation hardware.

It's important to note that a robust communications infrastructure and tools capable of supporting the interactive interplay and exchange of data are necessary but insufficient to foster collaboration. Collaborations are built around

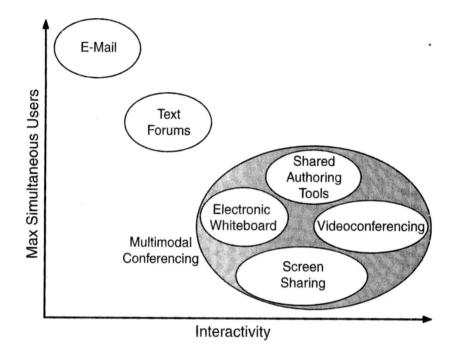

Figure 10-4 Interactivity versus Maximum Number of Users for Collaborative Technologies. The typical tradeoff is of interactivity versus the number of collaborators that can be accommodated.

interested, engaged, and motivated participants with a common vision. The concept of people- and project-centered communities of practice, as used in the field of knowledge management, seems most applicable here. The best collaborations, whether in real or virtual workspaces, can be facilitated by technology, but not dictated or even directed by it. In addition, some tasks are better performed in a hierarchical collaborative environment in which a team leader performs all of the work, based on suggestions from the other collaborators.

For example, consider that simulations are an excellent means of exploring what-if scenarios in an interactive format. As communication tools, simulations can be used to illustrate complex processes and dynamic relationships—such as protein docking—in an easy-to-understand, visual form. However, enabling peer-to-peer collaborative simulation building, in which each participant can take turns defining the parameters of the simulation from their perspective, isn't necessarily desirable. The exception is when collaborators have a shared vision of how the simulation should function and share the working assumptions of the underlying models. Without this shared vision, there is a significant risk that the resulting simulation won't reflect the best art of any of the collaborators.

The considerations of technology-enabled collaboration in bioinformatics aren't limited to small group projects such as constructing a molecule over the Internet, but extend to institutions and government supporters. For example, the Research Collaboratory for Structural Bioinformatics (RCSB), one of the major collaboratories in bioinformatics, is a consortium consisting of the Biochemistry Department of Rutgers, The State University of New Jersey, the San Diego Supercomputer Center (SDSC) at the University of California, San Diego (UCSD) and Department of Biochemistry, University of Wisconsin-Madison. Similarly, the funding of the RCSB is through an equally diverse collaboration. The PDB is operated by Rutgers, The State University of New Jersey; the SDSC at USCD; and the National Institute of Standards and Technology (NIST), with funds from the National Science Foundation, the Department of Energy, the National Institute of General Medical Sciences, and the National Library of Medicine.

STANDARDS

Communications and collaboration are based on standards that span low-level file formats and hardware signal protocols to high-level application program interfaces (APIs) and user interface designs. Standards don't simply appear overnight, but, as illustrated in Figure 10-5, they normally evolve over months and years along a stepwise path from independent niche solutions to full interoperability.

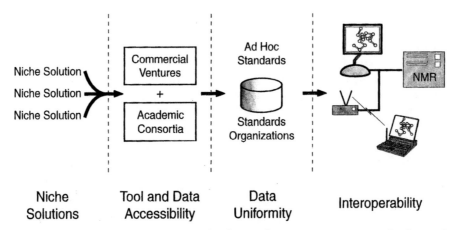

Figure 10-5 Evolution of Standards. The data uniformity stage represents the first real instantiation of standards.

The evolution of standards normally progresses from independent niche solutions to interdependent interoperability with multiple data sources, applications, and application areas. Niche solutions tend to be internally focused, addressing a particular need within a lab or project, such as the need to model a particular protein molecule. The tool and data accessibility stage of standards evolution involves sharing among groups with a common focus or problem area, such as structure analysis. The data uniformity stage of standards evolution involves active cooperation that may include the formation or participation of ad hoc or formal standards organizations. The interoperability stage of standards evolution is characterized by interaction with standards organizations outside of the bioinformatics community.

The progression from niche solution to interoperability represents a potential path of progression. However, most niche solutions never evolve to the tool and data accessibility stage of standards, and fewer still progress to the data uniformity or interoperability stages of standards evolution. Consider the characteristics of each stage of the evolution of standards in more detail in the following sections.

Niche Solutions

The path to standards typically starts as a body of niche solutions that are designed to satisfy specific needs, without regard (or time to regard) for connectivity with other systems in order to solve other problems. Examples of early niche solutions in bioinformatics include stand-alone dot-matrix alignment programs that required sequence data to be either typed or pasted into the program, and whose output had to be manually copied and pasted into other applications. Hundreds of other niche solutions have been developed as well, from programs that perform data conversion from a particular NMR file format to one compatible with a homegrown analysis program, to interface tools that facilitate low-level communications between applications. Most of these niche solutions never leave the laboratory in which they are developed because the niche solutions can't be generalized to other laboratories. The few applications that do address general problems in a typical bioinformatics laboratory may progress to the next phase of standards evolution, tool and data accessibility.

Tool and Data Accessibility

The tool and data accessibility phase of standards evolution involves restricted sharing of the niche solutions among the members of the bioinformatics R&D community. Applications that have the greatest general appeal to other researchers are typically either distributed through academic and government-sponsored consortia or transformed into commercial ventures. In either case, there is a lack of data uniformity, and applications may be very useful or of no practical value, depending on the problems that need to be addressed.

This stage of standards evolution represents the status of applications in many areas of bioinformatics today. For example, consider the many varied file formats in use by the relatively small number of bioinformatics-specific applications, illustrated in Table 10-1.

Table 10-1   Major Bioinformatics File Formats.

ASN.1
DNAStrider
EMBL
Fitch
GCG
GenBank/GBFF
IG/Stanford
MmCIF
MSF
NBRF
Olsen
PAUP/NEXUS
PDB
Pearson/FASTA
Phylip/Philip3.2
PIR/CODATA
Plain/Raw
Pretty
Zuker

The number and variation of file formats used for nucleotide and protein data is an indicator of the amount of variability in the applications used in bioinformatics computing. Although bioinformatics is moving toward file format and application standards, there are hundreds of file formats in use. Many of these formats are application-specific and associated with niche solutions that are designed to solve a local problem as quickly and as efficiently as possible.

Making niche tools, their file formats, and the data they generate generally accessible is a major step in the evolution of standards. This phase represents an opportunity for larger academic or commercial players to position their proprietary formats as standards. The advantage of making tools and data openly available to a group of potential collaborators is that the best tools tend to attract the greatest number of users. These users in turn perpetuate the tools and the data formats that they support throughout the bioinformatics community, eventually making some tools de facto standards, simply because they perform their functions very efficiently or effectively. The most popular tools are often rewritten to enable sharing by supporting a uniform data format.

Data Uniformity

There are numerous reasons for developing data uniformity or a common file format for popular applications. A common file format for applications reduces the cost of maintenance and data archiving, minimizes the likelihood of data loss and results in more efficient use of software tools. Another motivation for establishing data uniformity through standards is to improve the reliability of searching the online bioinformatics databases. However, evolving to the data-uniformity stage of standards requires more than simply publishing data format specifications; it requires active cooperation among software and hardware developers.

Although cooperation may occur though a one-on-one relationship, in most cases there are either ad hoc group collaborations or formal standards groups. In either case, politics and capital are typically major deciding factors in which tools establish the standards. For example, a group of universities collaborating on a project may informally agree on a particular hardware, operating system, and application standard to facilitate sharing of data and applications. Similarly, a commercial venture that has built its product around a particular file structure, for example, may stand to lose considerable money if their format isn't selected as the industry standard.

The data uniformity stage of standards evolution is product- and industry-specific. For example, there are competing standards for NMR data formats. Most of the more than 20 manufacturers of NMR equipment support their own proprietary data format exclusively. Moreover, there may be several different formats supported by different product lines from the same NMR manufacturer. For example, there are the GE Omega, GN, and QE file formats, the Varian Gemini, XL, Unity, Inova, and VXR formats, and the Nicolet 1180 and 1280 file formats.

While the NMR market has yet to crystallize around a single data format, the standards issue appears much more certain in the area of protein structure data. The macromolecular crystallographic information file (mmCIF) format has a good chance of becoming the industry standard, in part because of a collaboration between the NIST and the RCSB. The two organizations are working to develop data and data-exchange standards based on the mmCIF format and eXtensible Markup Language (XML) over the Web.

Interoperability

The final stage of standards evolution—interoperability—is the ability of a device or application to work seamlessly with tools and devices from multiple industries. True interoperability isn't limited to bioinformatics, but extends to general-purpose tools, such as databases and spreadsheets, and to other specialized areas, such as NMR equipment. Interoperability makes it possible for a Universal Serial Bus (USB) printer to work with a Dell workstation running Linux or a Macintosh computer running OS X, or for an NMR machine to output files directly to a format compatible with the PDB.

Ultimately, interoperability extends beyond bioinformatics and molecular biology, potentially to encompass devices and software in every industry. As such, a bioinformatics application should be able to share data and link seamlessly with applications used in other industries, including Microsoft's suite of office products, Adobe's line of graphics creation and editing tools, and Oracle's suite of database tools. Achieving true interoperability involves following industry standards for everything from APIs, database data structures, operating system and network protocols, and user interface design, to magnetic media formats and cable connector designs.

Achieving interoperability necessarily involves national and international standards organizations (see Table 10-2). Although organizations such as NIST may be peripherally involved in the data uniformity stage of standards development, these organizations are intimately involved in achieving interoperability. For example, in the digital imaging industry, which includes manufacturers of digital cameras, flash-RAM, and developers of photo-editing software, interoperability is due to the work of the Joint Photographic Experts Group (JPEG) and the Motion Picture Experts Group (MPEG). The JPEG standard is recognized worldwide as a standard for compressing continuous-tone still images (digital photographs), just as the MPEG standard is used for digital motion pictures. Many graphics applications support several industry standards to maximize the odds of interoperability with other graphics applications. For example, in addition to supporting its own proprietary file format, Adobe Photoshop can import most of the graphics formats used by the most popular graphics applications available for workstations. For the same reason, the RasMol molecular modeling program supports data in graphics interface format (GIF), encapsulated PostScript (EPS), ASCII or raw, Windows bitmap (BMP), Apple PICT, and Sun Rasterfile (RAST).

Table 10-2   Standards Organizations. In addition to this sampling of standards organizations that affect bioinformatics, there are hundreds of additional standards working committees that informally influence standards.

ACR/NEMA	American College of Radiology/National Electronic Manufacturers Association
ANSI	American National Standards Institute
ASTM	American Society for Testing and Materials
CEN	European Committee for Standardization
EDIFACT	Electronic Data Interchange for Administration, Commerce, and Transport
EUCLIDES	European Clinical Data Exchange Standard
FCC	Federal Communications Commission
HCFA	Health Care Financing Administration
HHCC	Georgetown Home Health Classification
HIPAA	Heath Insurance Portability and Accountability Act
HISP	Healthcare Informatics Standards Board
IEC	International Electrotechnical Commission
IEEE	Institute of Electrical and Electronics Engineers
ISO	International Standards Organization
JPEG	Joint Photographic Experts Group
NANDA	North American Nursing Diagnosis Association
NIST	National Institute of Standards and Technology
OSI	Open Systems Interconnection
UCC	Uniform Code Council

Some standards are holdovers from previous systems that no longer exist. For example, GIF was introduced in 1987 by the now-defunct CompuServe online service as a proprietary format. GIF remains popular as an image format for Web pages because the images are compact and can be interlaced. Loading an interlaced image, which produces a melting effect on the screen as the alternate lines of the image are loaded, is especially useful with low-bandwidth connections. Users aren't left staring at a blank screen, waiting for the complete graphics file to download. Even though CompuServe is no longer a contender in the online market, the standard it introduced remains. Similarly, some standards are based on technologies developed for other purposes. For example, EPS is based on PostScript, a device-dependent page-description language developed by Xerox and commercialized by Adobe Systems for laser printers. Other graphics standards are so popular on particular hardware platforms that they are supported to guarantee that those hardware devices can access the images. For example, the BMP format is native to Microsoft Windows, and PICT is native to Apple's Macintosh.

Interoperability entails more than simple file formats. For example, although JPEG and MPEG file formats have helped the digital imaging market, standards for physical media and the associated electronics are equally important. Many of these standards arose from organizations outside of the digital imaging industry. The same situation exists in bioinformatics, where external organizations have a major influence on standards.

Table 10-2 lists a sample of the standards organizations that either directly or indirectly affect bioinformatics standards. Applications and devices that follow standards established by these organizations are compatible with data and devices from multiple developers and vendors. Conversely, those who ignore the standards do so at their own peril. The downside of ignoring standards depends on whether they are enforced or voluntary. For example, the Institute of Electrical and Electronics Engineers (IEEE) establishes standards for everything from signal levels in cables to and from NMR machines to the data bus inside of a workstation. Because the IEEE is a self-policing industry-sponsored organization, it's up to individual manufacturers and developers to abide by the IEEE's published standard guidelines. If their software or hardware doesn't comply with the IEEE standards, then these components can't be marketed as IEEE-com. In contrast, the Federal Communications Commission (FCC), which deals with issues such as allowed operating frequencies and power levels, can enforce its rulings. Failure to heed FCC standards for handling signals from an NMR machine or a wireless network can result in fines for the developer.

Most of the standards organizations are established to make life easier, not harder, on developers and end-users. For example, NIST is a federal technology agency that works with industry to "develop and promote measurements, standards, and technology to enhance productivity, facilitate trade, and improve the quality of life". Similarly, the Uniform Code Council (UCC), which defines standards for the bar code labels that are used to track tissue specimens, microarray cartridges, and clinical radiographs, provides the guidelines on the use of barcodes that have helped revolutionize the workings of a modern experimental laboratory. Its mission is to enhance interoperability through establishing and promoting multi-industry standards for product identification and related electronic communication.

The extent of interoperability may be global, such as worldwide communications standards, or limited to a cluster of industries, such as healthcare. For example, in network communications, there are virtually universal standards for the communications infrastructure, including Ethernet, Fiber Distributed Data Interface (FDDI), Integrated Services Digital Network (ISDN), and x.25 (packet switching). These standards allow computer systems around the world to exchange data with each other, regardless of equipment manufacturer. An Ethernet-compatible device will work with an Ethernet network anywhere in the world. Similarly, when it comes to e-mail there are worldwide standards, including MIMI, BinHEX, ASCII, and Uuencode, that allow e-mail with an attached file to be sent by America On-Line (AOL) executing on a Macintosh computer to be received by a workstation running Microsoft Outlook under Microsoft Windows XP.

Similarly, in the medical industry, which encompasses computer systems dedicated to research and dozens of specialties in clinical medicine, there are standards that allow interoperability between devices and applications, especially clinical systems from different vendors. For example, when it comes to combining clinical data from one application with data from another, there are several coding systems available: the Systematized Nomenclature of Medicine (SNOMED), the Nursing Outcomes Classification (NOC), the European Clinical Data Exchange Standard (EUCLIDES) the World Health Organization (WHO) Drug Dictionary, and the Medical Subject Headings (MESH) coding system.

Operating systems and browser environments are areas where interoperability is possible because of standardization around a handful of operating systems and Web browsers (either the Netscape Navigator or Internet Explorer). Although Windows is the most popular operating system worldwide, the most popular operating systems used in bioinformatics are various flavors of UNIX, followed by Windows 95/98/NT/2000/XP and MacOS/OS X. Linux is the most popular version of UNIX used on Intel-compatible workstations. Systems based on the X-Windows System—a consortium-developed open source client-server system—running on top of UNIX are common on high-end workstation hardware from DEC and Sun Microsystems. Globus, the most popular distributed operating system for creating high-performance clusters, is typically used with dozens to hundreds of inexpensive PCs in order to create a grid computer.

However, there is often a connectivity issue with hardware running other operating systems, even though the major operating system companies provide software utilities to network computers running some version of their operating system. At the lowest level, most systems support file transfer between disparate systems. However, executing software designed for, say X-windows under MacOS requires an appropriate emulator—software that allows users of each platform to access and use programs written to run on the other. X-Windows emulators are available for both Windows and the MacOS. Similarly, there are built-in utilities to the MacOS that allow Macintosh users to read files from Windows-formatted disks, and emulator programs allow a Macintosh to execute programs written for Windows. However, emulators are typically too slow for many computationally intensive bioinformatics applications, many of which already tax the hardware platform running in native mode on the intended hardware.

Standard interfaces that enable communication between software applications and users (graphical user interfaces—GUIs) and between programs and the operating system (application programming interfaces—APIs) also support interoperability. For example, a common GUI decreases the learning curve for someone working with a new program. A user fluent with a few programs written for Windows should be able to quickly learn other Windows-based programs that follow the same GUI standards. Both Apple and Microsoft have published standard GUI guidelines for software developers in order to foster a common look-and-feel among applications running under the same operating system.

Similarly, the standardization of APIs, the interfaces between applications and the underlying operating system, reduces the burden on programmers who must otherwise devise novel methods of making operating system calls every time they create a new program. Following an API standard, such as the IEEE P1520 standard for networks, allows programmers to learn and use one set of programming routines, regardless of the application and differences in the underlying hardware.

Before discussing grass-roots methods of standardizing applications and application development, it's important to consider that interoperability doesn't imply identical results. For example, several protein structure rendering programs may be interoperable, in that they can read and write the same data formats and seamlessly share results with other applications. However, the results of each program may be different, depending on the underlying algorithm and assumptions used by the programmer. Rendering programs that use the PDB file format must interpret the bonding information, typically using different algorithms. One way around this dilemma is to use a file format such as the MMDB, which contains explicit bonding information. As a result, protein structures are consistently rendered.

Open Source

As noted in the discussion of standard tool and data accessibility, one way for a company or academic laboratory to influence the development of standards is to simply offer to let developers in other companies use the formerly proprietary standards with no or nominal license fees. Giving away a standard has benefits to all parties involved. For the original standards developer, offering a standard to the industry provides it with a competitive advantage in the marketplace. Not only does it have a high level of expertise, but its engineering investment in the standard may provide the developer with a depth of knowledge that would otherwise take years to attain.

Conversely, for laboratories without a standard of their own, it may make economic sense to use a system that has already been debugged and is available immediately, depending on the relationship of the developers. For example, rivals Oracle, Sun Microsystems, and Microsoft typically don't support the "standard" offered by each other. When Sun Microsystems offered its Java as a platform-independent programming language, many developers in software industries throughout the world began using it. What makes Java so attractive, and the reason it provides interoperability between hardware platforms, is because Sun Microsystems didn't simply offer the standard to the world in the form of a specifications document. Instead, it created tutorials, easy-to-use software installation utilities, code samples, and support. It also actively markets Java as a tool for interactive Web development. Today, Sun maintains Java for Windows and UNIX, while Apple Computer maintains a version for its Macintosh computers. Java isn't without its various flavors, however. To get a piece of this market, Microsoft sells J++ for Windows, which is a superset of Java.

Sun's backing of Java—its free programming language standard—is unusual. More common and increasingly significant are grass-roots activities that offer programming language standards and, most importantly, support. Open-source software has become the basis for much of the software development in bioinformatics. Open-source software isn't freeware or shareware, in which programs are simply given away or sold at a nominal price, respectively, but the product of an organic community of dedicated developers and users. The description of the Apache Software Foundation on its Web site provides an apt description of the concept of open-source software:

> "The Apache Software Foundation provides support for the Apache community of open-source software projects. The Apache projects are characterized by a collaborative consensus based development process, an open and pragmatic software license, and a desire to create high quality software that leads the way in its field. We consider ourselves not simply a group of projects sharing a server, but rather a community of developers and users."

What makes open-source software so special is that the source code is provided, free of charge. Programmers are encouraged to modify the code as they see fit. The main restriction is that the relevant open-source provider must be acknowledged on any products that incorporate any part of the open-source code. The Apache File Server, TCL, Python, PHP, PERL, the Linux operating system, Jakarta, and Apache XML are all examples of open-source languages and systems that have heavily influenced bioinformatics. These and other open-source languages and products are typically developed by volunteers, and there is no paid staff associated with development. Many of the applications developed in bioinformatics are based on open-source languages. For example, the Chimera Collaboratory Extension is written in Python, an extensible, easy-to-use language that is also used in data mining and natural language processing applications.

ISSUES

Despite a history of over a decade of international cooperation in sequencing the human genome, there remain several impediments to realizing the full potential of collaboration in bioinformatics. Many issues are external to the bioinformatics field, and are tied to the internal politics and economics of international pharmaceutical companies. In addition, there are several internal issues associated with establishing and maintaining collaborations. As described in the following paragraphs, these include platform dependence, security, intellectual property, and economics.

Platform Dependence

There's something to be said for a world in which everyone is limited to single make and model of desktop computer. For example, if the bioinformatics community standardized on vanilla 1 GHz Pentium IV computers running Linux, managing networks, creating applications, and sharing files and applications would be non-issues. However, computationally intensive applications, such as sequence alignment, might require weeks or months of processing time. Similarly, without a graphics hardware accelerator card, the rendering of protein structures on the screen would be excruciatingly slow. Many third-party software packages, including general-purpose office software and utilities, may not work as expected or at all.

For better or worse, we work in a world dominated by a few computer hardware manufacturers and operating system developers. As a result, users become accustomed to one kind of hardware or one set of tools, and come to depend on having the look and feel of a familiar interface available when they work. For example, to the regular user of a Sun workstation, the Mac's keyboard and mouse may feel foreign, and the slight difference in the layout of the keys may initially result in an abnormally large number of typing errors.

Most basic human-computer interface issues associated with platform dependence have yet to be resolved. This is especially true in a market that attempts to differentiate commodity computer hardware in terms of personality or even color—factors that don't directly affect the performance or usefulness of applications running on the computer.

One area in which platform dependence has been addressed is in tool development, especially in platform-independent programming languages and applications. For example, Java is popular in part because it's available for virtually every desktop hardware–operating system combination in general use. As a result, developers aren't limited to a particular hardware platform, but they can easily migrate an application written in Java from one platform to the next.

Security

Collaboration implies trust and requires a degree of connectivity between workstations and other devices. Whenever this connectivity takes the form of a wired or wireless connection to the Internet, internets, or an intranet, it represents a security risk. Every Web server or workstation connected to the Internet is a potential target for hackers, and wireless devices represent an easy portal of entry for sophisticated hackers. Although some cyberattacks, such as denial of service, are directed at specific servers, the greatest threats to the typical bioinformatics lab are computer viruses, worms, or Trojan horses.

Improving security entails the use of anti-virus utilities, software or hardware firewalls to protect a network from unauthorized external access, password protection of sensitive documents, and the ability to train staff on security procedures. A robust security infrastructure is especially critical in commercial laboratory settings where corporate espionage is a constant threat, and in academic laboratories working on sensitive projects that may be of interest to those who would use biologicals as weapons.

Intellectual Property

When it comes to collaboration, there are two major camps: academia and business. At the individual researcher level, the motivations for collaboration are typically the same in each camp—the thrill and challenge of pushing the envelope of scientific discovery while achieving personal career advancement. At higher levels in business and academia, the dimension of economics is usually added to the mix. Lab administrators are necessarily concerned with continuing funding from corporate, government, or other sources. With the prospect of substantial economic gain looming on the horizon, many organizations have taken steps to secure their intellectual property rights through the U.S. Patent and Trademark Office before revealing or sharing their research findings with other researchers.

This practice of obtaining temporary exclusivity to use a gene or gene sequence is much more prevalent in commercial laboratories than in academia. As in other industries, patents provide the holder with some degree of protection for their economic investment in developing a particular molecule. For example, a pharmaceutical firm would be foolish to invest millions of dollars toward the development of a molecule that it hadn't patented or licensed from the patent owner.

The publication of significant research findings is often delayed by years because of the slow review process used within the U.S. Patent and Trademark Office. Although some of this delay is attributable to the normal workings of the patent office, much of the delay is due to the huge number of genetic patent applications submitted to the office in the past few years. Companies are quick to patent every new sequence in the event that it might prove to be invaluable one day. As a lottery of sorts, the odds are very good that several patents will pay off handsomely in the near future, with big Pharma paying for licensing rights.

Although much has been made of the patent practices of companies such as Celera Genomics, academia has its own problems. For example, there are several suits pending over who should be credited with the original sequencing technology. Apparently, the sequencing method developed by a researcher was patented surreptitiously by the lab director. As a result, millions of dollars of income and the academic credit for the R&D were allegedly misdirected. The converse condition exists as well, in that there is a practice of intellectual property theft by researchers working in commercial and academic laboratories. This problem is apparently especially prevalent with foreign researchers who come to work in U.S. laboratories.

Economics

In every commercial or academic endeavor, progress is a function of operating costs and the availability of funding. For example, overhead, payroll, hardware, software, and infrastructure costs represent the main expenditures for a typical bioinformatics laboratory. Web servers, workstations, and network cables, routers, firewalls, and related hardware are fortunately commodity items that tend to follow a trend of decreasing price-to-performance ratio.

One of the largest variables in the economics of establishing and maintaining a bioinformatics laboratory capable of collaborating with the larger bioinformatics community is obtaining software for servers, workstations, and high-performance clusters. Throughout most of this book, the focus has been on open-source and freely available academic software. The intent is to introduce readers who are interested in gaining practical experience in bioinformatics computing to software that can be downloaded from the Web and run within a few minutes. However, from an economic perspective, "free" software isn't necessarily superior to commercial software.

Consider the criteria for evaluating the suitability of a commercial product for a hypothetical bioinformatics project. As illustrated in Figure 10-6, the typical criteria for evaluating a software or hardware solution range from price (the initial cost) to synergies with previously installed hardware and software. Assuming a typical software product, such as a database for storing sequence data, a primary concern is the technology fit, which is a measure of the compatibility of the product with existing hardware, operating systems, and other legacy technologies. Another key issue is support, as measured by the responsiveness of the vendor or developer to calls for help by way of phone, e-mail, or the Web. Product functionality, a reflection of the software's ability to supply needed tools, adherence to standards, licensing terms, and cultural fit

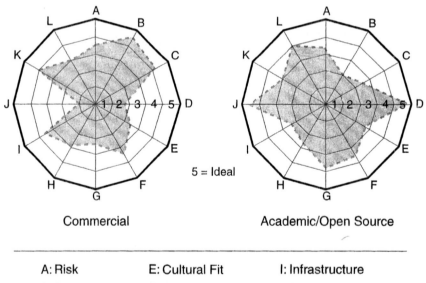

Commercial   Academic/Open Source

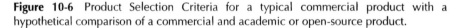

A: Risk	E: Cultural Fit	I: Infrastructure
B: Support	F: Technology Fit	J: Price
C: Standards	G: Cost	K: Functionality
D: Licenses	H: Synergies	L: Vendor/Developer

Figure 10-6 Product Selection Criteria for a typical commercial product with a hypothetical comparison of a commercial and academic or open-source product.

should be considered. For example, a tool designed for Microsoft Windows, even though functional, may not fit into the culture of a lab using computers based on the Linux operating system.

The comparison of any two software products should be performed on a case-by-case basis. The hypothetical comparison of two products illustrated in Figure 10-6 highlights the key issues of support, licensing arrangements, price, and cost in deciding between commercial and open-source/academic products. For example, even though the purchase price of a commercial database may be several thousand dollars, compared to a free open-source database, the overall cost of the open-source software to the laboratory may be greater. The initial purchase price plus any annual licensing and maintenance fees have to be balanced against the internal resources that would likely be required to properly configure and maintain open-source software. Depending on the maturity and popularity of the open-source software and the availability of computer-savvy staff, it may be less expensive over the operating lifetime of the software to purchase a commercial product. Because the availability of affordable assistants who are willing to work with, modify, and maintain non-commercial products differs from lab to lab and institution to institution, there isn't a clear rule for when to make the extra up-front investment in a commercial product.

Many open-source products, such as PERL, Python, and Linux are technically solid, with large user bases, and online tutorials and reference texts available for support. However, it's unreasonable to expect an open-source project that is staffed by volunteer programmers to provide 24-hour hotline support. If this level of handholding is required, then the options are either to go with a commercial product that offers full support or to use a commercial house that supports open-source products. Several successful companies make a handsome profit every year by providing telephone, e-mail, and even on-site support for open-source and other freely available software.

Inevitably, the products and processes that are the most accurate, useful, and useable enter the commercial arena in some form. As the current R&D projects associated with bioinformatics software evolve into maintenance and support projects, many of the research labs will focus their attention on the next new thing in bioinformatics. When this happens, the commercial houses will be left with the opportunity—and burden—of maintaining and upgrading the software tools, hardware, and various experimental devices that are still evolving in bioinformatics laboratories around the world.

ON THE HORIZON

The future of collaboration in bioinformatics is intimately tied to advances in the information technology industry and to establishing clear intellectual property rights agreements between industry, government, and academia. Technologically, several patterns are emerging. There appears to be a simultaneous move toward pervasive computing—the any-time, any-place access to data and computing power. Most of these capabilities will come about through advances in networking, such as new wireless network designs, improved network security measures, an emphasis on storage area networks and other distributed storage solutions, and high-speed (10 Gigabit) Ethernet.

The current Wi-Fi or 802.11b wireless standard, which operates at 11 Mbps, will soon be replaced by systems capable of both Wi-Fi and higher-speed 802.11a wireless communications, which provides 54 Mbps connectivity. Similarly, the current 10 Mbps Ethernet standard, which hasn't changed appreciably since 1979, is being upgraded industry-wide to 10 Gbps, starting with the backbone connections. Both of these developments are making network-based storage—a component of pervasive computing—a practical alternative to local storage.

With the threat of non-specific cyberterrorism and the increased motivation for the theft of bioinformatics research data, new security technologies and improved internal processes are inevitable. The bioinformatics laboratory of the next decade will likely resemble the work environment depicted in the science-fiction thriller *GATTACA*, in which a battery of biometric tests, including DNA analysis, are routinely used to identify every employee and track their movements—all in the name of national security.

ENDNOTE

Most, if not all, of the major technological advances of the 20th Century, from aviation and space flight to nuclear power, computers, and germ warfare, have been tied to military funding. For example, the first major advances in electronic computing were the direct result of military need for computer-based encryption and decryption systems in World War II. In their military-funded work to potentiate the effects of mustard gas in the battlefield, Goodman and Gilman developed the first cancer chemotherapy in the 1940s. The walkie-talkie, developed for troops in World War II, laid the foundation for the cellular phone service. Later, during the cold war with Russia, the U.S. military establishment funded the nascent field of AI as a means of automatically decoding Russian text. Similarly, the progenitor of the Internet was developed as a nuclear-proof communications link between military centers of operation and academic institutions involved in nuclear weapon R&D. Today, the U.S. military is the largest market for supercomputers and high-performance computing clusters.

One of the long-standing interests of the U.S. military has been offensive and defensive biological weapons. With the increase in military R&D funding following the events of September 11, 2001, this interest has taken on a new urgency. The first public information on next-generation biological warfare R&D was released in July of 2002, when it was reported that scientists at the State University of New York at Stony Brook had successfully synthesized the Polio virus. The research, funded by the Defense Advanced Research Projects Agency (DARPA), demonstrated that a living, lethal virus could be constructed in the laboratory, based on the published genetic sequence, like the one in Figure 10-7.

POLIO VIRUS SEQUENCE

```
   1 ctgcagtcct catgtactat ggtagtgcca tggattagca acaccacgta tcggcaaacc
  61 atagatgata gtttcaccga aggcggatac atcagcgtct tctaccaaac tagaatagtc
 121 gtccctcttt cgacacccag agagatggac atccttggtt ttgtgtcagc gtgtaatgac
 181 ttcagcgtgc gcttgttgcg agataccaca catatagagc aaaaagcgct agcacagggg
 241 ttaggtcaga tgcttgaaag catgattgac aacacagtcc gtgaaacggt gggggcggca
 301 acatctagag acgctctccc aaacactgaa gccagtggac caacacactc caaggaaatt
 361 ccggcactca ccgcagtgga aactggggcc acaaatccac tagtcccttc tgatacagtg
 421 caaaccagac atgttgtaca acataggtca aggtcagagt ctagcataga gtctttcttc
 481 gcgcggggtg catgcgtgac cattatgacc gtggataacc cagcttccac cacgaataag
 541 gataagctat ttgcagtgtg gaagatcact tataaagata ctgtccagtt acggaggaaa
 601 ttggagttct tcacctattc tagatttgat atggaactta cctttgtggt tactgcaaat
 661 ttcactgaga ctaacaatgg gcatgcctta aatcaagtgt accaaattat gtacgtacca
 721 ccaggcgctc cagtgccga aaaatgggac gactacacat ggcaaacctc atcaaatcca
 781 tcaatctttt acacctacgg aacagctcca gcccggatct cggtaccgta tgttggtatt
 841 tcgaacgcct attcacactt ttacgacggt ttttccaaag taccactgaa ggaccagtcg
 901 gcagcactag gtgactccct ttatggtgca gcatctctaa atgacttcgg tattttggct
 961 gttagagtag tcaatgatca caacccgacc aaggtcacct ccaaaatcag agtgtatcta
1021 aaacccaaac acatcagagt ctggtgcccg cgtccaccga gggcagtggc gtactacggc
1081 cctggagtgg attacaagga tggtacgctt acacccctct ccaccaagga tctgaccaca
1141 tatggattcg gacaccaaaa caaagcggtg tacactgcag gttacaaaat ttgcaactac
1201 cacttggcca ctcaggatga tttgcaaaac gcagtgaacg tcatgtggag tagagacctc
1261 ttagtcacag aatcaagagc ccagggcacc gattcaatcg caaggtgcaa ttgcaacgca
1321 ggggtgtact actgcgagtc tagaaggaaa tactacccag tatccttcgt tggcccaacg
```

Figure 10-7   Polio Virus Sequence from Entrez.

The creation of the Polio virus from scratch gives "textbook medicine" a new meaning. Although the technology used to create a deadly virus could also be used to create new vaccines, a group with access to a microbiology laboratory could create new, designer biological warfare agents that are far more deadly than the Ebola virus. As such, making the sequence data on deadly pathogens freely available on public databases, and even publishing the descriptions of basic microbiology techniques, could be deemed a threat to national security.

This research highlights numerous ethical, political, and social issues that directly affect researchers in the field of bioinformatics computing. For example, do the public biological databases amount to publishing the plans for weapons, complete with instructions on how to synthesize the biological payloads? Should a subset of biological data be off-limits to the public, non–U.S. laboratories, or anyone without a demonstrable "need to know?" Should the publication of any type biological data on known or potential biological warfare agents, such as Figure 10-7, be banned? What of the online databases maintained by other countries, such as SWISS-PROT? Should collaboration be limited or monitored by local governments, the WHO, or other organization?

An examination of the nuclear and computing industries and how threats have been addressed might provide some guidance on how to address the issue of synthetic biologicals. When Britain's Ministry of Defense recently made public the information describing in detail the make-up of a nuclear bomb, there was highly publicized opposition from those who contend that the disclosure amounts to giving potential terrorists a blueprint to create an atomic bomb. However, the Ministry of Defense countered that the Web is replete with plans to make atomic bombs (a Google search for "atomic bomb plans" in August of 2002 reveals 59,600 hits), and that the accusations were groundless. Others contend that the real issue is controlling plutonium, not the plans for a bomb. Some rebuke this position by highlighting the amount of weapons-grade plutonium that is "missing" from the dismantled Soviet atomic arsenal.

Another view is that information on how to build an atomic bomb from the Ministry of Defense is more likely to be believed by terrorists than are the plans posted anonymously on the Web. Assuming extensive testing isn't performed on the resultant bomb, if one or two key elements of the Ministry's plans are intentionally in error, then the terrorist's time, effort, and plutonium would be wasted on a failed attempt at building and exploding an atomic bomb.

Following this scenario, is it acceptable, in the interest of national security, to post erroneous information in the online biological databases? For example, should the sequence definition of potential biohazards, such as the Polio virus sequence in Figure 10-7, contain intentional errors that reduce the potency of the virus (the synthetic Polio virus created at State University of New York isn't as infectious as the natural virus because of 18 genetic markers intentionally inserted into the virus)? In addition, should the errors be used to indicate the source of the sequence data as well as render the viruses harmless?

In the computing industry, the U.S. has a long-standing practice of barring the export of computers, including desktop and laptop computers, capable of being used in weapons systems or in weapons design. As a workaround, groups in Asia, the Middle East, and elsewhere have developed high-performance computing clusters using Sony PlayStation II hardware, which is easy to purchase on the open market. In a similar vein, it's impossible to stop a country from importing every piece of medical equipment that might somehow be used develop bioterrorism materials.

Clearly, the culture of open collaboration and sharing of information in bioinformatics is at odds with recent national security concerns as well as those opposed to genetic research on religious or other grounds. It remains to be seen how concerns for privacy and security in the name of the common good will affect the efficiency and effectiveness of collaboration between researchers involved in bioinformatics and molecular biology research. What is certain is that molecular biology and bioinformatics computing aren't fields in which major decisions will be made by stereotypical scientists dressed in white lab coats, working quietly and diligently in a wet lab. Practitioners and practices in both fields will be open to public scrutiny. They'll also have to bear the brunt of political legislation regarding cloning, genetically modified foods, and designer drugs, and will likely be the focus of heated ethical debates. We do live in interesting times.

BIBLIOGRAPHY

Chapter One—The Central Dogma

Adlington, F. and C. Humphries, Eds. *Philip's Science & Technology: People, Dates & Events*. London: Octopus Publishing Group, 1999.

Anderson, J. *An Introduction to Neural Networks*. Cambridge: MIT Press, 1997.

Churchland, P. and T. Sejnowski. *The Computational Brain*. New York: Bradford Books, 1994.

Daives, K. *Cracking the Genome: Inside the Race to Unlock Human DNA*. New York: The Free Press, 2001.

Dorffner, G., Ed. *Neural Networks and a New Artificial Intelligence*. New York: International Thomson Computer Press, 1997.

Feynman, R. P., R. B. Leighton, et al. *The Feynman Lectures on Physics*. Reading, MA: Addison-Wesley Publishing Company, 1977.

Freiberger, P. and M. Swaine. *Fire in the Valley: The Making of the Personal Computer*. New York: McGraw-Hill, 1984.

Giarratano, J. and G. Riley. *Expert Systems: Principles and Programming*. Boston: PWS Publishing Company, 1994.

Jenness, R. *Analog Computation and Simulation: Laboratory Approach*. Boston: Allyn and Bacon, Inc., 1965.

Johnson, C. *Analog Computer Techniques*. New York: McGraw-Hill Book Company, 1963.

Karplus, W. and W. Soroka. *Analog Methods: Computation and Simulation.* New York: McGraw-Hill Book Company, Inc., 1959.

Korn, G. and T. Korn. *Electronic Analog Computers (DC Analog Computers).* New York: McGraw-Hill Book Company, Inc., 1956.

Kurzweil, R. *The Age of Spiritual Machines: When Computers Exceed Human Intelligence.* New York: Viking, 1999.

MacKay, D. and M. Fisher. *Analogue Computing at Ultra-High Speed.* New York: John Wiley & Sons, Inc., 1962.

Mitchell, T. *Machine Learning.* New York: McGraw-Hill, 1997.

Paul, J. *Fundamental Analogue Techniques.* New York: The Macmillan Company, 1965.

Peterson, G. *Basic Analog Computation.* New York: Macmillan Company, 1967.

Ricci, F. *Analog/Logic Computer Programming and Simulation.* New York: Spartan Books, 1972.

Rummer, D. *Introduction to Analog Computer Programming.* Dallas: Holt, Rinehart and Winston, Inc., 1969.

Russell, S. and P. Norvig. *Artificial Intelligence: A Modern Approach.* Englewood Cliffs, NJ: Prentice Hall Publishers, 1994.

Stice, J. and B. Swanson. *Electronic Analog Computer Primer.* New York: Blaisdell Publishing Company, 1965.

Tomovic, R. and W. Karplus. *High-Speed Analog Computers.* New York: John Wiley and Sons, Inc., 1962.

Wass, C. and K. Garner. *Introduction to Electronic Analogue Computers.* New York: Pergamon Press, 1965.

Chapter Two—Databases

Benson, D., I. Karsch-Mizrachi, D. Lipman, J. Ostell, B. Rapp and D. Wheeler. "GenBank." *Nucleic Acids Research* 28(2000): 15–8.

Bergeron, B. *Essentials of Knowledge Management.* New York: John Wiley & Sons, 2003.

Brackett, M. *Data Resource Quality.* New York: Addison-Wesley, 2000.

Celko, J. *Data & Databases: Concepts in Practice.* San Francisco, CA: Morgan-Kaufmann, 1999.

Conway, S. and C. Siligar. *Unlocking Knowledge Management*. Redmond, WA: Microsoft Press, 2002.

Garfinkel, S. and G. Spafford. *Web Security and Commerce*. Sebastopol, CA: O'Reilly & Associates, 1997.

Humphries, M., M. Hawkins and M. Dy. *Data Warehousing: Architecture and Implementation*. Upper Saddle River, NJ: Prentice Hall PTR., 1999.

Loshin, D. *Enterprise Knowledge Management*. San Francisco, CA: Morgan Kaufmann, 2001.

Prurba, S., Ed. *Data Management Handbook*. Boca Raton, FL: Auerbach Publications, 2000.

Ralston, A., E. Reily and D. Hemmendinger, Eds. *Encyclopedia of Computer Science*. New York: Groves Dictionaries, Inc., 2000.

Sanders, G. *Data Modeling*. New York: Boyd & Fraser Publishing Company, 1995.

Shortliffe, E., L. Perreault, G. Wiederhold and L. Fagan, Eds. *Medical Informatics: Computer Applications in Health Care and Biomedicine*. New York: Springer, 2001.

Taylor, D. *Object-Oriented Technology: A Manager's Guide*. New York: Addison-Wesley, 1990.

Warwick, A. "Knowledge management technology." *IBM Systems Journal* 40(4)(2001): 814–30.

Chapter Three—Networks

Anderson, D. and J. Kubiatowicz. "The Worldwide Computer." *Scientific American* 286(1)(2002): 40–7.

Bell, G. and J. Gray. "What's Next in High-Performance Computing?" *Communications of the ACM* 45(2)(2002): 91–5.

Bergeron, B. *The Wireless Web: How to Develop a Winning Wireless Strategy*. New York: McGraw-Hill, 2001.

Brand, S. "Founding Father." *Wired* (March 2001): 145–53.

Buderi, R. "Computing Goes Everywhere." *Technology Review* (Jan/Feb 2001): 53–9.

Dodd, A. *The Essential Guide to Telecommunications*. Upper Saddle River, NJ: Prentice Hall PTR, 1999.

Hecht, J. *City of Light: The Story of Fiber Optics*. New York: Oxford University Press, 1999.

Jackson, L. "Putting Sleeping PCs to Work." *Qwest Lightspeed* (Winter 2002): 22–4.

Newton, H. *Newton's Telecom Dictionary*. Gilroy, CA: Telecom Books, 2000.

Oppliger, R. *Internet and Intranet Security*. Boston: Artech House, 1998.

Ralston, A., E. Reily and D. Hemmendinger, Eds. *Encyclopedia of Computer Science*. New York: Groves Dictionaries, Inc., 2000.

Savage, N. "Building a Better Backbone." *Technology Review* 104(5)(2001): 40–7.

Stein, L. *Web Security*. New York: Addison-Wesley, 1997.

Stix, G. "The Triumph of the Light." *Scientific American* (Jan 2001): 80–99.

Tanenbaum, A. *Computer Networks*. Upper Saddle River, NJ: Prentice Hall PTR, 1996.

Chapter Four—Search Engines

Agarwal, P. and D. States. "Comparative Accuracy of Methods for Protein Similarity Search." *Bioinformatics* 14(1988): 40–7.

Altschul, S., M. Boguski, W. Gish and J. Wootton. "Issues in Searching Molecular Sequence Databases." *Nature Genetics* 6(1994): 119–29.

Balas, E., S. Boren and G. Brown, Eds. *Information Technology Strategies from the United States and the European Union*. Amsterdam: IOS Press, 2000.

Binstock, A. and J. Rex. *Practical Algorithms for Programmers*. New York: Addison-Wesley, 1995.

Cote, R., D. Rothwell, J. Palotay, R. Beckett and L. Brochu, Eds. *SNOMED International: The Systematized Nomenclature of Human and Veterinary Medicine*. Northfield, IL: College of American Pathologists, 1993.

Mack, R., Y. Ravin and R. Byrd. "Knowledge Portals and the Emerging Digital Knowledge Workplace." *IBM Systems Journal* 40(4)(2001): 814–30.

Newton, H. *Newton's Telecom Dictionary*. Gilroy, CA: Telecom Books, 2000.

Simon, S. *XML*. New York: McGraw-Hill, 2001.

Van Ginneken, A. "The Structure of Data in Medical Records." *Yearbook of Medical Informatics* (J. van Bemmel and A. McCay, Eds.). Stuttgart, Germany, Schattauer (1995): 61–70.

Chapter Five—Data Visualization

Banatao, R. "Visualization." *Bioinformatics Methods and Techniques*. Stanford University, Stanford Center for Professional Development, 2002.

Baxevanis, A. and B. Ouellette. *Bioinformatics: A Practical Guide to the Analysis of Genes and Proteins*. New York: John Wiley & Sons, 2001.

Gibas, C. and P. Jambeck. *Developing Bioinformatics Computer Skills*. Sebastopol, CA: O'Reilly & Associates, 2001.

Jagota, A. *Data Analysis and Classification for Bioinformatics*. Santa Cruz, CA: Arun Jagota, 2000.

Mount, D. *Bioinformatics Sequence and Genome Analysis*. Cold Spring Harbor, NY: Cold Spring Harbor Laboratory Press, 2001.

Ratledge, C. and B. Kristiansen, Eds. *Basic Biotechnology*. New York: Cambridge University Press, 2001.

Chapter Six—Statistics

Altman, R. "Microarray Cluster Analysis and Classification." *Bioinformatics Methods and Techniques*. Stanford University, Stanford Center for Professional Development, 2002.

Ewens, E. and G. Grant. *Statistical Methods in Bioinformatics*. New York: Springer-Verlag, 2001.

Friend, S. and R. Stoughton. "The Magic of Microarrays." *Scientific American* (Feb 2002): 44–9.

Jagota, A. *Data Analysis and Classification for Bioinformatics*. Santa Cruz, CA: Arun Jagota, 2000.

Kanehisa, M. *Post-Genome Informatics*. Oxford: Oxford University Press, 2001.

Pevzner, P. *Computational Molecular Biology*. Cambridge, MA: MIT Press, 2001.

Schnena, M., Ed. *Microarray Biochip Technology*. Natick, MA: Eaton Publishing, 2000.

Shortliffe, E., L. Perreault, G. Wiederhold and L. Fagan, Eds. *Medical Informatics: Computer Applications in Health Care and Biomedicine*. New York: Springer, 2001.

Chapter Seven—Data Mining

Arledge, E. and J. Cort. *Cracking the Code of Life*. Boston, MA: WGBH Boston Video, 2001.

Baxevanis, A. and B. Ouellette. *Bioinformatics: A Practical Guide to the Analysis of Genes and Proteins*. New York: John Wiley & Sons, 2001.

Deschaine, L., J. McCormack, D. Pyle and F. Francone. "Genetic Algorithms and Intelligent Agents Team Up: Techniques for Data Assembly, Preprocessing, Modeling, and Decision Optimization." *PC AI* 15(3)(2001): 35–40.

Friedman, C., S. Johnson, B. Forman and J. Staren. "Architectural Requirements for a Multipurpose Natural Language Processor in the Clinical Environment." *Nineteenth Annual Symposium on Computer Applications in Medical Care*. New Orleans, LA: AMIA, 1995.

Jagota, A. *Data Analysis and Classification for Bioinformatics*. Santa Cruz, CA: Arun Jagota, 2000.

Kanehisa, M. *Post-Genome Informatics*. Oxford: Oxford University Press, 2001.

Nasukawa, T. and T. Nagano. "Text Analysis and Knowledge Mining System," *IBM Systems Journal* 40(4)(2001): 814–30.

Pyle, D. *Data Preparation for Data Mining*. San Francisco, CA: Morgan Kaufmann Publishers, 1999.

Rubin, D. "Natural Language Processing," *Bioinformatics Methods and Techniques*. Stanford University, Stanford Center for Professional Development, 2002.

Tisdal, J. *Beginning PERL for Bioinformatics*. Sebastopol, CA: O'Reilly & Associates, Inc., 2001.

Chapter Eight—Pattern Matching

Altman, R. "Pairwise & Multiple Sequence Alignment," *Bioinformatics Methods and Techniques*. Stanford University, Stanford Center for Professional Development, 2002.

Altschul, S., W. Gish, W. Miller, E. Myers and D. Lipman. "Basic Local Alignment Search Tool." *Journal of Molecular Biology* 215(3)(1990): 403–10.

Apostolico, A. and R. Giancarlo. "Sequence Alignment in Molecular Biology." *Journal of Computational Biology* (5)(1998): 173–96.

Baxevanis, A. "Practical Aspects of Multiple Sequence Alignment." *Methods Biochem* (39)(1998): 172–88.

Binstock, A. and J. Rex. *Practical Algorithms for Programmers*. New York: Addison-Wesley, 1995.

Brutlag, D. "Multiple Sequence Alignment and Motifs." *Bioinformatics Methods and Techniques*. Stanford University, Stanford Center for Professional Development, 2002.

Charniak, E. and D. McDermont. *Introduction to Artificial Intelligence*. Reading, MA: Addison-Wesley Publishing Co., 1985.

Cheng, B. "Protein Structure Analysis." *Bioinformatics Methods and Techniques*. Stanford University, Stanford Center for Professional Development, 2002.

Eddy, S. "Hidden Markov Models." *Current Opinion in Structural Biology* 6(1996): 361-5.

Gribskov, M. and S. Veretnik. "Identification of Sequence Patterns with Profile Analysis." *Methods in Enzymology* 266(1996): 198–212.

Kanehisa, M. *Post-Genome Informatics*. Oxford: Oxford University Press, 2001.

Mount, D. *Bioinformatics Sequence and Genome Analysis*. Cold Spring Harbor, NY: Cold Spring Harbor Laboratory Press, 2001.

Pevzner, P. *Computational Molecular Biology*. Cambridge, MA: MIT Press, 2001.

Ralston, A., E. Reily and D. Hemmendinger, Eds. *Encyclopedia of Computer Science*. New York: Groves Dictionaries, Inc., 2000.

Schuler, G. "Sequence Alignment and Database Searching." *Meth Biochem Anal* 39(1998): 145–71.

Thompson, J., F. Plewniak and O. Poch. "A Comprehensive Comparison of Multiple Sequence Alignment Programs." *Nucleic Acids Research* 27(1999): 2682–90.

Chapter Nine—Modeling and Simulation

Beichl, I. and F. Sullivan. "The Metropolis Algorithm." *Computing in Science and Engineering* (Jan/Feb 2000): 65–9.

Bergeron, B. and R. Rouse. "Cognitive Aspects of Modeling and Simulating Complex Biological Systems." *Structuring Biological Systems: A Computer Modeling Approach* (S. Iyengar, Ed.). Boca Raton, FL: CRC Press (1992): 125–66.

Burge, C. and S. Karlin. "Prediction of Complete Gene Structures in Human Genomic DNA." *Journal of Molecular Biology* 268(1997): 78–94.

Cheng, B. "Protein Structure Prediction." *Bioinformatics Methods and Techniques*, Stanford University, Stanford Center for Professional Development, 2002.

Dudek, M., K. Ramnarayan and J. Ponder. "Protein Structure Prediction Using a Combination of Sequence Homology and Global Energy Minimization: II. Energy Functions." *J Comp Chem* 19(1998): 548–73.

Ezzell, C. "Proteins Rule." *Scientific American* 286(2)(2002): 42–7.

Hein, J., C. Wiuf, B. Knudsen, M. Moller and G. Wibling. "Statistical Alignment: Computational Properties, Homology Testing and Goodness-of-Fit." *Journal of Molecular Biology* 302(2000): 265–79.

Jagota, A. *Data Analysis and Classification for Bioinformatics.* Santa Cruz, CA: Arun Jagota, 2000.

Kreutzer, W. *System Simulation Programming Styles and Languages.* Menlo Park, CA: Addison-Wesley, 1986.

Krogh, A., M. Brown, I. Mian, K. Sjolander and D. Haussler. "Hidden Markov Models in Computational Biology: Applications to Protein Modeling." *Journal of Molecular Biology* 235(1994): 1501–31.

Law, A. M. and D. Kelton. *Simulation Modeling and Analysis.* New York: McGraw-Hill, 1982.

Marti-Renom, M., A. Struart, A. Fiser, R. Sanchez, F. Melo and A. Sali. "Comparative Protein Structure Modeling of Genes and Genomes." *Annual Review of Biophysics and Biomolecular Structure* 29(2000): 291–325.

Mount, D. *Bioinformatics Sequence and Genome Analysis.* Cold Spring Harbor, NY: Cold Spring Harbor Laboratory Press, 2001.

Randall, J. *Microcomputers and Physiological Simulation.* New York: Raven Press, 1987.

Ratledge, C. and B. Kristiansen, Eds. *Basic Biotechnology.* New York: Cambridge University Press, 2001.

Rost, B. and C. Sander. "Prediction of Protein Structure at Better than 70% Accuracy." *Journal of Molecular Biology* 232(1993): 584–99.

Saltman, A. "Pumping Big Iron." *Wired* (April 2001): 46.

Samuelson, P. "Intellectual Property for an Information Age." *Communications of the ACM* 44(2)(2001): 67–8.

Stikeman, A. "Systems Biology: Researchers Look for a Better Model of Diseases." *Technology Review* (March 2002): 31.

Taubes, G. "The Virtual Cell." *Technology Review* 105(3)(2002): 62–70.

Williams, T. "Fuzzy, Neural and Genetic Methods Train to Overcome Complexity." *Computer Design* 34(5)(1995): 59–76.

Chapter Ten—Collaboration

Alexander, B. "The Remastered Race." *Wired* (May 2002): 68–74.

Ford, W. and M. Baum. *Secure Electronic Commerce*. Upper Saddle River, NJ: Prentice Hall PTR, 1997.

Garfinkel, S. *Database Nation*. Sebastopol, CA: O'Reilly & Associates, 1997.

Niccol, A. *GATTACA*. Culver City, CA: Columbia Pictures, 1997.

Ratledge, C. and B. Kristiansen, Eds. *Basic Biotechnology*. New York: Cambridge University Press, 2001.

Skykes, C. *The End of Privacy*. New York: St. Martins Press, 1999.

Smith, D. *Java for the World Wide Web*. Berkley, CA: Peachpit Press, 1998.

Viega, J., T. Kohno and B. Potter. "Trust (and mistrust) in Secure Applications." *Communications of the ACM* 44(2)(2001): 31–6.

INDEX

Numerical